THE INDIAN ARMY IN THE FIRST WORLD WAR:
NEW PERSPECTIVES

War and Military Culture in South Asia, 1757-1947

www.helion.co.uk/warandmilitarycultureinsouthasia

Series Editors
Professor Emeritus Raymond Callahan, University of Delaware
Alan Jeffreys, Imperial War Museum
Professor Daniel Marston, Australian National University

Editorial Advisory Board
Squadron Leader (Retired) Rana Chhina, Centre of Armed Forces Historical Research, United Service Institution of India
Professor Anirudh Deshpande, University of Delhi
Professor Ashley Jackson, King's College London
Dr Robert Johnson, Oxford University
Lieutenant Commander Dr Kalesh Mohanan, Naval History Division, Ministry of Defence, India
Dr Tim Moreman
George Morton-Jack
Dr David Omissi, University of Hull
Professor Peter Stanley, University of New South Wales, Canberra
Dr Erica Wald, Goldsmiths, University of London

Submissions
The publishers would be pleased to receive submissions for this series. Please contact us via email (info@helion.co.uk), or in writing to Helion & Company Limited, 26 Willow Road, Solihull, West Midlands, B91 1UE

Titles
No 1 *'Swords Trembling In Their Scabbards'. The Changing Status of Indian Officers in the Indian Army 1757-1947* Michael Creese (ISBN 978-1-909982-81-9)

No 2 *'Discipline, System and Style'. The Sixteenth Lancers and British Soldiering in India 1822-1846* John H. Rumsby (ISBN 978-1-909982-91-8)

No 3 *Die in Battle, Do not Despair. The Indians on Gallipoli, 1915* Peter Stanley (ISBN 978-1-910294-67-3)

No 4 *Brave as a Lion. The Life and Times of Field Marshal Hugh Gough, 1st Viscount Gough* Christopher Brice (ISBN 978-1-910294-61-1)

No 5 *Approach to Battle. Training the Indian Army during the Second World War* Alan Jeffreys (ISBN 978-1-911096-51-1)

No 6 *The Indian Army in The First World War: New Perspectives* Edited by Alan Jeffreys (ISBN 978-1-911512-78-3)

THE INDIAN ARMY IN THE FIRST WORLD WAR

New Perspectives

War and Military Culture in South Asia, 1757–1947 No. 6

Edited by Alan Jeffreys

Published in association with the United Service Institution of India

Helion & Company

Helion & Company Limited
Unit 8 Amherst Business Centre
Budbrooke Road
Warwick
CV34 5WE
England
Tel. 01926 499 619
Email: info@helion.co.uk
Website: www.helion.co.uk
Twitter: @helionbooks
Visit our blog at blog.helion.co.uk

Published by Helion & Company in association with the United Service Institution of India 2018. Reprinted in paperback 2022
Designed and typeset by Mary Woolley, Battlefield Design (www.battlefield-design.co.uk)
Cover designed by Paul Hewitt, Battlefield Design (www.battlefield-design.co.uk)

Text © individual contributors 2018
Maps drawn by George Anderson © Helion & Company Limited 2018

Every reasonable effort has been made to trace copyright holders and to obtain their permission for the use of copyright material. The author and publisher apologize for any errors or omissions in this work, and would be grateful if notified of any corrections that should be incorporated in future reprints or editions of this book.

ISBN 978-1-804510-49-0

British Library Cataloguing-in-Publication Data.
A catalogue record for this book is available from the British Library.

All rights reserved. No part of this publication may be reproduced, stored in a retrieval system, or transmitted, in any form, or by any means, electronic, mechanical, photocopying, recording or otherwise, without the express written consent of Helion & Company Limited.

For details of other military history titles published by Helion & Company Limited contact the above address, or visit our website: http://www.helion.co.uk.

We always welcome receiving book proposals from prospective authors.

Contents

List of Maps		vii
List of Contributors		viii
Foreword by Rana Chhina		xi
Introduction		13
1	Neglected Soldiers *Raymond Callahan & Daniel Marston*	17
2	'I Shall Die Arms in Hand, Wearing the Warriors' Clothes': Mobilisation and Initial Operations of the Indian Army in France and Flanders *Rob Johnson*	40
3	The Mobilisation and Supply of India's Equine Army 1914: The chief arm of transport, artillery, cavalry and support units are their animals *Graham Winton*	52
4	Beyond the Hindu Kush: Imperial Defence, Expeditionary Warfare and the Role of the Indian Army *Joseph Moretz*	91
5	Keeping the 'Highway to India' Open: The Indian Army and the Defence of the Suez Canal 1914-15 *Adam Prime*	110
6	The Dark Shadow of the Dardanelles: Churchill's *World Crisis* and his Portrayal of the Indian Army at Gallipoli *Cat Wilson*	131
7	'The Greatest Muslim Power in the World': Islam, the Indian Army and the Grand Strategy of British India, 1914–1916 *David Omissi*	153
8	The Expansion of the Indian Army Officer Corps during the First World War *Alan Jeffreys*	174

9	The Sikh Experience *David Omissi*	187
10	Indian Prisoners of War in Germany during First World War *Andrew Jarboe*	207
11	The Indian Cavalry in Palestine 1917-19 *Michael Creese*	231
12	India and the Mesopotamia Campaign *Kristian Coates Ulrichsen*	249
13	Terriers in India: a preliminary report *Peter Stanley*	270
14	Tiger by the Tail: Demobilization of the Indian Army of War, 1918-1923 *Anirudh Deshpande*	281

Select Bibliography   299
Index   309

List of Maps

India 1914 55
The Suez Canal 1914-15 123

List of Contributors

RAYMOND CALLAHAN is an emeritus professor at the University of Delaware. He has a career long interest in the Indian Army of the British Raj which he has explored in a number of books and articles beginning with *Burma* 1942-1945 (1978) and continuing to the recent *Triumph at Imphal-Kohima: How the Indian Army Finally Stooped the Japanese Juggernaut* (2017). Professor Callahan is a Fellow of the Royal Historical Society.

MICHAEL CREESE is a retired headteacher and educational consultant. His doctoral thesis at the University of Leicester focused on the Indian officers in four cavalry regiments, drawing on material in Britain and India. The scope of the thesis was widened into the Helion publication: *'Swords Trembling in their Scabbards': The Changing Status of Indian Officers in the Indian Army 1757-1947* (2015). He has also written a history of the Jodhpur Lancers which is awaiting publication in India.

ANIRUDH DESHPANDE is an associate professor in the history department of Delhi University. He edited *The British Raj and its Indian Armed Forces, 1857 - 1939* (Oxford University Press, 2002) with the late Professor Partha Sarathi Gupta. His book, *British Military Policy in India 1900-1945: colonial constraints and declining power*, was published and simultaneously released in India and Pakistan by Manohar Publishers in 2005. His latest book, *Hope and Despair: Mutiny, Rebellion and Death in India, 1946* has been published by Primus Books in August 2016.

ANDREW JARBOE is an assistant professor of history at Berklee College of Music. He is the editor of *Empires in World War I: Shifting Frontiers and Imperial Dynamics in a Global Conflict* (2014) along with Richard Fogarty. He is also editor of *War News in India: The Punjabi Press during World War I* (2015).

ALAN JEFFREYS is the author of *Approach to Battle: Training the Indian Army during the Second World War* (2017). He is the founding series editor of Helion's 'War and Military Culture in South Asia, 1757-1947' and a senior curator at the Imperial War Museum. He is also a Visiting Research Fellow at the University of Greenwich and has been a Senior Research Fellow at the Centre of Armed Forces Historical Research, the United Service Institution of India.

ROBERT JOHNSON is the Director of the Changing Character of War Centre based at Pembroke College, a senior research fellow of Pembroke College, and an associate professor of the Department of Politics and International Relations, at the University of Oxford. His primary research interests are in strategy, unconventional operations, insurgency and information warfare. He conducts research on conflicts 'amongst the people' with particular reference to Afghanistan, Pakistan and the Middle East. He acts as a specialist advisor to the NATO armed forces on security, and broader developments in armed conflict. Nevertheless, as a historian, Dr Johnson is particularly focussed on the history of the First World War and published *The Great War and the Middle East* with Oxford University Press in 2016.

DANIEL MARSTON BA MA (McGill) DPhil (Oxon.) FRHistS holds a Professorship in Military Studies at the Australian National University. He previously held the Ike Skelton Distinguished Chair in the Art of War at the US Army Command and General Staff College. He has been a Visiting Fellow, on multiple occasions, with the Leverhulme Changing Character of War Program at the University of Oxford. His research focuses on the topic of transnational military culture and how armies learn and adapt to new environments. His first book *Phoenix from the Ashes*, an in-depth assessment of how the British/Indian Army turned defeat into victory in the Burma campaign of the Second World War, won the Field Marshal Templer Medal Book Prize in 2003. The second volume, *The Indian Army and the End of the Raj*, was Runner Up for the Templer Medal in 2014. He completed his doctorate as the Beit Research Scholar in Imperial and Commonwealth History at Balliol College, Oxford University, and is a Fellow of the Royal Historical Society.

JOSEPH MORETZ was born in 1956 and educated at King's College, London where he received his MA and PhD in War Studies. Retiring from the U.S. Department of Defense in 2010, he is now an independent writer specializing in British military and naval history with emphasis on education, training and doctrine. His publications include *The Royal Navy and the Capital Ship in the Interwar Period: An Operational Perspective*, *Thinking Wisely, Planning Boldly: The Higher Education and Training of Royal Navy Officers, 1919-39* and *Towards a Wider War: British Strategic Decision Making and Military Effectiveness in Scandinavia, 1939-40*. He is presently writing a history of British amphibious operations for the period 1882-1916.

DAVID OMISSI is senior lecturer in modern history at the University of Hull. His edited volume *Indian Voices of the Great War: Soldiers' Letters, 1914–1918* (1999) was reissued with a new preface by Penguin India in 2014. His publications include 'A Dismal Story? Britain, the Gurkhas and the Partition of India, 1945–1948' in A. Jeffreys and P. Rose (eds), *The Indian Army, 1939–47: Experience and Development* (2012); "A Most Arduous but a most Noble Duty': Gladstone and the British Raj in India, 1868–98' in Mary E. Daly and K. Theodore Hoppen (eds), *Gladstone: Ireland*

and Beyond (2011); and 'Europe Through Indian Eyes: Indian Soldiers Encounter England and France', *The English Historical Review*, 122/496 (2007).

ADAM PRIME is a PhD candidate with the School of History, Politics and International Relations, the University of Leicester. His thesis is a study of the Indian Army's British officer corps from the aftermath of the Great Rebellion of 1857 to the end of the First World War. Prior to this Adam studied for a MA in Military History at the University of Chester and a BA(Hons) in Contemporary Military and International History at the University of Salford. This is his first publication.

PETER STANLEY is research professor at the University of NSW Canberra. Formerly the Principal Historian at the Australian War Memorial, he has published over thirty books, in Australian and British imperial military history. His 2010 book, Bad Characters: Sex, Crime, Mutiny, Murder and the Australian Imperial Force, was jointly awarded the Prime Minister's Prize for Australian History. In 2015 he published *Die in Battle, Do not Despair, the Indians on Gallipoli, 1915*, the first account of the Indian Army's part in the campaign.

KRISTIAN COATES ULRICHSEN is the Fellow for the Middle East in the Baker Institute for Public Policy at Rice University and affiliate professor at the Henry M. Jackson School of International Studies, University of Washington. He is author of *The Logistics and Politics of the British Campaigns in the Middle East, 1914-22* and *The First World War in the Middle East*.

CAT WILSON was awarded her PhD from Hull University in 2013. Her research examined Winston Churchill's portrayal of the war in the Far East as set-out within his memoirs entitled *The Second World War*, and was published by Palgrave Macmillan a year later. Her research interests include British imperial history – particularly the *Raj* and the Indian Army during the First and Second World Wars – and Winston Churchill. She is currently researching her next book, provisionally entitled 'Churchill and India: the complexities of colonialism in the nineteenth and twentieth centuries'.

GRAHAM WINTON (PhD, FRHistS, FRGS), retired in 2008 as principal of an adult education college to concentrate on research, publishing and lecturing. A part-time tutor with the University of Cambridge Institute of Continuing Education for over twenty years, he has lectured in the USA, India and extensively in Britain on military and landscape history, particularly relating to the First World War. He has written widely on military horses, army remounts and veterinary services, recently publishing *Theirs Not To Reason Why: Horsing the British Army 1875-1925* (Solihull: Helion, 2014) and 'British-Indian Cavalry: From Mobilisation to the Western Front 1915', in *Courage Without Glory*, Spencer Jones (ed) (Solihull: Helion, 2015). He has also appeared on BBC radio and television programmes relating to horses and the Army Remount Department in the First World War.

Foreword

The First World War was arguably one of the defining events of the twentieth century. Tomes have been written of the war: its causes, conduct and impact have spawned an entire genre of both popular and scholarly writing. First World War studies are today a bona fide academic discipline. While conventionally the conflict was seen as a European war, global colonial networks ensured that it spread beyond the heartland until it embroiled large parts of the world. The war did not discriminate between colonized and colonizer; both suffered the consequences in equal measure. Yet the narratives of the war were largely shaped by the victors in the metropole and passed on to the colonies for uncritical adoption. These hollow narratives endured for as long as the colonial powers that generated them held sway. With the passing of empires, the narratives that they had spawned were unceremoniously discarded by the erstwhile colonies and replaced with nationalist histories of political struggle and emancipation. A war, even a global war of epic proportions, which was not rooted in the political soil of the newly independent nations was quickly consigned to the dustbins of history in the post-colonial world. Scant regard was paid to the myriad ways in which the war had affected colonial societies because it was felt by the successor states that the Great War was not 'their' war.

Yet the war did indisputably impact the lives of people in Africa, Asia and the Middle East. As the colonial experience recedes from memory, there has been a resurgence of interest in the role of the periphery in shaping the war in Europe and beyond, as well as the manner in which the war itself impacted upon these societies. That the war and its impact are open to multiple interpretations is evident from a study of the collection of censored letters of Indian soldiers held in the British library. These letters provide scholars with a much-needed subaltern 'voice' to help them come to a better understanding of the motives and motivations of an army that has long vanished with little trace of its passing. However, like all humans at all points in history, the views expressed in these fragments are often contradictory and do not speak with a single voice or to a single purpose. It is for the historian to untangle these, and other connected strands, and weave them into a coherent narrative.

A number of contributors to this volume have made the very valid point that the role of the Indian Army in the Great War has been ignored, if not forgotten. Their observation rings true. Until recently, the number of books on the subject could literally be counted on the fingers of the hand. The centenary of the war has however seen a revival of interest in the subject. The 'India and the Great War' centenary commemoration project undertaken by the United Service Institution of India with the support of the Government of India Ministry of External Affairs was a reflection of the changed socio-political perceptions within the country. It demonstrated that India had now moved out of the colonial shadow and matured sufficiently as a nation to be able to not just interrogate the past but also begin to take ownership of it.

The 'India and the Great War' centenary commemoration project commenced with an international conference at which a couple of the papers in this and its companion volume, were originally presented. The spread of subjects is indicative of both the holistic manner in which the conflict was examined as well as the multiple interpretations that were presented by scholars from different parts of the world. From a national point of view, the project is significant for having effected a change in the official narrative. For the first time since independence an official acknowledgement of India's involvement in the First World War has been forthcoming. This was exemplified by the fact that at the conference the Vice President of India delivered the inaugural address while the Foreign Secretary gave the valedictory speech.

The conference was just the beginning of academic evaluation of various aspects of India's role in the war. Professor Peter Stanley's book on the Indians at Gallipoli (*Die in Battle, Do not Despair: The Indians on Gallipoli, 1915*. Helion 2015), which preceded this volume in this series, and others that are to follow, are set to be important milestones in the historiography of the Great War and of the Indian Army. These works are also indicative of the immense potential for research and inquiry that still remains.

The authors of the papers published in this volume along with the editor are to be complimented for having added immensely to our knowledge of the subject. It is hoped that their labours will generate new awareness within India and around the world of the impact of the war and its consequences for the subcontinent and stimulate others to build upon the solid base of knowledge being now created.

Rana Chhina
New Delhi
August 2017

Introduction

This edited collection is a companion volume to one that was produced on the Indian Army during the Second World War and the period up to Independence.[1] David Omissi, a contributor to both volumes, stated in a talk for the National Army Museum that when he started researching this subject area in the 1990s, there were very few scholars studying the Indian Army but now it has become fashionable.[2] The range of recent material published on the Indian Army in both World Wars has amply demonstrated his assertion.[3]

The idea for this publication originated in late 2014 with the intention to show both the global nature of the conflict and demonstrate the wide role of the Indian Army. In Britain, recent narrative and illustrated histories have tended to concentrate on the Indian Army in France and Flanders but this has not been reciprocated in India, where recent work has covered the global nature of the army's role.[4] It was felt, that forty years after the publication of the excellent and perhaps less well-known edited volume produced by Ellinwood C. De Witt and S. D. Pradhan, *India and World War One*, a new edited collection was long overdue.[5] Thus, this publication both highlights some of the research that has been undertaken in the intervening period but is also

---

1   See Alan Jeffreys and Patrick Rose (eds.), *The Indian Army, 1939-47: Experience and Development* (Farnham: Ashgate, 2012).
2   National Army Museum talk given by David Omissi at the Army & Navy Club, 2 November 2015, entitled 'Illiterate but Literary: The Letters of Indian Soldiers on the Western Front, 1914-1918'.
3   See the Select Bibliography in this volume for the First World War period.
4   See for example In the UK and Europe: Shrabani Basu, *For King and Another Country: Indian Soldiers on the Western Front 1914-18* (London: Bloomsbury, 2015); David Olusoga, *The World's War* (London: Head of Zeus, 2014): Santanu Das, *1914-1918 India Troops in Europe* (Paris: Edition Gallimard, 2014) and Simon Doherty and Tom Donovan, *The Indian Corps on the Western Front: A Handbook and Battlefield Guide* (Brighton: Tom Donovan Editions, 2015). In India: Vedica Kant, *'If I die here, who will remember me?' India and the First World War* (New Delhi: Roli Books, 2014) and Amarinder Singh, *Honour and Fidelity: India's Military Contribution to the Great War 1914-18* (New Delhi: Roli Books, 2014) and Rana Chhina, *India and the First World War 1914-1918* (New Delhi: United Service Institution of India, 2014).
5   D. C. Ellinwood & S. D. Pradhan, *India and World War I* (New Delhi: Manohar, 1978).

a timely reminder that more research needs to be done in this area, even with the popularity of First World War studies. This volume covers the more traditional areas of the Indian Army on the Western Front, in Palestine, Mesopotamia and the defence of the Suez Canal. Other chapters focus on combined operations, Indian prisoners of war in Germany, the expansion of the officer corps, the role of religion, as well as the mobilisation of the equine army at the beginning of the war and demobilisation of the army in the period from 1918 until 1923. Two additional chapters are related to the theme: on the role of the Territorial Army in India and Winston Churchill's portrayal of the Indian Army during the Gallipoli campaign in his *World Crisis*.

There have also been a number of conferences, exhibitions and seminars in the UK, Europe but also more importantly in India. The conference held at the USI in March 2014 and the pioneering efforts of Squadron Leader Rana Chhina has awakened both academic and popular interest in the role of India and the Indian Army during the First World War that hitherto had been dismissed as part of the colonial legacy. Two of the chapters by Anirudh Deshpande and Alan Jeffreys originate in papers given at the aforementioned conference.[6] This book is published by Helion in the 'War and Military Culture in South Asia, 1757-1947' series in association with the Centre of Armed Forces Historical Research, at the United Service Institution (USI) of India in New Delhi.

The volume is an academic reassessment of the army by both established and early-career scholars of the Indian Army from Australia, Britain, India and the United States. In the opening essay, Raymond Callahan and Daniel Marston look at the historiography of the Indian Army and note how neglected it has been until recently. It also provides an overview of the Indian Army and the main theatres it fought in during the war. Rob Johnson next looks at the Indian Army on the Western Front in 1914-15, taking a more traditional historical line. The latest addition to the historiography is the work of George Morton-Jack that also warrants attention.[7]

In the early stages of the war India provided a colossal number of horses for the European war. This topic has not been covered by either historians of the Indian Army or the First World War, making Graham Winton's chapter a unique addition to the historiography. The fourth chapter is by the naval historian Joseph Moretz who looks at the important role that combined operations planning before the war played for the army and how unprepared it was for simultaneous campaigns. Adam Prime looks at the often neglected role of the army and the defence of the Suez Canal during the early years of the war. He assesses the training and acclimatisation of the army in Egypt and then examines their operational performance in defence of the canal.

---

6   The remaining papers will be published in the Helion series edited by Rana Chhina.
7   An earlier version of this chapter was published in *British Journal for Military History*, Vol. 2, Issue 2, February 2016. See George Morton- Jack, *The Indian Army on the Western Front: India's Expeditionary Force to France and Belgium in the First World War* (Cambridge: CUP, 2014).

His chapter paves the way for the fighting on the Gallipoli peninsula by 29th Indian Infantry Brigade, 7th Indian Mountain Artillery Brigade as well as detachments of the Indian Mule Corps and Indian Field Ambulance units.[8] Cat Wilson's chapter is a development of her work on Winston Churchill, India and the Indian Army during the Second World War by looking at Churchill, his First World War memoirs and the portrayal of Indian soldiers in the Gallipoli campaign.[9]

The important question of religion is explored in two chapters by David Omissi. He looks at the vital role to the Indian soldiers of the Muslim faith and the impact on their military service, as well as the wider strategy of British India in the first two years of the war towards the global community of Islam.[10] His other chapter is devoted to Sikhism. Omissi demonstrates the important links with the Sikhs of the Punjab and the Indian Army, resulting in the recruitment of large numbers of the Sikh community, and looking at what was the effect of the war on the Punjab. After the war and specifically after the Amritsar massacre of 1919, many former Sikh soldiers were instrumental in the Akali and Ghadr movements. Alan Jeffreys charts the expansion of the officer corps.

Andrew Jarboe draws upon his PhD thesis 'Soldiers of Empire: Indian Sepoys in and beyond the metropole during the First World War, 1914-1919' to provide a fascinating chapter on Indian prisoners of war in Germany looking at collaboration, dissent and repatriation.[11] Kristian Coates Ulrichsen and Michael Creese provide overviews of the campaigns in Mesopotamia and the Indian cavalry in Palestine respectively. Coates Ulrichsen has already written widely on the subject whilst Creese has produced work on the Jodhpur Lancers as well as on Indian officers.[12] Peter Stanley outlines his next project looking at British Territorial Army regiments and the soldiers' experience, who were transferred to India to replace Indian Army and British Army regular soldiers. In the final chapter, Anirudh Deshpande covers the demobilisation

---

8   See Peter Stanley, *Die in Battle, Do Not Despair: The Indians on Gallipoli, 1915* (Solihull: Helion, 2015).
9   See also Cat Wilson, *Churchill on the Far East in the Second World War: Hiding the History of the 'Special Relationship'* (Basingstoke: Palgrave Macmillan, 2014).
10 This important area has been largely neglected with the exception of Nile Green, *Islam and the Army in Colonial India* (Cambridge: Cambridge University Press, 2009).
11 See also Andrew Jarboe, 'The Long Road Home: Britain, Germany and the Repatriation of Indian Prisoners of War after the First World War' in Eric Storm and Ali Al Tuna (eds.), *Colonial Soldiers in Europe, 1914-1945: "Aliens in Uniform" in Wartime Societies* (London: Routledge, 2017) and Andrew Jarboe, 'The Prisoner Dilemma: Britain, Germany and the Repatriation of Indian Prisoners of War', *The Round Table: The Commonwealth Journal of International Affairs*, Vol. 103, No. 2, 2014.
12 See Kristian Coates Ulrichsen, *The Logistics and Politics of the British Campaigns in the Middle East, 1914-22* (Basingstoke: Palgrave Macmillan, 2011) and *The First World War in the Middle East* (London: Hurst, 2014). See also Michael Creese, *Swords Trembling in their Scabbards: The changing status of Indian officers in the Indian Army 1757-1947* (Solihull: Helion, 2015) and he has a history of the Jodhpur Lancers awaiting publication in India.

of the army and its economic situation after the war.¹³ The Indian Army continued to be in very heavy demand after 1918 with the third Afghan war and the campaign in Waziristan, 1919-20 in conjunction with the insurrection in Mesopotamia, 1920. Indeed the Indian Army was still providing troops to garrison Iraq in 1922 when regiments based there were being amalgamated to make 'super' regiments, as a result of the 1921-22 reforms, instigated after the recommendations of Esher Committee, formed in 1919, to examine the perceived setbacks of the Indian Army during the First World War. At the same time Indian Army troops continued to act as an 'Aid to Civil Power' especially with the rise of the nationalist movement, including the notorious Amritsar massacre. Simultaneously India was severely affected by the Spanish flu epidemic of 1919. It was the country most affected by the pandemic, with over 18 million dying. The half-hearted British response further fuelled resentment of Imperial rule and increased support of the nationalist movement.

In the last year of the centenary commemorations of the First World War, this collection demonstrates the ubiquitous role of the Indian Army. According to Vipul Dutta, 'The "success" of the centenary, morbid as it may sound, has been its ability to put First World War studies on a firm footing in the larger network of South Asia studies'.[14] It is hoped this volume will be of use to these students. Lastly, the editor is very grateful to all the contributors, Squadron Leader Rana Chhina for writing the preface and George Morton-Jack for all his help in the peer review process when preparing this volume.

---

13   See also Anirudh Deshpande, *British Military Policy in India, 1900-1945: Colonial Constraints and Declining Power* (Delhi: Manohar, 2005).
14   Vipul Dutta, 'India and the First World War', 29 June 2015, Defence in Depth blog, Defence Studies Department, King's College London, https://defenceindepth.co/?s=vipul+dutta, accessed 19 May 2017.

1

Neglected Soldiers[1]

Raymond Callahan & Daniel Marston

For two centuries, Britain was a global power – the first modern superpower. When considering the military dimension of that power, the Royal Navy comes first to mind, but as a French general is supposed to have once reminded a British counterpart, the Royal Navy did not run on wheels. Empires need armies. Britain's was never large enough for a global power. Constrained by the British aversion to conscription, as well as parliamentary reluctance to accept high military (as opposed to naval) costs, the British Army was always relatively small in relation to both European neighbours or imperial commitments. But Britain found, almost accidentally, another army. As it turned from merchant venturer to empire builder, the East India Company created an army that cost the British taxpayer almost nothing in blood or treasure. That army became the strategic reserve and expeditionary force that underpinned the growth and maintenance of Britain's vast Asian (and later Middle Eastern) imperium. In the two twentieth century total wars, its existence made possible a global war effort on a scale that Britain's own manpower resources simply would not have supported. In the aftermath of victory in 1945, it ceased to be available to Britain and, within two decades, the empire it had helped to create and defend went as well.

The memory of the Indian Army fell into a curious limbo after 1947. The centrality of the Indian Army not only to the Raj but to what Chris Bayly and Tim Harper have called the 'great arc' of British Asia might be thought to have won for it a certain amount of historical attention, but, until recently, that has not been the case. There is of course a great deal of older writing for the era of the Company and the Queen Empress – memoirs, barely readable official publications and dutiful regimental histories – but

---

1   This essay is not intended to be a detailed bibliographic survey, which would require a volume to itself. It is rather an overview of what the Indian Army did 1914-18, with an indication both of significant issues and the contribution of recent scholarship to the examination of those issues.

high quality modern scholarship is relatively sparse: studies like John Pemble's of the Company's war with Nepal, Douglas Peers' of the Company's military-fiscal state at its height and David Omissi's careful examination of the post-Mutiny army are relatively rare.[2] The one exception to this, of course, is the 1857 'Sepoy Mutiny,' which has always attracted writers (and readers) of popular history. But even that epochal event has not made much of a dent in general scholarly neglect of the Indian Army (the relevant volume of the *Oxford History of the British Empire* manages to deal with the collapse of the Company's Bengal Army in two very short paragraphs).[3] There is not even a good, recent survey of the Indian Army to which the beginning student can be directed. The last two Indian Army field marshals, Claude Auchinleck and Bill Slim, over forty years ago asked for the commissioning of an official history of the army they had led in its twilight. That suggestion was quietly ignored, and the only good general history remains the still useful *A Matter of Honour* written forty years ago by a former officer of the Indian Civil Service, Philip Mason – an elegant writer but his account is heavily anecdotal and drenched in nostalgia.[4]

The era of the first of the twentieth century's world wars has however recently seen a great deal of scholarly activity, including some significant work on the Indian Army, perhaps indicating a renewed interest in the most remarkable institution created by the British during their imperial adventure. The army that went to war in 1914 had taken the form it would retain until the end over the preceding three decades. The Eden Commission, sitting at the end of the Second Afghan War (1878-81), had recommended a range of modernizing measures that were slowly implemented over the next dozen years. Further reorganization was put in hand by the imperious Lord

---

2 John Pemble, *The Invasion of Nepal: John Company at War* (London: OUP, 1971); Douglas Peers, *Between Mars and Mammon: Colonial Armies and the Garrison State in Early Nineteenth Century India* (London: I. B. Tauris, 1995); David Omissi, *The Sepoy and the Raj: The Indian Army, 1860-1940* (Basingstoke: Macmillan, 1994). A collective volume, Daniel P. Marston and Chandar S. Sundaram (eds.), *A Military History of India and South Asia: From the East India Company to the Nuclear Era* (Westport, CT: Praeger, 2007) pulls together the work of a number of Indian and western scholars. A great deal of recent scholarly writing has appeared as articles in journals of limited circulation. In the absence of a comprehensive bibliographic survey, the source notes in the titles listed in the footnotes to this essay are an excellent starting point.

3 Andrew Porter (ed.), *The Oxford History of the British Empire, Vol. III: The Nineteenth Century* (Oxford: OUP, 1999), p. 418. The author of the chapter, 'India, 1818-1860,' D. A. Washbrook, manages to cram in, however, one major error about Bengal Army recruitment. A good recent survey is Saul David, *The Indian Mutiny, 1857* (London: Penguin, 2002).

4 Philip Mason, *A Matter of Honour: An account of the Indian Army, its officers and men* (London: Jonathan Cape, 1974). Lieutenant General S. L. Menezes, *Fidelity and Honour: The Indian Army from the Seventeenth to the Twenty-first Century* (New Delhi: OUP, 2001) is an interesting survey from a different perspective. General Menezes began his career in the twilight of the Raj. A good general history incorporating the finally growing body of recent scholarship is badly needed.

Kitchener (Commander-in-Chief, India, 1902-1909). One of Kitchener's acolytes, Sir Beauchamp Duff, led the army in 1914. The old Presidency armies, and their separate officer corps, were gone and the Indian Army was a unitary institution; its sepoys, although often serving in units whose names recalled the days of the Company and the Presidency armies, reflected in fact the 'martial races' preoccupations of Field Marshal Lord Roberts, the most influential Indian service officer of the 19th century.[5] The 1914 Army was configured to control the ever restive North West Frontier, support civil authority within the Raj, and function as an imperial reserve, ready to send expeditionary forces overseas. The modernization set in train by Kitchener had given the Indian Army its own staff college (established at Quetta in 1907), and its own general staff. The newly created Indian general staff was not yet a smoothly functioning planning body for operations outside India, however. The Indian Army Kitchener left had fine fighting qualities but also harboured quite a few weaknesses, some of long standing, that would quickly surface once it was committed to a war beyond anything anyone had foreseen.[6]

The Indian Army was 159,000 strong in 1914, with 35,000 reservists – a figure that turned out to be less impressive than it seemed. It had never been designed for extensive, lengthy, overseas deployments (and the incumbent Viceroy, Lord Hardinge, felt strongly that it should remain a 'small war' force). Nonetheless, at the war's outbreak India dispatched quickly and smoothly seven Indian Expeditionary Forces, designated 'A' through 'G.' 'A' went to France; 'B' and 'C' were destined for East

---

5 There is a new biography of Roberts: Rodney Atwood, *The Life of Field Marshal Lord Roberts* (London: Bloomsbury, 2015). The Roberts era is carefully surveyed by Douglas Peers, 'The Martial Races and the Indian Army in the Victorian Era' in Marston and Sundaram, *op. cit*, pp. 34-52 and in greater detail in Omissi, *The Sepoy and the Raj*. This is probably the place to point out that the 'Indian service' was completely separate from the British Army. In Company days, officers' commissions came from the Court of Directors, not the King, although after 1796 Company officers held 'concurrent' royal commissions, which meant that a Company officer had in effect an auxiliary royal commission in whatever rank he held in the Company's service. Company officers were trained separately, at the Company's 'military seminary' at Addiscombe. After the Company was replaced by the Crown both the Indian Army and its officer corps remained separate entities, even though now all officers were trained at Sandhurst. Thereafter however they went their separate ways for most of their careers. There were jealousies and tensions between the two services, originating in the eighteenth century, that lingered throughout the lifetime of the Raj. By 1914 it was common for British service officers to command higher Indian Army formations (brigades and divisions but never sepoy battalions). Although less common, Indian Army officers could be found in command of British formations. Nearly every British Army officer, at some point in his career, would do a tour in India, almost invariably with a British unit posted there. Again, the reverse was much less common.
6 A good, clear, brief guide to the structure and administration of the Indian Army under Company and Crown is T. A. Heathcote, *The Indian Army: The Garrison of British Imperial India, 1822-1922* (Newton Abbot: David & Charles, 1974). A study of Kitchener in India is badly needed.

Africa. Then 'D' was shipped to Mesopotamia (today's Iraq), E and F to Egypt and, finally G to Gallipoli. This was the beginning of a steady flow of Indian military units (as well as labor and support units) overseas. By 1918, all these commitments (to which a contribution to the Salonika force had been added, as well as units stationed at Aden and in the Persian Gulf) had ballooned the 1914 army to 3 cavalry and 13 infantry divisions, a force larger than the combined total raised by all the Dominions. To do this India had enlisted 877,068 combatants and 563, 369 non-combatants in support units ('followers'). On 11 November 1918 the Indian Army had 1, 123,264 men serving abroad (and of course there were internal security units and the garrison of the North West Frontier not included in this total). This prodigiously expanded force had suffered 53,486 dead and 64,350 wounded. It was a remarkable war effort wrung out of a country rich in little but manpower. It was also one that was relegated rapidly to the historical attic.[7]

World War I produced an avalanche of writing. In the Anglophone world that was overwhelmingly concentrated on the Western Front (or, in Australia, the epic of Anzac). There were, of course, official histories slowly making their appearance (the last Western Front volume not until 1948). The Government of India published a summary in 1924; there was an account by an 'official observer' of the service of IEFA – the Indian Corps in France – which went into a second edition.[8] But there was no Indian official history, as there would be after World War II. Inevitably historians were dependent on official histories as foundational sources for their accounts (under the then prevailing rules, World War I era documents would not be accessible for an indeterminate period, eventually set at fifty years in 1958 and reduced to thirty in 1967). Of course, Indian units were mentioned in the various series of official accounts – each theatre was accorded one (the East African campaign series was never completed). But no comprehensive treatment, official or otherwise, of the contribution of the Raj and its army to Britain's victory in 1918 appeared before a new war, followed shortly by the 'Transfer of Power,' swept both away. World War

---

7   These figures are taken from *Statistics of the Military Effort of the British Empire during the Great War 1944-1920* (London, 1922), p. 777. No two sources for the 1914-18 Indian war effort give exactly the same number but these given are as close as we are likely to get and very clearly establish the magnitude of the Indian war effort.

8   Government of India, *India's Contribution to the Great War* (Calcutta: Government of India, 1923); J. Merewether and F. E. Smith, *The Indian Corps in France*, 2nd ed. (London: John Murray, 1919). F. E. Smith, later 1st Earl of Birkenhead, wrote very favorably about the sepoys who fought in France. Later, as Secretary of State for India in Baldwin's 1924-29 Conservative government he was to oppose further movement towards Indian self-government. Had alcoholism not led to his early death, his good friend Winston Churchill would have had a powerful supporter in his diehard 1931-35 campaign to prevent the passage of the 1935 Government of India Act. Both Churchill and 'F. E.' understood that a link existed between control of the Indian Army and British global power. Neither understood the post 1919 impossibility of turning back the clock in India. At least F. E. was willing to assess the Indian Army generously, something Churchill would never do.

I only began to reclaim scholarly, and popular, attention in the last few decades, and the Indian Army's renaissance as a subject of serious historical study is even more recent. One reason for this neglect was the general turning away from imperial themes in Britain as the empire faded from the map – and the initial disinterest of post-1947 India in the army that had served the British Raj (even though it was the same army that won India's wars with Pakistan and, almost uniquely among post-colonial armies, respected civilian authority).[9] But changing foci of scholarly interest – and the book selling opportunity of a centenary – have now produced a rebirth of interest in the Indian Army's role in the first of the two total wars that would destroy the institution it served. The balance of this essay will address some of the works resulting from this renewal of focus on what, after all, was one of the pillars on which rested the huge structure of British power 'East of Suez.'

IEFA, which would go to France, initially mobilized on the assumption its destination would be Egypt, but that quickly shifted to France (the aged Roberts, consulted by the Cabinet, argued against involving the Indian Army in 'white man's wars' – although quite how this squared with his assumption that it could face the Russian Army on the North West Frontier is not clear). Given that mobilization was ordered during the summer leave season when many sepoys were scattered across the subcontinent in villages remote from roads and the telegraph, the speed with which the 3rd (Lahore) and 7th (Meerut) Indian divisions were mobilized, moved and concentrated within three weeks at their ports of embarkation (Bombay and Karachi) was impressive. The most careful study of IEFA by George Morton-Jack points out that the mobilization of the Indian Army for the 1911 Delhi Durbar had provided a sort of dress rehearsal for 1914.[10] By late September IEFA, 24,000 strong, the largest expedition ever to leave India, was disembarking at Marseilles. Within a month they were in action on the Western Front. It was a very remarkable display of improvisation, professionalism and efficiency by the Indian military machine.

The British Expeditionary Force's Indian Army Corps would remain on the Western Front until the end of 1915 when it redeployed to Mesopotamia (leaving the Indian Army Cavalry Corps behind – the horsemen, whose troopers were called sowars, would remain in France until early 1918). During that time, it fought at both Ypres and in the first major British offensive at Neuve Chapelle in the Spring of 1915. Although its performance, in a war for which it had never trained, was

---

9   This neglect cost history the memories of the 'jawans' (the replacement word for the venerable 'sepoy') of the World Wars. There is no real Indian counterpart to the Imperial War Museum's invaluable collection of letters, diaries, personal accounts and interviews that give us insight into experience of rank and file British soldiers. Even in 1939-45 most jawans were illiterate, so there will be no diaries, letters or accounts written in retirement. Only oral history interviews, never done, could have saved their experiences for posterity.
10 George Morton-Jack, *The Indian Army on the Western Front: India's Expeditionary Force to France and Belgium in the First World War* (Cambridge: CUP, 2014). This is a model monograph.

good, various controversies arose that reverberated in subsequent historical writing, controversies dealt with effectively by some recent publications. Beginning as gossip and rumor and ending as scholarly articles, the criticisms of the Indian Corps were that its performance rapidly degraded as the ranks of its British officers were thinned by casualties; that, confronted by industrialized total war, so different from what it had trained for (or experienced on the North West Frontier) its morale sank; that the cold, damp and gloom of France in autumn and winter further depressed men unused to it and ill clad for it. Declining morale was signalled by the appearance of self-inflicted wounds. It might seem that Roberts had been right – the Indian Army was unsuitable for a 'white man's war.' The whole question of the performance of the Indian Corps has however lately been revisited, and, as is so often the case, a second look has produced startlingly different judgments. Major Gordon Corrigan, a retired Gurkha officer, wrote a detailed, readable study *Sepoys in the Trenches* (of the 24 infantry battalions in the original IEFA, 25% were Gurkha).[11] Corrigan drew on a study of 1,000 wound cases conducted by Colonel Sir Bruce Seaton, commandant of the Kitchener Indian Hospital at Brighton, at the request of the Indian Corps Commander, Sir James Willcocks, which found that only 6 of the wounds could have been self-inflicted. George Morton-Jack's *The Indian Army on the Western Front*, an even more thorough monographic treatment of IEFA from mobilization to departure from France, concludes 'self-infliction of wounds was not endemic among the... Indian Corps.' Most cases occurred in October 1914 as the corps acclimated to the Western Front and were confined 'almost entirely to certain battalions or companies within just two brigades' in one division. Morton-Jack also points out that cases of self-inflicted wounds in the BEF ran into the hundreds in 1914 (and the problem persisted until 1918). Similar problems cropped up at the same time in the French and German armies. In fact it would seem that the most interesting question to ask about the whole non-issue is why was it so quickly and widely believed that the sepoys were prone to self-wounding. Colonel Seaton remarked at the time 'others claim it... it is not true.'[12] The obvious answer is that the rumors fed into a widely held stereotype – the inferiority of the non-white as a soldier, as well as the British Army prejudice against the Indian service. When Sir John French, the Commander-in-Chief of the BEF, inspected a brigade from each of the Indian Corps' divisions in January 1915, he marched stonily along the ranks of the assembled sepoys in silence (he spoke no Indian language and had not bothered to learn even a few phrases) and promptly left without a word to any of the British officers either – he shared their language but not their social class.[13]

---

11   Gordon Corrigan, *Sepoys in the Trenches: The Indian Corps on the Western Front, 1914-15* (Staplehurst: Spellmount, 1999).
12   The quotations are from Corrigan, *Sepoys in the Trenches*, pp. 178-80 and Morton-Jack, *The Indian Army on the Western Front*, pp. 174-75.
13   Corrigan, *Sepoys in the Trenches*, p. 134.

The best picture we have of the sepoys' own reactions to the experience into which they were plunged in France is David Omissi's edition of the letters, or extracts from them, preserved in the records of the British mail censorship office in France which had been set up to handle the surprising volume of mail the Indian Corps generated.[14] Some Viceroy Commissioned Officers (VCOs) could read and write. Many could not. Virtually all sepoys were illiterate. The letters were dictated to a battalion clerk, who may have 'improved' on the original phrasing. All wrote, or dictated, with the knowledge that the letters would be vetted before dispatch to India. There is in them, therefore, not only surprisingly flowery turns of phrase but many pious statements of loyalty. Even with all these filters, it is hard to read into these letters a sense of shaky morale or homesick depression – and very possible to see how shrewdly some of the VCOs and sepoys assessed their surroundings. If allegations of collapsing morale can now be dismissed, there is no doubt the Indian Corps faced a very considerable set of problems growing out of the 1914 structure of the army itself.[15]

The Indian Army had fewer than fifty reserve officers. There were sepoy reservists but it quickly became apparent that many, perhaps most, were no longer physically able to sustain active service, and, in any case, their training was badly out of date. Pre-1914 battalions did their own recruiting, something that caused few problems as long as casualties were relatively low, as was the case in Frontier soldiering. But replacements on the scale required in France (and, soon enough, other theatres) overwhelmed the system. In the early months of the war, the Indian Army was rapidly improvising new systems for officer recruitment and training, as well as a new system for feeding replacements to units overseas, scattered from Tanganyika to France. It was also embarked on a far more intensive recruitment effort than had ever before been needed – or, even, imagined. That effort (like the even greater effort of 1939-45) was remarkably successful as the 1918 size of the army indicates. When the decision was taken to withdraw the Indian Corps' two infantry divisions for deployment to the Middle East, it was not because of either the fragility of their morale, or their failure to cope with northern European weather, or the impossibility of sustaining

---

14   David Omissi, *Indian Voices of the Great War: Soldier's Letters, 1914-1918* (Basingstoke: Macmillan, 1999).
15   The VCOs were a crucial, and often overlooked, component of the Indian Army, and had no real counterpart in any Western army. In Company days they were called 'Indian Officers,' the VCO designation appearing after 1857. They were, in fact, officers commanding up to platoon level (and, if a unit's British officers became casualties, often companies as well). The most senior of them, the Subedar Major, functioned as the battalion commander's right hand man in all matters relating to sepoy customs, morale – and moods. However, although saluted by sepoys, they did not rate a salute from British Other Ranks, let alone officers, could not command above platoon level, were often only semi-literate at best (although this began to change after 1918) and had no opportunity for what is now called 'further military education.' Nonetheless, in both World Wars they were absolutely crucial to the Indian Army's cohesion. The position (although of course not the title) survives in the Indian Army today.

their fighting strength on the Western Front, but because the Government of India wanted them back to sustain its rapidly deepening involvement in a campaign of its own in Mesopotamia that was going very badly.

Even as the Indian Army grappled with logistical issues on the Western Front, it was beginning a tactical transformation that would ultimately contribute to its successes in northern Mesopotamia and Syria. By instituting a culture of learning and adaptation on the battlefield, the Indian Army, along with their British and Empire counterparts went through a series of significant organizational, tactical and operational reforms which enabled them to not only hold their own in the first modern European conflict, but emerge from battle in 1918 as a victorious and modern institution.[16]

Following their rapid deployment to France described earlier, the 3rd Lahore and 7th Meerut divisions went into the line in and around Ypres in late October and early November 1914. The Indian Corps helped relieve the British II Corps which had been fighting since August, and by the end of 1914 they represented nearly one-third of the British Expeditionary Force (BEF).

British authorities in London and Delhi had not anticipated the level of violence associated with the 'modern warfare' of 1914, and upon arrival in France the Indian Corps had been re-equipped with the newest rifles and equipment. Despite this, by the end of November, many Indian Army battalions had suffered close to 50% casualties on the front lines - as had the BEF's professional battalions. One Indian battalion, the 57th Wilde's Rifles, Frontier Force, had landed in France in August, with 14 British officers and 788 VCOs, NCOs and men. By the following August, after a year of more or less continuous combat, the unit was reporting 10 officers killed, 8 wounded, 16 Indian officers killed or wounded and 800 men killed or wounded.[17]

The Indian Corps gained numerous battle honours in France during this period, including Ypres, Neuvelle Chappelle, Aubers Ridge, Festubert and Loos. Five Indian soldiers won the Victoria Cross. Like British units before them and Canadians after, the Indian units and formations struggled to get to grips with the brutality of the Western Front. The Indian Army, similar to some regular BEF formations, had a solid core of officers, VCOs, NCOs and men who had active duty experience. It may have been on the North-West Frontier or in China, but it was still useful and many of these veterans attempted to adapt their knowledge to the unique environment

---

16 See Paddy Griffith, *Battle Tactics on the Western Front* (New Haven: Yale University Press, 1994); Bill Rawlins, *Surviving Trench Warfare: Technology and the Canadian Corps, 1914-1918* (Toronto: University of Toronto Press, 1992); Tim Travers, *The Killing Ground* (London: Unwin and Hyman, 1987); Tim Travers, *How the War was Won* (London: Routledge, 1992); Mark Grotelueschen, *The AEF Way of War: The American Army and Combat in World War One* (Cambridge: CUP, 2007) and Jonathan Boff, *Winning and Losing on the Western Front: The British Third Army and the Defeat of Germany in 1918* (Cambridge: CUP, 2012) for in-depth discussion of the learning curve for British Empire and US forces.

17 W.E.H. Condon, *Frontier Force Rifles* (Aldershot: Gale & Polden, 1953), p. 57.

of the Western Front. They used skirmish tactics learned on the Frontier, as their British counterparts adapted tactics from the Boer War to trench raids and control of no-man's land. The Indian Frontier Force units succeeded so well that they were commended in 1915 for their successes in scouting and dominating no-man's land.[18]

Throughout 1914 and 1915, Indian units honed their skills on the battlefields of the Western Front. They learned from veteran formations in the sector, consumed the various circulars developed by senior commands and carried out their own focused in-theatre training for replacements arriving from India. As with their British and Canadian allies, not all Indian Corps units performed at the same level, but the desire to learn and adapt was evident.[19] As Morton-Jack notes:

> up to the end of 1915, the British Army had adapted to the Western Front like the Indian Army. From August to December 1914, its pre-war regular battalions learned lessons much as the Indian troops did about how to hold trenches. Whether they were drawn from the Home Army or the Army in India, they frequently made the same mistakes overexposing themselves to German fire, before they improved through common sense, discussion with more experienced officers and men, and tactical circulars.[20]

World War I in the Middle East has exerted a continuing fascination for historians, scholarly and popular, in large part because the legacy of those complexities (and the attempts to resolve them) remains very much with us. Despite this however, the role of the Government of India, and its army, in the story remains underappreciated – perhaps because the rival Arab Bureau in Cairo harboured a talented writer among its officers, whose postwar narrative would permanently focus the story on the 'Arab Revolt.'[21] In fact, India was one of the main determinants of British policy in the region especially during the war's first two years – after which events moved along grooves already cut. Britain's relations with Persia (as it then was) and the Arab chieftaincies of the Gulf had always been managed from India since the Company had first intervened there in the eighteenth century. British diplomatic contacts and representation were handled by officers of the Indian Political Service and enforcement, when necessary,

---

18 See Morton-Jack, specifically the chapter 'Old tactics' for a much more detailed examination and discussion of the adaptability of the Indian Army to the new environment. See p. 203 for a humorous description of a scouting mission.
19 Morton-Jack, see the chapter 'New tactics' for a thorough discussion of the learning and adaptation that took place on the battlefield.
20 Morton-Jack, p. 242.
21 A recent survey of World War I in the Middle East, Kristian Coates Ulrichsen, *The First World War in the Middle East* (London: Hurst, 2014) is a balanced treatment, paying due attention to India's role. The best treatment of the Indian dimension of Britain's war in the Middle East remains however Briton Cooper Busch, *Britain, India and the Arabs, 1914-1921* (Berkeley, CA, 1971).

was carried out by the Indian Army transported by the Raj's navy, the Indian Marine. To secure Britain's interests in the Gulf – and the terminals from which the Anglo-Persian Oil Company (controlled by the British government) shipped the output of its south Persian fields – India had designated one of its overseas expeditionary forces (IEFD) for the Gulf. And duly dispatched to the Gulf it was, even before Turkey entered the war in November 1914. Thus began what may well stand as a classic example of 'mission creep,' as well as the first act in the birth of the modern Middle East. As one trenchant recent analysis of IEFD's fortunes put it, '…the campaign would provide the greatest challenge [the Indian Army] had yet faced. Apart from bitter fighting against a tenacious opponent, it would have to endure some of the most difficult climatic and health conditions while operating at the end of a very long and precarious supply chain.'[22] This sounds, of course, rather like a description of the Burma campaign, the Indian Army's main effort in the next global war. The two leading figures in the Indian Army's World War II story, Claude Auchinleck and Bill Slim, were in fact both veterans of the Mesopotamia campaign and London, the ultimate authority in both cases, displayed the same pattern of intermittent attention and inadequate support until a disaster forced brief heed to be paid. Initially however things went quite smoothly for IEFD. The oil terminals were secured and Basra occupied. Then a variety of factors conspired to create a 'forward policy.' The Viceroy became enamoured of Mesopotamia as a possible new component of the Indian Empire; British success against the Turks, it was thought, would dampen the impact of the Sultan-Caliph's proclamation of jihad against Britain (and France) in November 1914, and, finally, and perhaps most influentially, victory in Mesopotamia, signalled by the taking of Baghdad, would, it was believed, go far to offset the deepening debacle at Gallipoli (it was an article of faith among the managers of Britain's Asian empire that prestige, 'face,' was a crucial component of British power, to be protected at all costs). And so Brigadier Delamain's brigade turned into Major General Charles Townshend's 6th Indian Division. Another improvised division – 12th Indian – was added, as was a lieutenant general as theatre commander. Early successes against the weak Ottoman forces bred overconfidence, which fed ambition, personal and institutional, and 6th Indian Division's drive on Baghdad began in the early autumn of 1915. All the while a logistic and medical disaster took shape in the background. Kitchener's reforms had separated operations from logistics (then known as administration) in the Indian Army. Government of India financial parsimony had compounded the weakness. Mesopotamia was not France – there was no infrastructure in place that could be adapted to military needs. Basra was not a functioning port in any real sense of the word. There were almost no roads and absolutely no railways. The Tigris and Euphrates were perforce, IEFD's line of communications – difficult rivers

---

22   Ross Anderson, 'Logistics of Expeditionary Force D in Mesopotamia: 1914-1918' in Kaushik Roy (ed.), *The Indian Army in the Two World Wars* (Leiden: Brill, 2012), p. 105. This is a very important study.

to navigate and undersupplied with rivercraft useful to an army's supply services. Medical arrangements, in a very unhealthy climate, would be flattered by the adjective 'medieval.' If there were some, mostly overblown, concerns about sepoy morale and loyalty in France, the issue was much more of a concern in IEFD. The Indian Army of 1914 was heavily Muslim – about 40%. The Germans were not Muslims but the Turks were. Southern Mesopotamia moreover contained a number of Muslim holy sites (Shia rather than Sunni). Turkish propaganda constantly played on these issues. It seems to have found some echoes among the army's 'trans-frontier Pathans' – i.e. Pashtun tribesmen from beyond the formal borders of the Raj (and whose families and lands were therefore immune from the Raj's anger). There were some desertions; some units were moved out of the combat zone because of concerns over their loyalty. In February, 1915 a whole Muslim unit, the 15th Lancers, refused to leave Basra to fight fellow Muslims near sacred sites.[23] The problems of replacing veteran Indian Army officers who became casualties with new, wartime officers unknown to their men (and without the language skills to bond in any way with them) as well as of getting appropriate (in caste and class terms) replacements for sepoy casualties, which had been concerns in France, were even greater problems in Mesopotamia. And yet, in spite of everything, 6th Indian Division almost pulled it off.[24]

23 There were three unit mutinies in the Indian Army during World War I. All three were in Muslim units and connected to service in Mesopotamia. In addition to the 15th Lancers at Basra (Feb., 1916), the 130th Baluchis refused in January 1915 to embark from Rangoon for service in Mesopotamia. Both these episodes were bloodless but the February 1915 mutiny by the 5th Light Infantry at Singapore was not – the sepoys killed 10 officers and, in the aftermath, forty one of them were shot by firing squads, while 126 were sentenced to transportation or imprisonment. However, while concern over being shipped to Mesopotamia was a factor in the mutiny of the 5th Light Infantry, it was not the only, nor perhaps the most important, one. Mason, *A Matter of Honour*, pp. 425-27 points out that the 5th was not a happy unit – poor officers and discontented VCOs and NCOs. Mesopotamia may have been the trigger (like the famous greased cartridges in 1857) but was not the underlying cause. There is an excellent account of the whole episode in Malcolm Murfett, John N. Miksic, Brian P. Farrell & Chiang Ming Shun, *Between Two Oceans: A Military History of Singapore from First Settlement to Final British Withdrawal* (Oxford: OUP, 1999), pp. 125-136. In long retrospect, the relatively small number of cases of unrest is what seems surprising, given the rapid expansion of the army, the dilution of the officer and VCO corps by that expansion and the deployment of a heavily Muslim army against the leading Muslim power of the day. The Indian Army's institutional framework proved to be surprisingly resilient – as would be the case when it faced the even greater stresses of 1939-45.
24 There is of course an official history of the campaign – F. J. Moberley, *The Campaign in Mesopotamia, 1914-1918*, 4 vols. (London: HMSO, 1923-1927). A very good military history of the campaign is A. J. Barker's *The Neglected War: The Mesopotamian Campaign, 1914-1918* (London: Faber & Faber, 1967). For some reason the American edition came out under the curious title *The Bastard War*. Barker, a British Army officer, served in Burma during World War II. Although more recent, Charles Townshend's *When God Made Hell: The British Invasion of Mesopotamia and the Creation of Iraq, 1914-1921* (London: Faber & Faber,

At Ctesiphon, eighteen miles south of Baghdad – and at the end of a 465-mile line of communications stretching back to the 'base' at Basra where ships waited months to be unloaded – Townshend attacked a much superior Turkish force (an intelligence failure deprived him of knowledge of that fact, although, given his character this might not have mattered). He was comprehensively beaten. The 6th Indian Division lost nearly 50% of its remaining British officers, while VCO casualties exceeded 50% (four of 6th Division's battalions had 11 British officers between them). Despite these shattering losses to its command structure, it held together and executed a 90-mile retreat under pressure to its advanced base at Kut-al-Amara where it was besieged.

The siege of Kut lasted until April when the garrison, worn down by illness and fatigue, with its food supplies exhausted, and relief efforts stymied, capitulated. Most of Kut's defenders (over 8,000 of the original 11,000 combatants, plus 3,500 non-combatant followers) were Indians. There has been considerable discussion of the deterioration of the sepoys during the siege. As food supplies dwindled, horses and mules were slaughtered – but the sepoys declined until the bitter end to eat either, largely for cultural rather than religious reasons ('dispensations,' secured from religious leaders in India and made known to the sepoys, made no difference precisely because culture not theology dictated their actions). The desertion rate began to rise – 147 sepoys deserted during the four month siege (the actual number is probably somewhat higher as it does not include those caught in the act and shot). By the time Townshend capitulated on 23 April most of his Indian troops were nearly incapable of fighting any longer (his British troops, who had eaten better, were in only slightly better shape).

If the drive to take Baghdad was recklessly undertaken with one rapidly weakening division, the attempt to relieve the 6th Indian Division, once it was immured in Kut, was even worse conceived and executed. The redeployment of the now veteran 3rd and 7th Indian Divisions from France to Mesopotamia would seem to have given IEFD a powerful force with which to relieve Townsend. But the circumstances of their arrival meant they were handicapped from the start. The planning for their transfer from France to IEFD was carelessly handled; landing at Basra in bits and pieces they were denied any opportunity to regain coherence as divisions. Pushed upriver, they encountered quickly the full range of 'Mespot' woes: rain and mud, inadequate rations, a collapsing transport system and a barely visible medical establishment. The contrast with the situation in France was painful. Moreover the 'Tigris Corps' into which they were grouped was poorly commanded (as was the theatre for that matter). The Turks, however, energized by their victory at Gallipoli, remained full of fight. As futile attack succeeded futile attack on the Turkish positions covering their siege lines

---

2010), is less satisfactory as far as the Indian Army is concerned (there is no index entry for it). Townshend, nearly all of whose previous research has been on Ireland, is clearly less well informed about the Indian Army than Barker, a graduate of the Quetta Staff College. This is a handicap when writing about a campaign that depended on that army.

around Kut, the Tigris Corps commander, Lieutenant General Sir Fenton Alymer (a British service officer), detected a reluctance to attack in the sepoys. Given the handicaps under which they were operating, this would not be terribly surprising, although the facts show that Tigris Corps kept trying despite circumstances that would have dampened the enthusiasm of any troops. What may have been in play once again is the suspicion lurking in many British minds since 1857 that in the last analysis, sepoy loyalty was conditional (Winston Churchill would give voice to this as late as August, 1941). And so, in some respects it was – the sepoys were professional soldiers fighting not for 'King and Country' but for their regiment plus a defined 'pay and benefits' package, as well as status, in their communities. As long as this implicit contract was honoured they fought as well as any soldiers anywhere. In Mesopotamia in a badly conceived and poorly supported campaign and with their command structure depleted by casualties to their officers and VCOs, their morale and effectiveness suffered. What they could and would do in different circumstances was shown dramatically in the aftermath of Kut.[25]

The loss of the 6th Indian Division, coming on the heels of the failure at Gallipoli, caught London's attention – imperial prestige seemed at risk. The inevitable

---

25 The 1915-16 campaign in Mesopotamia, culminating in the fall of Kut has attracted more attention than any other part of the 4 year war there – understandably, perhaps, since it was the largest surrender in British military history to that point (much larger than that of Cornwallis at Yorktown). Barker, *Neglected War*, and Townsend, *When God Made Hell*, both provide good overviews, although Townsend seems ready to accept statements of declining sepoy morale and combat effectiveness without asking whether they originated with British officers (many already prone to be suspicious of sepoys) or more knowledgeable Indian Army officers who actually understood their units. Nor does he adequately consider the effect on command effectiveness in the Indian units of the catastrophically heavy losses not only of British officers (which he mentions) but of VCOs, the glue of Indian battalions (a factor he ignores entirely). The best studies of the campaign and siege is Nikolas Gardner's recent *The Siege of Kut-al-Amara: At War in Mesopotamia, 1915-1916* (Bloomington, IN: Indiana University Press, 2014). Gardner concludes: '…Townshend did not 'thoroughly understand Indian troops.' This was the principal factor in the defeat of the 6th Indian Division at Kut-al-Amara in 1916' (p. 171). This may seem a strange charge to make against an Indian Army officer but Townshend, who transferred to the Indian Army from the Royal Marines, had spent much time away from Indian soldiering pursuing his personal ambitions, only resuming his Indian Army career on the eve of the war. Gardner has examined the issue of Indian Army morale in the campaign as a whole in 'Morale of the Indian Army in the Mesopotamian Campaign: 1914-1917' in Kaushik Roy (ed.), *The Indian Army in the Two World Wars*, pp. 393-417. Two other detailed scholarly assessments are crucial to understanding 1914-16 in Mesopotamia: Andrew Syk, 'Command in the Indian Expeditionary Force D in Mesopotamia, 1915-1916' and Ross Anderson's 'Logistics of the Indian Expeditionary Force D in Mesopotamia: 1914-1918' in Kaushik Roy (ed.), *The Indian Army in the Two World Wars*, pp. 63-144.

Townshend, whose post-surrender behaviour damned him more thoroughly than his military mistakes, has been ferociously deconstructed by Norman Dixon in his brilliant *On the Psychology of Military Incompetence* (London: Jonathan Cape, 1976), pp. 95-109.

Parliamentary Commission was convened but long before it reported in 1917 there was a thorough shake-up of the command structure in Mesopotamia. The theatre commander, Sir Percy Lake, a former chief of the Indian General Staff, who initiated the organizational improvements was removed in favour of Lieutenant General Stanley Maude who had arrived with the 13th Division, a British 'New Army' division that had been at Gallipoli (and in whose ranks Bill Slim served). In India, Hardinge, never comfortable with military affairs, was replaced by Lord Chelmsford, and Kitchener's inept protégé, Sir Beauchamp Duff, gave way to a new commander-in-chief, Sir Charles Monro. The War Office would now manage the campaign with India providing troops and support services. Monro and Maude were both British service officers but competent soldiers and good managers, a quality hitherto sadly absent in the direction of IEFD. The key figure was Maude.[26]

A methodical rather than charismatic commander, Maude (known as 'Systematic Joe') was powerfully aided by the appointment of the energetic Major General George MacMunn as Inspector General of Communications. Basra was finally sorted out, as were the medical services. Himself a Guardsman, Maude learned Urdu (the Indian Army's *lingua franca*) and used it in touring units and hospitals. Effective leadership as well as improved food and healthcare, the result of better logistics (including the arrival of motor transport companies) produced a remarkable turnaround in what was now known as the Mesopotamian Expeditionary Force – which would seem to indicate, since so much of it was now made up of newly raised Indian Army units, that any sag in Indian morale during the Kut debacle was circumstantial rather than systemic. Maude had been appointed by Sir William Robertson, the Chief of the Imperial General Staff in London, to reorganize the battered forces in Mesopotamia and to stabilize that front enough to ensure that it would not require the commitment of resources needed on the Western Front. But rebuilding an army's morale and fighting effectiveness is not compatible with standing pat and in February 1917 Maude took Baghdad.

General Maude set out to reform the army as a whole. He created a stronger logistic and sustainment system, and medical wastage began to decrease. Replacements arrived more efficiently to fill the depleted numbers in various units. The quality of British officers also began to improve, although this issue was never entirely resolved.[27]

---

26 There is a curious parallel between the post-Kut shakeup in Mesopotamia and what happened after the fiasco of the first Arakan offensive in 1942-43. As in 1916 an Indian Army operation, badly conceived and poorly supported had ended in an embarrassing debacle. Churchill revamped the command structure, placing operations in Burma under a new South East Asia Command that reported directly to London, leaving Indian Army HQ in Delhi to train troops and deal with logistics. Common to both experiences was this: both campaigns continued to depend on the Indian Army.

27 Specifically see Morton-Jack, pp. 221-2, where a veteran Sikh soldier described the officer issues in his battalion by late 1915. Many veteran officers had been killed or wounded in France, Mesopotamia, and elsewhere. There were many young officers with minimal time

Corps, divisions, brigades, battalions and regiments were all rested and re-trained. Battlefield experience and lessons from the fighting in Mesopotamia as well as from other theatres were disseminated throughout the force. Battalion records highlight these improvements: the 51st and 53rd Sikhs (Frontier Force) documented how 'their war-worn units required rebuilding, their newly arrived officers needed training and knowledge of their men. . . . [A] thorough overhaul of the Army on the Tigris, with measures to restore morale, was undertaken.'[28] The 1/8th Gurkha Rifles noted that 'the men were well trained and full [of] confidence.'[29] The 45th Rattray Sikhs noted repeatedly in their histories 'a period of intensive training. Company training . . . carried out in the morning with the Battalion drill in the afternoons. The Brigade worked together . . . practicing attack, retirement and night operations.'[30]

Equally important, better equipment and more artillery were brought into the IEFD to deal with the lack of fire support that had plagued the earlier phases of the campaign.[31] The IEFD, with more than 150,000 men, was ready by the end of 1916 to carry out their counteroffensive towards Baghdad. Kut was recaptured in February 1917, and Baghdad in March. General Maude noted that 'the men are tremendously pleased with themselves as well they may be, for their conduct has been splendid.'[32] For his part, General Maude had shown that he was more than just a solid administrator and reformer; he was also a sound commander on the field of battle. The IEFD stopped their advance and shored up their forces. The lessons and training transformation continued; in April 1917, the 45th Sikhs recorded that the month had passed in 'quiet training and re-organisation. . . . [T]raining in all branches was carried on.'[33] Other units carried out similar efforts. The 56th Rifles (Frontier Force) noted that 'during the summer (1917) the depleted strength of the regiment was made up to 805, and much training, both individual and collective, was necessary.' The offensive began in October and by November 1917, Tikrit had been taken. In November General Maude died of cholera, but the Army continued to make progress.

In 1918, the campaign in Mesopotamia entered into a different phase. With the German offensives on the Western Front, the War Office in London began shifting forces between fronts. In an effort to support the final offensives in Palestine, IEFD units were shipped from Mesopotamia and Indian Cavalry units from France. These forces were sent expressly to stiffen and spread lessons identified from the fighting,

in theatre as well as inadequate language skills, leadership abilities, and experience. This was an issue that would occur again in the Second World War.
28 W.E.H. Condon, *The Frontier Force Regiment* (Aldershot: Gale and Polden, 1962), p. 112.
29 H.T. Huxford, *The 8th Gurkha Rifles, 1824-1949* (Aldershot: Gale and Polden, 1952), p. 95.
30 R.H. Anderson, *Regimental History of the 45th Rattray's Sikhs: During the Great War and After* (London: Sifton Praed & Co., 1925), p. 43.
31 See Ross Anderson for much more detail.
32 Quoted in Morton-Jack, p. 253.
33 Anderson, *45th Rattray's*, pp. 84-5.

both in Mesopotamia and on the Western Front. The 3rd and 7th Divisions were among those sent to Palestine; these two divisions had left India in August 1914 to serve in France and Mesopotamia, and would end the war in Palestine and Syria.

Five divisions strong at the end, its one cavalry and four infantry divisions numbered some 155,000 fighting men and 162,000 followers – the largest Indian Army force in any theatre. By October 1918, when the Turks signed an armistice, the MEF had taken most of present day Iraq; they entered Mosul, the last large city not occupied, in early November 1918. The MEF's transformation was complete - from defeat in 1916, it had risen, phoenix-like, to destroy the Turkish Army in Mesopotamia by late 1918. One interested observer of the change wrought under Maude's leadership was Slim, who would transfer to the Indian Army after the war and himself preside over the even more dramatic transformation of a largely Indian, thoroughly beaten and badly under-supported force a quarter century later.

But by the time the MEF reached the Kurdish highlands, its theatre had become secondary, as many of its Indian units were switched to Palestine where, as part of the Egyptian Expeditionary Force, they took part in the great British victory at Megiddo in September 1918, a victory that rang down the curtain on Britain's war with Ottoman Turkey.

Prospective Turkish entry into the war in 1914 imperilled the Suez Canal, an even more sensitive point in the strategic geography of the British Empire than the Persian Gulf. As IEFA passed through Egypt on its way to France one of its brigades was briefly detached to strengthen the British garrison there and two of India's Expeditionary Forces, E and F, quickly followed. By the time the Turks mounted their assault on the Canal, in January 1915, there were in addition to a British division two Indian Divisions in Egypt, 10th and 11th, as well as an Indian State unit, the Bikaner Camel Corps.[34] The Turkish assault on the Canal failed quickly and completely (although their success in traversing the brutal Sinai Desert even to get there might have indicated that, despite the generally shambolic state of Ottoman administration, their army would fight with determination). The Indian component in the Egyptian Expeditionary Force would be present throughout the conflict, and, by its end, would be the largest of its imperial contingents. For most of the EEF's existence however the Indian Army was not an overwhelming presence on the battlefield being used largely on garrison and line of communication duties. That changed dramatically in 1917-18. David Lloyd George, who became prime minister at the end of 1916, was skeptical of the value of Western Front offensives, and more than skeptical about the BEF

---

34 A large number of India's 560 odd 'Princely States' – about 40% of the land area of the Raj – maintained military forces. Most were simply for prestige purposes and display. A minority however were wealthy enough – and determined enough – to have their forces trained up to Indian Army standards. Those State Forces, when placed by the ruler at the disposal of the Raj (to display the ruler's loyalty and enhance his prestige) constituted Imperial Service Troops. They were officered by Indians but had an attached British advisor.

commander, General Sir Douglas Haig, and his principal supporter in London, the CIGS, General Sir William Robertson. Haig was politically untouchable (although Lloyd George levered Robertson out early in 1918) and the Western Front inescapable for reasons of alliance politics, but the prime minister could at least tilt in the direction of his 'Easterner' instincts in the EEF's area of operations. That force had, very slowly, inched its way across the Sinai Desert, unspooling a railroad and water pipeline behind it. By the time Lloyd George became prime minister it stood at the gates of Palestine, stalled by the Turkish defenses anchored on Gaza and Beersheba. As Lloyd George's focus shifted to the theatre and, above all, to the morale enhancing prospects of an offensive that would take Jerusalem, General Sir Archibald Murray, who had supervised the careful build up of the Egyptian base and the slow crawl across the Sinai, was replaced by the dynamic (and, as it proved, very able) Edmund Allenby. Allenby broke the Turkish front at Gaza and gave the prime minister the 'Christmas present' he wanted for the war-weary British public, entering Jerusalem on 11 December 1917. Up to this point, Allenby's army was largely British, plus an Australian and New Zealand cavalry division. The cost of the 1917 operations on the Western Front however, especially the horrific losses in Haig's Passchendaele offensive, left Britain facing a manpower crisis in a war that most saw stretching into at least 1919. Looking at a 600,000 man shortfall, London began to pull British troops out of secondary theatres. The MEF had only one complete British division which the Government of India regarded as a back-up for the maintenance of order in India in an emergency. If it had to remain, that left only the EEF. And the only source of replacements for the British units recalled to the Western Front was the Indian Army. When the great German offensive burst upon the BEF in March 1918, plans already made and underway were dramatically accelerated.

As 1918 opened, in addition to the 49th Indian Brigade serving on the lines of communication, there were already five Indian battalions serving in the newly constituted 75th British division. The 7th Indian Division was getting ready to move from Mesopotamia to the EEF. It would be followed by the 3rd – the Meerut and Lahore divisions were about to fight in their third theatre since 1914 as noted previously. They were also about to be reunited with the cavalry that had accompanied them to France, the Indian elements of 4th and 5th Cavalry Divisions, 13,000 strong, moving to the EEF as well. When Ludendorff's hammer blows fell upon the BEF in March – Haig lost 38,500 men on the first day – the pace of transferring British units to France accelerated. 'British' EEF infantry brigades were now to be turned into Indian pattern units made up of one British and three Indian battalions. The Indian Army found the necessary units either by moving battalions from India or the MEF or by 'milking' existing formations of a company that would become the nucleus of a new battalion which would be completed with new recruits from India. By the time Allenby's campaign ended in October 1918, of his 13 divisions, only two, a British infantry division, and the Anzac mounted division, contained no Indian troops – although all his Indian divisions still carried the 'British' designation. As in Mesopotamia, there was British concern that Turkish propaganda might stir up unrest among Muslim sepoys. In fact none appeared.

This massive reorganisation took months to complete and for units and formations to settle into their new roles. Throughout the process, Indian and British continued to distil lessons from previous campaigns, preparing their men for what was to come. The lessons from the Western Front, captured in doctrinal pamphlets such as *Training and Employment of a Platoon, 1918* and *Training and Deployment of Divisions, 1918*, were being implemented in numerous training programmes.[35] In one example of this, the 1/8th GR described how, 'owing to the reorganisation in this Command [EEF], and the necessity for training and reorganisation, the battalion was not called upon for active operations for about three months. The time was well spent in training and assimilating new ideas under new conditions.'[36] Units received additional practical training by carrying out raids and patrols.

General Allenby and his staff had turned their focus to the last major objectives in the Palestine campaign: the destruction of the Turkish armies to the north. The offensive began in September, with the famous battle of Megiddo on the Plain of Sharon, 19-25 September. Damascus fell on 1 October, Beirut on the 8th, and Aleppo soon afterwards. James Kitchen characterized the Palestine campaign as 'one of the triumphs of the Indian Army', highlighting their tactical flexibility and military professionalism.

Allenby, however, would have preferred to keep his British units. Indeed, at one point he asked if he could be supplied with Japanese divisions in preference to Indians. But it was the Indian Army he got, and it was heavily sepoy units that battered in the Turkish front at the beginning of the battle of Megiddo in September and Indian sowars that played a major role in the devastating pursuit to Damascus and Aleppo that shattered the Turkish forces beyond the possibility of recovery (rather like Slim's 'Sea or Bust' drive after his victory at Meiktila in 1945). When a Free French army landed in southern France in August 1944, the French command immediately began a process known as 'whitening,' replacing Moroccan, Algerian and Tunisian units with French conscripts and resistance formations turned overnight into regular soldiers. A similar process was operating in reverse in the EEF in 1918 – 'Indianization,' turning British units, in effect, into Indian divisions, without diminution of fighting qualities. The same change would have taken place in the British units serving on the Salonika Front had the war not unexpectedly ended in November.[37]

---

35   See James Kitchen, *The British Imperial Army in the Middle East: Morale and Identity in the Sinai and Palestine Campaigns, 1916-1918* (London: Bloomsbury, 2014) for a more detailed description of this transformation.
36   Huxford, p. 105.
37   The Egypt-Palestine campaigns of 1914-18 has attracted more attention than that in Mesopotamia, largely because of the career of T. E. Lawrence (and the great film by Sir David Lean). Cyril Falls was the principal author of the official history, *Military Operations Egypt and Palestine*, 2 vols. (London, 1930). Archibald Wavell, who served under Allenby

In addition to the major commitments in France, Mesopotamia and Egypt-Palestine, the Indian Army contributed to two other campaigns. IEFG, the 29th Indian Infantry Brigade, took part in the Gallipoli campaign. Its four battalions were Sikh and Gurkha – it did not include the usual British battalion (Gurkhas and Sikhs, of course, had been prominent among the Indian troops who had fought with the British in 1857). It was the 1/6 Gurkhas under Major Cecil Allanson, who, briefly, got the summit of 'Hill Q' on 8 August 1915, the high point of the offensive it was hoped would break the stalemated campaign and carry the British to victory. With them was a Royal Warwicks subaltern, Bill Slim, who, transferring to the Indian Army in 1920, would join the 1/6 and become the regiment's most famous alumnus.[38]

There was a very large Indian Army presence in what is perhaps World War I's most obscure British campaign – the four years of fighting in 'German East Africa' – Tanganyika (now Tanzania). Two IEFs were destined for East Africa – one to reinforce the battalions of the King's African Rifles in Kenya; the other to assault the port of Tanga in German East Africa. It is fate of the latter that is the best remembered part of the Indian Army's role in the East African campaign. IEF B was a hastily thrown together force – only one brigade of regulars, the balance made up of contingents from princely states (not up to Imperial Service Troops standards). There was unwarranted optimism about the ease with which Indian regulars would dispose of the German officered askaris. The art of amphibious operations was unpracticed – indeed virtually non-existent. The result was an epic fiasco. Despite this awkward beginning the

---

in Palestine (and who would become successively Commander-in-Chief, Middle East; Commander-in-Chief, India and Viceroy, 1939-47), produced a one volume account, *The Palestine Campaigns* (London: Constable, 1928) – which has precisely two index entries for the Indian Army. Wavell also wrote a two volume biography of Allenby, *Allenby: A Study in Greatness* (London: George G. Harrap & Co., 1940) and *Allenby in Egypt* (London: George G. Harrap & Co., 1943) – a remarkable achievement while holding high command in a global war. There is no recent study of Allenby as a soldier. Two very incisive essays on the Indian Army in the Egypt-Palestine campaign reveal both how much Allenby owed to the Indian Army and how much more there is to be learned about this campaign when the gaze is wrenched from Lawrence and the Arabs and focused on the troops who carried it to victory: Dennis Showalter, 'The Indianization of the Egyptian Expeditionary Force, 1917-1918: An Imperial Turning Point' and James Kitchen, 'The Indianization of the Egyptian Expeditionary Force: Palestine, 1918' both in Kaushik Roy (ed.), *The Indian Army in the Two World Wars*, pp. 145-190. The Palestine campaign also saw the employment of Imperial Service Troops. Their performance was excellent – the Jodhpur Lancers took Haifa in a mounted charge during Allenby's final offensive.

38 The saga of the 29th Indian Infantry Brigade has finally found appropriate memorialization in Peter Stanley's fine monograph, *Die In Battle, Do Not Despair: The Indians on Gallipoli* (Solihull: Helion, 2015). It is worth noting that what is almost certainly still the most widely read single book on Gallipoli, Alan Moorehead's *Gallipoli* (London: Hamish Hamilton, 1956), while it covers Allanson and his Gurkhas, never mentions the 29th Indian Infantry Brigade, nor does anything Indian rate an entry in his index.

Indian Army presence in East Africa grew steadily until the wartime expansion of the King's African Rifles allowed the war to be 'Africanized' in 1917-18. At that point twenty-two battalions of Indian infantry (the infantry strength of two divisions) were returned to India – in time to help support the 'Indianization' of the imperial war effort in the Middle East.[39]

Behind the eightfold expansion of the Indian Army lay, of course, India's Home Front. The Raj undertook, before 1914, a limited number of functions. When, in *Passage to India*, E. M. Forster, no admirer of British India, put into the mouth of an Indian Civil Service character, drawn to be unattractive, the line 'we are here to do justice and keep the peace,' he succinctly expressed an important part of the Raj ethos. Of course there was more to it than that. Assessing and collecting the revenue had always been job one, for Company and Crown Raj alike. The revenue yield paid for the whole vast edifice, of which the army was the key component and the most expensive – absorbing nearly half the revenues. But the Raj also built a complex civil administration and an infrastructure – roads, canals, ports, bridges, telegraph and postal systems and, above all, a railway network that unified the country in an unprecedented fashion. And, in the shadow of the Raj, there grew up not only the beginnings of an Indian industrial economy but an Anglicized political class that had already extracted concessions before 1914 – the thin end of a wedge. The impact of total war on the complex but delicate fabric of the Raj was bound to be significant. Much of that impact lies outside the remit of this essay, but one point needs to be stressed. The army's homeland, the Punjab, was badly stressed and the officering of the army finally became a question whose resolution could no longer be postponed.

Recruitment for the Indian Army had always been voluntary, but the demands had always been modest. The 'martial races' could easily keep the army up to strength as long as casualties were light, as was the case in Frontier wars or pre-1914

---

39   The official history, C. Hodern, *Military Operations East Africa*, was never completed. Only Volume I, covering events up to September 1916 appeared in 1941. The best recent account of the war in East Africa is the summary in Hew Strahan's *The First World War: Vol. I: To Arms* (Oxford: OUP, 2001), pp. 569-643. While he does not discuss the Indian contribution to the campaign in any detail (beyond a brief description of the Tanga debacle), he does point out (p. 586) that there was friction between the Indian Army and the locally recruited KAR, the former regarding the latter as local levies. Curiously, that would be the complaint of British Indian Army officers in Burma about British Army attitudes toward the Indian Army. British officers of African formations in Burma (three African divisions served there) felt Indian Army officers, in turn, looked down on African units. Perhaps the best commentary on this comes from Slim: 'The young British officer commanding native troops is often asked if he likes his men. An absurd question, for there is always one answer. They are *his* men... the young officer will tell you that his particular fellows possess a combination of military virtues denied to any other race. Good soldiers! He is prepared to back them against the Brigade of Guards itself!' *Unofficial History* (London: Cassell, 1959), p. 27. The essay from which this comes was written prior to World War II.

overseas expeditions like that sent to confront the 'Mad Mullah' in Somaliland. The unprecedented casualties and unexpected duration of the war presented challenges that stressed the recruiting system to the breaking point. Conscription was discussed but never instituted in India. What was done however was to create a network of district and provincial recruiting committees that could by 1917-18 only meet their assigned quotas by measures that amounted to compulsion – applied of course to only a small fraction of India's huge population. When the Commander-in-Chief committed to 40 new battalions in 1918 the system had been wrung dry. The Raj had armed itself with a variety of legal and administrative tools to contain dissent and there was no serious unrest during the war, but clearly the Indian war effort would have to be met by significant political concession if the situation was to remain stable. This was done in the 1917 'August Declaration' – the commitment to Dominion status for India to contain the aspirations of Indian politicians. The military dimension of this has often been ignored but it was the crucial moment for the future of the army.[40]

The question of giving royal commissions – that is full officer status – to Indians was not a new one. Periodically it had been raised – and brushed aside. A half-hearted pre-war attempt to meet growing Indian pressure for Indian officers in the Indian Army, the Imperial Cadet Corps, confined to the sons of the Indian princely class, made little difference, and it is hard to believe that it was intended to. The war however changed everything. As noted above it was simply impossible to rapidly replace the prewar British regulars who either became casualties or were elevated by the growth of the army into positions above company and battalion level. Officers were, of course, found but their lack of linguistic skills and/or cultural understanding threw a very heavy burden on the Viceroy Commissioned Officers whose own prewar ranks were both decimated by casualties and diluted by promotions from the NCO corps. The successful performance of the army in the second half of the war owed much to these men, while the increasing degree of modernization in the army pointed to the limitations of men with little or no education in command positions. Furthermore units of the Imperial Service Troops – from princely states but trained up to regular Indian Army standards, and officered by Indians - performed well, especially in the EEF. It was becoming harder to construct a rationale for maintaining an all-British commissioned officer corps – and yet, not to do so would change, in a fundamental and irreversible way, the dynamics of the Raj. An Indian officered Indian Army would make self-government inescapable, and sooner rather than later. The commitment made on 20 August 1917 by Edwin Montagu, the Secretary of State for India,

---

40 There is an excellent study of the impact of the war on the Indian Army's heartland, the Punjab, in Tan Tai Yong, *The Garrison State: The Military, Government and Society in Colonial Punjab, 1849-1947* (Delhi: Sage, 2005). The extent of the wartime pressures on the Punjab can be gauged by the fact that this 'loyalist' province was the epicenter of unrest in 1919. Rajit K. Mazumdar's 'From Loyalty to Dissent: Punjabis from the Great War to World War II,' in Kaushik Roy (ed.), *The Indian Army in the Two World Wars*, pp. 461-491 is also very illuminating.

that Indians would henceforth be eligible for the King's Commission is therefore a key moment in the road to 1947. Its importance also is the reason that its actual implementation was so hesitant and fraught with difficulty. Without the war however it would not have happened or, at any rate, not as quickly. Claude Auchinleck would later say that the British got no credit from Indian opinion for this concession because there was no grace in the giving and no one should have known better than he, but what has been called 'the other August declaration,' once made, was a commitment virtually impossible to revoke, one that would eventually lay a foundation upon which the next total war would build a large body of Indian officers who would carry their army (armies after 1947) into a new era.[41]

If there is a constant in the complex story of the Indian Army in World War I it is the mixture of distrust and underestimation with which it was regarded by all but its British officers, even as it was called upon to carry an ever greater burden of the imperial war effort in several theatres. Sepoys were alleged to be stunned by the violence of European industrialized war (and the intensity of northern European winters) and to have resorted to the frequent infliction of disabling wounds upon themselves to escape – allegations that largely evaporated under careful scrutiny. Their morale was alleged to be shaky in Mesopotamia but given competent generalship and logistic support they carried Maude to victory. Fighting fellow Muslims might compromise their loyalty it was thought – but only a trickle of desertions occurred in Mesopotamia, and those mostly by trans-frontier Pathans who were a special case (and whose recruitment was discontinued after 1916). Allenby preferred Japanese soldiers but it was Indian sepoys and sowars who carried the EEF to its final smashing victory (and Allenby to a peerage and a field marshal's baton). Looking at its World War I record (which it would better twenty-five years later) it seems clear that it was both an effective fighting force and a very resilient one.[42] Throughout the First World War, the Indian Army had undergone fundamental changes to deal with the exigencies of a modern global war – as had its counterparts across the British Empire's forces. All had no choice but to contend with rapid expansion of units, administrative issues,

---

41 The best introduction to the complexities of the 'Indianization' of the Indian Army's officer corps is Chandar Sundaram, 'Grudging Concessions: The Officer Corps and Its Indianisation, 1817-1940' in Daniel P. Marston and Chandar S. Sundaram (eds.), *A Military History of India and South Asia*, pp. 88-101. See also Pradeep Barua's *Gentlemen of the Raj: The Indian Army Officer Corps, 1817-1949* (Westport, CT, 2003) picks up the story and carries it to the end of the Raj.
42 The last stages of the story have attracted some very fine historical writing, in particular Daniel Marston's two excellent monographs, the prize winning *Phoenix from the Ashes: The Indian Army and the Burma Campaign* (Westport, CT, 2003) and *The Indian Army and the End of the Raj* (Cambridge, 2014). Tim Moreman's *The Jungle, The Japanese and the British Commonwealth Armies at War, 1941-1945* (London, 2005), deals with the doctrinal changes in the Indian Army that helped turn defeat into victory in 1942-45. See also Alan Jeffreys, *Approach to Battle: Training the Indian Army during the Second World War* (Solihull: Helion, 2017).

logistic difficulties, and tactical deficiencies; and by 1918, British Empire forces in Europe, Palestine, and Mesopotamia could declare that they had overcome most of these issues and emerged among the best troops in their respective theatres of war. The almost accidental 18th century marriage of European technology and technique with Indian martial traditions created a unique institution, a creature of a moment in history that had already begun to pass by 1918 but which, while it lasted, made possible much of a small, foggy, European island's global power.

2

'I Shall Die Arms in Hand, Wearing the Warriors' Clothes': Mobilisation and Initial Operations of the Indian Army in France and Flanders[1]

Rob Johnson

The performance of the Indian Army in the first months of the war was decidedly mixed. While there were episodes of great courage, resolution and resilience, there was also setback, chaotic haste and disorganisation. On the one hand, the outbreak of war was greeted with the same enthusiasm that prevailed in Europe, with only a handful of dissenting voices, and India went on to produce almost 1.4 million volunteers. These men fought as far afield as France and Flanders, in East Africa, at Gallipoli, in Palestine and Mesopotamia. Some 53,486 were killed in the course of their duties, and a further 64,350 were wounded, the greatest toll being caused by disease. The Indian Army earned a number of gallantry awards, and the citations for the Victoria Cross are inspirational. Yet, on the other hand, the bulk of the Indian Corps was withdrawn from Europe after a few months of fighting because its losses, particularly the high proportion of officers, were unsustainable. The apparent deterioration of the Indian Corps in France confirmed widespread fears at the time that Indian troops might not be reliable in a European war. The reason for these mixed results lies in the pre-war period and offers an important insight: in 1903, the Army in India had been composed to provide internal and border security, with a very small expeditionary force. It was simply not designed for a major war fought in multiple theatres and its weaknesses in being able to generate sufficient numbers of qualified junior officers or trained reservists were painfully exposed.

---

1   Indar Singh to Chattar Singh, letter in Urdu, Somme, 15 September 1916, cited in David Omisi, *Indian Voices of the Great War: Soldier's Letters, 1914-18* (Basingstoke and New York: Palgrave, 1999). This paper was delivered at the Royal Military Academy Sandhurst, 29 November 2014, and the author wishes to thank the Academy for that opportunity.

Mobilisation

When the Viceroy declared war on India's behalf, there was a sincere and positive response from many Indian leaders and organisations: the All India Muslim League, Punjab Provincial Congress, the princely states and many thousands of individuals expressed their loyalty to the British Empire and its King-Emperor. Gandhi, not yet well-known across the subcontinent tendered a resolution to the Indian National Congress for unconditional service to the Empire in 1918. Offers of money, horses, medics, hospital ships and ambulances were made, and 21 of the 27 princes' Imperial Service Troops contingents, a percentage of whom had been trained to the same standards of the British Indian Army, were mobilised. The Nizam of Hyderabad committed troops and gave 60 lakhs of rupees (£400,000). The Maharajah of Mysore gave a further 50 lakhs (£333,000). In some rural districts there were more volunteers than could be taken into the army, although wealthy landowners competed with each other to 'give' larger and larger numbers of men they had selected.[2] Enthusiasm and cohesion were not in doubt: the Jodhpur Lancers, for example, were even commanded by their septuagenarian Regent-Maharajah, Major General Sir Pratab Singh. Problems lay in the organisation, training and capabilities of the force.

The Indian Army of 1914 was a long-service profession but lacked sufficient trained reserves to be able to regenerate in the event of significant casualties.[3] Its primary task had been to act as a frontier force. Many of its personnel were drawn from the north and west, close to the most sensitive frontiers where guerrilla warfare waged by recalcitrant tribes and opportunist Afghan incursions were the most frequent threat, although until 1905 there remained the more distant possibility of a Russian confrontation. Frontier fighting had required well-trained units with the cohesion to withstand demoralising insurgency, but casualties had, on the whole, been light.[4] The fighting had offered sufficient hazard to reinforce one's personal *izzat* (honour) or sense of fate, demonstrate attachment to one's officer and unit, and earn decorations and promotion without a high probability of death. The Pashtun tribes' habit of murdering the wounded and mutilating the dead meant that heroic efforts were always made to recover casualties, which again reinforced cohesion.

Service in Indian regiments tended to deter the rapid turnover of personnel and therefore didn't generate a large cadre of reservists.[5] To qualify for a pension,

---

2   Philip Mason, *The Men Who Ruled India* (London: Guild, 1985; previously *The Guardians*, II, publd. 1954), p. 283.
3   Government of India, *The Army in India and its Evolution* (Calcutta: Superintendant Government Publishing, 1924), p.219.
4   The most significant losses of the frontier wars occurred in the 1897-98 Pathan Rising. On the Tirah expedition, some 287 were killed and a further 853 were wounded, but this was exceptional. Captain H.L. Nevill, *Campaigns on the North West Frontier* (London, 1912), p. 301.
5   Government of India, *The Army in India and its Evolution. Op. Cit.*

soldiers had to serve 25 years. By contrast, three year short service men, who could take opportunities for periodic retraining, were few and far between and in any case insufficiently trained to be useful. Often, sickness and civilian employment rendered ex-soldiers unfit for further military service. The result was an army of some experience in mountain warfare, cohesive, with a strong sense of its exclusive identity, but without any notion of formation level operations or high-intensity European war.

The other peculiarity of the Indian Army was the organisation of the officers. Each infantry battalion had 12 European officers, and subordinated to them, regardless of experience, were 17 Indian Officers carrying the Viceroy's Commission. Together they commanded 729 ranks and 42 civilian 'commissariat' followers. In the cavalry, the proportions were the same. In 1914 there were 139 infantry battalions and 39 cavalry regiments, supported by mountain artillery, sappers and miners, pioneer battalions and logisticians. The Indian units were brigaded with British regiments to form the Army in India, an amalgamation of the old Presidency armies.[6] There were obvious cultural differences between British and Indian Army units, but they were also evident amongst the officer corps.[7] In the Indian cavalry, the legacy of being 'irregular' and under the personal command of pioneering individuals gave rise to an attitude that praised initiative, carried disdain for parade ground precision (while exhibiting pride in the most splendid Indian uniforms) and cherished the horses and sowars above all else. The fact that troopers owned their own mounts in the sillidar system made the men particularly responsible. In the infantry, Auchinleck described a similar atmosphere of respectful relations between officers and men: 'there was no question of ordering them about – they were yeomen really and that made all the difference'.[8] Geoff Hamilton described his Indian regiment as: 'a happy band and I was intensely proud to be their leader, and they knew it. We fought and played together undeterred by race, rank, class or creed, or age for that matter'.[9] Brigadier F.J. Dillon recorded that new recruits 'became yours in a much more personal way than in the British Army. You knew all about him, where he came from, what his family [trade] was. You probably visited his village and knew his parents'.[10] Viceroy Commissioned Officers, despite their subordination, were the most respected of all, and guided young British officers in their role. They were referred to as 'God's Own Gentlemen'. In contrast to most European armies which expected their 'native' soldiers to learn the Europeans' language, in the Indian Army every officer had to

---

6   TNA, CAB 6/2, Redistribution of the Army in India, 1904, Committee of Imperial Defence 58-D.
7   George Morton-Jack, *The Indian Army on the Western Front: India's Expeditionary Force to France and Belgium in the First World War* (Cambridge, 2014), p.3.
8   Charles Allen, *Plain Tales From the Raj*, (London: Andre Deutsch-Penguin, 1975), pp. 239-40.
9   Cited in Victoria Schofield, *Every Rock, Every Hill: A Plain Tale of the North West Frontier of India and Afghanistan* (London: Buchan and Enright, 1984), p. 159.
10 Allen, *Plain Tales*, p. 240.

learn to speak to his soldiers in their vernacular, not least because he was regarded as the neutral arbiter in any local disputes.[11] The emphasis on personal leadership led to a tendency to lead from the front in combat, but that had its own attractions for young British officers. The appeal of command in the Indian Army was so high that, in 1913, of the top 25 cadets at the Royal Military Academy Sandhurst, 20 of them opted to join the Indian Army.[12]

The motivation of the Indian Army was initially not in doubt. A hierarchy of prestige, based on 'fighting quality' and physique, ran through a number of ethnic groups that constituted the army, and each was eager to assert its martial prowess.[13] This competitiveness existed between units recruited on the basis of territorial demarcation as much as on ethnicity, and it was common in 'mixed' units where companies were made up of a particular 'class'. The 6th Bengal Lancers, for example, consisted of one Muslim squadron, one Hindu and one Sikh, with the Headquarters Squadron made up of troops from all three 'classes'.[14] Half of the regular army was drawn from the Punjab, and even regiments designated with particular regional titles, might actually contain a cross section of more competitive groups.[15] However, there was also a trait amongst some groups to enlist for the 'fight' rather than identity *per se*. There are countless accounts of British personnel describing the characteristics of classes, and of reciprocal responses by the men themselves.[16] Alongside exceptional courage, Mahsuds had a reputation for fanatical behaviour and the occasional murder of their officers; they prided themselves on being 'Mizh der beitabora khalqi-i'.[17] Pathans generally were 'athletic' but possessed a 'swaggering gait'.[18] Sikhs were 'sturdy lions' with a 'stately bearing'. Dogras were allegedly 'quiet, reliable, well-behaved, courageous but lacked the Pathans' native cunning.'[19] Jats were 'worthy and slightly

---

11 There were two examinations, with further training in specialist languages as required.
12 Incidentally, Auchinleck succeeded; Montgomery failed. Charles Chenevix Trench, *The Indian Army and the King's Enemies, 1900-1947* (London: Thames and Hudson, 1988), p. 25.
13 There is an extensive literature on the martial races, but a clear explanation is given in David Omissi, *The Sepoy and the Raj: The Politics of the Indian Army, 1860-1940* (London: Macmillan, 1994). For a contemporary view, see George MacMunn, *The Martial Races of India* (London: Sampson Low, 1933).
14 Francis Ingall, *The Last of the Bengal Lancers* (London: Leo Cooper, 1988), p.5.
15 The 129th Baluchis, for example, despite the title, contained no Baluchis but was made up of Pashtuns, Mahsuds and Punjabis. In Wilde's Rifles, there were companies consisting of Dogras, Pathans, Punjabis and Sikhs.
16 Santanu Das, *Race, Empire and First World War Writing* (Cambridge: Cambridge University Press, 2011).
17 This translates as: 'we are an untrustworthy people' from the British moral point of view but not necessarily that untrustworthiness was objectively a point of tribe pride.
18 J.W.B Merewhether, *The Indian Corps in France* (London: John Murray, 1919).
19 Trench, *Indian Army*, p. 28.

dull', while Gurkhas were 'nice little fellows, excellent, aggressive infantry though a trifle thick, liable (like everyone else) to have their off-days.'[20]

It was to the credit of the pre-war planners that the Indian Army had a scheme for mobilisation and deployment, with specialist equipment, in place when the war broke out. India had two infantry divisions and one cavalry brigade available for immediate operations.[21] Nevertheless, there were problems from the outset. The call-up occurred in August, when most personnel were on leave, and, in an age before information technologies, it took a little while to make contact with everyone, especially soldiers up in the hills. The depot system, which was supposed to operate as the rear link for deploying units, handling call ups, reservists, pensions and discharges, was completely overwhelmed and remained chaotic well into 1915. While units made their way to Bombay relatively quickly, the entire force was deficient in artillery and possessed only two machine guns per battalion.[22] Insufficient numbers of troop ships meant 30 vessels had to be hurriedly converted. As bewildered sepoys embarked, many of them on a ship for the first time, their officers struggled to contain the rumours about their destination, which varied from guarding the Suez Canal to joining the fighting in Europe. Most thought the greatest risk was that the war would be over before they arrived, but, in the short term, there were more prosaic preoccupations about rations, stores and orders to re-organise from their standard eight companies into the British model of four companies.[23] While the Lahore and Meerut Divisions (Force 'A') assembled, efforts were also made to get back British officers on the reserve list with the Indian Army. Of the 47 available, half were swept up in the corresponding British mobilisation. There also were too few Indian reservists to provide for the ten per cent of the strength anticipated for battle casualty replacements.

Deployment to France

The initial deployments were also a mixed success. It was remarkable that two entire divisions could be transported with most of their equipment, so rapidly to the far side of the world, prepared for any operations. Nevertheless, there were still significant gaps in the readiness and the ability to sustain enduring operations in the Indian

---

20   Trench, *Indian Army*, p. 28.
21   IOR, L/MIL/17/5/3088, A further 5 cavalry brigades could be deployed with sufficient notice. Indian Expeditionary Force A, War Diary, Simla, October 1914, p.136.
22   Sir Moore Creagh, the former CiCI, had demanded modern arms and equipment to fulful Kitchener's planned expeditionary force capabilities, but the government and his successor as CiCI, deferred the decision on grounds of cost. Even after six months of war, the Government of India remained on a peacetime footing with regard to military expenditure.
23   IOR, L/MIL/7/120 Reorganisation, 1861-1936.

Corps.[24] Force A had disembarked briefly at Suez before setting off for France, where the first division landed at Marseilles on 26 September. There it was issued with the newer Mark III Lee Enfield Rifle, conducted marches, organised stores, was allocated liaison officers and established a camp. Transport was provided in the form of London butchers' carts, but, apart from the distribution of some greatcoats, the troops wore their light tropical uniforms. There was considerable enthusiasm amongst the French for the newly arrived Indian troops, and the soldiers experienced a form of culture shock, remarking in their letters on the existence of aircraft, women working in agriculture, strange food, and, for Muslim troops, the alleged idolatry of the pork-eating French.

From Marseilles, the Indian Corps was moved by rail to Ypres to relieve the shattered British Second Corps and their contribution helped stabilise the line at a time when manpower shortages were critical.[25] From the railheads, the 129th Baluchis and Wilde's Rifles were transported by bus and rushed into the shallow trenches and ditches to relieve the British cavalry at Wytschaete and Messines. Neither the British cavalry nor the Indian troops, divided into company groups, were supported by sufficient artillery.[26] On 22 October, a German thrust was only held with the greatest difficulty, most of the casualties being caused by German shell fire. Trenches were flattened, and reinforcing sepoys were forced to lie in the open to repel a German infantry assault. The Baluchis' machine guns, placed in a prominent farm house, took a direct hit. One machine gun unit was entirely overrun and wiped out, but for the sole survivor Khuda Dad Khan. A similar fate befell the Dogra company of Wilde's Rifles: Jemadar Kapur Singh, realising he was the only survivor, shot himself to prevent his capture; Havildar Gagna, having killed five Germans around him, broke his bayonet in the close quarter action, but snatched up a German officer's sword and accounted for more: he was later found, alive, with six wounds.[27] At Neuve Chapelle the village was lost on 28 October when Indian Sapper and Miners were overwhelmed in another close quarter battle: all their officers and over 100 of the 300 men available were killed or wounded. After a week's further fighting, some 500 sepoys were killed.

The accounts of the troops indicate the typical problems of these early days of the war. The Poona Horse sowars did not initially take cover in their unfamiliar dismounted role and they had little training in infantry tactics or trench warfare. Consequently their casualties were severe. Fresh night operations were stalled by the inability to seize the high ground that lay to the east of Neuve Chappelle, by the

24 Logistics, for example, had to fit into a British Army system, with which the Indian Army was unfamiliar. H Alexander, *On Two Fronts, Being the Adventures of an Indian Mule Corps in France and Gallipoli* (New York: Dutton, 1917), p.42.
25 TNA, WO 95/1090, Indian Corps War Diary (October-December 1914).
26 J. Willcocks, *With the Indians in France* (London: Constable, 1920), ch. 20.
27 The Battalion had deployed with 11 British officers and 729 Indian Other Ranks; three days' later, five officers and 274 Indians returned: a casualty rate of 63 per cent.

abysmal autumn weather and the evident confusion of troops unfamiliar with the environment.[28]

From personal accounts we know that some officers struggled to keep their men in place. Captain 'Roly' Grimshaw (Poona Horse) came across some Gurkhas attempting to seek out Germans in No Man's Land on their own initiative, while others were clearly shirking in culverts, ditches and ruins. He explained that 'the sight which met the eyes at daybreak was perfectly revolting ... corpses choked the trenches ... fragments of human beings everywhere. Most of the dead seemed to have been bayoneted, but some had their heads blown clean off.'[29]

Between the shelling and sniping, the greatest hazard was the environment itself. None of the men had waterproofs, braziers, or 'rugs' (blankets). By November, the troops were occupying trenches almost brim full of water. At Festubert, two men of the 8th Gurkhas drowned within hours of occupying their 'miniature canals'. On 23 November, the Germans broke into the Indian lines and several trenches were lost. Close quarter fighting over the next 24 hours resulted in some of those positions being recovered, but the cost was high. Sikhs and Pathans were described as having lost turbans, revealing their long and straggling hair, matted with mud. All ranks were terribly filthy and often exhausted. Some Gurkhas discarded their boots, complaining that sore feet were worse inside their footwear. There were other unseen and unexpected enemies: a German mine detonated under the Indian lines killed 200 and induced profound shock.

Under these conditions, it is more understandable that Jemadar Mir Mast and 14 Afridis deserted to the relative comfort of the German lines that winter, that there were higher than 'average' statistics of Self-Inflicted Wounds amongst Indian Other Ranks, and that censor reports recorded a lowering of morale.[30] Officer casualties were difficult to replace, but the sheer numbers of losses and the nature of the conditions evidently had its effect too.

Operations Around Neuve Chappelle

By the following spring, the Indian Corps had to some extent recovered from its emergency deployment. New equipment had arrived and much needed winter clothing, along with rifle grenades, mills bombs, mortars and trench periscopes.

---

28   Morton-Jack, *Indian Army on the Western Front*, p.15. He lists the authors endorsing the suffering caused by the climate.
29   Captain R. Grimshaw, *Indian Cavalry Officer, 1914-15* (London, 1986), cited in Trench, *Indian Army*, p. 35.
30   J. Greenhut, ' "Sahib and Sepoy" An Enquiry into the Relationship between British Officers and Native Soldiers of the British Indian Army', *Military Affairs*, 48 (1984), pp.16-17; IOR, L/Mil/17/5/2403 List A, 'Nominal Roll of Indian prisoners of war suspected of having deserted to the enemy or to have given information or to have otherwise assisted the enemy after capture', secret.

Morale improved. Nevertheless, what the Corps lacked was artillery and without a superior weight of fire support, it was difficult to see how they could retake the objective of Neuve Chappelle, lost to the Germans in October 1914. Since then the village had been prepared extensively for defence, was ringed with wire and its approaches were criss-crossed with water-filled ditches and flooded ground, and the whole area was dominated by German guns on and behind the Aubers Ridge. When the order to retake the village came, all the Allied artillery fire that was available was concentrated into a short bombardment at dawn on 10 March 1915, and the initial assault by the Garhwali Brigade was successful. By 0930 that day, the Garhwalis were inside the village although their British officers, characteristically leading from the front, had suffered heavy casualties and the 2/3rd Gurkhas had lost direction and become separated. The usual problems of communication across the debris of the battlefield delayed the arrival of the Dehra Dun Brigade, which was forced to take up a temporary defensive position along Layes Brook, to the west of the village. The Germans counter-attacked, determined to recover their forward strongpoints. This was defeated, despite a blizzard of shelling, and yet another crop of casualties for the Indian Corps.

Attempts to restart the offensive failed repeatedly. Subsequent attacks in April and May at Festubert and Aubers Ridge were also unsuccessful. Explanations were sought in terms of inadequate artillery support, shell shortages, and criticism of Indian Army staff work.[31] Senior Indian Army officers have been criticised for valuing seniority over merit, failing to have sufficient numbers put through staff college, and being unfamiliar with large formation manoeuvres that characterised European warfare. Diversionary operations at Moulin St Piètre by the Indian Corps during the Battle of Loos were marked by a successful assault, but a failure in staff work meant that there were no reserves or supports so that captured ground was enveloped and the leading battalions were compelled to make a fighting retreat.[32] Yet, as elsewhere during the First World War, the relentless mathematics of modern warfare was the true cause of failure, and the engineering capabilities of the German Army. During the assault on Aubers Ridge on 9th May, Allied artillery fire had failed to make much impression on German trenches or their well-revetted strongpoints. As the Dehra Dun brigade rose from the ground some yards ahead of their sodden trenches, following unseasonably heavy rain, the German infantry and machine gunners had a clear field of fire. The German Maxims had been calibrated in advance to fire at just eight inches above the ground, and they scythed down the extended lines with impunity.[33] In one leading

---

31 The latter is strongly refuted by Gordon Corrigan, *Sepoys in the Trenches: the Indian Corps on the Western Front, 1914-15* (Stroud: Spellmount, 2006), pp.168 and 247. See Nikolas Gardner, *Trial by Fire: Command and the British Expeditionary Force in 1914* (Westport, CT: Praeger, 2003), pp.177-82.
32 John Buchan, *A History of the Great War*, I, (New York: Houghton Mifflin, 1923), pp.150-49.
33 Corrigan, *Sepoys in the Trenches*, pp.204-207.

company of 6th Jats, every man was killed or wounded before they advanced 100 yards. The 2/2nd Gurkhas lost all their officers and NCOs, but the survivors dashed forward and got to the German trenches where they were all killed or wounded. Just 20 minutes after the assault had begun, the battlefield was empty, save for handfuls of men sheltering in craters and ditches, and strewn across the ground were the wounded and the dead.

Other divisions on alternative axes were also checked, and a second wave, scheduled to take place on the same front of the Dehra Dun Brigade, was cancelled. Nevertheless, it was determined that the Bareilly Brigade would continue with its attack once the communication trenches had been cleared of the wounded. This second assault got barely 30 yards from its start line before it was cut down. Vaughan's Rifles lost 50 per cent killed and wounded in this advance, and the 41st Dogras lost 401 casualties of a strength of 645, including all its officers. The Garwhal Brigade suffered the same fate on 15 and 16 May, being decimated by the sheer weight of fire. When the action concluded on 18 May, the gains were pitifully small and the landscape was a scene of Dantean desolation.

The Indian Corps was not limited to operations at Neuve Chappelle and Aubers Ridge. In April, the Germans used poison gas to the north-east of Ypres and the Lahore Division was thrust into the gap in the line. Due to confusion about the geography, the division attempted to reach what it believed was the original French front line, only to find that the position had long been abandoned, and, as they pressed on to their objective, vaguely defined as 'the enemy trench', they had to storm across over 1,000 yards of No Man's Land. The attack, with derisory artillery support, was broken up by German fire.[34] The Ferozepore Brigade was then subjected to a retaliatory gas attack, which, for troops without any respirators or protection, inflicted severe casualties. Some terrified sepoys fled, but others were rallied by junior leaders like Jemadar Mir Dast, who, for his determined resistance, courageous inspiration to others and his insistence on going back out into No Man's Land to recover wounded comrades was awarded the Victoria Cross.[35] A handful of survivors under the command of Major Deacon of the Connaughts with survivors of the Manchesters, far in advance of the rest, grimly clung to the mud and drove off German counterattacks.[36] The division held on, but the gas attack had been another profound shock to the troops.

For some time, the deterioration of the Indian Corps had been noted. British regiments in the Army in India had not had the same dislocation over officers, despite similar losses.[37] Some British officers, posted in to the Indian regiments, did not speak the language of the soldiers. Losses in Viceroy Commissioned Officers were

---

34 Willcocks, *With the Indians in France*, pp.266-67.
35 Mir Dast was awarded the VC, and was, ironically, the brother of the deserter, who allegedly received an Iron Cross.
36 Corrigan, *Sepoys in the Trenches*, pp. 189-90.
37 Morton-Jack, *Indian Army on the Western Front*, p.168.

also severe. Familiar faces, who knew the men well, were often now gone.[38] Moreover, Indian units had to be reinforced with drafts, and although efforts were made to replace class companies with men of the same background, in the confusion of the early months of the war, this had not been possible.[39] Despite the larger numbers of reinforcements available by June 1915, the cohesion of the Corps could no longer be guaranteed.[40]

The decision was taken to move the Indian infantry out of France and relocate them in Middle Eastern theatres where communications with India were shorter and, for those from the plains of India at least, the climate more familiar.[41] In any case, the expansion of the campaigns in the Middle East demanded more manpower and the Mesopotamian operations came under the direction of the Indian government.[42] The cavalry stayed on, of course, and took part in the larger actions of the war on the Somme, without success, but the unique composition of the Indian Army, while a strength on frontier operations, had suffered severely under the pressures of very heavy losses and such trying conditions in France and Flanders.[43]

Assessments

By the autumn of 1915, the Indian Army had been through a transformative experience, a crucible of war that no one could have conceived of even twelve months before. From a strategic perspective, India was secure, and, despite German efforts to ignite unrest through Ghadr subversion and Bengali revolutionaries, the subcontinent did not show signs of unrest. Although on the truculent North West Frontier, there was a series of operations including a brief period of resistance by Mahsuds in 1917 and a Mohmand blockade in 1916. Territorial battalions from Britain released British and Indian Army units for service overseas, thus maintaining the strength of the garrison.[44] Beyond the frontier, despite the widespread fighting inside Persia, Afghanistan was curiously quiet. In Mesopotamia and East Africa there had been significant defeats and evidence of poor performance, including the lacklustre actions

---

38 Morton-Jack, *Indian Army on the Western Front*, p.185.
39 John Merewhether and Sir Frederick Smith, *The Indian Corps in France* (London: John Murray, 1919), pp. 462-89; Morton-Jack, *Indian Army on the Western Front*, pp. 19 and 162-5.
40 Merewhether and Smith, *The Indian Corps in France*, p.463; Morton-Jack, *Indian Army on the Western Front*, p. 18.
41 George Morton-Jack refutes the idea that the Indian Corps was withdrawn because of suffering from the northern European climate or operational underperformance. See, *Indian Army on the Western Front*, p.157.
42 Morton-Jack, *Indian Army on the Western Front*, p.154.
43 Robin Prior and Trevor Wilson, *The Somme* (New Haven: Yale University Press, 2005), p.139.
44 Although, it should be noted, that the regular contingent was down to 15,000 men, too few to garrison 300 million in the event of a major insurrection.

of the Indian cavalry near Ctesiphon, but overall, despite the British authorities' anxiety that there would be widespread disaffection, desertion or even mutiny, the Indian Army remained cohesive.

In France and Flanders, there had been a handful of desertions by Muslim soldiers, but never to the extent that some British officers had feared, and the cases were usually related to the appalling conditions of the fighting front. Some deterioration of performance was to be expected in subsequent deployments when one considers that the forces being despatched overseas at short notice were far in excess of what the pre-war planners had prepared for. On the Western Front, morale had been an issue, but this is hardly surprising given the casualties and winter conditions in which the sepoys and sowars served. It is surely more remarkable that their spirit of cohesion and the quality of the leadership enabled the Indian Corps to remain intact under such stresses. While most units fought well, making use of frontier warfare training and experience, there were exceptions. The 9th Bhopal Regiment tried to cross No Man's Land at Neuve Chappelle by crawling under German fire, but their slow rate of movement exposed them to heavy casualties and there had been no attempt to co-ordinate fire and movement tactics, although the battalion redeemed itself with a fighting withdrawal.[45] By contrast, the 2/3rd Gurkhas utilised the tactics they had cleared in clearing sangars at Dargai on the North West Frontier in 1898 to assault building in Neuve Chappelle. Their skirmishing tactics enabled them to co-ordinate movements and covering fire and clear machine gun posts which would otherwise have pinned down the entire brigade.[46] The verdict on the performance of the Indian Corps is therefore a mixture of success and setback.

It was understandable that, during and after the war, Indian Army officers would emphasise the excellent examples of courage and determination shown by Indian units and their soldiers.[47] Critics would place greater significance on the incidence of self-inflicted wounds to show that Indian troops' morale made them unsuitable for the European theatre. Champions and critics alike had their agendas.[48] In recent years, these have been replaced with new historiographical trends. There have been efforts to show that the Indian Army was merely an issue of race and coercion, apparently representing the organising principles of the British Empire. The problem with this interpretation is it was clearly not the way the soldiers and officers of the Indian Army saw it themselves at the time.[49] They were organised primarily as an army, with a distinct cultural emphasis that could and often did generate fierce loyalty, competitiveness and *espirit de corps*. However, it was an army built around certain

---

45 Corrigan, *Sepoys in the Trenches*, p.71.
46 Morton-Jack, *Indian Army on the Western Front*, p.231.
47 Willcocks, *With the Indians in France*, p. 9.
48 See Morton-Jack, *The Indian Army on the Western Front*, p.13; Merewhether and Smith, *The Indian Corps in France*, pp. vii, ch 2 and 14.
49 See 'Introduction' in Rob Johnson (ed), *The Indian Army: Virtue and Necessity* (Cambridge Scholars Press, 2014).

assumptions about the character of the war they would be called upon to fight. No one could have foreseen the demands that were to be placed upon it, and we should remember that the Indian Army was pitched hastily into a conflict without the luxury of preparation, in order to hold the line in France, replace shattered divisions or secure vulnerable parts of the empire. Crucially, it had insufficient numbers of qualified young officers or experienced Indian offcers to the replace the casualties it suffered. Although largely withdrawn from France and Flanders, from 1917, the Indian Army that took the offensive in Palestine, Mesopotamia, and Africa was a significantly different organisation from that in 1914. Better equipped, seasoned, expanded, with better staffs, intelligence, logistics and *materiel*, it would go on to provide a great contribution to Allied victory in all these theatres.

3

The Mobilisation and Supply of India's Equine Army 1914[1]:The chief arm of transport, artillery, cavalry and support units are their animals[2]

Graham Winton

In August 1914 India immediately committed substantial military and economic resources to the Allied war effort; the total minimum value of which was some £479 million.[3] From this initial commitment India made available appropriate resources from its approximately 1.3 million animals, for Home defence and overseas expeditionary forces.[4] In October the Indian Army Department confirmed it would

---

1   The 'Army of India' consisted of two elements. The 'Indian Army' (composed of native Indians) and the 'British Army in India' composed of British regiments stationed in India. British India included what became independent India, Pakistan, Bangladesh and Burma. My thanks to Squadron Leader Rana T.S. China, United Services Institute of India, for his generous help in supplying materials and photographs, and making valuable comments on a draft of this chapter.
2   Adapted from Stephen Badsey, *Doctrine and Reform in the British Cavalry 1880-1918*, (Hampshire: Ashgate, 2008), p. 274. The Army Act,1912 gives the military definition of the 'horse' as: including the mule, and any other beast of whatever description used for burden, or draught or carrying persons, for example donkey and camel.
3   Krishan Saini, 'The Economic Aspects of India's Participation in the First World War', in Ellinwood De Witt (ed), *India and World War One*, (Delhi: Manohar, 1978), Chapter 8, pp.143-144. Saini offers a range of figures, which should be taken as approximate. India's full economic contribution to the war effort involved changes by the Indian Legislative Council to statutes governing India's relationship with Great Britain, see Saini, pp.141-143,146, 152,173. See also *Statistics 1914-1920, The Military Effort of The British Empire During the Great War*, (War Office, 1922), p.777 and India's Contribution to the Great War, Calcutta: Government of India, 1923.
4   John Moore, *Army Veterinary Service in War*, (London: H & W Brown, 1921), p.40.

continue to meet ordinary maintenance charges for animals with Expeditionary Force 'A' [IEFA], which would have been met had they remained in India.[5]

Official statistics for the number of animals India sent overseas are:[6]

102,840	Mesopotamia
51,776	France
17,736	Egypt
6,995	Persian Gulf
3,500	Aden
1,501	East Africa
2	Gallipoli
184,350	Total

The above table does not provide the total number of animals mobilised for military service in India, or the type of animals involved. The organisation and transportation of animals from across India, to ports of embarkation and then overseas, was a major, but often ignored, logistic achievement.

India's military forces depended on animals (horse, pony, mule, donkey, camel and bullock), as the principal means of motive power and mobility. Sufficient animals were required of the appropriate class, type, conformation and size to perform the specific tasks required of them. An adequate supply of fit trained animals was needed; with safe transportation by rail and ship to the various theatres of war. An efficient remount service and most importantly a veterinary service for the care of animals was imperative to maintaining supply and effectiveness in the field. Speedy mobilisation could only be achieved with successful pre-war planning to meet wartime expansion and sustainability, developing the crucial elements of supply, care and organisation e.g. farriers, harness, saddlery, shoes, tools, blankets, nose bags and appropriate buildings.

The Naval Commander-in-Chief, East Indies, wrote (30 July), 'War is imminent between Great Britain and certain Foreign Powers'.[7] The Director of the Royal Indian

---

5   IOR, L/MIL/17/5/2431, General Staff Branch European War, War Diary, Diary Number (hereafter DN) 5589, 13 October 1914.
6   *Statistics 1914-1920*, p.779. In contrast Saini, 'Economic Aspects', p.143, lists 172,815 animals.
7   IOR, L/MIL/17/5/2421, General Staff Branch European War, War Diary (hereafter GSB), DN.8, 30 July, 1914. See also L/MIL/17/5/3151, IEFB, Appendix 66, 23 September 1914, footnote 62, which makes it clear the reference to a Naval C-in-C is not for India but the East Indies. A memorandum was also sent from the Secretary, Foreign and Political Department, to the Government of India, Army Department [AD], to the Local Administrations and Political Officers throughout India, informing them

Marine [RIM] was informed that, 'it may conceivably become necessary to send to Europe a cavalry brigade and two or three infantry divisions at very short notice', and arrangements for 'possibly having to take up shipping for the transport of the above troops [and animals] in the event of war'. He was to:

> At once consider the arrangements required to meet the above contingency and any enquiries he may have to make from shipping companies should be made very confidentially. A Cavalry Brigade would require seven ships and each division 23 ships of about 5,000 tons.[8]

The maintenance of this Force was understood by India to mean the replacement of wastage in Indian troops and animals. British units, stationed in India, would be supplied from England. In addition, the resources of the semi-autonomous 'Princely States' (including their Imperial Service Troops [IST]) were volunteered and placed at the disposal of His Majesty's Government.[9]

The Maharaja of Rewa, for example, enquired if there were 'any orders for me and my army':[10]

> There is an old regulation in the State that all men fit to carry arms are liable for military service when an emergency arises ... I think you know very well that our men and horses are quite fit for service according to the population of the State.

---

    of precautionary measures being adopted: Honourable Resident of Hyderabad, Mysore, Baroda, Nepal and Kashmir, the Agent to the Governor of Central India, of Rajputana and of Baluchistan, Chief Commissioner and Agent to Governor General North West Frontier Province. Copies also to the Political Resident in Persian Gulf, in Aden and His Britannic Majesty's Minister at Tehran, IOR, L/MIL/17/5/2421, GSB, DN.35, 30 July 1914.

8 IOR, L/MIL/17/5/2421, GSB, DN.37, 30 July 1914.
9 Over 600 Princely States, some only minor fiefdoms, were not governed directly by British India but co-existed through a series of subsidiary alliances retaining autonomy within the State except for external affairs. After 1885 the British created a small military reserve force recruited from these States (Imperial Service Troops), trained and equipped by the Indian Army, but paid for by the State. These forces were largely restricted to ceremonial and internal policing. The States also made a cash contribution of some £5 million. Gordon Corrigan, *Sepoys in the Trenches*, (Gloucestershire: Spellmount, 2004), p.22. Peter Duckers, *The British-Indian Army 1860-1914*, (Buckinghamshire: Shire Publications, 2003), pp.32-33. Arnold Wright (ed), *Indian States: A Biographical History & Administrative Survey*, (London, 1922). Saini, 'Economic Aspects', p.152. IOR, L/MIL/17/5/2421, GSB, DN.68, 30 July 1914. L/MIL/17/5/2422, GSB, DN.952, 11 August 1914. See also *The Maharaja's Paltans: A history of the Indian State Forces 1888-1948*, Head. R, and McClenaghan, T, (New Delhi: Manohar, 2013).
10 IOR, L/MIL/17/5/2425, GSB, DN.2846, 15 August 1914.

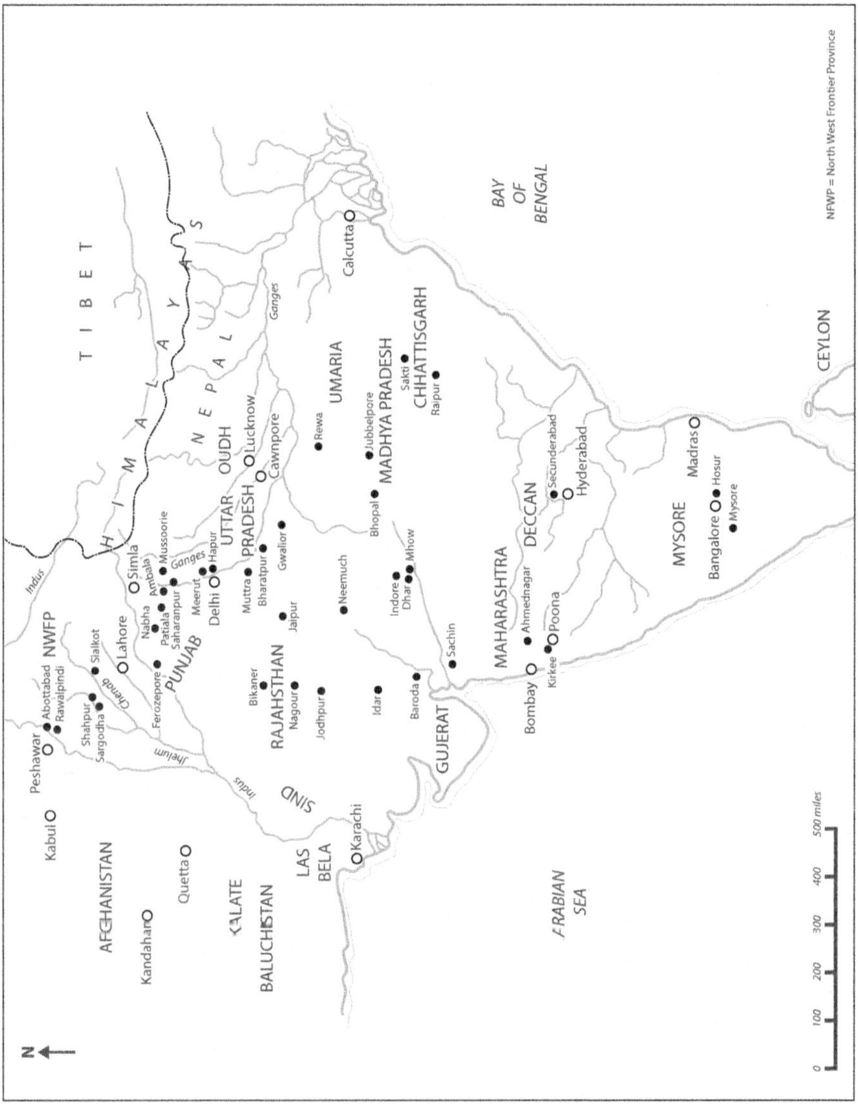

The Mobilisation and Supply of India's Equine Army 1914

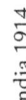

India 1914

The Raja Liladhar Singh telegraphed (4 September), 'As war has broken out I place my personal services and entire resources of my state at His Majesty's disposal'.[11] The Maharaja of Rewa enquired whether his colliery, or leather factor at Umaria, could be used by the Government for the war effort. The supply of leather was crucial to mobilisation demands for harness and saddlery. Not all were so loyal to the Empire. The Officiating Political Resident in Turkish Arabia, Baghdad, wrote to the Secretary of the Foreign and Political Department, Simla, stating the military authorities categorically refused to give up transport animals and horses requisitioned for mobilisation.[12]

Shipping to provide military transports was taken up as it arrived into Indian ports. From the issue of mobilisation orders all government dockyards, Port Trusts, railway, sapper and miners workshops, worked continually making up horse and mule fittings. If animals were to cross the Arabian Sea alive during the monsoon it was deemed essential that all fittings were thoroughly reliable.[13]

The Director, RIM, enquired whether the possibility of war was so far advanced as to warrant the detention of suitable ships at ports.[14] He was not to detain any ships, but keep a list of foreign shipping in harbour and all subsequent arrivals and departures. Orders were then received (8 August) to permanently detain enemy merchant ships.[15]

The Army Department was notified (5th August), 'War with Germany has started'. Local Governments of India, Administrations and Political Officers were also informed.[16]

Major Edward Tennant (Deccan Horse) wrote:

> On conclusion of spring field training in 1914 there were no rumours of war; by the end of July speculation was rife but the consensus was that the crises would blow over. Even when war was declared there appeared small likelihood the Indian Army would be required, then suddenly on the evening 9 August came orders for mobilisation for service out of India.[17]

---

11 IOR, L/MIL/17/5/2426, GSB, DN.3142, 4 September 1914. Liladhar Singh, Feudatory Chief, Sakti State to Political Agent Chhattisgharh Feudatories, Raipur.
12 Umaria (Madhya Pradesh, Central India). IOR, L/MIL/17/5/2424, GSB,DN.1958, 21 August and L/MIL/17/5/2422, GSB, DN. 954, 6 August 1914. Turkish Arabia came under British India's broad political orbit and was part of British India's Residency System, see James Onley, 'The Raj Reconsidered", *Asian Affairs*, Vol. XL, No.1 (March 2009), pp.4-62.
13 IOR, L/MIL/17/5/2425, GSB, DN.2714, 2 September.
14 At an approximate cost of roughly Rs.750 (£50) per day, per ship. Conversion into pounds sterling using an exchange rate of £1 to 15 rupees, in Saini, 'Economic Aspects', p.175, note 22, IOR, L/MIL/17/5/2421, GSB, DN.102, 31 July 1914.
15 IOR, L /MIL/17/5/2422,GSB,DN.748, 8 August 1914.
16 IOR, L/MIL/17/5/2421,GSB,DN.324-5 and 370, 5 August 1914.
17 Edward Tennant ('A' Squadron (Sikh) Deccan Horse, *Royal Deccan Horse in the Great War*, (Aldershot: Gale & Polden,1939), p.7.

The Indian Government committed (30 July) to sending the IEFA of two infantry divisions and a cavalry brigade to Egypt (6 August), with a view to its possible deployment in Europe. First line transport (animals and vehicles) was to be modified to operate in Egypt if necessary, but always with the possibility of employment in Europe.[18] Finally (28 August) the decision was made for the IEFA to be sent to Europe. By the end of 1914 India had formed and despatched, with animals, six overseas expeditionary forces: 'A' (France), 'B' – 'C' (East Africa), 'D' (Mesopotamia) and 'E' – 'F' (Egypt).[19]

Official peacetime and wartime, or paper strengths, of units usually differed from what actually existed in the field. On mobilisation the animal establishments for units of the British-Indian Army serving in India, differed from those sent overseas.[20] For example, the decision to use draught or pack transport with 1st line regimental transport depended on whether they mobilised with, or without, tents. As few of the expeditionary force units took anything like the number of animals listed in official wartime establishments, when serving in India, it is difficult to calculate the numbers actually sent overseas with individual units.

An Indian infantry division, serving in India, consisting of three brigades of four infantry regiments (three Indian and one British) plus divisional units, attached transport and miscellaneous units, on paper, required a wartime establishment of approximately 9,051 animals:[21]

18   On 8 August, 1914, the Secretary of State for Indian informed The Viceroy [AD] that a separate expeditionary force to German East Africa was being considered, IOR, L/MIL/17/5/2422,GSB, DN.750, 8 August 1914. Michael Healy, 'Operation 'Nathi' and the Old Contemptibles, The Decision to Reinforce the BEF with Indian troops in 1914', in *Durbar, Journal of the Indian Military Historical Society*, Vol.31, No.3 (2014), pp.109-20. L/MIL/17/5/2421, GSB, DN.672 & 675-676, 6-7 August. On 16 September 1914 changes were made to the Act for the Better Government of India,1858, Section 55, allowing the resources of the States to be used beyond India's external frontiers. Saini, 'Economic Aspects', p.142. L/MIL/17/5/2422, GSB, DN.845, 9 August 1914.
19   Expeditionary Force 'G' (Gallipoli) was added in 1915. The Viceroy [AD] to Secretary of State for India, 10 August wrote that, with a 'view to preserve secrecy, suggest Force destined for East Africa be alluded to as IEF 'B' and Force for Egypt IEF 'A'. IOR, L/MIL/17/5/3086, Army HQs India, War Dairy IEFA (hereafter IEFA), DN.2427, 28 August. L/MIL/17/5/2422, GSB, DN.934, 10 August. L/MIL/17/5/2424, GSB, DN.2399, 28 August and DN.1967, 22 August, 'Two separate forces are being sent to East Africa, one is for operations in German East Africa and is known as 'B', the other is for British East Africa and is known as 'C'.' David Payne, 'The Indian Army on the Western Front', 21 May, 2008. James Edward Edmonds, *History of the Great War*, (London: Macmillan, 1927), Vol. II, p.8.
20   The actual units forming, for example, a corps, division and brigade, vary considerably between historians and sources. Few include all units and many do not give the date of their listings.
21   Figures taken from *Field Service Pocket Book 1914* (London: HMSO,1914) (hereafter FSPB), pp.14,22 and included: Divisional HQs, 3 Infantry Brigades, Indian Cavalry Regiment, Indian Pioneer Battalion, HQs Divisional Artillery, Field Artillery Brigade,

1,064	riding horses
490	pack horses
700	draught horses
178	ponies
2,646	pack mules
595	draught mules
8	riding camels
3,270	draught camels
100	bullocks

The 3rd (Lahore) Indian Division, IEFA, sailed with about 3,233 (1,507 mules and 1,726 horses). On paper, an Indian infantry regiment with headquarters and machine gun section required 223 animals:

20	riding horses
2	ponies
24	pack mules
6	camels (mess transport)
106	pack mules (attached transport)
65	camels (attached transport)

Infantry regiments with the 3rd (Lahore) Division each sailed with between 80 to 94 horses and mules.[22]

Of the 45 peacetime British-Indian Army cavalry regiments stationed in India, by the end of 1914, 20 were in France (14 Indian and six British). A cavalry brigade in India consisted of three regiments, one British and two Indian.[23] The war establishment of a

---

Indian Mountain Artillery Brigade, Divisional Ammunition Column, HQs Divisional Engineers with two Field Companies and Signal Company, 2 British and 3 Indian Field Ambulances, Divisional Supply Column and Supply Park, Transport HQs, Field Veterinary Section, Printing Section, Litho Section, Coolie Corps, Carrier Corps, Survey Section, 1st and 2nd Class Post Offices. Compare this with, for example, Chris Kempton, 'Duty and Fidelity: *The Indian Army 1914-1922, Part 1, Divisions*, pp.29, 63.

22 TNA, WO 95/3911/1, General Staff, 3rd Indian Division, War Diary, Appendix 27, 18th September, 1914.

23 *FSPB*, pp.12-23. TNA, WO 95/1176-3, 6th Inniskilling Dragoons, War Diary, November 1914 and April 1915. David Kenyon, *Horsemen in No Man's Land*, (Barnsley: Pen and Sword, 2011), p.33 and private correspondence. TNA, WO 95/1167, 1st Indian Cavalry Division, War Diary, Appendix 1. Graham Winton, 'British-Indian Army Cavalry: From Mobilisation to the Western Front 1915', in Spencer Jones (ed) *Courage Without Glory: The British Army on the Western Front 1915*, (Solihull: Helion & Company, 2015), Chapter 6.

British regiment, stationed in India, at sabre strength plus headquarters and machine gun section, was 742 animals:

542	riding horses
24	pack horses
2	ponies
2	camels (mess transport)
70	pack mules (attached transport)
92	draught mules (attached transport)

The 6th (Inniskilling) Dragoons, 2nd Indian Cavalry Division, sailed from Bombay with 485 horses (transport not included) and on departure from Orleans 608 animals (559 horses, 3 ponies and 46 mules). In April 1915 the strength is given as 621:

565	riding horses
20	Army Service Corps draught horses
4	ponies
10	Supply and Transport mules
22	Ammunition column (horses or mules)

An Indian cavalry regiment differed. When mobilised with draught transport, at sabre strength plus headquarters and machine gun section, the strength was 750 animals (figures when mobilised with pack transport (total 948) are given in brackets):

550	riding horses	(550)
24	pack horses	(24)
2	ponies	(2)
76	pack mules	(314)
8	riding camels	(8)
6	camels (mess transport)	(6)
84	draught mules (transport)	(44)

The 15th Lancers, attached to the 3rd (Lahore) Division) sailed with 565 horses and 44 mules.[24]

---

24 The Jodhpur Imperial Service Lancers, initially with the 9th (Secunderabad) Cavalry Brigade, IEFA, mobilised with a strength of 499 riding horses. TNA, WO 95/3911/1, 3rd Indian Division, Appendix 27, 18 September, 1914. IOR, L/MIL/17/5/2424, GSB,

An Indian cavalry brigade (figures for a division (8,997) are given in brackets), serving in India, required about 2,999 animals:[25]

1,723	riding horses	(5,169)
42	pack horses	(126)
226	draught horses	(678)
30	ponies	(90)
70	riding mules	(210)
249	pack mules	(747)
627	draught mules	(1,881)
16	riding camels	(48)
16	draught camels (mess transport)	(48)

With three brigades to a Cavalry division the total would be about 8,997 animals including 96 camels. The 1st Indian Cavalry Division, November 1914 (France), lists an approximate strength of 8,624 animals:[26]

6,413	riding horses and ponies
754	draught horses
246	ponies (including 168 draught)
12	Ordnance 1st Line equipment mules
872	draught mules
327	pack mules (Small Arms Ammunition section and troop reserves)

DN.2220, 26 August. Gurcharn Singh Sandhu, *The Indian Cavalry*, (Delhi: Vision Books,1981), Vol.1, p.56, gives the combat strength of an Indian cavalry regiment as 520 horses, employing 584 non-combatants, or followers, including 260 syces and 260 grass cutters.

25 TNA, WO 95/1167,1st Indian Cavalry Division, War Diary, Appendix1 (includes some figures for the 9th (Secunderabad) Cavalry Brigade), gives a total of 2,017 animals in a brigade but does not include the 964 given in the FSPB, pp.11-12, for artillery, ammunition and supply columns, field ambulances and transport headquarters. The actual difference is 18 fewer animals from the War Diary for the comparable figures between the two above sources, but the figures making the totals for the various types of animals vary considerably.

26 TNA, WO 95/1167, 1st Cavalry Division, War Diary. The figures given are confusing, possibly some are repeated and do not always add up.

These figures show a difference of only 373 animals, but with a significant increase in certain types: riding horses, ponies and draught horses (the latter supplied by the War Office [WO]) and a decrease in mules. No riding mules, or camels, are listed.

The most significant difference between the structure and composition of Indian and British cavalry regiments was the unique Silladar System of recruitment and supply.[27] All except three of the 39 Indian regular line cavalry regiments were part of this system. Government control of 'Indian Army' horses only related to mounting the three non-silladar regiments and British cavalry.[28] Silladar regiments recruited individually and were maintained and funded with no linking structure to other regiments, or centralised veterinary and remount services. The quality of saddlery, horses and equipment depended on the wealth and discretion of the individual regiment. They were simultaneously a fighting organisation and commercial concern, purchasing, breeding and training their own horses and mules; farming on a large scale, purchasing wholesale grain, saddlery and other equipment, which was then sold within the regiment.[29] On mobilisation no horses, or horse equipment could be drawn from government supply depots. The system was totally unsuited to a major and lengthy destructive European war as can be seen in India's response (15 October) to a War Office request for a second cavalry division in France. By completing the 1st Indian Cavalry Division, regiments had already been depleted of horses and equipment. The 9th Secunderabad Cavalry Brigade, ordered to make up deficiencies in horses and saddlery from the 26th Light Cavalry (non-silladar) and the 34th Horse, indented for 157 horses and equipment from the 26th.[30] The Secretary of State wrote of 'two non-silladar regiments still in existence but which have apparently been demolished by your [Army Department] action in stripping them of horses'.[31] The process was made more difficult as the Government had no

---

27 Silladar, probably an adaptation of the Persian sillahbardar, or soldier bearing arms. It was an irregular cavalry system of recruitment, descended from the Mughal and Maratha cavalry and adopted by the East India Company because of its cheapness. Sandhu, *Indian Cavalry*, p.87.
28 The 26th, 27th, 28th Light Cavalry, the three surviving pre Indian Mutiny (1878) regular regiments of the old Madras Presidency cavalry. George MacMunn, *The Armies of India*, (Bristol: Crecy Books,1911), pp.12- 3, 176-80. The Silladar System was abolished in 1922.
29 Philip Mason, *A Matter of Honour*, (London: Jonathan Cape, 1974) p.377. *Army In India and Its Evolution*, (Government of India, 1924), pp.91-98; Sandhu, *Indian Cavalry*, pp. 409-10; George MacMunn, *Behind The Scenes in Many Wars*, (London: John Murray, 1930), pp.333-4.
30 The 26th (King George's Own) Light Cavalry, ex Madras Presidency, served in South Yemen as part of The Aden Field Force (IEFD). 34th (Prince Albert Victor's Own) Poona Horse, 9th (Secunderabad) Cavalry Brigade. IOR, L/MIL/17/5/3086, IEFA, Appendix 16, 8 August. For British cavalry regiments in India see L/MIL/17/5/2425, GSB, DN.2907, 5 September 1914.
31 IOR, L/MIL/17/5/3151, Army Headquarters India, IEF 'B' War Diary (hereafter IEFB),DN.3254, 9 September 1914.

powers to compulsorily transfer horses and equipment between silladar regiments, which were reliant, as was the entire army, on volunteering. With only a negligible reserve and no other immediate source from which India could supply trained remounts to replace wastage, this depletion would continue.

Improvements in the quality of Indian bred country horses were made in the late 19thC, allowing some reduction in the Indian Army's dependence on imported remounts and breeding stock. In the Punjab for example, a series of new canal colonies were founded from 1885 with significant military involvement in the allocation of land grants to ex-soldiers. A process that increased as new areas were colonised. This military involvement secured a labour force and extensive areas of land for the breeding and maintenance of animals for military use, camels, mules and cavalry horses (initially for British regiments stationed in India and later also for Indian silladar regiments). This colonisation process formed part of the 'paramount importance' for an internal supply of cavalry horses and reduction in the reliance on imported animals.[32] Some Arab horses were imported but the main source was from New South Wales, Australia, known as the 'Waler'. Mules came from a variety of sources, Indian country bred, from China, Tibet and Persia. Larger mules were imported from the Argentine or America.[33]

Horse artillery for British-Indian Army cavalry brigades was supplied by the British Royal Horse Artillery [RHA]. A horsed battery totalled 281 animals (98 riding horses, 132 draught, 1 pony, 2 mess transport camels, with attached transport of 12 pack and 36 draught mules). On mobilisation useless horses were not to be transferred to depots but destroyed or sold; unless useful for training purposes. Line bullocks with RHA and Royal Field Artillery [RFA] units proceeding on service reverted to the Supply and Transport Department.[34]

Shipping

Transport for the Indian expeditionary forces was crucial to the success of mobilisation and continued supply. Units were raised to war strength and transported to the ports of embarkation, mainly Bombay (Mumbai) and Karachi, embarking in ships requisitioned and converted for the purpose.[35] Embarkation and convoy timetables

---

32 Something India did not achieve as in 1932 over a 1,000 cavalry horses were purchased annually from Australia. Imran Ali, *The Punjab Under Imperialism, 1885-1947* (New Jersey: Princetown University Press, 1988), pp.8, 129-130, 153. I am grateful to Rana Chhina for bringing this publication to my attention.
33 See for example *The Victorian Society*, 'Transport Mules'.
34 During the Indian Mutiny (1857) artillery proved the mutineer's most effective arm. Consequently, except for a small number of mountain artillery batteries, all artillery in India was manned by British gunners, of the Royal Regiment of Artillery. *FSPB*, p.20. IOR, L/MIL/17/5/2429, GSB, DN.5018, Statement A.
35 IOR, L/MIL/17/5/3087, IEFA, Appendix 11, 2 September 1914.

were co-ordinated, including their naval escorts. The Director, RIM, was informed (9 August) that the IEFA urgently required transport and to make all the necessary arrangements for acquiring and fitting ships.

The unexpected scale of mobilisation and number of ships required could be summarised in the Army Department's response to a demand for some 65 troopships, but with only a limited number of horse fittings maintained in peacetime:

> Had we been aware from the first, of the great demand for troopships, which we would have to supply, we might have been able to expedite matters by being able to begin at once preparation on that scale.[36]

Fittings, such as animal stalls, were a major difficulty, as prior to the war India only maintained 620 mule and 700 horse fittings in Bombay. The Director, RIM, requested authorisation (31 July) to increase the stock of horse fittings by 500. However, the Indian Government sanctioned (4 August) an increase in fittings to 1,889 for mules and 4,114 for horses.[37] Owing to the scarcity of ships the Director advised that horses could be placed at closer quarters than Army Regulations allowed. No objection was raised provided sufficient air space was ensured and there was no overcrowding. Even with this 'no overcrowding' the Quartermaster General [QMG], India, requested ships carrying the 9th (Secunderabad) Cavalry Brigade take an extra charger for each British officer.[38]

Not only large ocean going transport ships were required. The QMG, India, wrote (15 August) that for expeditionary forces there was no immediate hurry for ordering boats for landing transport and animals on an open beach. If further boats were required notification was needed as early as possible as horse boats could not be built in less than two months.[39]

The Government entered into negotiations with shipping companies about rates for the hire of transports, some were asking exorbitant rates, and the approximate length of time they would be required. The Director, RIM, was anxious not to interfere more than necessary with trade, or enforce legislation regarding the compulsory acquisition

---

36 IOR, L/MIL/17/5/2425, GSB, DN.2714, 2 September 1914. Many telegrams requested detailed information on the size of transport vessels and number of animals they could carry, for example, the Army Department (22 September) noted that the 'Norseman' could carry 774 horses and the 'Atlantian' 670. L/MIL/17/5/2428, GSB, DN.4215, 22 September 1914.
37 IOR, L/MIL/17/5/2421, GSB, DN.279, 4 August 1914 & DN.101, 31 July 1914.
38 An officers riding horse, or charger; originally a horse suitable for riding into battle. British officers in possession of a suitable third charger were given permission to take them overseas. IOR, L/MIL/17/5/2423, GSB, DN.1847, 20 August 1914. L/MIL/17/5/2425,GSB,DN.2505, 30 August; DN.2806 & DN.2931, 4 September 1914. L/MIL/17/5/2426, GSB, DN.3032, 7 September 1914.
39 IOR, L/MIL/17/5/2423, GSB, DN.1375, 15 August. L/MIL/17/5/2422, GSB, DN.1214, 13 August 1914.

of ships.⁴⁰ On 12-13 August all German ships in Indian ports were placed at the Director's disposal and Austrian ships detained with the notification, 'We are at war with Austria'.⁴¹ Charters for enemy vessels (prizes) were agreed at a minimum of six months, as officers and engineers would not sign on for a lesser period.⁴²

Transport ships sailed in convoy as some travelled at a maximum speed of only seven knots. There was also a very real threat from the German raiding cruisers *Emden* and *Konigsberg*.⁴³ The minimum strength for naval convoy support was two ships, of which one had to be superior to the *Konigsberg*; not including armed transports. An additional regular warship was to be added to a large convoy.⁴⁴ By 21 August rumours were circulating that some ships had already been sunk and those leaving Calcutta (Kolkata) would fall prey to German warships. Such rumours made recruitment of lascars (sailors) difficult and with many desertions some sailings were delayed. The 3rd (Lahore) Division war diary records that the day before sailing (27 August) the *Konigsberg* was in wireless contact with the *Ziethen* about 500 miles south of Bombay.⁴⁵

Expeditionary Forces

IEF 'A'

The IEFA was originally only to be used on a defensive basis in the Mediterranean, not outside Egypt (which accounts for indecision about the mobilisation of camels).

---

40 IOR, L/MIL/17/5/2422, GSB,DN.719, 8 August; DN.823, 9 August; DN.988,11 August & DN.888,10 August 1914.
41 IOR, L/MIL/17/5/2422, GSB, DN.129/30, 13 August; DN.805, 9 August & DN.1077, 12 August 1914.
42 IOR, L/MIL/17/5/2426, GSB, DN.3167, 8 September & DN.3368, 9 September 1914.
43 The *Konigsberg* was reported off Socotra (now part of the Yemen), Indian Ocean, part of the Aden Governorate (24 August) and later in the vicinity of Zanzibar. IOR, L/MIL/17/5/2424,GSB, DN.2409, 29 August. L/MIL/17/5/2428, GSB, DN.4039A, 20 September (Intelligence from Aden and Nairobi). L/MIL/17/5/2422, GSB, DN.1042, 11 August 1914.
44 For example, the *Swiftsure, Dartmouth, Hardinge* and *Dufferin* and other RIM ships, when ready, were to constitute the convoy squadron. The *Minto* and *Northbrook* were also being prepared for Naval service and immediately placed under orders of the Naval C-in-C. The 'Dalhousie' was added 11 August. IOR, L/MIL/17/5/2422, GSB, DN.862, 10 August & DN.864, 9 August & DN.957, 11 August 1914.
45 SMS *Zieten*. German torpedo vessel built at the Thames Ironworks, Blackwall, London 1875-6. TNA, WO 95/3911/1, 3rd (Lahore) Division War Diary, 25 August, Karachi. IOR, L/MIL/17/5/2423,GSB, DN.1852, 21 August. The 'Emden' was reported (13 September) 200 miles east of Vizagapatam (with four prizes), in the Bay of Bengal (15th) sinking merchant vessels (five already sunk) and off Rangoon, Burma (18th). L/MIL/17/5/2427,GSB,DN.3560 & 3647, 15 September 1914. A cruiser was reported bombarding Madras (22nd); by the 29th *Emden* had sunk another four ships, capturing several more. L/MIL/17/5/2428,GSB,DN.4238, 22 September. Between 15-19 October she sank five to six steamers.

Eventually, the IEFA proceeded to Marseilles with India also providing a complete cavalry division of four brigades.⁴⁶ By the end of 1914 the IEFA consisted of two infantry divisions (3rd Lahore and 7th Meerut), each with an attached divisional cavalry regiment (15th Lancers (Cureton's Multanis), and 4th Cavalry), forming the Indian Army Corps, and the 9th (Secunderabad) Cavalry Brigade (mobilised 9 August) until December when it was placed with the 2nd Indian Cavalry Division. Two Indian cavalry divisions (1st and 2nd) were formed into the Indian Cavalry Corps.⁴⁷ On paper, animals with the IEFA infantry divisions numbered about 19,310 (horses and mules) and another 1,058 animals (including pack) with the two attached cavalry regiments, and over 17,000 with the two cavalry divisions (about 11,800 regimental horses plus artillery, transport horses and mules).

The War Office was to provide Indian forces with horses and mules for artillery and engineer units, also wagons, horses and drivers for supply trains. Thereby reducing the number of animals shipped from India to Europe. The IEFA was despatched without supply parks and supply columns, but ammunition columns were sent complete with wagons, horses, mules and carts. Army transport carts accompanied 1st Line Transport. Pack mules were also taken for Maxim machine guns, Section Reserve Small Arms Ammunition [SAA] and technical equipment other than medical supplies.⁴⁸ The IEFA was accompanied by a 10% first reinforcement for animals; other reinforcements, for example, 480 mules were to follow after the fighting formations. Supplies were to be provided en-voyage, including an additional 30 days reserve of grain and fodder and a further 15 days reserve in freight ships.⁴⁹

The Lahore Division sailed from Bombay and Karachi between 24-29 August (arriving Marseilles 26 September).⁵⁰ A shortage of transports and escort vessels delayed the remainder of the IEFA until 20 September. The Meerut Division and 9th (Secunderabad) Cavalry Brigade arrived Marseilles 12-14 October.⁵¹ Convoys sailed

---

46 Under the command of General Sir James Willcocks. 25 August. IOR, L/MIL/17/5/3086, IEFA, Appendix 113, 25-28 August & Appendix 116, 28 August 1914.
47 Notification of Indian Cavalry Corps formation was issued on 27 November. See for example, Edmonds, *History of the Great War*, Vol. II, pp. 8-9, 92,481- 486; TNA, WO 95/1167,1st Indian Cavalry Division War Diary, 23 November 1914.
48 Motor cars were required for staff.
49 As agreed with reference to *Paper Z* and *War Establishments India 1913*. IOR, L/MIL/17/5/2422, GSB, DN.1121, 12 August & DN.1122, 13 August 1914. Meerut Division transport mules mostly from the Argentine were fed bran and barley which they disliked whereas the Chinese mules 'ate anything'. TNA, WO 95/3938/8, MuleTransport War Diary, Meerut Division, p.2, 'Notes on Voyage'.
50 The nomenclature of all Indian brigades and divisions was changed to avoid confusion with British formations, retaining only a territorial name. For example 3rd (Lahore) to the Lahore Division and 9th (Secunderabad) to Secunderabad Cavalry Brigade. Edmonds, *History of the Great War*, Vol. II, pp.8-9.
51 The following units were also attached to the Indian Army Corps from 12 October-23 December, when transferred to the Indian Cavalry Corps: Signal troop and Cavalry Field Ambulance, 'N' Battery RHA, 'H' Section Ammunition Column,1st Indian Field Troop,

via the Arabian Sea, Indian Ocean, Red Sea, Suez Canal and Mediterranean. Units disembarked in Egypt re-embarking for the journey to Marseilles, travelling some 5,000 miles in seven weeks.

The 9th (Secunderabad) Cavalry Brigade, moved units in two stages, by rail from Secunderabad to Bombay, 5-8 and 31 August, sailing 3 September and 20 September in nine ships. Embarkation staff at Bombay had been informed of the necessity to prepare billeting (also for animals, see Grimshaw below) in anticipation of an unexpected delay in port. This was not done and heavy rain caused damage to equipment and discomfort for animals. The majority of the Brigade sailed on the 20th in a fleet of 33 ships part of an eventual convoy of 412 vessels. Passing through the Suez Canal (4-5 October) to Port Said, then Malta (10 October) arriving Marseilles during 12-13 October. The Brigade disembarked marching nine miles to camp, experiencing heavy rain. Moving to Orleans for refitting between 25-28 October.[52]

Only veterinary officers, distributed amongst the transports, sailed with the Brigade. The remainder of the veterinary staff being left behind due to an outbreak of smallpox. Eighteen horses died on the worst day off Aden as stalls were without ventilation. This loss was considered avoidable if the ships had been more effectively converted to horse transports.[53] The 6th (Inniskilling) Dragoons recorded a good voyage with the loss of only three horses and the Meerut Divisional Mule Transport only one out of 1,600 mules.[54]

The period off Aden (Red Sea) and Port Said appears to have been the most difficult for the horses due to intensive heat, with temperatures ranging from 80-94 degrees Fahrenheit. As many horses as possible were taken on deck for air. Captain Grimshaw, 34th Horse (which lost seven horses) met his regiment at Port Said. Inspecting the horses he thought those kept outside 'in pelting rain' two weeks before embarkation from India suffered most on the sea journey.[55]

An entry in the Brigade war diary (Mediterranean Sea, south of Italy) provides valuable insight into the transportation of animals during this early period:[56]

Jodhpur Lancers and Jodhpur Cavalry Field Ambulance. Edmonds, *History of the Great War*, Vol. II, pp. 8-9, 92, 481-486.
52 TNA, WO 95/1887, 9th (Secunderabad) Brigade War Diary.
53 TNA, WO 95/1887, 9th (Secunderabad) Cavalry Brigade War Diary, 6 October. IOR, L/MIL/17/5/3088, IEFA, Appendix 25, 5 October & Appendix 165, 27 October 1914. Tennant, *Royal Deccan Horse*, pp.11-12.
54 5th (Mhow) Cavalry Brigade, 1st Indian Cavalry Division. TNA, WO 95/1176, 6th (Inniskilling) Dragoons War Diary; on departure for Orleans its strength was 559 horses, 3 ponies and 46 mules. See also TNA, WO 95/3938/8, Mule Transport, War Diary, Meerut Division.
55 Roly Grimshaw, *Indian Cavalry Officer 1914-1915*, (Kent: Costello, 1986), 6 October, p.63. TNA, WO 95/1187, 34th Poona Horse War Diary, September, pp.15-17.
56 8 October. The above is my paraphrased part of the Report. The Report was sent to the Brigade GOC in reply to the QMG, India's request for suggestions on the suitability of

When shipping troops on board transports for a voyage of any length, it was essential that a certain scale of cleaning materials was allowed. This had not been sanctioned on this present voyage. Spanners and saws for refining horse boxes, shovels and brooms for litter (manure) removal were also required together with an ample supply of cresol disinfectant, not carbolic, which was apt to damage the horse's feet. More harness and saddle rooms should be provided. Ventilation was of primary importance when shipping horses in hastily prepared ships. Ports or openings could be placed in the ship's side giving direct access of light and air to troop decks, also enabling litter (manure) to be thrown directly overboard instead of being brought up on deck first. All horse decks should be provided with some sort of drainage system to enable swilling down with water and draining of urine. Exercise mats for animals should be wider and of rougher material, with room next to the bulkheads where horses could then be exercised all round the 'tween' deck. Staunchions of every sixth stall should be easily removable facilitating getting horses out for exercise and corners of gangways should all be padded. Head collars should be large enough for horses.

The immediate result of this report was an order that horses should not be placed in parts of a ship without satisfactory ventilation, unless prevented by unforeseen circumstances.

Animals travelled from India via Egypt to Marseilles, a distance of about 5,300 miles. Leaving the heat of India and Egypt and moving into the cold, damp wet, winter conditions of France was problematic. On arrival at Marseilles some animals were piquetted outside in constant heavy rain. Regular exercising was difficult and appears to have been done in hand. Grimshaw commented on receiving orders 'for another change in fodder' ... 'back on grain after being accustomed to oats; how can one expect to keep animals fit and well'. Acclimatisation and recuperation were vital if the Army was to have effective cavalry and mule transport. Failure to supply fit and healthy animals in a theatre of war was clearly shown when two brigades of the 1st Indian Cavalry Division were delayed reaching the front owing to sickness amongst transport horses provided by the War Office.[57] There were few outbreaks of mange

---

Indian Force transports and their fittings for the conveyance of horses. Addressed to the Base Commandant Marseilles. TNA, WO 95/1887, 9th (Secunderabad) Cavalry Brigade War Diary.

57 25 November. Sialkot and Lucknow Brigades were delayed leaving Orleans owing to outbreaks of pink eye (conjunctivitis, an inflammation of the conjunctiva, which can be highly infectious) in draught-transport horses from Le Havre. The Division was informed 353 horses had been sent to them and no fit horses remained at HQ, but everything possible was being done to obtain more, hopefully from Rouen. On 1 December a batch of 221 horses were at Rouen, having landed four days previously at Le Havre but the whole batch was infected. The Brigades finally entrained 5 December. GHQ was to be notified of the absolute necessity for improving arrangements under which horses were sent from

and glanders, diseases common to military campaigning; cases were treated quickly and effectively.[58]

The 9th (Secunderabad) Cavalry Brigade listed the number of reinforcements from their landing in France to the end of December 1914 as: 67 mules for Transport HQ, 103 horses for the Poona Horse and 3 for the 7th Dragoon Guards.[59]

IEF 'B' and 'C'

Initially it was not clear where the IEFB was to be sent. The Secretary of State, India, wrote (2 September) 'events will probably soon settle the question of destination'. The Director, RIM asked (10 September) whether Forces 'B' and 'C' would be despatched to similar destinations, or if not, what was the destination of IEFB? Followed by (15 September), 'we should like to know whether the words 'East Africa' refer to German, or British East Africa?' The Cabinet finally decided (14 September) that the remainder of the IEFC must be despatched immediately to Mombasa and IEFB as soon as possible to East Africa.[60] Deliberations over destination directly affected the mobilisation of animals and support services, equipment and shipping.[61] For example, whether to take mounted units, camels or horses, the type of animal shoes and type and number of fittings required for each transport ship; whether transport animals would be taken and if so, what type and in what numbers. Also what remount and veterinary arrangements would be required.

England. TNA, WO 95/1167, 1st Indian Cavalry Division War Diary, November 1914. Sandhu, *Indian Cavalry*, p.293.
58 Mange: parasitic skin disease not usually fatal. Glanders: seriously infectious disease common in wartime, can result in large numbers of animals being destroyed if not dealt with quickly and effectively. TNA, WO 95/1177, Mhow Cavalry Brigade, Mobile Veterinary Section War Diary, May 1915. WO 95/1188, 9th (Secunderabad) Cavalry Brigade, Mobile Veterinary Section War Diary, 6 April 1915.
59 TNA, WO 95/1187, 9th (Secunderabad) Cavalry Brigade War Diary, 'Reinforcements', note at the end of December 1914.
60 IOR, L/MIL/17/5/3151, IEFB,DN.2984, 5 September; Appendix 7, September & Appendix 8, September 1914. The Colonial Office was informed about postponing IEFB 'for the present'. Also Appendix 10; Appendix 11,10 September; Appendix 16,10 September; Appendix 34,15 September; Appendix 35,16 September; Appendix 28, 14 September; Appendix 22, 14 September. L/MIL/17/5/3220,IEFC, Appendix 46, 49-50, 15 September 1914.
61 For units changes see for example: IOR, L/MIL/17/5, 3150, IEFB, Appendix 44, 16 August. Also Appendix 52, 17 August; Appendix 102, 28 August; Appendix 106, 30 August; Appendix 112, 3 September 1914. L/MIL/17/5/3151, IEFB, Appendix 11-13, 10 September & Appendix 28, 14 September 1914.

The IEFB (formed 9 September) was eventually sent to Tanganyika (Tanzania) to invade and hold the principal port of German East Africa and the IEFC (formed 12 August), primarily to guard the Mombasa-Nairobi railway line and Zanzibar.[62]

The construction of fittings for shipping these forces was to begin immediately. The Director, RIM, reported (15 August) that the IEFB and IEFC would sail in five ships from Bombay and one from Karachi; the seven ships for the Cavalry Division (IEFA) were being fitted in Calcutta. On the 29 August the QMG, India, stated the despatch of the IEFA including the Jodhpur Lancers, but not the Bikaner Camel Corps (both Imperial Service units), 'must be completed without delay'. The IEFB was to be held in abeyance but the IEFC was required immediately. Ships previously earmarked for the IEFB, subject to availability, could be taken for shipping additional artillery and cavalry.[63] On the 23 September the Naval C-in-C, East Indies, was notified of a proposal to despatch nine ships from Bombay for the IEFB and three from Karachi, depending on the opening of the Bay of Bengal for the movement of fitted transports and availability of naval escorts.[64]

By the 22 August there were in rest camps with their units, 981 horses, 22 ponies, 1,221 mules and in a segregation camp, 13 horses and 12 mules. On the 17 September there were 2,488 animals in relief camps in Bombay waiting for transportation overseas.[65]

The IEFB and IEFC were to consist of one British and eight Indian battalions, a sapper and miner company, one heavy and one mountain artillery battery. On paper, the total war establishment of these infantry units, serving in India, would have been approximately 2,500 animals. The actual composition and number of animals with the IEFB and IEFC is given (14 August) as 542:[66]

---

62 'IEFB' under the command of Major General Arthur Aitken and 'IEFC' under Brigadier General J. M. Stewart. IOR, L/MIL/17/5/3150, IEFB, Appendix 10, 13 August 1914. The Army Department informed the Admiralty (13 August) that to reduce difficulties with shipping, the leading divisions of IEFA, IEFB and 29th Punjabis (IEFC), were to leave together, followed by remaining IEFA units with the Cavalry Divison going last.
63 IOR, L/MIL/17/5/3150, IEFB, Appendix 40, 15 August & Appendix 107, 29 August 1914.
64 IOR, L/MIL/17/5/3151, IEFB, Appendix 66, 23 September 1914.
65 17 September, composed of the Bangalore Brigade (comprising 63rd Carnatics made up to field strength, the Loyal North Lancashire Regiment, 98th Infantry, 101st Grenadiers plus 28th Mountain Battery, 61st Pioneers, a Kashmir Battalion, the Faridkot Sappers, a composite battalion of Gwalior and Nabha Infantry. IOR, L/MIL/17/5/2427,GSB, DN.3799,17 September & L/MIL/17/5/3086, IEFA, Appendix 96, 22 August 1914.
66 IOR, L/MIL/17/5/3150, IEFB, Appendix 16-17, 14 August. This telegram revised down the number of animals given in a telegram, Appendix 9 of 13 August, for an IEFB Indian infantry battalion from 14 horses and 76 mules, mountain battery 7 horses and 173 mules, Sapper and Miner Company 5 horses and 63 mules, howitzer battery 50 horses and 3 mules (it was proposed to substitute this battery for a four gun 30 pounder battery without horses and drivers. There is no revised figure given for the mountain battery. L/MIL/17/5/2423, GSB, DN1392, 14 August 1914.

One British battalion	12 horses and	16 mules
Eight Indian battalions, each with	14 (112)	17 (136)
Sapper and Miner company	5	52
Heavy artillery battery	24	5
	(153)	(209) (Total 362)
Mountain battery	7	173
	(160)	(382) (Total 542)

Many telegrams state that transport animals, ponies and officers chargers were not to be taken. The IEFB finally sailed (16-17 October) in 10 ships from Bombay (eight carrying animals) and three from Karachi (two carrying animals), with a total of only 340 animals and horse equipment (IEFC would sail with 251).[67] Landing at Tanga (2-3 November) the Force was defeated in battle (4 November) and re-embarked arriving Mombasa on 8 November.[68] The Force's mountain battery had not disembarked and after three weeks on board ship its mules were incapable of hard work. Reinforcements for the 27th-28th Indian Mountain Batteries (despatched from Abbottabad Depot to Bombay, 15 November) consisted of one shoeing smith and 50 ordnance mules. Further reinforcements (sailed 19-20 November) included 25 ordnance mules for mountain batteries and 48 for the 36th Mule Corps. A request for a mounted unit was met by the East African Mounted Rifles [EAMR], although the Calcutta Light Horse was suggested (9 August). The EAMR consisted of British colonial volunteers and mounted infantry using locally sourced animals; reportedly mostly inferior mules. The Commander of the IEFC, suggested purchasing 200 ponies in India which, he believed, were selling cheaply.[69]

The first contingent of the IEFC sailed from Karachi (19 August), the remainder 18-20 September, reaching Mombasa 3 October.[70] The Loyal North Lancashire Regiment records a long cramped confinement aboard ship, for some two weeks before

---

67   IEFC 213 plus 38 (251). On paper the number of animals required for IEFB with two infantry brigades and Force troops, if serving in India, was approximately 2,700 of all types. IOR, L/MIL/17/5/3152, IEFB, Appendix 60-1, 23 & 25 October 1914.
68   Tanga, Indian ocean (a military post of German East Africa in 1889) and most northerly seaport of Tanzania, about 50 miles (80Kms) from the Kenyan border. IOR, L/MIL/17/5/3152, IEFB, Appendix 73, 3 November. L/MIL/17/5/3153, IEFB, DN.6853, 15th November. The IEFB moved to Mombasa with units moving to Nairobi and Voli in Southern Kenya at the end of the Uganda Railway line. Also DN.6876, 5 November; DN.7032,7 November; Appendix 43,10 November; DN.7828, 20 November & DN.8369, 28 November 1914.
69   The EAMR was formed in Nairobi (5 August) gradually absorbing a collection of independent units, such as Bowker's Horse and Cole's Scouts, into one corps of mounted volunteers. IOR, L/MIL/17/5/3153, IEFB, DN.8112, 25 November & DN.8291, 28 November 1914.
70   IOR, L/MIL/17/5/3220, IEFB, Appendix 97, 3 October 1914.

final departure; reducing the effectiveness of men and animals.[71] An engagement, 3 October (Battle Kilimanjaro), was a failure with heavy causalities. A German mounted patrol ambushed a supply column capturing about 100 mules carrying water for the troops. The IEFC was joined by the IEFB at Mombasa (8 November) and amalgamated from 23 November.[72]

The various figures given for the number and type of animals sailing with the IEFC are confusing. The Director, RIM, was informed shipping for three Indian infantry battalions was required, each with a strength of 14 horses (42) and 17 mules (51); total 93 animals. Fittings for ships were to be constructed immediately. Approximately 251 animals sailed with the IEFC during August and September. The *Nairung* sailed on the 19th carrying 35, or 38 animals. Due at Zanzibar 31 August it was diverted (en-route) to Mombasa (26 August).[73] The remainder of the IEFC sailed on the 20 September from Bombay with 213 animals:[74]

'Begum' (88 animals)
    14 horses   - two for each of the four companies IST (without transport or officers' chargers) and six for 27th Mountain Battery
    74 mules   - 27th Mountain Battery (part of)

'Bandra' (122 plus 10 animals)
    90 mules   - 27th Mountain Battery (part of)
    32 mules   - Maxim Gun Company (not listed 5 horses?)
    10 horses   - Calcutta Volunteer Battery. Although none are listed as sailing.

'Umfuli' (3 animals)
    2 horses   - Clearing hospital
    1 horse   - Divisional Supply Column

---

71   2nd Battalion, The Duke of Lancaster's Regiment. *2nd Loyals in East Africa 1914-1917.* www.lancashireinfantrymuseum.org.uk.
72   The War Office took control of operations and reorganised the Forces into two commands, Mombasa Area and Nairobi Area, with units redistributed between them. IOR, L/Mil/17/5/3219, IEFC, DN.1813, 20 August 1914. For the East African Campaign, see for example, *Purnell's History of the First World War*, (ed) Barrie Pitt, (London:Purnell,1966): Vol.1, R. Sibley, 'East Africa: Fiasco at Tanga', pp.354-60 & Vol.4, Sibley, 'East Africa', pp.1370-6. *Battle of Kilimanjaro* (Wikipedia, November 2015).
73   *Nairung* could embark 76 mules and 14 horses; total of 90 animals. Owned by the Asiatic Steam Navigation Company, speed 10.5 knots. IOR, L/MIL/17/5/3219, IEFC, DN.1678, 19 August 1914. Also Appendix 15,14 August; Appendix 29, 26 August; Appendix 5-7,12 and14 August; Appendix 10-11,13 August; Appendix 25-27, 19-20 August 1914. Appendix 25 gives16 horses, 19 mules and ponies. Appendix 26 gives 18 horses and 20 mules. L/MIL/17/5/2424, GSB, DN.1967, 22 August 1914.
74   IOR, L/MIL/17/5/3151, IEFB, Appendix 54, 22 September 1914. Gives only 6 horses for the 27th Mountain Battery on 'Begum'. L/MIL/17/5/3220, IEFC, Appendix 77, 22 September 1914.

The 29th Punjabis, for example, embarked without transport. The only animals taken were officers' chargers, Maxim gun mules and one water mule per company (four per battalion).[75] The C-in-C (IEFC) had been informed there were plenty of bullock and mule carts available for his Force, but all other supplies 'must come from India'. However, the civil veterinary officer, after making further enquiries amongst tribesmen, reported bullocks were not recommended for pack work.[76]

Two volunteer companies were formed (12 September). The Calcutta Volunteer Mobile Battery, to be oxen drawn, and the Indian Volunteer Maxim Machine Gun Company with pack mules. The mobile battery was to take 10 riding horses with 50 sets of harness for mules measuring 12.1 hands.[77] Officers' chargers, draught mules and oxen for 15 pounder guns were to be arranged locally. The HQ (Bombay) of the Maxim Company received (15 September), 16 machine gun mules with saddlery and six drabies.[78] The Company would take one horse for the commanding officer, one for each section subaltern (4), eight mules per gun section for privates (32); total of five horses and 32 mules.[79]

At the outset of war there was no military veterinary organisation in the East African Protectorate, this was created from the Civil Veterinary Department becoming the East African Veterinary Corps [EAVC]. Captain Hart from the EAVC was detailed for duty with the IEFB in October.[80] The C-in-C, IEFC, had been informed by his veterinary officer that horse sickness was prevalent in German East Africa and that

75   A telegram notes, 'if in possession, bicycles may be useful'.14 days rations plus 50% spare, including fodder bales, accompanied the 29th; the same amounts were to be issued to each vessel carrying IEFB and IEFC units.
76   Moore, *Army Veterinary Service*, p.146, wrote, Bullocks 'are unsatisfactory war animals. They are of no use for the transport of fighting formations, their only place is for transport service on Lines of Communication'. IOR, L/MIL/17/5/3219, IEFC, Appendix 8-9, 12 August; Appendix 32, 1 September 1914. L/Mil/17/5/2422, IEFC, DN.1300, 14 August. L/MIL/17/5/2426, IEFC, DN.2969, 5 September. L/MIL/17/5/3150, IEFB, Appendix 91, 24 August 1914.
77   A Hand is the unit of length, standardized at 4 inches (10.16 cm) for measuring the height of horses from the ground to the withers (top of the shoulders). The unit was originally defined as the breadth of the palm including the thumb. Donkeys are measured in inches.
78   Drabies: men tending mules.
79   The Maxim Company was formed from 1st Punjab Rifles, Mussoorie Volunteer Rifles, Lucknow Volunteer Rifles, Nagour Volunteer Rifles, Bombay Volunteer Rifles, Poona and Bangalore Volunteer Rifles. IOR, L/MIL/17/5/3220, IEFC, Appendix 68, 18 September 1914. 'Indian Volunteers in the Great War, East African Campaign', Westernfrontassociation.com.
80   In 1916 an Assistant Director of Remounts was sent out by the WO to take charge of the Remount Service; separating the veterinary and remount services until re-united later in the Campaign. The Deputy Director of Supplies and Transport took over live-stock. As the campaign progressed veterinary services were found from four allied armies. For Captain Hart's appointment see IOR, L/MIL/17/5/3152, IEFB, Appendix 6, 6 October 1914.

tsetse fly (deadly for horses and artillery mules) was bad. As a large number of oxen were available in British East Africa he suggested using them as pack or draught transport for guns. The Director of the EAVC (Remounts and Veterinary) had to purchase large numbers of animals and construct depots at two main remount purchasing centres.[81] Animal wastage in 1914 was the smallest for the campaign and not abnormal for Africa, until it moved into the tsetse-fly areas in 1916 against veterinary advice. Out of some 98,000 horses, mules and donkeys employed in the East African Campaign, only 3,126 survived. There is no parallel for such a preventable colossal wastage of animals in any other 1914-1918 campaign.[82]

Remount and Veterinary - the 'Silent' Services

Often overlooked but key services. The Remount Service being the 'Providers' and 'Finishers', and Veterinary Service the 'Menders.' 'A broad line of policy, the 'Fit' and 'Unfit' for supplying animals for military purposes.'[83]

On the outbreak of war the Remount Department in India was one of three organisations responsible for the supply of remounts including the Supply and Transport Corps and Silladar regiments.[84] The Department was only responsible for mounting British cavalry stationed in India, the three non-silladar Indian cavalry regiments, artillery (field and mountain batteries) and purchasing most transport mules. It was not responsible for providing horses for the 36 Silladar cavalry regiments, camels or bullocks, or the remuneration of India's animal resources for wartime requirements.[85] Quite early in the war Silladar units began to be supplied with animals by the Remount Department with veterinary officers attached to each regiment.[86] In 1913 the Remount Department maintained an establishment of: 5,049 British cavalry horses, 14,845 RHA and RFA horses, 3,760 Mountain Artillery mules, 1,536 Non-Silladar Indian cavalry horses and a further miscellaneous 386 horses and 2,294 mules.[87]

---

81   IOR, L/MIL/17/5/3151, IEFB, Appendix 1, 3 September 1914.
82   See Blenkinsop, L.J, & Rainey, J.W, *Official History of the Great War: Veterinary Services*, (London: HMSO, 1925), pp.407-427. Graham Winton, *Theirs Not to Reason Why: Horsing the British Army 1875-1925*, (Solihull: Helion & Company, 2013), pp.409-11.
83   Moore, *Army Veterinary Service*, p.48.
84   The development of Indian Remount and Veterinary services differs from that of the British Army. An Indian Army Remount Department was established in 1876 but did not include Silladar regiments. A central British Remount Department (WO), abolishing the regimental system of remounting was established in 1887. See for example: Walter Gilbey, *Horse-Breeding in England and India and Army Horses Abroad*, (London: Vinton & Co, 1906) and Winton, *Theirs Not To Reason Why*, p.39.
85   MacMunn, *Behind the Scenes*, p.351.
86   Shahid, S, Hamid, *So They Rode and Fought*, (Kent: Midas Books, 1983), p.170.
87   Heathcote, T.A, *The Indian Army*, (London: David & Charles, 1974), p.67.

The Supply and Transport Corps maintained a separate remount transport service and depots.[88] The range of animals employed included: pack-mules and ponies, horse and mule drawn carts and wagons, bullock carts, camels, pack-bullocks and pack-donkeys. Following reorganisation (1899-1904) regular corps and cadres of camel, mule and cart transport were formed.[89] A mule corps, supporting cavalry brigades had a total strength of 936 mules; those supporting infantry brigades approximately 840 mules.[90] The 2nd and 9th Mule Corps with the 3rd (Meerut) Infantry Division mobilised with 864 and 840 mules respectively. Doherty and Donovan list a Mule Corps with a strength of 768 mules with its own veterinary assistants, farriers, blacksmiths, carpenters, saddlers and bellow boys.[91]

The Remount Department was organised for service within India. Major remount depots existed at Hapur (United Provinces, now Uttar Pradesh), Hosur (Mysore), Saharanpur (United Provinces, now Uttar Pradesh), Ahmednagar (Bombay, now Maharashtra), Jhelum Colony at Mona (Shahpur) and Sargodha (Punjab). Each mule unit had its own depot in divisional areas.[92] Cavalry Base Horse Depots [CBHD] supplied trained remounts on mobilisation. All horses returning from veterinary hospitals were transferred to a CBHD. Temporary Remount Training Depots [TRTD] with 500 horses were founded for breaking and training before issue to non-mobilised regiments, making up for deficiencies from supplying regiments going on active service. On mobilisation in 1914, new TRTD were established at Meerut and Bangalore (1 October) and Neemuch (5 December).[93]

There was little in the way of pre-war organisation for overseas expeditionary forces and no remount officer, or subordinate personnel, accompanied them on mobilisation in 1914. A remount depot was established with the IEFA at Marseilles, but in Mesopotamia (IEFD), for example, from November 1914 to December 1915,

---

88 Established 1889 when the three Presidency transport and commissariat departments were amalgamated forming one corps for the whole Indian Army. See for example Heathcote, *Indian Army*, p.62; *Imperial Gazetteer of India* (Oxford: Clarendon, 1907/8), Vol.3.
89 Cadres: nucleus of trained officers and men forming the basis for the training of new units on expansion. The cadres included 21 mule transport corps, 18 mule transport cadres, 9 silladar camel cadres and 2 pony-cart trained cadres.
90 When supporting cavalry brigades they were divided into six draught and four pack-troops. Supporting infantry brigades they were divided into nine pack-troops. Heathcote, *Indian Army*, p.62. I am grateful to Andy Smerdon for sharing his expert knowledge on military mules.
91 With 200 army transport carts, divided into eight troops of 96 mules. TNA, WO 95/3911/1, General Staff, 3rd (Lahore) Division War Diary, 10 August, 1914. Simon Doherty and Tom Donovan, *The Indian Corps on the Western Front*, (Brighton: Tom Donovan, 2014), p.16.
92 For example, Sialkot, Lahore and Meerut. See J.S. Bhalla, *History of the Remount and Veterinary Corps 1794-1987*, (New Delhi: Directorate General Remount and Veterinary, 1988), pp.37-39.
93 Bhalla, *History of the Remount*, p.40.

the Veterinary Department was made responsible for providing remounts from casualties.[94]

The Army Department enquired (16 September) whether the War Office 'would be upset if arrangements were made for a base at Marseilles for Indian cavalry remounts'. The advantages were seen as an economy in transport, earlier readiness for the field and better climatic conditions. The War Office responded positively and a base remount depot was established, on an Imperial organisation, holding 2,600 animals, to supply all transport horses and mules. The Base Transport Depot was to either join the remount depot or hand over its mules. The main sections of the depot sailed (2 November) in two ships with 236 followers and 1,239 animals. This included drafts for Indian cavalry regiments (IEFA) with 1,600 horses.[95] 'Followers', an essential component of British and Indian horsed units, were predominantly Indian non-combatants. The majority employed in animal welfare.[96]

The Depot establishment (23 September) was to consist of a HQ and four sections.[97] On 6 November the establishment was stated to be:

Headquarters:
    British ranks: Commandant, 1 Adjutant and Quartermaster,
                           1 Veterinary officer, 2 farriers, 1 European clerk.
    Indian ranks: 2 clerks, 2 dafadars, 81 sowars, 2 veterinary assistants.

---

94 Bhalla, *History of the Remount*, p.40.
95 IOR, L/MIL/17/5/2427, GSB, DN.3702, 16 September. L/MIL/17/5/2431, GSB, DN.5547, 14 October 1914. L/MIL/17/5/3089, IEFA, Appendix 20, 3 November. L/MIL/17/5/3088, IEFA, Appendix 86, 17 October.
96 'Official followers', authorised by headquarters, performing a wide range of essential tasks. 'Public Followers' were generally skilled, such as mistry smith (caste status: craftsmen), syces (attendants, or grooms) and grass cutters, nalbands (farriers), motchie (saddler/cobbler), langri (cook), cutler (sharpener). When asking about arrangements for exercising horses the C-in-C, India commented that 'few syces could ride at any pace other than a walk'. 'Private followers' were unskilled performing more menial tasks such as sweepers (disposal of waste, latrines and refuse) and pakhalis, or bhistis the vital water carriers. Sandhu, *Indian Cavalry*, p.56. Heathcote, *Indian Army*, pp.113-4. George Morton-Jack, *The Indian Army on the Western Front*, (New York: Cambridge University Press, 2014), p.36. IOR, L/MIL/17/5/2429, GSB, DN.4920, 3 October 1914.
97 The figures for personnel and animals are confusing as various telegrams give differing numbers. See establishment (for above) in IOR, L/MIL/17/5/2428, GSB, DN.4293, 23 September. Also L/MIL/17/5/3089, IEFA, Appendix 82, 6 November 1914, that the remainder of the establishment included 1,000 Indian cavalry horses, 500 mules and horse gear with 500 artillery horses being despatched about 19 November; also Appendix 119, 9 November 1914, the establishment and number of remounts given as having actually sailed on 2 November had changed again.

Four Sections:
> British ranks: 3 Section Commanders
> Indian ranks: 12 officers, 4 kot dafadars, 7 veterinary assistants, 38 nalbands, 38 jemadar syces, 16 bhisties, 16 sweepers, 4 mochies.

There were practical issues to be resolved. The War Office had authorised the GOC Egypt to disembark one section of the Remount Depot and any cavalry and artillery horses required for remounting troops in Egypt. The C-in-C India raised the undesirability of disembarking any portion of the Depot, which had not been organised into sections before embarkation, and the 1,000 horses dispatched were for Indian cavalry; urging the GOC to state his requirements and not draw on Depot shipments. The War Office reply was to the point. The GOC had a large force to remount and disembarking part of the Depot was the only suitable solution; cavalry divisions in France would be provided with English horses to replace any disembarked in Egypt. 'All Indian horses and remount depots formed part of a general pool'. Indian horses and mules, where possible, would go to Indian units.[98]

The 2,600 animals to be held in the Depot consisted of approximately 500 artillery horses, 600 British cavalry horses, 1,000 Indian cavalry horses and 500 mules. The 600 trained British cavalry horses, complete with sets of line gear, were initially to be supplied by three cavalry regiments at 200 each, despatched to port of embarkation accompanied by suitable men who would then return to their regiments.[99] The Remount Department would then replace the horses of these regiments. 1,000 reinforcement sowars (Indian cavalryman), detailed for service from silladar cavalry regiments not on field service, would take a horse each to the port of embarkation. The C-in-C India notified the War Office (21 October) they had depended on British cavalry regiments in India supplying the 600 horses. However, this source of supply was no longer available, as two additional cavalry brigades had been mobilised for France. For the trained British cavalry horses, the Army Department could send 250 early in December and 200 more in January, 'the most we can do' as until May (1915) 'our supply will be exhausted'. The War Office was notified that 1,000 Indian cavalry horses, 500 mules and horse gear was to sail about 2 November, with 500 artillery horses about 19 November.[100]

---

98 India was also arranging for remounting the Imperial Service Cavalry in Egypt. IOR, L/MIL/17/5/3089, IEFA, Appendix 63, 6 November. Also Appendix143, 17 November; Appendix169, 14 November; Appendix 191, 17 November 1914.
99 6th (Inniskilling) Dragoons (at Muttra), 7th Hussars (at Secunderabad) and 14th Hussars (at Mhow). Line gear: equipment for keeping horses on a picket line including, ropes, water/feed buckets, rugs.
100 IOR, L/MIL/17/5/3088, IEFA, Appendix 59, 12 October. L/MIL/17/5/2431, GSB, DN5932, 21 October. L/MIL/17/5/ 3089, IEFA, Appendix 82, 6 November 1914.

Indian Remounts from Australia

India imported large numbers of Australian horses for remounts and breeding stock.[101] On mobilization this remained the major source of remounts for the Army in India. However, pressure on Australia's equine population increased considerably with the mobilisation of its own Expeditionary Force [AIF]. The Governor General of Australia requested a supply of 1,000 trained horses from India, for Field Artillery and general transport for the AIF.[102] An immediate shipment to India of unbroken horses was proposed by Australia to replace any of the 1,000 horses India could spare. However, India much regretted no spare horses were available as, 'we ourselves now have to purchase largely in Australia'.

The first of a number of supply problems from Australia appeared when the Army Department wrote to the Governor General (12 August) following a cable from one of their Australian horse shippers reporting an embargo on the export of horses. Trusting 'this would not be enforced' for horses purchased by the Indian Government, which 'are essential to us'.[103] The Army Department was informed (2 October) that with the necessity for conserving future production, the Commonwealth of Australia had prohibited the export of mares and these conditions had to be observed. However, permission was later granted for export.[104] The War Office responded (11 October) that the embargo be lifted, 'as horse supply throughout the world was having heavy demands made upon it, we must hope to obtain the full number demanded from Australia and New Zealand'. The War Office further stated that suitable commissions were to be sent to Australia and New Zealand, 'requiring energetic action'; offering (11 October) to assist by sending good purchasers to Australia if needed, such as Colonel Goad.[105]

India was anxious to ship remounts already ordered in Australia at the earliest possible date, but was concerned about difficulties with the Australian freight markets in Melbourne, Sidney, Brisbane and Townsville. Australia recommended using

---

101 I am grateful to Dr Jean Bou, Strategic and Defence Studies Centre, Australian Command and Staff College, Malcolm and Katy Brain, Jeremy Sibbald of the National Archives of Australia for assistance with Australian records.
102 Governor-General, Ronald Craufurd Munro Ferguson, 1st Viscount Novar, sixth Governor- General (1914–1920). There were also State Premiers and Governors for New South Wales, Victoria, Queensland, South Australia, Western Australia and Tasmania. IOR, L/MIL/17/5/2422,GSB, DN.1194,13 August & DN.1278, 14 August 1914.
103 IOR, L/MIL/17/5/2422, GSB, DN.1136, 12 August 1914.
104 IOR, L/MIL/17/5/2429, GSB, DN.4937, 2 October. L/MIL/17/5/2431, GSB, DN.5809, 17 October 1914.
105 Colonel Howard Goad, Director General, Army Remount Department, India, 1903-1908. In 1908 Goad visited Australia and New Zealand to assess the horse markets, equine resources and purchase of remounts for India. My thanks to Brian Hill (WFA) for his detailed knowledge on Remount and Veterinary personnel records. IOR, L/MIL/17/5/2429, GSB, DN.5401, 11 October 1914.

ships sent from India for horses awaiting immediate and then later shipments, as its freight market was very uncertain.[106] The Governor General was later thanked for his assistance with the supply of oats and hay.[107]

India proposed establishing remount agencies at Melbourne and Sidney for the purchase of mature and broken horses and requested information as to what extent Australia was drawing on its own horse supply for military purposes. Australia did not object to establishing the remount agencies, but as their requirements were for the same class of animals, demand would be considerable. India proposed sending two remount officers, using their own importers, with orders not to clash with Australian interests and work entirely in conjunction with the Commonwealth Defence Department. This would not create any difficulties in obtaining equal facilities for exportation and controlling prices. Australia accepted that freight facilities and exportation of horses ordered by both Indian silladar cavalry regiments and the Government of India would receive equal facilities. India responded that 'Assistance rendered by your Government in these matters has considerably helped India'.[108]

The RIM was to arrange shipment of horses for the Imperial Service Cavalry Brigade and 2,100 remounts for France. With only two ships available in Calcutta that could be fitted for shipment from Australia, the Indian Department of Commerce suggested carrying a cargo of gunnies loaded at Bombay. The horse fittings would be undertaken in Australia, after the gunnies were unloaded, by a Melbourne company at 30/- per stall.[109]

The War Office depended on India replacing IEFA wastage for six months at 5% per month for all units and 10% for cavalry; also requiring India to purchase some 50,000 cavalry and artillery horses for them in Australia and New Zealand. The Army Department suggested that if the War Office extended timings a larger market would be available, including untrained horses which could be broken for the War Office in India. After India had fulfilled its own Home defence arrangements and for France any horses left were to sail to Southampton, but 'the number would be small'.[110]

The Secretary of State, India requested (10 August) that Colonel Peacocke, Army Remount Department, India [ARD], on leave in England be detained for employment

---

106 IOR, L/MIL/17/5/2425, GSB, DN.2704, 2 September. L/MIL/17/5/2429, GSB, DN4937, 2 October 1914.
107 For example, having secured and shipped, 1,000 tons of oaten chaff at £3 per ton.
108 IOR, L/MIL/17/5/2427, GSB, DN.3592, 14 September & DN3466, 13 September. L/MIL/17/5/2429,GSB, DN.4634, 28 September & DN. 4937, 2 October. L/MIL/17/5/3087, IEFA, Appendix 79, 13 September.
109 The ships *Orteric* and *Kumeric*. Gunnies, a strong, coarse material commonly produced from Jute. IOR, L/MIL/17/5/2431, GSB, DN.5505 Enclosure 1 & 3, 7-9 October. L/MIL/17/5/2429,GSB, DN5461,12 October 1914.
110 IOR, L/MIL/17/5/2429, GSB, DN.4634, 28 September & DN.5463, 13 October. L/MIL/17/5/2428,GSB, DN.4299, 23 September. L/MIL/17/5/ 3087,IEFA, Appendix136, 23 September & Appendix 6, 1 September. L/MIL/17/5/3088, IEFA, Appendix 31, 6 October 1914.

in Argentina purchasing mules on behalf of the Indian Government. He proceeded to Argentina to inspect mules for shipment from Buenos Aires.[111] The Army Department was arranging to supply approximately 120 ordnance and 800 other class mules, with the first consignment ready in October. 1,000 army transport class mules (4 to 7 years and 12.7 to 14.2 hands) had already been purchased in Argentina (19 August), to meet 5% wastage. They were to be shipped uninsured to Calcutta, at an inclusive price not to exceed £50.[112] A bonus of 4/- was paid to the crew for every mule landed alive. The Army Department informed the Secretary of State (23 September) that Howard Brothers were offering 80 ordnance mules available in Argentina at £32.10s, uninsured. The offer was to be accepted and shipped with the 1,000 army transport class mules.[113]

Peacocke sailed for Melbourne (9 October), presumably from the Argentine, in charge of the Indian Purchasing Commission to Australia with instructions to communicate on arrival with the Commonwealth Defence Department.[114] The War Office argued that Peacocke was of insufficient seniority for such a large and complicated commission suggesting Colonel Goad be placed in overall command. The estimated outlay (December 1914) for purchases from Australia was £2million. Peacocke had already sailed for Australia with full instructions regarding the special conditions under which the Australian Government required India to act. With full confidence in his ability the C-in-C India 'preferred to let arrangements stand'.[115]

Camels

Major-General Sir John Moore wrote that there was no more useful animal in existence than the baggage camel for military purposes and under certain circumstances

---

111 Lieutenant-Colonel T.G. Peacocke appears on the 1911 Delhi Durbar medal roll as Superintendant, ARD. Also on the India General Service Medal Roll qualifying for the Relief of Chitral 1895 clasp as a Veterinary Lieutenant, AVD. Hart's Army List 1914 gives him as Major 7/1/1906, Lt- Col 6/1/1911, transferred from AVD to Indian Army Remount Department, 20/11/1907. My thanks to Brian Hill (WFA) and Clare Boulton, Librarian, Royal College of Veterinary Surgeons Library. IOR, L/MIL/17/5/2422, GSB, DN.889, 10 August & DN.1027, 11 August. L/MIL/17/5/2423, GSB, DN.1712, 19 August 1914.
112 In addition, the War Office required India to purchase another 1,600 from Argentina of the same type and terms.
113 IOR, L/MIL/17/5/2423, GSB, DN.1712, 19 August & DN.2331, 27 August. L/MIL/17/5/2428,GSB, DN.4276, 23 September. The War Office also suggested using their agents Guyton and Harrington, Kansas City, Missouri. Mules had been purchased from them and shipped to India, for example, in 1902. L/MIL/17/5/2429, GSB, DN.5249, 8 October 1914.
114 IOR, L/MIL/17/5/2431, GSB, DN.5743, 17 October 1914.
115 IOR, L/MIL/17/5/2429, GSB, DN.5463, 13 October. L/MIL/17/5/2431, GSB, DN.5850,19 October & DN.5995, 21 October. L/MIL/2436, GSB, DN.8499, 1 December 1914.

absolutely indispensable. The camel's carrying power depended on the breed and the climate in which it was employed. It could carry heavier loads than other transport animals and work under circumstances, or situations unsuitable for other forms of transport.[116] Camels were purchased from various sources, India, Persia and Arabia. Riding camels were quite distinct from baggage or burden animals. Indian camels were broadly the plains type (desert riding camels), or riverine (baggage camels). Bikanir, Jaisalmeri and Rajputana camels were considered the best for riding. Baggage camels came, for example, from Uttar Pradesh, Gujerat, Sind (Sindhi, Pakistan), Baluchistan (Balochistan, Pakistan) and the Punjab.[117] In the Punjab for example, one of the early canal colonies was devised for the breeding of fit camels (camel grants) and supply of sarwan attendants (attendants accompanying camels on military service) for military use by the Silladari Camel Corps. Problems in maintaining the camel service grants led to the sanctioning of their abolition in 1913; but with the outbreak of war in 1914 and before the decision could be implemented, the four camels corps (59th, 60th, 61st and 62nd) were retained for war service in India and abroad.[118]

Indian cavalry regiments were authorised (1904) an establishment of eight camels replacing the same number of horses, for carrying first-line transport loads such as ammunition and officers' mess camps.[119] Each silladar camel corps consisted of four subdivisions with an establishment of 357 camels, increasing to 1,068 on mobilisation.[120] The GOC, Egypt was informed (18 August) that an additional 5,500 camels and 2,100 mules would be required should the IEFA be employed, 'in a country on which wheeled vehicles could not be used'. Camels were to be obtained locally.[121] Gradually IEFA units were informed to take additional horses not camels.[122] The Native States also offered camels for the war effort. The State of Kalat offered a free

116 Moore, *Army Veterinary Service in War*, p.150.
117 See for example, *Army Veterinary Service*, pp.149-156. George Watt, *Dictionary of Economic Products of India*, Vol.2, pp.52-55 (Calcutta 1889; reprinted Cambridge University Press, 2014). Porter, Alderson, Hall, Sponenberg, *Masons World Encyclopaedia of Livestock Breeds and Breeding*, Vol.1, pp.54-59, (Oxfordshire, CABI, 2016).
118 Chebab Colony 1892. The first colonies were founded primarily on uncultivated land sparsely inhabited by semi-nomadic cattle graziers and camel owners. The unpopular bonding or service tenure placed upon a sarwan, when other employment opportunities developed, led to a severe labour shortage exacerbated by the demands of war. *Punjab Under Imperialism*, pp.8-9, 123-129.
119 Sandhu, *Indian Cavalry*, pp. 77-79.
120 Silladar Camel Corps were based on a similar principle to silladar cavalry. Riding and burden camels were purchased from various sources in India, Persia, Arabia, Egypt, Somalia and Abyssinia. Heathcote, *Indian Army*, pp.60-63.
121 IOR, L/MIL/17/5/2423, GSB, DN.1589, 18 August 1914.
122 The GOC, 3rd (Lahore) Division, thought the eight camels with Indian cavalry regiments would be useless in Europe and those disembarked in Egypt should be retained there. The 4th Cavalry were told (11 September) not to take their riding camels and those of the 15th Lancers were to be disembarked and retained in Egypt. IOR, L/MIL/17/5/2427, GSB, DN.3716, 16 September. L/MIL/17/5/2429,GSB, DN.5178, 7 October. L/

gift of 2,000 loading camels and drivers for service, all to be paid for by the State for a period of six months. The Agent in Baluchistan wrote (4 September) that rulers had shown great keenness and begun to provide and equip the camels, 'it would have been impolitic to interfere with this, as it was obviously desirable to strike while the iron was hot'.[123] The Bikanir Camel Corps sailed from Karachi (17 October) for Egypt on two transports with 603 animals.[124]

Remounts from the Indian Native States

As well as horsing their own army units many Indian States also made available resources and remounts for the Indian Government, some at their own expense. Various Agents and Government officials stressed the political importance of accepting the many offers of support. Remount officers moved between the States inspecting animals for suitability against laid down specifications.[125] Horses were to be aged 5-10 years and 14.2-15.3 hands in height. Remount animals were also sent for war training to those States with training establishments and paid 5/- for each horse trained. NCOs and men of British and Indian units were paid 5/- to 10/- per horse, or mule trained.[126]

The Maharaja Scindia, of Gwalior (10 August) listed all his serviceable horses at 2,000, with a possible additional 2,000. 'If it is horses that are wanted' he was ready to offer the whole 4,000. This offer is not referred to again as he placed at the Government's immediate disposal (21 August) 700 horses, free, from his State Irregular cavalry. Also, 'as many additional horses' as Gwalior State could provide, 'together with 200 ponies with harness and personnel from his Imperial Service Transport'. General Rimington (13 October) having inspected the transport ponies did not consider them fit for service.[127] Major Templer (ARD) travelled to Gwalior (10

MIL/17/5/2426,GSB,DN.3039,7 September. Also DN.3040,7 September, DN 3324/3325, 11 September 1914.
123 Jam of Las Bela and Khan and Sardars of Kalat. IOR, L/MIL/17/5/2423,GSB, DN.1722, 8 August, from Hon Agent to Governor-General in Baluchistan. L/MIL/17/5/2426, GSB, DN.3103, 4 September 1914.
124 IOR, L/MIL/17/5/2423, GSB, DN.1516, 17 August. L/MIL/17/5/2424, GSB, DN.2220, 26 August. L/MIL/17/5/2431, GSB, DN.5609, 15 October & DN.5891, 20 October 1914.
125 As laid down in the 1905 regulations for *the Purchase of Horses from Native States*.
126 A makeshift and unsatisfactory wartime payment system. IOR, L/MIL/17/5/2423, GSB, DN.1714, 18 August. Bhalla, *History of the Remount*, p.42. Bhalla quotes Rs.5/- to Rs10/- which I have inferred as 5/- and 10/-
127 Lieutenant-General M.F. Rimington 1858-1928. Served 6th (Inniskilling) Dragoons and 1899-1902 South African war. Commanded 1st Indian Cavalry Division and Indian Cavalry Corps on the Western Front. The Gwalior Transport Corps was at Orleans, France on 20th November 1914, see for example, IOR, R/2/775/396, 'Reports of good work performed by men of the Gwalior Transport Corps whilst on active service in France and other places'.

September) to urgently select, as many artillery and cavalry horses as possible, 'strong and in hard condition'. The original number of 700 cavalry horses had been calculated before the Maharaja received the requirements regarding age and height, therefore, a large proportion failed to meet the required standard.[128]

With a general relaxation in the specifications more useful animals became available.

This would appear to have happened prior to 17 September, when Captain Anderson (ARD) returned to the Maharaja of Rewa (Central India) and purchased additional horses.[129] The Agent for Bharatpur (Rajputana, Abu) reported, 'the State cavalry were mounted on light weedy country breeds whose condition after a year of scarcity [poor harvest?] was very poor'. The Durbar was willing to assist by 'selling (formy) horses, but after inspection the Agent did not think they were suitable and doubted if the remount officer would select more than one or two'.[130] The Bharatpur cavalry horses were to be re-inspected when conditions improved, meanwhile permission was requested to select from the State stables, 'as horses urgently needed and even a dozen would be useful'.[131]

The Political Agent to the Maharajah of Rewah was asked to ascertain how many artillery and cavalry horses could be placed, without payment, at the Government's disposal. Captain Anderson selected 85 horses that met all specifications.[132] The Raja Dhar (Central India) offered all the horses belonging to his State. 28 were selected as meeting all specifications (11 for horse artillery, 4 light cavalry and 13 transport).[133] The Maharaja Holkar (Central India) also placed free of charge all cavalry and artillery horses in his State army. 135 complied with requirements (72 artillery and 63 cavalry). This number was exclusive of horses in the Imperial Service Escort, being maintained in expectation of mobilisation. In addition, the Maharaja hoped the Durbar would be allowed to meet the cost of their despatch, fodder and maintenance during the war.

---

128 Major, C.F. Templer, Indian ARD 1907. Lieutenant-Colonel Director-General ARD, September 1915. IOR, L/MIL/17/5/2422, GSB, DN.912, 10 August. L/MIL/17/5/2425, GSB, DN.2846, 3 September 1914. L/MIL/17/5/2426, GSB, Enclosure 1 to DN 3237, 8 September & DN.3373, 10 September 1914. L/MIL/17/5/2431, GSB, Enclosure to DN.5672, 13 October 1914, from General Rimington.
129 W.H. Anderson, Indian ARD from 1913. Superintendant 1918 and temporary Lt-Col.
130 A Durbar - formal meeting called by the head of state to administer affairs. It could also be a purely ceremonial gathering as used during the period of British rule in India.
131 IOR, L/MIL/17/5/2429, GSB, DN.4512, 25 September 1914.
132 The Viceroy, on a previous visit to Umaria, had commented that these horses were 'quite good'. IOR, L/MIL/17/5/2425, GSB, Enclosures 2 & 5 to DN.2846, 21 & 25 August & DN.2787, 2 September 1914. L/MIL/17/5/2427, GSB, DN.3995, 17 September & DN.3996 & Enclosure, 19 September 1914.
133 The horses personally offered by Raja Dhar were from his private stable and described as English and Australian coach team and carriage horses useful for horse artillery, saddle horses for light cavalry and polo ponies, 'of which several are first class transport animals'. IOR, L/MIL/17/5/2427, GSB, Enclosures 1 & 2, & DN.3907, 17-18 September 1914.

This offer was turned down as inconvenient, owing to the difficulty of assessing the amount involved.[134]

Mules were also offered. The Maharaja of Patiala (Punjab) placed his mules at the Government's disposal of which the Agent thought about 400 would initially be serviceable.[135] The Maharaja Idar State (Gujerat) offered 'six more despatch riders' attached to his Brigade, with four mules for their baggage.[136]

Veterinary Services

The Army Veterinary Department [AVD] was only organised and trained for active service essentially in India, not for a major European War.[137] Major General Sir John Moore wrote (1921) that the Veterinary Service in India:

> As it stands at present, is in no way yet adapted for its success in a war of any big undertaking. It is a curious mixture of elements seeking the light of day and inviting the process of welding into one common interest and organisation ... A different system was followed in wartime to what existed in peacetime ... such a state of affairs does not commend itself to efficiency, and particularly with personnel for the most part untrained.[138]

Veterinary Surgeons (officers) were sent to India by the War Office on a tour of 5 to 7 years. From 1889 they were not attached to regiments and only responsible for the horses of British units, cavalry, artillery and non-silladar cavalry. There was no organisation

---

134 IOR, L/MIL/17/5/2426, GSB, DN.3011, 5 September & DN.3372, 10 September. L/MIL/17/5/2427,GSB, DN.3973, 17 September & DN.3974, 19 September 1914.
135 IOR, L/MIL/17/5/2429, GSB, DN.4928, 30 September & 1 October 1914.
136 State of Idar, within the Gujarat Division of the old Bombay Presidency. The State provided a small detachment of lancers and 12 despatch riders for the 15th (Imperial Service) Cavalry Brigade for the Sinai and Palestine Campaign. IOR, L/MIL/17/5/2431, GSB, DN.5941, 21 October 1914.
137 The AVD made significant developments in its organisation between 1903 and 1914. Veterinary treatment had been carried out in Veterinary Hospitals and Branch Stations. These designations were changed in 1907 to Class I and Class II Veterinary Hospitals (totalling 23 and 18 respectively in 1909). A separate Civil Veterinary Department [CVD] was created in1892; in theory to act as a reserve for the AVD. In 1884 Indian veterinary services were organised into an AVD. The Principal Veterinary Officer was on the Staff of the C-in-C at Army HQs with an Inspecting Veterinary Officer with each command. Bhalla, *History of the Remount*, pp.78-81, 83, 85. G.A. West (ed), *History of Overseas Veterinary Services*, (London: British Veterinary, 1961), Part1, 'India' (Frank Ware), pp.11-47.
138 Moore, *Army Veterinary Service*, p.2. Moore served in India 1890-96, 1905-1910. Deputy Principal Veterinary Officer, Simla from 1907 and 1919-21 as Director Veterinary Services. From 1914 to 1919 he was Director Veterinary Services with the British Expeditionary Force, France.

for permanent subordinate staff. On the eve of war AVD personnel numbered 63 officers (including eight for the Remount Department) and 23 Non-Commissioned Officers on the Unattached List (part of the Indian Subordinate Veterinary Corps).[139]

Veterinary care in transport units, silladar cavalry, mountain and heavy artillery batteries and other native establishments was the responsibility of subordinate Indian qualified regimental veterinary staff (salutries).[140] AVD officers were only called to these units for periodic inspections and outbreaks of contagious disease. The Transport Corps engaged college graduates, as did Silladar cavalry sending sowars to the Punjab Veterinary College, Lahore, graduating after a three year course as salutries or veterinary assistants. In peacetime transport animals, not with permanent Transport Corps units, were the responsibility of civilian contractors who provided them.

From 1903 mobilisation equipment was sanctioned for all units, with a reserve of medicines and instruments. Each veterinary stores department was to provide for 20,000 animals for three months; veterinary equipment was standardised, regularly checked and replaced.[141]

The designation of veterinary field units was changed in 1911. Veterinary hospitals became Veterinary Sections and veterinary store depots designated Base Depot Veterinary Stores [BDVS] bringing them in line with similar units in the British Army. Field units were still only raised on mobilisation with personnel taken from station veterinary hospitals. Revised Veterinary Field Service Regulations laid down the principles of veterinary organisation in the field. Ordinary veterinary cases were to be treated in corps or regimental sick lines by their own veterinary staff, under AVD supervision. Only serious cases such as immobility were to be admitted to Field Veterinary Sections [FVS]. Transport provision for one FVS was six mules.[142]

Moore considered this pre-war system a:

> Purely scratch arrangement of borrowing personnel from units for departmental purposes, totally excluding from skilled veterinary care and treatment the great majority of Indian Cavalry, and the whole of the Transport.[143]

---

139 A register was kept in each command (1895) with names of qualified NCOs and men wanting to transfer onto the unattached list. If chosen, they were posted to station veterinary hospitals, but returned to their regiments when no longer required. Moore, *Army Veterinary Service*, pp.2-3. Bhalla, *History of the Remount*, p.83.
140 Qualifying from Indian veterinary colleges, first established, Madras 1810. Subordinate attendant personnel such as dressers and grooms were detailed from various army units. Bhalla, *History of the Remount*, p.56.
141 Bhalla, *History of the Remount*, pp.87, 92.
142 Bhalla, *History of the Remount*, pp.87, 89.
143 Moore, *Army Veterinary Service*, p.3.

On the outbreak of war 94 veterinary officers were required for the field army and 32 for Home service in India. These numbers were not met during the war.[144] In the early days of the war divisions mobilised with their allotted veterinary sections, but establishments soon dwindled and few replacements were available during 1914.[145] An Assistant Director Veterinary Services was appointed (17 September) for each of the Lahore, Meerut and 1st Cavalry Divisions (IEFA); further appointments were made (22 September) and to the 2nd Indian Cavalry Division (12 November).[146] No appointments were listed for the IEFB/C.

Veterinary Officers could take two horses and each batman one horse.[147] FVS No's.18, 19 and 23 were mobilised (8-9 August). No.23 was at Secunderabad (Sikandarabad) with subordinate personnel taken from the station veterinary hospital and No.19 at Meerut (Mirat) taken from No.2 Station Veterinary Hospital. 99 grooming syces for each FVS were mobilised from mounted units in Secunderabad and Meerut. No.7 FVS, Lahore, was mobilised (September) for duty with 6th Division (IEFA). A staff sergeant farrier (unattached list), shoeing smith and clerk were to be taken from the Station Veterinary Hospital with 99 grooming syces from 10th Field Artillery Brigade, Kirkee (Khadki). No.3 BDVS, Calcutta, mobilised with subordinate personnel, including a Farrier Staff Sergeant from the Station Veterinary Hospital, Sialkot. For all of the above, Line orderly, Supply and Transport personnel, veterinary dafadars and followers were as laid down in the Field Service Manual, Veterinary.[148]

Veterinary personnel (599) for the Base Remount Depot Marseilles, required from about the end of October, were to be taken from the Artillery Depots in Ambala and Jubbulpore (Jabalpur). Additional syces (80) required as veterinary reinforcements with the IEFA were taken from supernumerary enrolled artillery syces at Jubbulpore.[149] In December the WO sanctioned a Mobile Veterinary Section [MVS] for each infantry division and cavalry brigade of the two IEFA Indian cavalry divisions. These eight sections each required a British Veterinary Officer, a Non-Commissioned Veterinary Assistant, five Daffadars, two Naiks, 14 Sowars and one Nalband (21 officers and

---

144 Moore, *Army Veterinary Service*, p.2. Bhalla, *History of the Remount*, p.92.
145 Saini, *Economic Aspects*, p.146, states '165 veterinary staff were sent overseas during the war'. However, he does not state whether they were Indian, British, or their rank.
146 17 September. One at Army HQs, two veterinary officers each for the three divisions and one for each cavalry brigade. An ADVS for the 2nd Indian Cavalry Division and two veterinary officers for the cavalry brigades (12 November). IOR, L/MIL/17/5/3087,IEFA, Appendix 110,17 September & Appendix 129, 22 September 1914.
147 IOR, L/MIL/17/5/2426, GSB, DN.3204, 9 September & DN.3265, 10 September 1914.
148 IOR, L/MIL/17/5/3086, IEFA, Appendix 27-29, 8-9 August. L/MIL/17/5/3087, IEFA, Appendix 27, 2 September & Appendix 28, 28 September 1914.
149 From each: 16 naik syces, 216 syces, 8 bhistis, 8 sweepers and 2 mochis (total 500). In addition 50 syces (Ambala) and 49 (Jubbulpore) were required for the 20th FVS, Meerut, also mobilising for duty with the Marseilles Depot. IOR, L/MIL/17/5/3088,IEFA, Appendix 64,13 October & Appendix 66, 14 October 1914.

personnel). Personal servants or attached batmen and two Supply and Transport drivers brought the total to 27.¹⁵⁰ At the end of November 1914, IEFA Administrative Services on Lines of Communication included: No's 11, 19, 21, 22, and 23 FVS and at Base, No 20 FVS and No's 2 and 3 BDVS.

Only seven veterinary officers were left in India to look after the needs of the whole country including the North West Frontier Province. With the onset of war Veterinary Officers had suddenly to handle and screen many thousands of hurriedly purchased or hired animals from all sources. Glanders was reported in the 7th Lancers (15 September) and 17th Cavalry. The latter was replaced for service overseas by the 29th Lancers (1st Indian Cavalry Division) as the only regiment that could reach Bombay to sail with the convoy.¹⁵¹ A serious spread of glanders in Lahore District (August 1914) was blamed on the heavy demands placed on military officers and no fulltime veterinary officer available to cope effectively with the spread of disease. In September suspected cases of glanders were reported in the Jaipur Transport Corps. A veterinary officer was despatched to inspect and inoculate ponies of the Corps, which was due to provide about 300 carts complete with personnel and ponies for overseas service with 6th (Poona) Division (IEFD). The Corps was replaced by Government transport.¹⁵² A special veterinary branch of the Indian Army Reserve of Officers was formed in an attempt to overcome the shortage of qualified veterinarians. Limited help was provided by the Civil Veterinary Department [CVD], which had difficulty sparing a fulltime veterinary officer for military duties.¹⁵³

Shoeing, harness and saddlery

Effective shoeing is a vital element if animals are to remain healthy and fit for purpose. Especially during the mobilisation period, and generally in war time, there were insufficient numbers of trained farriers and shoeing smiths. In 1914 shoeing arrangements for horses and mules at depots in India was to continue as in peacetime. Spare shoes, with 30 nails, were to be carried as part of mobilisation equipment, replacements being provided by the Ordnance Depot.¹⁵⁴ The Army Department

---

150 IOR, L/MIL/17/5/3090, IEFA, Appendix 222, 22 December 1914.
151 Two squadrons of the 7th Lancers served in Persia from July 1915 mounted on camels, the remainder of the regiment arrived November. The 17th Cavalry (Robartes Horse), included three of its own squadrons (one served in East Africa from 1915) and one of the 27th Light Cavalry. The latter remained in India during the war but squadrons served in Mesopotamia, Persia and East Africa, as well as supplying drafts to other regiments serving overseas. IOR, L/MIL/17/5/2427,GSB, DN.3612,15 September & DN.3749, 16 September. L/MIL/17/5/2429, GSB, DN.5428, 12 October 1914.
152 IOR, L/MIL/17/5/2423, GSB, DN.1367, 15 August. L/MIL/17/5/2426, GSB, DN.3192, 9 September 1914.
153 Bhalla, *History of the Remount*, p.93.
154 From 1866 shoeing was subject to veterinary inspection with farriers undertaking veterinary instruction. Native shoeing smiths were permanently transferred from British

requested the WO provide frost nails, not available in India, for mounted units. The estimated number required for shoeing animals in Europe, before winter, was: 72,000 for ponies, 2.5 million for horses and 8,500 for mules. In December, the Meerut Division (IEFA) Mule Transport had no 'frost' shoes and frost nails purchased in Bethune (France) were useless. 'If the shoes did arrive every mule would have to be re-shod.'[155]

The War Office had, 'presumed an adequate supply of mule shoes were sent with the Ordnance Park from India for shoeing all mules of the Indian Division (IEFA) and that supplies would be maintained from India'.[156] In the dry climate of India only a small percentage of mules where shod. In the damp climate of France experience soon showed that on hard, often paved roads, the mule's feet were quickly worn down and became tender. Between the two mule corps with the Lahore Division only 5 nalbands (farriers) were available for roughly 1,500 mules. The Division requested 11 additional nalbands and a supply of shoes.

As there were no arrangements for shoeing Maxim gun and Equipment mules of Pioneer regiments and Sappers and Miners, their shoeing devolved to Mule Transport HQ. No arrangements had been made for replacing casualties amongst Maxim gun and Equipment mules so this also devolved to the HQ. The same was true in the Meerut Division. Only 45% of the shoe requirement had sailed with the Division and more than half of these had been left at base. A set of shoes had been sent back to the Ordnance Department in India to be copied and sets manufactured. Iron was purchased locally in France and every forge within a six mile radius (of Hinges) was making shoes and in some cases shoeing. The lack of shoeing meant many mules soon went lame.[157] In November, India was notified that the Army Ordnance Corps, Abbeville, France was taking responsibility for the supply of mule shoes. The GOC Lahore Divisional Area was instructed that reinforcements of Indian ranks for IEFA artillery units were to include 14 shoeing smiths.[158]

The requirement for military harness and saddlery created an immediate supply problem. In addition to supplying harness for its own units and notably for some Silladar cavalry regiments, India received requests from the War Office (31 August) and New Zealand (8 September). The New Zealand Government requested Indian

---

cavalry to Station Veterinary Hospitals (1892). Cold shoeing was introduced (1913) with shoes and nails imported from England for Government horses. Bhalla, *History of the Remount*, pp.64, 79, 92. IOR, L/MIL/17/5/3088, IEFA, Appendix 8, 29 September 1914.
155 IOR, L/MIL/17/5/3087, IEFA, Appendix 109, 17 September. TNA:WO95/3938/8, Divisional Mule Transport, War Diary, 7th (Meerut) Division, 3 December, 1914.
156 IOR, L/MIL/17/5/2429, GSB, DN.4833, 1 October 1914.
157 TNA, WO 95/3921/15, HQ Indian Mule Corps, Lahore Division, 26 October 1914. Transport HQ of the Division was formed from the HQs of 7th and 9th Mules Corps, 18 October 1914, at Orleans. WO 95/3938/8, Divisional Mule Transport, War Diary, Meerut Division, 24 November 1914.
158 IOR, L/MIL/17/5/3088, IEFA, Appendix 52, 11 October. L/MIL/17/5/3089, IEFA, Appendix 287, 24 November 1914.

Government contractors provide and ship complete harness sets for 18 gun teams. This was impossible as full production of artillery harness and saddlery, for the next 12 months, from all sources, meant India was already fully extended.[159] The War Office requested India purchase and ship to Woolwich some 35,000 sets of harness and saddlery from a company in Cawnpore (Kanpur). After much discussion and compromise the Company agreed to concentrate on saddlery and not manufacture harness. To avoid delay in the despatch of saddlery the War Office requested that Indian Ordnance quality control standards and procedures should not detain supplies because of 'small discrepancies not affecting ultimate efficiency in war'.[160] The C-in-C India was informed (14 October) that batteries of Field and Horse Artillery returning Home from India would take all their harness, which was 'very urgently needed'.[161]

Mechanisation

Unlike the peacetime British Army where motor vehicles had replaced most horse drawn transport, the Army in India depended totally on animal power.[162] This is not to say the Army in India was ignorant of developments in, or the benefits of, mechanical transport for military purposes. India has a history of experimenting with steam traction from the 1870s.[163] By the end of 1901 the Indian Government had committed itself to participating in War Office developments for the use of motor vehicles for military purposes; but no progress appears to have been made in mechanising Indian military transport by August 1914. During March and June 1914 proposals were made for the employment of petrol driven lorries for transport purposes and training of personnel from the Supply and Transport Corps. In July questions about the advisability of introducing motor transport into India were raised with the WO but little positive action was taken.[164] With the mobilisation of India's expeditionary

---

159   IOR, L/MIL/17/5/2426, GSB, DN.3099, 8 September & DN.3133, 8 September 1914.
160   Shipments of both would finally take place between January and September 1915 due to difficulties obtaining leather in India. Some harness parts such as pads and collars were all imported from England. IOR, L/MIL/17/5/3086, IEFA, Appendix 138, 31 August. L/MIL/17/5/3087, IEFA, Appendix 52, 7 September. L/MIL/17/5/2425, GSB, DN.2610, 31 August. L/MIL/17/5/2426, GSB,DN.3066, 7 September. L/MIL/17/5/2427, GSB, DN.3460, 12 September. L/MIL/17/5/2428,GSB, DN.4342, 23 September. L/MIL/17/5/2429, GSB, DN.4632, 28 September & DN.4673, 28 September 1914.
161   IOR, L/MIL/17/5/2431, GSB, DN.5916, 2 October & DN.5588, 14 October.
162   Winton, *Theirs Not To Reason Why*, Chapter Five, for example p.207.
163   The War Office formed (1901) a special Motor Transport Committee which included the Ordnance Consulting Officer for India, Colonel Scott, RA, Motor Transport Committee. The Financial Secretary, Lord Stanley as President. I am grateful to Alexandra Fisher, Museum of Rural Life, University of Reading, for information on India and Fowler Steam Engines.
164   IOR, L/MIL/7/6733, Supply and Transport Corp. 'Introduction of Motor Transport into India', 19 March and 25 June, 1914. India Office, London, 31 July 1914, Military No.74, to 'His Excellency the Right Honourable the Governor General of India in Council',

forces the Army Department requested (September) five motor lorries be provided on disembarkation for each of five pack wireless stations of the Signal Squadron.[165] The Secretary of State, India, was informed (2 October) that 46 motor cars were being obtained in India for two infantry divisions and one Cavalry division (IEFA). The cavalry 'should be specially considered in the allotment of motor lorries'.[166] Finally (October) some recognition came from the War Office, that motor cars were being provided on the same scale as the British Expeditionary Force (BEF) for all Indian troops in France and that it was unnecessary for India to send further cars. The QMGs Branch (WO) took over 'the supply of mechanical transport in motor lorries, motor cars and their drivers ... not the motor cycles of volunteer cyclists.'[167]

A number of States offered their private vehicles for war use. For example the Maharaja Scindia gave £15,000 to purchase vehicles for use with Indian Army troops in France and £1,000 for motor lorries in India.[168] The Maharaja of Patiala gave 12 of his private motor cars and the Nawab of Sachin offered two motors, (seven seated touring bodies), for ambulance work or other use; equipped with tools, spares and lamps.[169]

Conclusion

The Allied armies during the 1914-1918 war commanded the majority of the world's most useful animals and particularly those essential for artillery and transport draught purposes. In a war of such long duration and severity for some animals, the frequently overlooked equine resources of India, including personnel, equipment, fodder and shipping, was an important contribution to the war effort in 1914. The mobilization and transportation of the largest number of Indian troops and mounted forces with

---

    response to Despatch No.35 19th March 1914 (a) Training of officers and subordinates in Motor Transport.
165 Wireless Squadron 231 horses: 145 riding, 44 pack and 42 draught. When published in 1914, The *FSPB*, p.20, noted these had not yet been sanctioned. IOR, L/MIL/17/5/2426, GSB, DN.3260, 10 September 1914.
166 To the question of purchasing lorries for experimental purposes, the Military Secretary, London responded 'there was no prospect of lorries being supplied at that time'. IOR, L/MIL/17/5/2429, GSB, DN.4866 & DN.4867, 2 October 1914. L/MIL/7/6733, Supply and Transport Corps, 'Introduction of Motor Transport into India', 9 October, reply 13 October 1914. See also 'British-Indian Cavalry: From Mobilization to the Western Front 1915', in *Courage Without Glory*, Chapter 6, (ed) Dr Spencer Jones (Solihull: Helion, 2015, in the Wolverhampton Military Studies Series).
167 IOR, L/MIL/17/5/2429,GSB,DN.5124, 6 October. L/MIL/17/5/2427, GSB, DN.3796, 17 September 1914.
168 IOR, L/MIL/17/5/2428, GSB, DN.4313, 24 September. L/Mil/17/5/2429, GSB, DN.4628, 26 September 1914. He also gave £5,000 for relief of Belgium sufferers.
169 IOR, L/MIL/17/5/2428, GSB, DN.4264, 22 September & DN.4353, 23 September 1914.

their animals, was a logistical achievement on a monumental scale. All these factors should be 'viewed as an element in the ultimate Allied victory in 1918'.[170]

The Army in India as with most major European powers was in the process of evolving when war broke out in August 1914. At this point it was organised, trained and equipped for conflict in greater India, not for a lengthy major European war. In some cases its pre-war attempts to 'modernise' and reduce dependency on animal power by the introduction of motor transport had been severely restricted by the powers in London. Veterinary services made significant progress by moving into line with the British AVD, even though in 1921 Sir john Moore would write that, 'As it stands at present, it is in no way yet adapted for its success in a war or any big undertaking'.[171] The cheaper but decentralized Silladar system of mounting, supplying and supporting units relying on animals such as cavalry, transport and supply, would be finally abolished in 1922. Ultimately, with increasing mechanisation, the post-war peacetime Army in India would reduce its total reliance on animals for power and mobility.

Honour, therefore, to those noble creatures, who, under circumstances indescribable in their awfulness ... suffered with a dumb obedience, and helped to 'win the war.' [172]

---

170 Moore, *Army Veterinary Service*, p.41. Moore's statement is supported by mapping where Great Britain and her Allies and the Central Powers could obtain the type, class and stamp of animals, and numbers required for military purposes, could be obtained. The Central Powers did not have access to the vast resources of the American Continent.
171 Moore, *Army Veterinary Service*, p.2.
172 Moore, *Army Veterinary Service*, p.41.

4

Beyond the Hindu Kush: Imperial Defence, Expeditionary Warfare and the Role of the Indian Army

Joseph Moretz

Defence of the subcontinent and aid to the civil power may pass without comment as duties befitting its military, but after the South African War (1899-1902) supporting out-of-area operations increasingly became a further mission that India had to account for in the training and equipping of its army. In truth, this had long been a task of the Indian Army with plans dating from 1890 and updated in 1897 for a *coup de main* against the French naval base at Diego Suarez, Madagascar being one example of it at play.[1] More recently providing a composite battalion for duty in East Africa, a similar unit to Aden, or the sending of emergency forces during the Boxer Rebellion featured. In the last instance, over 16,000 Indian troops deployed to China under Lieutenant-General Sir Alfred Gaselee.[2] The attachment of a Sikh battalion to the King's African Rifles (KAR) and serving in East Africa paralleled the use of West Indian troops in West Africa with both demonstrating the use of regularly trained troops to serve as a backstop to those locally raised.[3] Such were held to be less at risk to the religious and tribal influences prevailing and these considerations again applied when the question of reinforcing Egypt with Indian troops was on the table in 1905 with the despatch of Sikh or Ghurka units preferred.[4]

Creation of the Committee of Imperial Defence (CID) in 1902 with its ever expanding body of sub-committees investigating strategic questions, though, brought

1 TNA, CAB 38/4, Military Department to Secretary of State for India signal of 10 March 1904 and CID minutes of 30 March 1904.
2 *Hansard*, House of Commons debate of 18 February 1901, vol. 89, cc302-04.
3 S. C. Ukpabi, 'The Origins of the West African Frontier Force,' *Journal of the Historical Society of Nigeria*, Vol. 3, No. 3 (December 1966), p. 491.
4 TNA, CO 534/3, Uganda Protectorate to Colonial Office letter of 16 August 1905 and CAB 38/12, CID minutes of 26 July 1906.

a degree of systemization and forethought to the question previously lacking. This agency came under direct prime ministerial control in November 1903 and though its membership was inherently flexible, invariably the political heads of the Admiralty and War Office now attended alongside those of the Exchequer, Foreign, Colonial and India Offices. So too did the Chief of the General Staff and the First Sea Lord, the leading professional officers of the Services.[5] The problems the CID weighed were wide-ranging and, befitting a global empire of the first rank, defending isolated and vulnerable areas were often at the fore of its deliberations. That Britain was the premier maritime power both commercially and militarily allowed risks to be run such that adequate garrisons to protect all need not be the only form of defence considered. This played to Britain's strategic strength, but it also made the problem more manageable financially. This was especially true in Africa where European settlements were small and tax revenue to support constabulary and local forces even smaller. Consequently, the defence schemes prepared for Uganda and Kenya assumed their augmentation by Indian forces if ever they were threatened by external aggression.[6]

Still, a by-product of War Office reform and the establishment of the CID was a lessening of Britain's traditional maritime orientation. Officially, the War Office continued to avow that the British Army was the handmaiden to a maritime oriented approach; a viewed doubtlessly shared by Arthur Balfour, the prime minister, when he moved that a permanent sub-committee to consider combined naval and military operations be created.[7] This shift owed something to the quality of input originating from the General Staff to CID deliberations, but, more fundamentally, it owed much to the political accommodation reached with France. Planning for combined operations necessarily assumed the existence of an expeditionary force. Now, the Anglo-French entente established the political conditions for its commitment to the European mainland.

The events of the World War and, especially of the period through 1916, demonstrate what was attempted in out-of-area operations did not equal what was planned. Here, the findings of the Mesopotamia Commission chartered to review the origin, inception and conduct of that campaign found particular fault with both the Indian Army and the Government of India. More remains to be said about the workings and findings of that Commission, but it remains that the conclusions reached by Lord George Hamilton, no less that the minority report drafted by Commander Josiah Wedgwood, were always more about addressing the political fallout of one campaign rather than offering a dispassionate analysis of true cause and effect.[8] Fundamentally, in 1914 Britain elected to create an army of continental proportions whilst simultaneously

5   TNA, CAB 38/3, CID minutes of 4 December 1903.
6   TNA, CO 534/5, Officer Commanding, Troops Uganda Protectorate to Deputy Commissioner, Uganda Protectorate letter of 1 July 1907.
7   TNA, CAB 38/9, CID minutes of 20 July 1905.
8   TNA, CAB 19/26, Cd. 8610, 'Report of the Commission Appointed by Act of Parliament to Enquire into the Operations of War in Mesopotamia Together with a Separate Report

pursuing its traditional maritime strategy. Unfortunately, the wherewithal to follow both approaches did not exist in 1914 and would only come to be much later. The failure of the War Council to prioritize the essential from the desirable occurred during the first week of war when key decisions were taken. Administratively, the transition from peace to war went relatively smoothly demonstrating the thoroughness of prior planning with the preparation of the *War Book* maintained by Major Adrian Duff from the Black Watch and Captain James Longridge of the Indian Army paying dividends. Yet, options considered in peacetime could not account for the actual strategic setting found when war arose. This applied no less to the several military ventures Britain soon initiated.

Britain's last experience of major war had been in South Africa which, if offering many useful lessons, remained a limited conflict by the standards of 1914. British operations against the Boers, if eventually crowned with success, had exposed serious shortcomings across the spectrum of war. Consequently, a period of introspection and reform proved natural giving rise to newer bodies of political oversight, changes in War Office administration and committees to weigh the operational and tactical lessons of war. This spur to reform applied no less to the Indian Army with the agent overseeing this transition being no less than General Lord Kitchener, the late Commander-in-Chief directing British operations in South Africa. That Kitchener when serving as *Sirdar* had taken a hand in reorganizing the Egyptian Army offered yet a further reason for the appointment.[9] In truth, that effort had been uneven with mutiny just below the surface. Imperious, duplicitous and lacking experience of India, some cautioned Lord Curzon against the appointment. A reformer himself, the Viceroy saw Kitchener as a complement in his greater efforts.[10]

With its recent experience of the Tirah and frontier warfare, the lessons of South Africa were not the only one on offer, but in what followed, Kitchener willingly drew upon the recommendations of Viscount Esher's War Office (Reconstitution) Committee, as he sought to reshape the Indian Army.[11] Ironically, just as the post of Commander-in-Chief was being abolished in Britain, Kitchener would strengthen the parameters of its Indian variant with responsibilities for command and administration being devolved to a single officer.[12] Though the administrative underpinnings of the

 By Commander J. Wedgwood, D.S.O., M.P., and Appendices, 1917' and, hereafter 'Mesopotamia Report.'
9 'Lord Kitchener,' *The Times*, 7 June 1916, p. 14.
10 David Gilmour, *Curzon: Imperial Statesman, 1859-1925* (London: John Murray, 2003), p. 249.
11 George Morton-Jack, *The Indian Army on the Western Front: India's Expeditionary Force to France and Belgium in the First World War* (New York: Cambridge University Press, 2014), pp. 68, 98.
12 TNA, CAB 38/4, 'The Administration of the Army in India,' Kitchener memorandum of 26 April 1904. Admiral Sir John Fisher (Commander-in-Chief, Portsmouth) and Sir George Clarke (Secretary to the CID) served as the additional members to the committee.

British and Indian Armies were different, the desire remained that in the not too distant future the two establishments would share a common strategic view such that coordination between both in wartime would be enhanced. To be sure, this aim animated also within the Dominions or those forces such as the KAR falling directly under the auspices of the Colonial Office. Accordingly, concurrence was reached that all military establishments would be organized, trained and equipped to a common standard leading General Sir William Nicholson to exchange the title of Chief of the General Staff to the more expansive incarnation, Chief of the Imperial General Staff (CIGS).[13] Time would demonstrate that it was easier to establish broad, overarching goals than appropriate the funds required to secure the desired ends and this remained true in India. Nevertheless, the Indian Army accepted the divisional structure of the British Army for out-of-area operations.[14]

Though Kitchener was not a graduate of the Staff College, he was an officer who had spent his share of time in staff appointments and understood the vital necessity for effective staff work in planning, organizing and conducting operations. This was appreciated as a particular shortcoming of the Indian Army. That all was not as it should be had been raised in parliament in the previous decade when Duncan Pirie, a Liberal member and veteran of the Egyptian campaign, questioned the paucity of qualified officers found in the Indian Staff Corps. In 1897 only 30 of 142 held the coveted *psc* designation denoting successful completion of the Staff Course; a figure Lord George Hamilton, the Tory Secretary of State for India, conceded was substantially correct.[15] Given the need for officers to alternate between staff and regimental assignments, the shortfall was not apt to be alleviated if matters continued as presently ordained with events in South Africa providing fresh ammunition. Some now argued for the establishment of a separate school.[16] If Kitchener had not fathered the idea, he nonetheless grasped the reins of educational reform with alacrity. Nor was he finished. Much of what he pursued was done absent the consensus of Curzon, the India Council or receiving proper debate in parliament. Temperament and style aside, the Commander-in-Chief pursued his ends to make the Indian Army ready for a great war.[17]

Scale and distance increased the complexity of modern military operations and never the more so than in supporting the demands of out-of-theatre expeditionary warfare. In this regard, the Indian Army suffered two key hurdles. Firstly, it was officered by a mix of British and native officers with numbers for the former, however,

---

13   TNA, CAB 38/18, 'The Progress of the Imperial General Staff and the Development of its Functions,' General Staff memorandum of 19 May 1911.
14   TNA, CAB 38/7, 'Scheme of Re-distribution of the Army in India and Preparation of the Army in India for War,' 1904.
15   *Hansard*, House of Commons debate of 15 July 1897, vol. 51, cc161-62.
16   H. M. S., 'Proposed Indian Staff College,' *The Times*, 26 December 1900, p. 5.
17   Kenneth Rose, *Superior Person: A Portrait of Curzon and His Circle in Late Victorian England* (London: Phoenix Press, 2001), pp. 362-63.

rarely equalling their authorized strength. Vacancies owing to secondments, leave and training exasperated the problem and, if manageable in peacetime, spelled only trouble in war. A lesson derived from South African experience was that additional British officers needed to be attached to Indian formations with General Sir Arthur Palmer, the Commander-in-Chief, warning, 'it is no economy to keep up a native army during times of peace which, owing to its being under-officered, will be unfit efficiently to meet the numerous demands on the outbreak of war.'[18]

Even if the first constraint had not been present, the only venue for training staff officers to the required standard resided at Camberley. Here, three or four officers a year of the Indian Army attended its two-year course. Personal finance was one reason why more officers did not seek to attend Camberley for the reality remained that many served in India owing to the prohibitive costs of maintaining oneself in a domestic regiment. Still, a further restraint was that the course as presently conducted could not readily handle more qualifiers. Such might be forthcoming if funds to support expansion came from parliament, but Kitchener side-stepped that issue by securing the approval of the Government of India.[19] Thus, one of the most important steps taken and serving as an enabler for many of the further reforms to follow was the establishment of a dedicated Staff College to meet the needs of the Indian Army. To this end, a class of 24 qualifiers with instructors drawn from the infantry, cavalry, engineer and artillery arms convened at Deolali on 1 July 1905 under the auspices of Major-General Alfred Bayly.[20]

If Kitchener had successfully negotiated the shoals of financial scrutiny, opposition to the Staff College remained and would continue to fester for some time emanating from Camberley, the War Office, Simla or their acolytes in the press.[21] Of the last, the criticisms of Charles à Court Repington, the noted military correspondent of *The Times*, focused on the centrality of combined operations in the curricula of Camberley and the Naval War Course. The latter of recent vintage sought to prepare officers for command by focusing on the higher aspects of war and the essentials of naval tactics. Initiated in 1900 at Greenwich but subsequently transferring to Portsmouth, close links had developed between it and the Staff College residing at Camberley.[22] Distance alone meant that it would not be possible to replicate these ties with the new

---

18 TNA, CAB 38/3, 'Defence of India,' War Office report of 23 June 1903.
19 Untitled Leader, *The Times*, 9 June 1904, p. 11.
20 'The Indian Staff College,' *The Times*, 10 April 1905, p. 10.
21 A. R. Godwin-Austen, *The Staff and the Staff College* (London: Constable and Company, Ltd., 1927), pp. 249-50.
22 On pre-1914 affairs, see Andrew Lambert, 'The Naval War Course, *Some Principles of Maritime Strategy* and the Origins of 'The British Way in Warfare',' in Keith Neilson and Greg Kennedy, eds., *the British Way in Warfare: Power and the International System, 1856-1956: Essays in Honour of David French* (Farnham: Ashgate Publishing Limited, 2010). On the postwar period, see Joseph Moretz, *Thinking Wisely, Planning Boldly: The Higher Education and Training of Royal Navy Officers, 1919-1939* (Solihull: Helion & Company Limited, 2014).

Staff College.²³ This concern was not ill-founded, but other means existed to ensure a commonality of approach between what was imparted at Camberley and that taught at Quetta which in 1907 became the permanent home of the Indian Staff College.

Hence, the judicious appointment of instructors was critical. Kitchener sought to resolve any doubts on that score by securing the appointment of Colonel Thompson Capper to replace Bayly as commandant. Seen as a gifted instructor at Camberley—perhaps too gifted—Capper had been present during the Russo-Japanese War. This recent campaign offered the best contemporary lessons on the value of combined operations and featured as an important case study in the curricula at Camberley and Portsmouth with Japanese officers appearing at times to discuss its salient features. Now, it served the same purpose in India and whilst Quetta might not witness the presence of Japanese veterans to testify to the operations conducted, sending Capper, Lieutenant-Colonel Wilkinson Bird of the Directing Staff and twenty qualifiers to Manchuria in April 1907 to study the war *in situ* possessed a value all of its own. Drawing on attaché reports and contemporary accounts including Lieutenant-General Sir Ian Hamilton's recently penned *A Staff Officer's Scrap-Book*, qualifiers studied and prepared essays on important phases of the war during their voyage east.²⁴ Arriving in Manchuria, Japanese officers accompanied all to the scene of the recent battles providing expert commentary to those momentous events.²⁵

Notwithstanding Capper's unique approach to the study of combined operations, Repington's cautionary warning went beyond the principles to be distilled from a single example. Julian Corbett, the noted naval historian and influential maritime theorist, surveyed the progress of warfare and fastened onto combined operations as the salient feature of British experience as contrasted to continental practice in his lectures to the War Course. Drawing examples from the War of Spanish Succession, the Seven Years War, the Napoleonic Era, the Crimean War, and, of course, the Russo-Japanese War, if those attending Camberley did not receive such fulsome treatment, it remained that Corbett shared his views to qualifiers there on the utility of combined operations in a future European War in his lecture 'The Army in Relation to Gaining Command of the Seas.'

Though historical study was important for divining appropriate lessons, the conduct of operations demanded practical application and not mere theory. Consequently, both Camberley and the Naval War Course arranged joint exercises in the field in what would later be recognized as Tactical Exercises Without Troops to consider questions

---

23   'Rival Staff Colleges,' *The Times*, 29 May 1905, p. 10.
24   Ian Hamilton, *A Staff Officer's Scrap-Book during the Russo-Japanese War* (London: Edward Arnold, 1906).
25   Liddell Hart Centre for Military Archives, hereafter LHCMA, King's College, London, Major-General Sir Thompson Capper Papers, 2/1, 'Deductions from Accounts of Night Attacks during the Manchurian War, with Examples,' 1908.

of coastal defence and combined operations against a known objective.[26] Finally, the Royal Naval War College lent its support to Army Home establishments, such as Western Command in March 1909, when practical amphibious exercises featured in its training programme.[27]

Not all of these measures were possible in India and so it becomes apparent that training in combined operations necessarily diverged between Portsmouth, Camberley and Quetta. Yet, the Indian Army did more than just study the problem. Real-world operations provided ready opportunities to put theory to practice with the skills of planning, beach reconnaissance, loading, transfer and landing honed such as during the expedition mounted against the Mullah in Somaliland in 1902/04. If the landing of troops, animals and stores at Obbia was of an administrative nature, the conditions remained severe as all occurred during the height of a monsoon. In the event, troops making passage in open boats became thoroughly drenched during the transfer with some craft swamped; unsurprisingly, not all successfully negotiated the landing.[28]

Indeed, so central was the subject of combined operations and the case study of the Russo-Japanese War to its understanding that it indirectly resulted in the supersession of Capper. The specific crisis was the appointment of Major Berkeley Vincent, a recently appointed instructor to the Indian Staff College, made at the behest of Capper which Kitchener accepted in August 1909. How closely the Commander-in-Chief scrutinized the appointment as he was preparing to depart India is unknown, but upon leaving the following month those holding against Vincent struck. This included Henry Wilson, the present commandant at Camberley. A cavalry officer, Vincent had demonstrated only marginal abilities when studying at Staff College the previous year though why is the more interesting question. The evidence available points to a clash of personalities between Wilson and Vincent combined with fundamental differences over the doctrine being espoused at the Staff College by Wilson which Vincent had deprecated.[29] All this was enough to make Wilson apoplectic:

> The news about Vincent's is confirmed. It leaves us all in a rather breathless condition. We cannot think who is responsible for the selection. I suppose my report on him was seen. We can scarcely believe it unless indeed which seems likely, the opinions in Simla of a Camberley Staff College report is that it is

---

26 LHCMA, Sir Julian Corbett Papers, Box 1, 'Lecture Notes' and Box 2, Henry Rawlinson to Corbett letter of 2 October 1905.
27 TNA, ADM 196/43 (G. Hope).
28 *London Gazette*, No. 27710, 2 September 1904, Brigadier-General W. H. Manning, 'Report Upon the Operations of the Somaliland Field Force.'
29 Keith Jeffrey, *Field Marshal Sir Henry Wilson: A Political Soldier* (Oxford: Oxford University Press, 2006), pp. 82-83. Further considerations in the dispute must be the close association of Vincent to Ian Hamilton and the role of mounted infantry. To this end, Vincent retained close ties to Brigadier-General Henry de Beauvoir de Lisle, an officer seen as a *bête noire* to cavalry traditionalists such as Wilson and Douglas Haig.

not worth the paper it is written on. In this, as in every case, it represents the opinion, the unanimous opinion, of the whole Staff here. <u>Eleven of us</u>. I feel inclined to ask for permission to be relieved from reporting on officers of the I.A. [Indian Army] in future as it appears to me to be rather a waste of time. The personal part of all this is a very small matter. What we all feel is that the selection & appointment of Vincent is by far the worst thing that has happened to the Quetta S.C. [Staff College] up to date. For this reason we are most awfully upset about the business. And don't think I have any down on Vincent. In some appointments he would do admirably but Quetta – good Lord.[30]

Conceding the officer had decided limitations, Capper appreciated the strong suit of Vincent was his time spent as an observer to the Japanese Army during the Manchurian War. As the only other member of Quetta having direct experience of that war, this quality for Capper stood above all else. That argument carried little water with others including Major General Douglas Haig who faulted Vincent's understanding of the *Field Service Regulations* and the proper use of cavalry. After a year at Quetta, General Sir O'Moore Creagh, the new Commander-in-Chief, sanctioned Vincent's return to regimental duties prompting Capper's request to be relieved as commandant.[31]

The previous demonstrates the difficulty of harmonizing instruction between Camberley and Quetta when other equities were at play and it remains that the Russo-Japanese War was but one vehicle for imparting the underlying principles of combined operations. Challenging to secure reform within a single service, ever the more so when multiple services were involved and the strategic environment facing the British Empire was undergoing a fundamental realignment. Thus, the changes implemented following the Anglo-Boer War whilst correcting immediate deficiencies needed to operate in concert with the evolving strategic environment, account for the disparate political nature of the Empire and be financially sustainable over the long-term. The last is ever a problem and proving equally so at this moment with the reach of reform exceeding the grasp of economy.

Manifestly, the Empire was a function of Britain's maritime orientation, but an irony of its creation was that its furthest dominions inhabited by growing numbers of expatriates increasingly turned Britain into a power with continental responsibilities. If the responsibilities were acknowledged, the implications towards its traditional maritime-centric strategy were more difficult to square and never the more so than with respect to India. Britain might be able to keep the sea lanes open to the subcontinent in war, but only a large garrison could buy the necessary time to allow reinforcements arriving from elsewhere to meet an external threat. Traditionally, the enemy posited was Russia acting alone, or more worryingly, acting in tandem with Germany or

---

30 LHCMA, Capper Papers, 2/4/17, Wilson to Capper letter of 2 October 1908. Original emphasis.
31 Ibid, Capper to Chief of General Staff letter, no date, but *c*. January 1911.

France.³² Unable to meet the costs of every conceivable contingency, London at last eschewed 'Splendid Isolation' and aligned herself with Japan in 1902 before finding accommodation with France in 1904. This reduced, but did not eliminate all points of friction with the latter, but a rising German threat in home waters was increasingly seen as the greatest danger.

A superior battlefleet concentrated in the North Sea became the cornerstone for meeting the threat from invasion by Germany augmented with such military forces to meet any landing effected. Obsolete ships were paid off to free up funds for new warship construction and distant British squadrons were reduced to allow this concentration with the *quid pro quo* entertained being a formal commitment towards Japan and an informal obligation to France. In 1907, Britain reached a limited settlement over Persia with Russia who having a formal alliance already with France dating from 1892 evidenced that Germany had become threat number one in British eyes.³³

Though it was difficult to posit the actual conditions that might give rise to war with Germany, how to meet such an eventuality was more readily defined. First and foremost, Britain would apply a maritime blockade against Germany, though legally the term contraband control applied. British command of the greater seas would ensure that remote German colonies in the Pacific quickly fell. Their capture by local Dominion and Commonwealth troops denied any German shipping—commercial or otherwise—logistical support, but such when in British hands also removed the passing of intelligence as their associated wireless and cable facilities would cease transmitting. In Africa, where German colonial holdings were more substantial similar operations were posited against Cameroon, Southwest Africa and German East Africa. Seeing to the first two contingencies would be forces drawn from the West African Frontier Force (WAFF) stationed in Sierra Leone and the Niger and troops serving on the Cape Station with both serials supported by the Navy. East Africa represented a more formidable problem and an expedition drawn from India would concentrate at Zanzibar to subdue the colony. Such were the general lines of War Office thinking in 1903 and endorsed two years later by Admiral Sir John Fisher, the First Sea Lord. In the main, they applied when Britain found itself at war in August 1914.³⁴

Europe, however, was not ignored as a possible theatre of deployment and during Haig's period as Chief of Staff in India, the manner of sending an expeditionary force

---

32 Churchill Archives Centre, Cambridge, hereafter CAC, Admiral of the Fleet Lord Fisher Papers, CAC/FISR/1/4/139, Rear-Admiral Prince Louis of Battenberg to Admiral Fisher letter of 7 November 1904.
33 Beryl J. Williams, 'The Strategic Background to the Anglo-Russian Entente of August 1907,' *Historical Journal*, Vol. 9, No. 3 (1966), p. 369.
34 TNA, CAB 38/4, 'The Military Resources of Germany, and Probable Method of their Employment in a War Germany and England,' 7 February 1903 and CAC/FISR/5/12/4225, 'Disposition of the Fleet in England, preparatory to an outbreak of War with Germany,' no date, but *c.* June 1905.

to the continent featured in the exercises and staff rides conducted.[35] If such planning supported the ends of imperial strategy and was facilitated by the attachment of officers who had previously served on the General Staff, then it did not follow that it met with the approval of the Government of India. Why is not hard to discern for the budgetary implications of developing forces to engage a European army of the first-rank were substantial. Indeed, Lord Crewe, the Secretary of State, posited that spending on the Indian Army ought to be reduced at this moment owing to the rapprochement secured with Russia.[36] That that rapprochement was effected to meet a threat arising elsewhere testifies to the difficulties of adopting a unified strategy in the construct which was the British Empire where financial responsibility for military forces remained decentralized. This tension has received far too little focus as the underlying issue separating the differences of view held amongst principals.

The experience of South Africa, the Spanish-American and the Russo-Japanese Wars indicated that amphibious operations remained viable, but evidence suggested executing an opposed landing in the face of naval mines, fixed-torpedo defences, barbed wire and coastal batteries made discretion the better part of valour. To wit, the General Staff of the War Office advised the CID, 'It is only of very recent years that naval and military authorities have come to recognise the tactical principle that under modern conditions an opposed landing is one of the most difficult operations of war.'[37] The administrative landings made at Obbia had tested all concerned though enemy resistance had not even been a factor. Within limits, then, it was accepted a combined operation, or what are now known as joint amphibious operations, could still be executed.

This assessment was vital for a maritime empire and one protected primarily by its navy. Thus, the CID accepted Balfour's proposal for a dedicated committee to assess and develop options for combined operations against anticipated enemy state(s). By keeping such measures continuously up to date, they would be available for rapid execution upon the outbreak of war. The importance and restricted nature of the planning attached to these efforts may be gauged by its limited and focused membership: the prime minister, the First Sea Lord, the Director of Naval Intelligence, the Chief of the General Staff and the Director of Military Operations (DMO) along with subsidiary officers from the Admiralty and War Office responsible for strategic war planning. Absent were the political heads of the Services and the Foreign, India and Colonial Offices or officers coming from the imperial forces that might be employed. As the CID would approve any contingencies prepared, the opportunity of those offices to shape the plans drafted remained for a subsequent date. Yet, they would not have been privy to all the assumptions and details previously weighed rendering their

---

35 John Terraine, *Douglas Haig: The Educated Soldier* (London: Cassell, 1963), pp. 46-48.
36 TNA, CAB 38/18, CID minutes of 26 May 1911.
37 TNA, CAB 38/11, 'Infantry Garrisons of Gibraltar and Malta,' General Staff memorandum of 29 May 1906.

actual influence marginal.[38] Moreover, it is the case that those drafting such plans had not a true appreciation of the operational limitations facing imperial forces. It was also at this same proximate moment that the Chief of the General Staff, Lieutenant General the Hon. Sir Neville Lyttelton, led a staff conference of senior military officers at Camberley to weigh a host of pressing and contentious subjects. Ranging from the tactics governing modern rifle fire to the defence of India, they also listened to Captain Edmond Slade, presently directing the Naval War Course, expound on the 'Co-operation between the Navy and the Army in Over-sea Expeditions.'[39]

From HMS *Terpsichore* and the Naval War Course Slade would become the Director of Naval Intelligence. This put Slade at the heart of strategic planning both within the Admiralty and within the CID. In March 1909, Rear Admiral Slade assumed command of the East Indies Squadron being responsible for naval operations in the Persian Gulf, the east coast of Africa and, of course, India. Though wearing his flag at sea, Slade nevertheless chaired a committee examining the work and administration of the Royal Indian Marine. Returning to the Admiralty in April 1912, Slade served on a further committee investigating transport services before traveling to Persia as head of an expedition supporting the Anglo-Persian Oil Company. Upon his return the Admiralty in 1914, he served on the Admiralty-War Office committee weighing the transportation requirements for deploying an expeditionary force.[40]

Proximity made Persia of interest to India; petroleum made Persia a priority for the Royal Navy as it transitioned its ships from burning coal to steaming on oil. The East Indies Squadron presence in the Persian Gulf predated the discovery of oil, but that occasion made control of that body and its headwaters yet more vital for having the oil counted for nothing if it could not be shipped from Abadan. Unfortunately, control of the headwaters remained in dispute and, if that narrow issue was not troublesome enough for Admiral Slade, German encroachment via the Berlin to Baghdad railway threatened to undermine British commercial interests along Mesopotamia's major rivers. If ever Turkey turned openly hostile, an expedition to control Fao and Basra was advised.[41]

Hence, before August 1914 considerations of sending expeditions based on elements of the Indian Army to East Africa, Mesopotamia, Egypt and even Europe itself existed to varying degrees. Measuring how mature the plans for each of these contingencies is necessarily speculative, but given the existence of formal defence schemes for East Africa and Uganda which had already identified the use of Indian troops and the ongoing worries about defending the Canal, serials for these must be assumed. More recently, as Slade's correspondence confirms, Mesopotamia had come

---

38   TNA, CAB 38/9, appendix to CID minutes of 26 July 1905.
39   'Naval and Military Intelligence,' *The Times*, 13 January 1906, p. 7.
40   TNA, ADM 196/87 (E. Slade).
41   TNA, CAB 38/18, Commander-in-Chief, East Indies to Government of India letter of 22 April 1911.

to the fore as a contingency deserving attention whilst Haig's preparations indicate that operations further afield were within the realm of possibilities to the army if not to the Government of India.

Having opted for war on August 4, an immediate step implemented was the formation of a War Council to direct affairs. Such was not the Cabinet which remained in the background nor even the CID which continued to meet as necessary at the prompting of the War Council. Meeting for the first time the next day, the War Council confirmed that an expeditionary force should be readied and tasked the War Office to request a division of Indian troops to defend Egypt. In addition to these measures, British officers on secondment to colonial and imperial establishments were recalled home to round-out second-line establishments. The measure did not stop there with 280 Indian Army officers being similarly recalled.[42] Where, though, an expeditionary force was to proceed remained open with Sir Edward Grey, the Foreign Secretary, advising parliament and Paris both that defence of India and Egypt had first claim on British resources.[43] A further measure taken by Herbert Asquith at the prompting of Maurice Hankey was to reconstitute the Committee on Combined Operations in Foreign Territory under Admiral Sir Henry Jackson. Joining Jackson were two representatives from the War Office: General Sir Ian Hamilton and Major General Charles Callwell, the DMO. Aston, the foremost Marine officer on the question of combined operations and appointed Assistant Director of the Operations Division within the Admiralty only two days previous, completed the naval contribution.[44] Rowland Sperling from the Foreign Office and George Fiddes of the Colonial Office made up the balance of the body for the participation of General Sir Edmund Barrow proved to be more circumscribed attending only when matters affected the interests of India.[45]

Working to a frantic pace, Jackson's group met on 5 August 1914 *sans* the initial participation of the Foreign Office which missed three of the four initial sittings. This was little better than Hamilton who only attended the first session. Present, though, were others including the Inspectors General of the WAFF and the KAR—Brigadier General Charles Dobell and Colonel Reginald Hoskins, respectively. Conveniently, they were found in London on war's declaration. Further attendees were Colonel Alister Dallas from the War Office and Maurice Hankey, the redoubtable Secretary to the CID. Collectively, they proposed that a combined operation be initiated against German East Africa with the object of denying Dar es Salaam to the German Navy. This would protect British shipping in the Indian Ocean and further the defence of the East Africa Protectorate. Other possibilities weighed included attacks on German

---

42 TNA, CAB 42/6, War Committee minutes of 1 December 1915.
43 *Hansard*, House of Commons debate of 3 August 1914, vol. 65, cc1809-32 and TNA FO 800/166, Francis Bertie to William Tyrrell letter of 4 August 1914.
44 TNA, ADM 196/61 (G. Aston).
45 TNA, CAB 38/28, 'Committee on Combined Operations in Foreign Territory.'

Southwest Africa, Togoland and Cameroon in that theatre along with Yap, New Guinea, Samoa and Nauru in the Pacific. Here, the aim was primarily to disrupt German global wireless and cable communications and deny her anchorages and ports operating across the lines of communications leading to imperial territories.[46]

Though accepted in principle and with the details of its deployment previously worked out, the situation found on 5 August 1914 did not conform to the facts Germany had already created on the ground. Planning had assumed the despatch of an expeditionary force from Bristol, Newhaven and Southampton with its concentration on Maubeuge. This no longer appeared tenable with the alternate site of Amiens now proposed. The problem featured at the first meeting of the War Council with a decision deferred until the following day, August 6th.[47] The tenor of this meeting was that of experts wrestling with a technical question. Namely, where to deploy and not whether to deploy an expeditionary force. Those attending were overwhelmingly from the War Office and the designated senior officers to the force being mobilized with Asquith in the chair. Surprisingly, neither Callwell as DMO nor Jackson attended this conference, though Ian Hamilton did. To say the least, this was deeply troubling. Only five days earlier it had been decided to pursue a naval strategy in the event of hostilities.[48] That decision was not explicitly overturned, but it was in danger of being compromised for the act of sending an expeditionary force stood not alone from the deliberations of the Combined Operations Committee. Every decision taken needed to be measured against their place in Britain's greater war effort. Little purpose was served in insisting that proposals should only be considered that did not require forces destined for the main theatre, if the lines of that commitment remained unresolved.[49]

The War Council endorsed the recommendation of the Committee on Combined Operations to capture Dar es Salaam on August 6 tasking India to find the necessary troops for the effort.[50] Not waiting until then, the cruiser HMS *Astraea* left Zanzibar and raided the German port three days later destroying the wireless station, an auxiliary cruiser and sinking a floating dock. The last effectively blocking the channel.[51] These measures alone secured, if only temporarily, a primary object of any intended military operations against German East Africa. Thus, by the middle of August a limited campaign against German East Africa to secure its ports had been approved, raids against German territories in the Pacific had already commenced and

46 Ibid, Combined Operations Committee minutes of 5 August 1914.
47 TNA, CAB 42/1, War Council minutes of 5 August 1914.
48 TNA, CAB 38/28, 'Report on the Opening of the War,' Historical Section, CID, 1 November 1914 and Avner Offer, 'The Working Classes, British Naval Plans and the Coming of the Great War,' *Past and Present*, no. 107, (May 1985) p. 221.
49 TNA, CAB 38/28, 'Report on the Opening of the War,' Historical Section, CID, 1 November 1914.
50 TNA, CAB 42/1, War Council minutes of 6 August 1914.
51 TNA, CAB 38/28, 'Report on the Opening of the War,' Historical Section, CID, 1 November 1914.

operations against Cameroon were pending. Two companies from the WAFF were earmarked for redistribution from Sierra Leone to Lome, a coastal town in German controlled Togoland, for use there or to support Dobell's pending campaign against Cameroon,[52] while a half-company had been approved for removal from Gambia.[53]

In Egypt, Indian Expeditionary Force 'E' under the command of Major General Charles Melliss arrived in November to reinforce that quarter. In turn, a second element referred to as Expedition 'C' was readied for Zanzibar and the East Africa Protectorate and, again, coming from India. The aim of the latter force was to implement the prewar defence scheme for both areas to guard against a possible German attack. Offensively, a third element, Expedition 'B', again from the subcontinent, was being organized to conduct operations against German East Africa. On those occasions when elements of Expedition 'C' operated in German territory, they were to fall under the tactical control of Brigadier General Arthur Aitken, the Commander of Expedition 'B'.[54] The initial foray against German East Africa was to be a limited operation, but Belgium, following upon British actions against Dar es Salaam, proposed a joint operation to reduce the colony to eliminate the threat facing the Congo. This prodding expanded the objectives of the campaign, though it is likely Britain would have reached this decision at some point without any outside prompting. Always the risk existed that if Belgium was defeated by Germany, Brussels would not be the only territory occupied.[55]

Meanwhile, Indian Expeditionary Force 'D', landed at Basra on 5 November 1914. The town provided access but not much more as the infrastructure such as wharves to support a military campaign were totally lacking. That was from the sea, landward marshes predominated and to this the area was soon inundated with floods.[56] Ottoman forces stood not idle and a force moved from Mesopotamia into Persian Arabistan (present day, Iranian Khuzestan) and succeeded in cutting the pipeline which the occupation had meant to forestall. Consequently, initial British efforts witnessed the augmentation of forces, the improvement of the Basra logistics hub and the securing of the surrounding area by the 6th and 12th Indian Divisions which formed the heart of IEF 'D'. In January 1915, British troops occupied Qurna, northwest of Basra while another detachment held Ahwaz in southern Persia. Necessarily, a campaign fought in Mesopotamia required direct naval support if progress from Basra was to be made. Thus, whilst the initial landings were of an administrative nature, subsequent

---

52 Ibid, Combined Operations Committee minutes of 17 August 1914.
53 Ibid, Combined Operations Committee minutes of 25 August 1914.
54 Ibid, 'Expedition against German East Africa,' Barrow memorandum of 18 September 1914.
55 TNA, CAB 24/3, Appendix K, Sub-Committee on Territorial Changes, Third Interim Report, 28 March 1917.
56 *London Gazette*, No. 29536, 5 April 1916, p. 3655.

operations assumed the proportion of riverine warfare for the corps-size force deployed and were governed by the navigability of the Tigris and Euphrates Rivers.[57]

Once anchored at Basra, pressure to advance towards Baghdad became palpable. This owed something to the desire to maintain pressure on Ottoman forces in the region to forestall their deployment elsewhere. Yet, it also reflected broader considerations. Baghdad dominated the communications of southern Iraq and standing pat presented its own set of problems as Major General Sir Arthur Barrett appreciated. Moreover, the occupation of Iraq and, especially Mosul, was desirous for other strategic reasons. Having conceded to Russia control of the Straits if the Dardanelles campaign ended successfully, and anticipating French control of Syria, Britain eyed occupying Alexandretta as a counterbalance to ensure the defence of Egypt and of Mesopotamia from her ostensible allies. Having Alexandretta though would be reckless unless Mesopotamia proper belonged to Britain and, if she did not take it, then Russia assuredly would upon Turkey's defeat.[58] This assessment was fully endorsed by the Admiralty in a separate paper. Noting the sacrifices being incurred in the war and drawing upon the history of earlier British endeavours as documented by Corbett, compensation elsewhere was demanded with Mesopotamia the obvious choice.[59] Indeed, Admiral Jackson going further and not mincing his words argued the 'positions should be prevented from falling into the hands of our future possible enemies; this is best effected by holding them ourselves.'[60] Only in April 1915 did Britain first take stock what her greater objectives were in fighting Turkey when Maurice De Bunsen's body began considering the matter. Convening multiples times over the course of the next two months, their report laid the groundwork for a more expansive campaign in Mesopotamia and in the greater Near East in general. With regard to the former, they proposed that Britain should set her eyes beyond Baghdad and consider occupying the province of Mosul and its approaches.[61]

From the beginning, command and control arrangements posed problems for a simple, direct line did not flow from Westminster through Whitehall to the forces being deployed. While the War Council might ordain, it could not control. Distance was partly the reason why, but where operations were to be conducted explained the more so. Egypt fell under the auspices of the Foreign Office, whilst British East Africa and Zanzibar came under the eyes of the Colonial Office. Following upon the

---

57 TNA, CAB 42/6, 'Operations in Mesopotamia,' Naval War Staff notes, no date, but *c.* December 1915.
58 TNA, CAB 24/1, 'Alexandretta and Mesopotamia,' Kitchener to CID memorandum of 16 March 1915.
59 Ibid, 'Alexandretta and Mesopotamia,' Admiralty to CID memorandum of 17 March 1915.
60 Ibid, 'Alexandretta,' Jackson memorandum of 15 March 1915.
61 Edward Peter Fitzgerald, 'France's Middle Eastern Ambitions, the Sykes-Picot Negotiations, and the Oil Fields of Mosul, 1915-1918,' *Journal of Modern History*, Vol. 66, No. 4 (December 1994) p. 706.

experience of the Boxer Rebellion, the decision was taken that India would direct certain out-of-theatre operations. Politically and militarily, this made perfect sense for East Africa and southern Mesopotamia were problems of more saliency to India and this nominally freed London to focus on Europe, the Mediterranean environ, West Africa and the Americas. To this end, the Intelligence Departments found in England and in India had divided areas into separate spheres of responsibility for collecting topographical and local intelligence.[62] From a maritime viewpoint, the question was much finer. The Royal Indian Marine assumed more the lines of a constabulary force with the East Indies Squadron under direct Admiralty control being the real font of local naval power. Always latent was the conflict between the demands of general naval strategy and Indian military strategy compounded by the fact that India paid a portion of the operating costs of the squadron.[63] Still, the Government in India did not operate in a vacuum receiving policy direction from the India Office in London and, ultimately, from Cabinet and parliament. How closely those in London understood the situation in India and on the ground in Mesopotamia and Africa would be greatly tested in what came to follow.

By mutual agreement, warring amongst Europeans in Africa was deprecated. This was codified by treaty which went so far as to claim that European powers at war with each other would not affect the neutrality of central Africa.[64] More than this, though, Britain had even lent a hand helping Germany suppress a revolt in Southwest Africa.[65] While London could not assume such respect would continue after August 1914 and the more so after the violation of Belgium neutrality by Germany, whether active operations should have been initiated was another matter entirely. To this end, Belgium approached Britain soon after the war's start raising the possibility of adhering to the terms of the 1885 Act of Berlin. Timing though dictated otherwise for the Royal Navy had already attacked Dar es Salaam in contravention to the Article 11 of the Act, so, in effect, the matter had become moot in British eyes. Not though, in German, who relayed to the United States on 22 August 1914 that they would respect the neutrality of Equatorial Africa if the Allies made a similar pledge.[66] The standing defence scheme for Uganda assumed the violation of neutral African areas and the naval action taken was in keeping with the tenor of the military plan. Manifestly, it was in conformance with the broader aim of securing command of the sea. If the

62 TNA, CAB 19/26, 'Mesopotamia Report,' p. 96.
63 E. R. Fremantle, *The Navy as I Have Known It* (London: Cassell and Company, 1914), 335 and Lady Wester Wemyss, *The Life and Letters of Lord Wester Wemyss, G.C.B., C.M.G, M.V.O., Admiral of the Fleet* (London: Eyre and Spottiswoode, 1935), p. 277.
64 TNA, CAB 24/3, Sub-Committee on Territorial Changes,' Fourth Interim Report, 17 July 1917.
65 Matthew S. Seligmann, ed., *Military Intelligence from Germany, 1906-1914, Army Records Society, Vol. 34* (Stroud: The History Press, 2014), p. 60.
66 TNA, CAB 24/3, Sub-Committee on Territorial Changes,' Fourth Interim Report, 17 July 1917.

above did not feature in the calculations of the Committee on Combined Operations, then it should have raised concerns to Lewis Harcourt and Edward Grey, the Colonial and Foreign Secretaries, respectively.

Britain declared war on Tuesday, August 4th, agreed to send an expedition to East Africa on Wednesday and then committed to sending an expeditionary force to the continent on the Thursday.[67] This day also saw Field Marshal the Earl Kitchener, presently home on leave from Egypt, appointed to the Privy Council becoming the Secretary of State for War, though forsaking the whip of the Liberals.[68] Thus, it proved that the initial decision for war and where first measures would be pursued occurred whilst the War Office portfolio was held by the prime minister since the resignation of Colonel John Seely following upon the Curragh incident. One did not cause the other, but it is surely the case that Asquith had more than enough on his plate before weighing the recommendations coming fast and furious from Jackson's body. Within a fortnight, raids on enemy Pacific islands, an attack on Cameroon and another on Southwest Africa had been approved all the while sending reinforcements to Egypt from India. In the case of the last contingency, the 3rd Indian Division under Lieutenant General Henry Watkis landed on 19 August 1914.[69] In the event, Egypt was calm and they soon departed for service in France to be replaced by other Indian troops. Inexplicably, the War Council, the Cabinet-level body created to direct the war, met on 5 and 6 August 1914 and would not sit again until 25 November.[70] Consequently, the actions proposed by Jackson and company did not receive the level of scrutiny required and this failure accounts for much of the problems later experienced.

These serials were in keeping with prewar plans to deny the enemy the ability to communicate with shipping and naval warships and securing the defence of Egypt. They can also be seen as an extension of the naval blockade against Germany to areas beyond the North Sea and posited by the Admiralty in 1906.[71] Initially, they demanded few resources of the Navy beyond employing a number of small, older warships already on station.[72] As such, the decision to execute did not rise to the War Council for consideration. Meanwhile, other serials were debated by that body such as a combined operation against Zeebrugge, a landing at Borkum and an assault on Alexandretta, but were referred to the Admiralty or the War Office for further

---

67 TNA, CAB 42/1, War Council minutes of 5 and 6 August 1914.
68 'Court Circular,' *The Times*, 7 August 1914, p. 9.
69 TNA, FO 800/48, General Officer Commanding, Egypt to War Office signal of 19 August 1914.
70 TNA, CAB 42/1, War Council minutes of 5 and 6 August and 25 November 1914.
71 TNA, CAB 24/2, 'The General View of the War,' Hankey to War Committee memorandum of 31 October 1916.
72 Ibid, 'Summary of Naval Situation,' First Sea Lord (Jackson) memorandum of 8 February 1916.

investigation given the size, complexity and likely cost.[73] For those attacks sanctioned, such as the one against Dar es Salaam, the conclusion must be they went forward because they were viewed as easy to accomplish and not apt to demand much more in the way of resources. This was a mistake for militarily the Admiralty, the War Office and India would yet have to up the ante of support. In the case of the Navy, to meet the expanding scope of operations as initial objectives were met in the case of Mesopotamia and West Africa; for the War Office and India, to secure what had been ordained but not yet realized in East Africa. Moreover, fresh commitments would follow including a naval demonstration in the Dardanelles that soon expanded into a major combined operation when its assumptions of quick victory proved false.

These operations demanded much of India. It was one thing to conduct operations along the Northwest Frontier quite another to deploy forces where a sound infrastructure already existed such as in France and recourse to the sources of supply were near at hand. More difficult it remained to initiate and sustain campaigns where communications were poor, local support was minimal and climatic conditions governed the tempo of operations. It also remained that the administrative underpinnings of the Indian Army were not robust notwithstanding the groundwork laid since South Africa. Each contingency supported taxed the means available and operated against each other. It was for this reason the Indian Government sought to eschew sending additional forces to East Africa for it reduced the wherewithal to send to Basra in late 1914.[74] It was overruled. To these difficulties, a further remained: the expeditions were secondary operations and tangential to the greater strategy of the war which quickly devolved to meeting the German threat at its strongest point. Ironically, the greater the burden assumed by the British Army in France and Belgium, the more it fell to India to meet the needs of Britain's traditional maritime strategy. Curzon and those in his wake may have sought to escape such commitments, but previous experience and present reality argued otherwise.

In the accountings which followed in the wake of the twin disasters of the Mesopotamia and Dardanelles-Gallipoli campaigns critics fashioned on the trees and not the forest. Failings in command and control, transport, ammunition supply, and especially medical support received particular attention. The listings of failures were not wrong; they were, though, incomplete and of the second tier. The accountings failed to place the campaigns within the greater strategic context that gave rise to them and the machinery existing for managing the higher direction of war. This was fundamentally a political failing and it was a failing that Asquith and company were at pains to escape. As to why the War Council sanctioned so many concurrent out-of-theatre operations, the best explanation remains they believed the war would end in a negotiated settlement and not assume the proportions that it eventually did. This after all was the record of previous experience. Hence, German African colonies might

---

73   TNA, CAB 42/1, War Council minutes of 1 December 1914 and 7 and 8 January 1915.
74   TNA, CAB 19/26, 'Mesopotamia Report,' p. 11.

prove useful at a subsequent peace conference or so avowed Kitchener. To the extent Britain and India saw benefits in controlling Mesopotamia, concessions elsewhere to France might have to be the price paid. Better still if it was paid in German coin.[75]

The reforms introduced by Kitchener and pursued in opposition to Curzon have been cited as a major reason why the Indian Army faltered in the campaigns that followed during the World War.[76] Certainly, Lord Cromer held as much in July 1916.[77] That is to claim too much. The reforms may have only suited one man, but the failures experienced in Mesopotamia, East Africa or even those occurring in France owed more to decisions made in Whitehall than on the subcontinent. 'He that commands the sea is at great liberty and may take as much and as little of the war as he will,' or so avowed Francis Bacon.[78] Bacon was not wrong, but judgment is still required. Plans developed beforehand needed to be considered anew based on the situation actually arising, the forces available and the capabilities existing. This presumably was where Foreign Office input was desired, yet Sperling was an infrequent participant in the deliberations of the Combined Operations Committee attending only two of the first nine sessions and not making his first appearance until August 8. In 1914/15, operational difficulties were all too easily dismissed and those doing the dismissing were mainly found in London.

The changes that had been embarked upon were important in their own right intended to resolve systemic and institutional issues. Systems and institutions, however, rely on people and are typically the product of compromise. Rarely ideal, rarely do they remain so over time as circumstances change. What had been fashioned was better than what had preceded it; that it remained insufficient for war was mostly assumed. Aston, the thoughtful Marine writer on amphibious operations and instructor at Camberley held as much in 1907 and so too did Brigadier General Sir Henry Rawlinson, the late commandant of the Staff College at Camberley.[79] In truth, Asquith felt the same in 1912. The British Army was ill-prepared to fight the style, pace and breadth of war that became manifest in 1914/15. Even more was this the case with the Indian Army. The immediate problem was the lack of wherewithal to fight simultaneous campaigns with prewar financial stringency being the underlying reason. More fundamental, though, remained Britain's higher direction of war; until that was corrected further setbacks would follow.

75 TNA, CAB 24/1, 'Alexandretta and Mesopotamia,' Kitchener to CID memorandum of 16 March 1915.
76 TNA, CAB 19/26, 'Mesopotamia Report,' p. 100.
77 Rose, *Superior Person*, p. 365.
78 Bacon cited in W. D. Bird, *A Précis of Strategy* (London: Hugh Rees, Ltd., 1910), p. 52.
79 'Combined Strategy for Fleets and Armies,' *The Times*, 16 July 1907, p. 15.

5

Keeping the 'Highway to India' Open: The Indian Army and the Defence of the Suez Canal 1914-15

Adam Prime[1]

For Britain's strategic planners the defence of the Suez Canal had always been intrinsically linked to the defence of India. The canal across the Suez Isthmus was the fastest route to India and therefore the quickest way of communicating with the sub-continent as well as for transporting men and supplies in times of crisis. In 1914, with the British Expeditionary Force needing reinforcements in Northern Europe, the defence of the Suez Canal fell largely to the 10th and 11th Indian Divisions and the Indian Imperial Service Cavalry Brigade. These troops, alongside the territorial soldiers of the East Lancashire Division, were able to repulse an Ottoman attack against the canal. When writing about the defenders of the Suez Canal, as a prelude to the much more infamous events in the Gallipoli Peninsular, noted military writer and theorist Charles Callwell wrote 'the Indian troops being for the most part regulars were fully qualified to take part in serious military operations'.[2] The purpose of this chapter is to use the training, preparations, and acclimatisation of the Indian Army in Egypt to assess Callwell's statement and examine their operational performance to place the defence of the Suez Canal in the broader British strategy of the First World War.

Background

When it was opened in November 1869 the Suez Canal measured one hundred and two miles long and twenty-six feet deep, flowing through the larger Lake Timsah

---

1 The author would like to thank Nikolas Gardner and Steve Marti for their helpful comments during the drafting process.
2 Charles Callwell, *The Dardanelles* (Boston: Houghton Miflin, 1919) p. 28.

and Great Bitter Lake, with a series of bypasses to allow ships to pass each other. The purpose of the canal was to connect the Mediterranean Sea with the Red Sea; creating a shorter route for maritime communication, trade, and travel which would usually have to take the much longer sea route around the Cape of Good Hope. Developer, Frenchman Ferdinand de Lesseps, was the driving force behind the canal's creation. The concept of a canal across the Isthmus of Suez was nothing revolutionary, however. Ancient Egyptian Pharoahs, the Persian ruler Darius, and Roman Emperor Trajan had all attempted, some with limited success, to effect a canal across the Isthmus of Suez. The great early-modern traders, the Republic of Venice, gave thought to opening the canal again but they lacked the means with which to carry through the idea. King Louis XIV of France considered conquering Egypt and opening a canal; had Napoleon's military expedition to Egypt, 1798-1801, proved more successful he too would have attempted to install a new canal. Bonaparte toured the Isthmus of Suez in 1798, hiring an engineer, Le Pere, to carry out a detailed survey of the area. Le Pere's work would prove a vital guide for future surveyors.[3]

The French eviction from Egypt in 1801 saw the country descend into civil war. The ruling class had been virtually wiped out by the French; a power struggle ensued. Britain unsuccessfully intervened on the losing side and subsequently retreated from Egyptian internal affairs. Once the situation in Egypt settled a series of progressive rulers, or *Khedives* (Viceroys), were able to oversee modernising reforms. Agriculture, industry, and education were all updated. Unfortunately, in 1858, de Lesseps and his Universal Suez Ship Canal Company (USSCC) struck a deal with the then *Khedive* which eventually saw the country bankrupt. As Europeans profited from the canal Egypt suffered. Rather than bring Egypt wealth the Suez Canal brought the country rising international debt. Egypt was forced to sell its share of the canal to Britain. This payment only eased Egypt's troubles for a short time, by 1876 the country was bankrupt.[4]

Britain had been initially sceptical about investing in de Lessep's canal project. Whilst on an official visit to the isthmus in 1869, the Prince of Wales expressed his disappointment in Lord Palmerstone's government for not supporting the initiative given its importance to communication with India. Six years later when passing through the completed canal the Prince would repeat his opinion and state that the Suez Canal was the 'highway to India'.[5] Britain's late interest in the canal was to benefit them immensely; purchasing Egypt's shares in the canal gave the government a majority share. Bankruptcy saw the European powers take control of Egypt's finances. This loss of independence proved unpopular. The country had spent the 19th century moving themselves away from the Ottoman Empire, although they were still

---

3   R E B Duff, *100 Years of the Suez Canal* (Brighton: Clifton Books, 1969) pp. 9-11.
4   Ibid. pp. 11-13, 114-5.
5   Lord Kinross, *Between Two Seas, The Creation of the Suez Canal* (London: John Murray, 1969) pp. 233-4.

nominally a part of it. Riots ensued. In 1881, Colonel Ahmed Urabi headed a revolt which aimed to overthrow the *Khedive* and remove all foreign influence from the country.

In May 1882, an Anglo-French fleet was dispatched and anchored threateningly in the harbour of Alexandria. Urabi was not deterred and began to fortify the waterfront. Rioting in Alexandria in June saw fifty Europeans killed; this prompted the British to take action. The French withdrew at the last minute but the Royal Navy bombarded Alexandria and landed an army, seizing the town. In Whitehall Gladstone's cabinet decided to send an army and put an end to Urabi's 'Egypt for Egyptians'. The British campaign that followed was short, efficient, and successful. General Sir Garnet Wolseley quickly seized the Suez Canal, landed his force, and defeated Urabi at Tel-el-Kabir. The war was ended less than two months after the decision had been taken in London to dispatch an army.[6]

Taking control of Egypt brought with it the problem of controlling the Sudan too. Egypt had invaded and exercised haphazard control of the Sudan since 1822. Whilst the Egyptians had been focused on their own country an Islamic leader calling himself the *Mahdi* (Messiah) united the tribes of the Sudan and began to take control of the country west of the Nile. The *Mahdi's* influence continued to spread and London ordered the authorities in Egypt to evacuate the Sudan. General Charles 'Chinese' Gordon, tasked with overseeing the withdrawal, was besieged at Khartoum by the *Mahdi's* forces in March 1884. A relief column under Wolseley reached Khartoum on 28 January 1885, two days after the *Mahdi's* forces had stormed Khartoum and slayed Gordon.[7] It was during the attempts to relieve Khartoum that Horatio Herbert Kitchener first came to prominence. Kitchener acted as intelligence officer for the relief column and was featured in many leading newspapers for his heroics ahead of the main force disguised as an Arab. Kitchener subsequently had several roles within the Egyptian Army, becoming *Sirdar* (Commander-in-Chief) in 1892. In this role he oversaw the reform of the Egyptian Army into a much more efficient, and modern, fighting force; a process he would attempt to imitate in India. Kitchener's main goal in Egypt was the avenge Gordon and reclaim the Sudan. In 1896 Kitchener got his wish. Kitchener's force swept through Sudan; his most famous victory came outside Khartoum at the Battle of Omdurman in September 1898. Kitchener went on to serve as Governor General of the Sudan until 1899 and Commander-in-Chief of the Indian Army between 1902 and 1909.[8]

---

6   Byron Farwell, *Queen Victoria's Little War* (London: Allen Lane, 1973) pp. 253-68; Dominic Green, *Three Empires on the Nile: The Victorian Jihad, 1869-1899* (New York: Free Press, 2007) 120-2.
7   Edward M. Spiers, *The Late Victorian Army 1868-1902* (Manchester: Manchester University Press, 1992) pp. 183-4; Farwell, *Queen Victoria's Little Wars* pp. 287-94.
8   George Morton-Jack, *The Indian Army on the Western Front, India's Expeditionary Force to France and Belgium in the First World War* (Cambridge: Cambridge University Press,

The significance of the Suez Canal would not have been lost on the British officers of the Indian Army. Whether heading out to India for the first time or heading to and from Britain on leave their transports would have travelled along the canal. More often than not stopping at Port Said along the way.

The Suez Canal in British Strategy

In the last decade of the 19th and first decade of the 20th centuries the defence of Egypt was planned in the event of war with France or Russia. It was calculated that there would be an interval of four days between a declaration of war and the arrival of an invading army. The British aim would be to hold Alexandria for as long as was practicable then retreat to Cairo. To meet such a threat the British kept a garrison of little over 4,000 troops in Egypt, along with 13,000 combatants of the Egyptian Army.[9]

From 1906 the prospect of war with the Ottomans began to be considered thoroughly by the Committee of Imperial Defence. This included the defence of the Suez Canal and also the possibility of a move against the Dardanelles. As part of these considerations, the then Colonel, Charles Callwell undertook an assessment of the forces and defences of Egypt. Callwell concluded that with repairs to the railways of Syria an attack from the East was a distinct possibility. Callwell recommended the acceleration of an increase in troops in Egypt as the present garrison would not have been able to concentrate its force in any meaningful number.[10] Though this recommendation was not taken up, the situation continued to be monitored. In 1910 a series of hypotheticals were considered including the cancellation of an attack against the Dardanelles, the local Senussi tribesmen taking up arms against the British, and internal unrest in both Egypt and the Sudan. In this instance, forward units would attempt to delay the Turkish advance, allowing reinforcements and naval support to take up position along the canal.[11] Reinforcements were always intended to come from Britain and South Africa, not India.

For Kitchener it was always important that his spiritual home, Egypt, should be well defended in order to safeguard Britain's prize possession, India. At a conference in 1902 he suggested raising four new Sudanese battalions under British officers to add to the force defending the Canal should a war break out. Kitchener was keen to see the canal more strongly defended so that lines to India could be kept open.

2014) pp. 48-9; George H. Cassar, *Kitchener's War, British Strategy from 1914 to 1916* (Washington DC: Potomac, 2004) pp. 2-14.

9   The National Archives (TNA) WO 106/42 Proposed Force available for service in Egypt, and time required to despatch re-inforcements from England and South Africa (C2/3); John Gooch, *The Plans of War, The General Staff and British Military Strategy c. 1900-1916* (London: Routledge, 1974) pp. 238-40.

10 TNA WO 106/42 Conclusion reached in the event of a war with Turkey (C3/21 B).

11 TNA WO 106/42 Defence of the Suez Canal - G.O.C. Egypt (C3/11).

Kitchener, who became Secretary of State for War at the commencement of hostilities, and others with experience of India and the Middle East feared Ottoman entry into the war despite not considering them a military or naval threat. He feared a Turkish declaration of war would stir up pan-Islamic sentiment. Kitchener was almost certain one of the Ottoman's first moves would be to cross the Sinai and attempt to take the Suez Canal.[12]

On 9 August 1914 orders were received from the War Office that two infantry divisions and a cavalry brigade were to be dispatched from India to Egypt. The purpose of these Indian units was to relieve the British units in Egypt, freeing them up for a return to Britain and then service in France. Just nine days later new orders were received. The two Indian infantry divisions were to go straight to Marseilles without disembarking in Egypt. It was felt politically astute to send Indian units to France as soon as possible in line with the strategic need as well as a symbol of the high esteem Indian soldiers were held in by their British overlords. It was hoped such a move would boost Indian support for the war effort. The British garrison was still to be relieved but by a territorial division. The commander in Egypt at this time was Major General Julian Byng. Byng was recalled to Britain and replaced by Sir John Maxwell. Maxwell had spent the majority of his military career in Egypt since 1882, commanding the British forces there between 1908 and 1912, he was very well acquainted with all aspects of the country.[13]

The Ottomans had not initially envisaged a multifront war involving Britain. For their allies in Berlin however, cutting British communications with India was of great importance. To strike at the British in Egypt, and cut their communications with Asia and Oceania, a new army, the Fourth, was created and based at Damascus. Djemal Pasha, Minister of the Navy and one of the ruling triumvirate, was nominated to take command of the Fourth Army and lead the offensive. Djemal arrived in Damascus on 18th November 1914 but it would take time for the army to be organised and for the Syrian road and rail systems to be improved.[14] This build-up was not helped by the actions of the British cruiser HMS *Doris*. Under Captain Frank Larkin the *Doris* spent December, 1914, and January, 1915, interdicting Ottoman supplies and communications. Telegraphs, railway tracks, bridges, and locomotives were all destroyed either by the *Doris'* guns or by landing parties.[15]

12　Cassar, *Kitchener's War* pp. 44-5; Gooch, *The Plans of War* pp. 244-5.
13　Lt-General Sir George MacMunn and Captain Cyril Falls, *Military Operations Egypt & Palestine, Front the Outbreak of War with Germany to June 1917* (London; His Majesty's Stationery Office, 1928) pp. 12-3; India Office Records (IOR)/L/MIL/17/5/1618 Private correspondence between General Sir Beauchamp Duff and Earl Kitchener. Simla: GSI, 1916.
14　Michael A. Reynolds, *Shattering Empires: The Clash and Collapse of the Ottoman and Russian Empires, 1908-1918* (Cambridge: Cambridge University Press, 2011) p. 127.
15　Edward J. Erickson, 'Captain Larkin and the Turks: The Strategic Impact of the Operations of *HMS Doris* in Early 1915' in *Middle Eastern Studies Vol. 46, No. 1* (January

Djemal faced difficulties raising this new Fourth Army. The Ottomans had unsuccessfully launched an attack against the Russians at Sarikamish, in the Caucasus Region. This offensive, led by Enver Pasha another of the ruling triumvirate, was an abject failure. Men were needed to reinforce this front and were also needed to protect Istanbul and the Bosphorus Strait. Djemal had to cobble together a force of regular soldiers from the Arab provinces and supplemented with irregular troops such as Bedouin tribesmen. Djemal had 50,000 men at his disposal but 20,000 of these were required to remain garrisoning the Arab provinces. Another 5,000 to 10,000 men would have to be kept as a reserve. Djemal could attack the Suez Canal with no more than 25,000 men. Facing this relatively small Fourth Army of Djemal's was 50,000 British-Indian troops, a number of warships, and the not inconsiderable obstacle of the canal itself. Djemal's plan relied on two important but unlikely events. Firstly, Djemal hoped to take a small section of the canal by catching the British by surprise. Secondly, Djemal hoped that this success would encourage the people of Egypt to rise up against the British. Djemal overestimated the Egyptian sympathies for the Turks, their former masters.[16] Djemal's plan may have been over optimistic but it was fully supported by Berlin. The Suez Canal was not the sole means of transportation for troops and supplies from India, Australia or New Zealand, but any attack against the canal would at least slow the British imperial chain of supply. If Djemal could achieve his objective of surprise and take a portion of the canal even for only two or three days it would enable the Turks to sink a number of ships in the canal, blocking it.[17]

On 19 September the 3rd (Lahore) Division sailed from Alexandria to Marseilles. It had arrived in Egypt on the 8th September, given that it was quiet in Egypt Maxwell had allowed the division to continue its journey to Europe as per the War Office's request. The 9th (Sirhind) Brigade was left behind, however, and sent to guard the canal. Soon after the territorial East Lancashire Division also arrived in Egypt. In early October Kitchener began to press Maxwell for the dispatch of the Sirhind Brigade to France also. The Sirhind Brigade were the only fully trained soldiers presently in Egypt. This concerned Maxwell. Reports were being received from across the Sinai of repairs being made to roads in Gaza and German officers being sighted at frontier posts. Maxwell was permitted to retain the Sirhind Brigade until the 22nd (Lucknow)

2010) pp. 151-5.
16 Eugene Rogan, *The Fall of the Ottomans, The Great War in the Middle East, 1914-1920* (London: Allen Lane, 2015) pp. 115-6; MacMunn & Falls, *Military Operations Egypt & Palestine* p. 36.
17 Rogan, *The Fall of the Ottomans* p. 116; MacMunn & Falls, *Military Operations Egypt & Palestine* pp. 35-6.

Brigade arrived from India to replace them.[18] Maxwell was also made aware that the East Lancashire Division's training and acclimatisation was progressing well.[19]

The Turks declared war on 28 October 1914. The East Lancashire Division was paraded through the streets of Cairo to impress the inhabitants. A number of prominent Ottoman subjects who were regarded as dangerous were arrested. Martial law was declared in Egypt on 2 November. In December the absent *Khedive* was replaced by his nephew and Egypt was proclaimed a British protectorate; the *Khedive* was known to be pro-Turkish, and had been in Turkey when war was declared, a fortunate occurrence for the British. The Ottoman Sultan, recognised as the spiritual head of the global Muslim community, declared a Holy War on Britain and France hoping to encourage Muslims in Africa and Asia to rise up against their colonial masters. The Sultan's call fell flat. Though at the time this declaration caused great concern both in Egypt and India.[20] On 16 November the Indian troops allocated for the defence of the Suez Canal arrived in the canal itself from India. With them arrived Major General Alexander Wilson, who was named General Officer Commanding (GOC) Canal Defence by Maxwell. The arrival of these troops had been held up by the activities of the SMS *Emden* which had been active in the India Ocean, even bombarding Madras in September 1914, before running aground at the Cocos Islands.[21]

For a number of the officers of the Indian Army being posted to Egypt was a bitter disappointment. Captain H.V. Gell of the 69th Punjabis is one such example. As reservists re-enlisted, officers were recalled from leave, and orders came to draw warm clothes Gell felt his battalion were earmarked for France. As they set sail from Karachi in early November 1914 the general impression was still that the battalion, as part of 29th Indian Brigade, were headed for France. Such was the impression that 29th Brigade's commander, Brigadier General Cox, ordered his officers to lecture their men on German fighting methods and how to meet them, along with others on protection from aircraft, night attacks, and fire discipline. The 29th Brigade made a detour. The brigade took part in a combined operation against Turkish artillery positions at Sheikh Syed, which threatened British held Perim in the Strait of Mandeb. HMS *Duke of Edinburgh* shelled two Turkish held forts whilst men of the 69th and 89th Punjabis and 14th Sikhs landed and destroyed what the cruiser could not hit. Gell was delighted to have seen his first action but hoped this did not affect his chances of going to France. Even as they disembarked at Suez on 16 November he hoped to get to France should the Ottomans not attack the canal. By January 1915

---

18   The Sirhind Brigade joined the 3rd Lahore Division in France on 9 December 1914. Its replacement the 22nd Lucknow Brigade was from the 8th Lucknow Division. The 8th Division spent the Great War on internal security duties with the exception of the 22nd Brigade which was sent to Egypt, eventually being incorporated in 11th Division, and the 8th Lucknow Cavalry Brigade which was sent to the Western Front.
19   MacMunn & Falls, *Military Operations Egypt & Palestine* pp. 14-5.
20   Ibid. pp. 15-8.
21   Ibid. pp. 19-20.

the reality of his situation had dawned on Gell. He bitterly wrote in his diary: 'I quite believe that the German officers who are bringing them [the Turks] know quite well it is a forlorn hope.' Gell appreciated that for the Germans keeping men away from the Western Front was imperative and he was disappointed to have been caught up in this strategy.[22]

The opening shots of the war in Egypt came on 17 November 1914. A detachment of the Bikaner Camel Corps were patrolling near Bir-el-Nuss. As the men bedded down for the night they were attacked by a group of Arab horsemen. The sentry fired his rifle to warn the sleeping cameleers of the impending attack but the Arabs managed to carry off a small number of the detachment; some of which managed to escape and returned to Kantara on foot. Three days later on 20 November a second detachment of the Bikaner Camel Corps, under a Captain Chope of the 2nd Gurkhas, were attacked again by Arabs. As Chope readied his men to face an estimated 100 Arab horsemen in front of him he realised that a similar number were massing behind him to envelope his detachment. Chope managed to get his men from between the two groups of horsemen and make it to higher ground under heavy fire. Upon reaching the higher ground the Bikaners regrouped and returned fire for around five minutes before retreating to the main road to Kantara. Once the cameleers had reached the road the Arab advance faltered and they resorted to long range sniping. The Camel Corps was accompanied by Sudanese cameleers of the Egyptian Coastguard but appear to have allowed themselves be taken prisoner by the Arabs without resisting.[23]

Chope received the Distinguished Service Order for the action; Sepoys Ali Khan and Faiz Ali Khan received the Indian Order of Merit and Indian Distinguished Service Medal respectively. The Official History states that Chope had 20 men with him whilst his own report states he had 44. One Indian Officer and twelve other ranks were killed during the skirmish, three sepoys were wounded. This would suggest Chope's own figure is more accurate as to accept MacMunn and Falls' figure would mean accepting by the end of the skirmish the Arabs allowed the cameleers to withdraw despite having just four able bodied men. The instance was taken by GOC Alexander Wilson to highlight the unreliability of the Egyptian Coastguard against their co-religionists. The Coastguard had been officered by British officers prior to the War but these had been transferred elsewhere to meet shortages. The Egyptian officers who replaced them had neither the training nor the experience to do so.[24]

22 Imperial War Museum (IWM) 10048, Private Papers of Lieutenant Colonel H V Gell.
23 IOR/L/MIL/17/5/3897, War diary, Army Headquarters India, Indian Expeditionary Force 'E'/'E' & 'G'/Egypt. GSI, 1914-19. 45 vols: Vol 5, February 1915.
24 Ibid.; MacMunn & Falls, *Military Operations Egypt and Palestine* p. 20.

The Indian Army to 1914

Indian troops had been involved in Wolseley's campaign of 1882 and also his ill-fated relief of Khartoum. Seven Indian regiments were present at the Battle of Tel-el-Kabir and a cavalry regiment and an infantry brigade were part of Wolseley's 1884 relief force. Service outside of India, particularly as far West as North Africa, was not a regular experience for Indian soldiers, however. Throughout the nineteenth and early twentieth centuries the Army of India's main defensive concern was the hilly country of the North West Frontier which presented unique military challenges. In his seminal work *Small Wars*, the aforementioned Charles Callwell observed: 'hill warfare may fairly be said to constitute a special branch of military art'.[25] As such there was no formal learning process for the men who defended the frontier; knowledge of how to fight on the frontier was simply 'passed on'. Firstly, the ways and means of hill warfare were passed on and learnt 'on the job' during periods of fighting against the local tribesmen who inhabited the frontier. Alternatively, when there was a lull in the fighting, mock battles would be arranged, one regiment would attack as if a native *lashkar* (war party) and another would defend using their usual tactics.[26]

Kitchener's arrival in India as Commander-in-Chief in 1902 saw a surge in reform. Kitchener felt he had to prepare the Army of India to face a potential Russia invasion through Afghanistan. The objective would be to keep the Russian advance at bay until British Army reinforcements could arrive. A regular war the Indian Army was ill prepared for. Kitchener began by renumbering the Indian regiments consecutively, disbanding those with the least efficient, and replacing them with new regiments raised in the more 'martial' north of the country. At Quetta, a Staff College was set up and run in a similar manner to Camberley. This Staff College helped the officers of the Indian Army absorb the lessons of the Boer War, in which only a few officers had been involved. From 1900 two new types of training manuals were produced. The first of these concerned regular warfare and was based mainly on the British experiences in South Africa. The second was for the North West Frontier and based largely on the Tirrah Campaign of 1897-8. With these new instructions distributed Kitchener was able to reform Indian Army training from the regiment level upwards. He introduced tests under active service conditions to assess a regiment's ability for war.[27] When Kitchener arrived in India, regiments were unevenly equipped and trained. The continually lingering spectre of 1857 meant that the authorities of the Raj had maintained a policy whereby potentially mutinous Indian troops were armed

---

25 Colonel C E Callwell, *Small Wars, A Tactical Textbook for Imperial Soldiers*. (London; Greenhill Books, 1990) p 286.
26 T R Moreman, *The Army in India and the Development of Frontier Warfare, 1849-1947* (Basingstoke; MacMillan, 1998) pp. 19-23.
27 Philip Mason, *A Matter of Honour, An Account of the Indian Army its Officers and Men* (London: Jonathan Cape, 1974) pp. 398-400; George Morton-Jack, *The Indian Army on the Western Front* pp. 67-9.

with inferior weaponry to their British counterparts. Upon Kitchener's arrival in 1902, the Indian Army were still issued with outdated Martini-Henry Rifles. These breech-loading weapons, used black powder, were accurate up to 1,500 yards and fired approximately twelve rounds per minute. In comparison British Army units were equipped with state of the art .303 Lee-Metford Rifles. The Lee-Metford was accurate up to 2,000 yards and used smokeless powder. Kitchener saw to it that Indian soldiers were also issued with the Lee-Metford.[28] All of these changes were designed to make the Indian Army a more effective fighting force as it had lagged behind its British counterpart. Kitchener's input certainly reinvigorated the Indian Army but the emphasis, both of training and planning, was always kept on the defence of the North West Frontier and the pacification of its unruly tribes.

Life in Egypt, 1914

The period between the German and Austro-Hungarian declarations of war and that of the Ottoman Empire saw Egypt used as a staging post for troops from India heading to France and Belgium. Captain Roly Grimshaw, of the Poona Horse, was on leave in England when war broke out. He was ordered back to India to retake his post. Grimshaw's regiment was earmarked for service in France and so he was able to meet them in Egypt. He spent around six weeks in Cairo before sailing for Marseilles with his squadron. Grimshaw found the August climate in Egypt to be similar to that of Bombay and Cairo to be much like Calcutta if the British aspect of Calcutta were substituted for French influences in Cairo. There was a social club and a sports club also, where Grimshaw played squash.[29] Social clubs played a large role in the social lives of Indian Army officers on the subcontinent. For the men who would defend the canal, the Suez Canal Company made every officer of the Egyptian Expeditionary Force an honorary member of their club in Ismailia.[30]

Whilst in Cairo, Grimshaw was able to visit the museums and see the ancient mummies on display; he found this exhibition of dead bodies distasteful. A couple of days later he visited the Pyramids and Sphinx. Grimshaw did not enjoy this visit either, describing the structures as dilapidating and claiming in his diary that the Ellora Caves in Northern India were a far better representation of 'our forefathers' skill and energy'.[31] In comparison, Private Norman Dunkerley, of 10th Battalion, Manchester Regiment, visited the Pyramids and Sphinx on several occasions. On his

---

28 Morton-Jack, *The Indian Army on the Western Front* pp. 66-7.
29 Col. J Wakefield and Lt. Col. J.M. Weippert (eds.) *Indian Cavalry Officer 1914-15, Captain Roly Grimshaw* (Tunbridge Wells: Costello, 1986) pp. 18-9.
30 TNA WO 95/4423, War Diary 32 Imperial Service Infantry Brigade Headquarters, 1914 October - 1915 September, Appendix A: Orders by General Watson.
31 Wakefield and Weippert (eds.) *Indian Cavalry Officer 1914-15* pp. 18-23.

second visit, Dunkerley was able to witness archaeologists at work excavating a nearby temple, much to his enjoyment.[32]

Indian soldiers may have seen action in Egypt in 1882 and 1898 but the First World War brought Indians and Egyptians into contact with each other on a scale never seen before in either nation's history. Indian soldiers not only mingled with local Egyptians but also with Indian soldiers of other castes or religions. When serving in India caste would be kept separate and officers would try to ensure all of their men's religious sensibilities were not offended. In Egypt, as in other parts of the world during active service, Indian soldiers had to abandon many of their religious and social values. One soldier, M.L. Tilhet, noted:

> 'There is no doubt that I had not practiced abstinence because I could not continue to remain hungry…In Egypt not only I but numbers of other Hindus – some of whom would, formerly, have rejected their food if only the shadow of a passer-by had fallen on it – have eaten from the hands of sweepers. Had we not done so there would have been no alternative but starvation, which could not be tolerated.'[33]

Religious sensibility may have had to be forsaken during the Indian Army's time in Egypt but the British and Indian authorities did ensure a good supply of traditional Indian ingredients for the sepoy's food. For instance in late January 1915, Wilson asked Commander-in-Chief of India, General Sir Beauchamp Duff, for an increase in the volume of dal, chillies, and ginger being sent from India. Wilson informed Duff that the monthly requirements of the forces in Egypt were 200,000lbs of dal, 8,500lbs of chillies, and 17,000lbs of ginger.[34]

Roly Grimshaw may have found the Egyptian climate very favourable in August but by December and January the Indian troops found themselves short of warm clothes such as mufflers, cardigans, shorts, and flannel pyjamas. The Indian units in France had sailed without these same items and a charity, the Indian Soldiers' Fund, had been set up in Britain to raise money in order to send these items across the Channel to France and Belgium. Whilst the Egyptian winter was mild in comparison to that of Northern Europe the temperature dropped significantly at night. H V Gell recorded in his diary the weather being 'beastly cold at night' and having to

---

32 Tameside Local Studies & Archive Centre, MR4/17/305/2/1, Norman Dunkerley Papers, Letters and Correspondence. The author is much obliged to archivist Liam Hart for helping him access these papers.
33 David Omissi, *Indian Voices of the Great War, Soldiers' Letters, 1914-18* (Basinstoke: Palgrave MacMillan, 1999) p. 155; Mario M. Ruiz, 'Manly Spectacles and Imperial Soldiers in Wartime Egypt, 1914-19' in *Middle Eastern Studies* Vol. 45, No. 3, (May 2009) p. 355.
34 India Office Records IOR/L/MIL/17/5/3896 War Diary Army Headquarters India, IEF E Vol 4.

wear scarf and mittens.³⁵ The Secretary of State for India, the Earl of Crewe, and the Viceroy, Lord Hardinge, had to request that some of the supplies being sent by the Indian Soldiers' Fund be diverted to Egypt.³⁶ Arrangements were also made to have Surgeon General William Babtie and an assistant spend six weeks in Egypt to assess the medical needs of the forces there. Medical supplies came from both Britain and India. Three motorised ambulances were also supplied from Britain.³⁷ On the whole the Indian Army did not suffer from ill health whilst in Egypt. The history of the 1/5th Gurkhas notes that the health of the battalion was generally good during their stay. Dysentery or fever was rare. The only regular complaint the men had was that of lice. Though the battalion received steam disinfectors to remedy this shortly after the Turkish attack.³⁸

Sports were a very important part of Indian army life. Officers actively encouraged their men to partake. The most obvious benefit of sport in the military is the promotion of physical exercise. It also promoted aggression and masculinity, helped build *espirit de corps*, and inter-rank relations. The Indian units in Egypt were no different. Even as the Canal Defence Force began to prepare the defences the amusement of the troops was not neglected. A football tournament for the four Gurkha battalions in Egypt was organised in January 1915. The 1/5th Royal Gurkha Rifles defeated the 1/7th Gurkha Rifles in the final. Their reward was a trophy in the form of a bronze sphinx. This trophy would find its way to the 5th Gurkhas mess at Abbottabad.³⁹ The Gurkhas had regularly played football, and a variety of other sports, on cantonment in India. In 1907 the 2nd battalion of the 5th even went to trouble of extending its playing field to accommodate a football tournament.⁴⁰ The Gurkhas may have been serving outside of India and Afghanistan for the first time in their history but sport remaining a constant would have kept the feeling of upheaval to a minimum. Turkish scouts reported seeing officers and men playing football on the banks of the canal when the main body of the Turkish force was as close as fifteen miles away.⁴¹

The effort put into providing the sepoys with traditional Indian ingredients, maintaining hygiene standards, supplying warm clothing, and encouraging sport served to maintain the morale of the Indian troops in Egypt. High morale may account for the soldiers' willingness to forego their usual dietary habits. In comparison the Mesopotamia Campaign, which required a more complex logistical system, saw the supply of the appropriate food and clothing diminish as forces headed further

---

35 IWM 10048, Private Papers of Lieutenant Colonel H V Gell.
36 IOR/L/MIL/17/5/3896, War diary, Army Headquarters India, Indian Expeditionary Force 'E'/'E' & 'G'/Egypt. GSI, 1914-19. 45 vols: Vol 4, January 1915.
37 Ibid.
38 Col. H.E. Weekes, *History of the 5th Royal Gurkha Rifles (Frontier Force) 1858 to 1928* (Uckfield: Naval & Military Press, 2003) p. 207.
39 Ibid. pp. 207-8.
40 Ibid. pp. 120-1.
41 Liman von Sanders, *Five Years in Turkey* (London: Bailliere, Tindall & Cox, 1928) p. 44.

inland. Lack of such supplies lead to a drop in morale amongst the Indian troops. The siege of Kut-al-Amara exasperated the situation. Goat was the Indian soldiers' main source of protein but when this ceased to be available Indian troops refused to eat horse flesh on religious grounds. As a result sepoys were malnourished and incapable of performing their duties.[42]

Being in close proximity to Turkey encouraged a small number of Muslim soldiers to desert and attempt to cross the Sinai. In late December four Khattak, Pashtun, men deserted. The first instance reported on the night of 23 December saw four Khattaks desert and though a search party was sent out the men were not found. Eight days later another four Khattaks attempted to desert. This time a cavalry search party had more success. All four men were picked up. A summary court martial found all four men guilty of desertion and sentenced them to death. The sentence was confirmed on three of the Khattaks, whilst the sentence of the fourth was commuted to penal servitude for life.[43] There were no further reports of desertion for at least the next two months. This suggests that the capture, trial, and execution of the second band of deserts served as an example to the Muslim soldiers in Egypt, discouraging further attempts to abscond. The use of example to quell indiscipline or desertion was commonplace within the Indian Army. Courts-martial would often dole out dismissals, demotions, flogging, and, in extreme cases, execution to a small number of soldiers in order to deter the rest from further action.

The Canal Defences

Turkey's entry into the war and the arrival of the 10th and 11th Indian Divisions provided stimulus for the improvement of the canal defences. The canal was a natural obstacle for any army to cross and so was used as the main defensive line. The main British defences were on the western, African, side of the canal with advanced outposts on the Asian side. The defences constructed were simple in comparison to those that would be constructed later in 1916. The purpose of the outposts on the eastern side was to protect a bridgehead so that if necessary troops could get across to the eastern side. These posts were dug into the ground and revetted with sandbags. The most elaborate outpost was at Ismailia which was to act as the main bridgehead in the event of a counterattack. Floating bridges were created using the boats of the Suez Canal Company to further aid crossing the canal. On the western bank trenches were dug. Where possible portions of the desert were flooded to prevent those areas coming under attack.[44] The Indian troops spent considerable time in December and January

---

42 Nikolas Gardner, *The Siege of Kut-al-Amara, at War in Mesopotamia, 1915-1916* (Bloomington: Indiana University Press, 2014) pp. 118-25.
43 IOR/L/MIL/17/5/3895, War diary, Army Headquarters India, Indian Expeditionary Force 'E'/'E' & 'G'/Egypt. GSI, 1914-19. 45 vols: Vol 3 15-31 December 1914.
44 Ibid. p. 25; Roger Parkinson, *The Auk: Auchinleck, Victor at Alamein* (London: Granada Publishing, 1977) pp. 17-8; Philip Warner, *Auchinleck, The Lonely Soldier* (Barnsley: Pen &

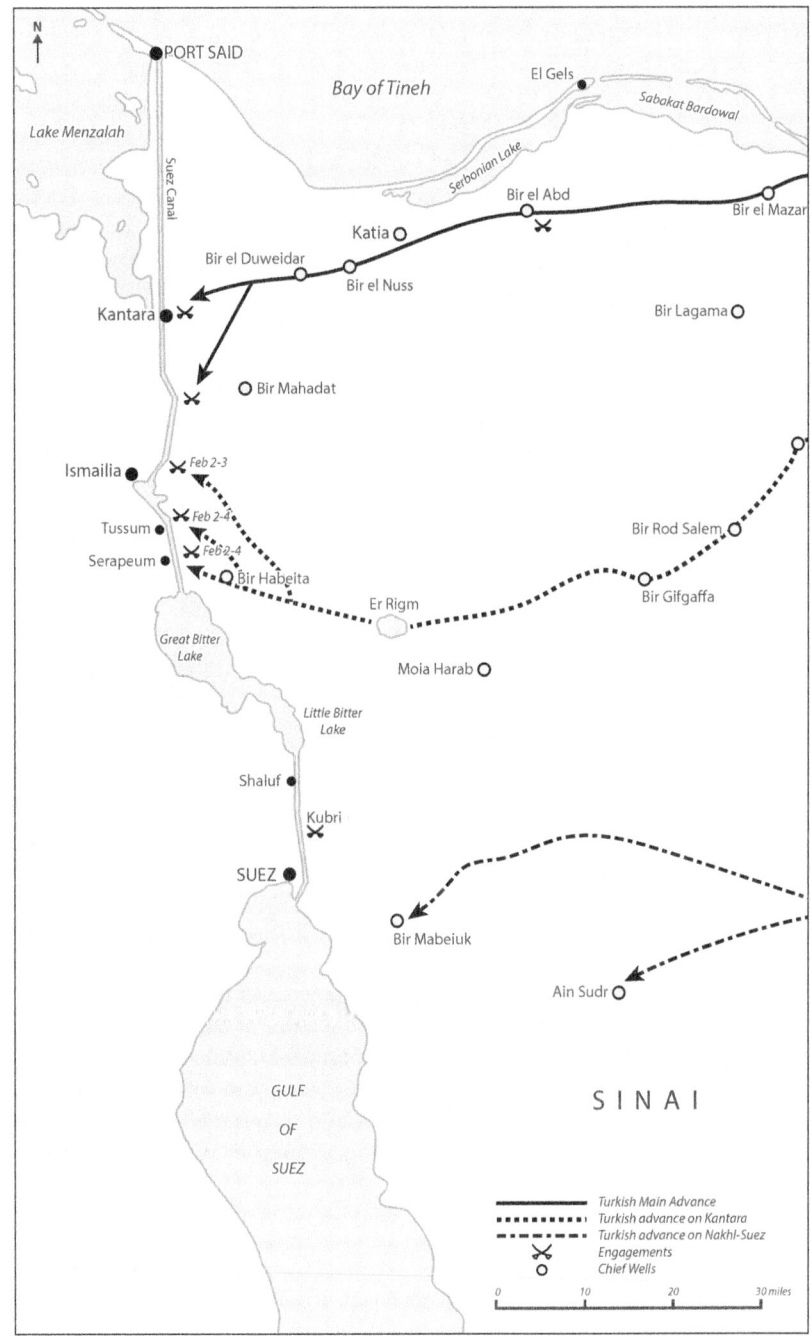

The Suez Canal 1914-15

digging trenches and strengthening earthworks. The war diary of the 93rd Burma Infantry for example, makes more references to working parties than training.[45]

The canal was divided into three sectors. The first of these was from Suez to the Bitter Lakes. The second sector ran from Deversoir, north of the Great Bitter Lake, to El Ferdan. The final zone was from El Ferdan to Port Said; the defences for sector included an armoured train. The headquarters for the Canal Defence Force was positioned at Ismailia. The Great and Little Bitter Lakes covered 22 miles of the 100 mile canal; Lake Timsah a further seven miles. These areas were the natural boundaries for the three sectors of the defensive sectors. Attacks against these lakes was highly impracticable and so the lakes were only lightly defended. The 10th and 11th Indian Divisions were given the responsibility of defending the canal. These divisions would usually contain at least one British Army battalion but this practice had been abandoned owing to the demand for trained battalions in Europe. The troops of the East Lancashire Division were left behind the lines to continue their training. The division's two artillery brigades were included in the defensive arrangements however. A pack-gun battery of the Egyptian Army was also included, they would be the only Egyptians involved in the defence of the Suez Canal. Australian and New Zealand troops were also left behind the lines to continue their training. In the event of an attack the East Lancashire Division, the Australian, and New Zealand contingents were to form a reserve.[46]

The Turkish attack on the canal was the first action for a man who would return to North Africa during the Second World War as Commander-in-Chief Middle East, Claude Auchinleck. The then Captain Auchinleck and his regiment, the 62nd Punjabis, were mobilised for overseas service on 28 October, the same day Turkey declared war, initially earmarked for France. In early November they were informed of their change of destination. The 62nd, part of 22nd Brigade, were to defend the Timsah-Bitter Lake section of the canal. It was this sector that was to repulse the main Turkish thrust. Transport complications meant that the 62nd did not arrive at their final defensive position until the 23 January 1915, just eleven days before the Turks launched their attack.[47]

Three Maurice Farman aircraft and three pilots were despatched from Britain to Egypt, upon the outbreak of war with Turkey, in order to assist in the event of an attack against the canal. One of these pilots, Captain S.D. Massy, was seconded from the 29th Punjabis as he had formerly been the commander of the Indian Central Flying School. From these humble beginnings would sprout the Middle East Brigade which went on to play a large role in the Mesopotamia and Palestine theatres. Further

---

Sword, 2006) pp. 22-3.
45 TNA, WO 95/4422 War Diary 31 Indian Infantry Brigade, 93 Battalion Burma Infantry, 1914 October - 1915 September.
46 MacMunn & Falls, *Military Operations Egypt and Palestine* pp. 22-4.
47 Parkinson, *The Auk* pp. 17-9.

aircraft were supplied from India minus engines, along with mechanics from the Indian Central Flying School. The pilots and engines for these craft were sent from Britain.[48] Demands elsewhere meant that the authorities in India could not despatch any further aircraft from India but one craft was sent to Egypt, gifted to the military by the Rajah of Rewa. The Rajah's plane was accompanied by Captain Reilly of the Indian Central Flying School as pilot.[49] These aircraft were able to survey the whole length of the canal at 4,000 feet. Reconnaissance of the Sinai itself was a little more difficult. From Ismailia, the portions of the Sinai opposite Port Said and Suez were some 50 miles away. This was over half of the flying time of a Maurice Farman. The RFC had to create a system of advanced landing grounds in the desert. This greatly extended the range of aerial scouting. Meanwhile French seaplanes were able to keep track of Ottoman forces building up in Beersheba. This aerial observation kept Maxwell and Wilson very well informed.[50]

When time allowed to prepare for an attack against the canal, just as they would prepare for action on the North West Frontier, the Indian units staged mock battles. For example on 17 January 1915 a field day was held by 11th Division. Two infantry battalions of 31st brigade and two squadrons of Imperial Service Cavalry made up White Force. Three battalions of 32nd Brigade and seven squadrons of Imperial Service Cavalry made up Khaki Force. White Force were to defend the canal from an attack by Khaki Force. White Force were successful. The mock battle was followed by a debrief.[51] Similarly, Brigadier General Cox, 29th Indian Brigade, tested the defensive scheme for Kantara by having the 14th Sikhs attack it whilst the remainder of his brigade defended the post. The War diary states that the defenders made a decisive counterattack.[52]

The Turkish Attack

By mid-January reports from the aerial reconnaissance began to report of a build-up of Turkish troops and activity in the Sinai. On the 21 January an advanced party of around 700 infantry and 200 cavalry was sighted by aircraft. This prompted Wilson to command that the main defences on the western bank of the canal to be manned a

---

48 Walter Raleigh, *The War in the Air: Being the Story of the part played in the Great War by the Royal Air Force, Vol.1* (Oxford: Clarendon Press, 1922) pp. 410-1; Stuart Hadaway, *Pyramids and Fleshpot, The Egyptian, Senussi and Eastern Mediterranean Campaigns, 1914-16* (Stroud: Spellmount, 2014) p. 58.
49 IOR/L/MIL/17/5/3896, War diary, Army Headquarters India, Indian Expeditionary Force 'E'/'E' & 'G'/Egypt. GSI, 1914-19. 45 vols: Vol 4, January 1915.
50 Hadaway, *Fleshpots and Pyramids* p 58; MacMunn & Falls, *Military Operations Egypt and Palestine* pp. 28-9.
51 TNA, WO 95/4422 War Diary 31 Infantry Brigade Headquarters, 1914 December - 1916 February.
52 TNA, WO 95/4422 War Diary 31 Indian Infantry Brigade, 93 Battalion Burma Infantry, 1914 October - 1915 September.

day later on the 22nd; this was done only by small detachments. It was decided that all troops should take up their positions on the 26 January when reports came in of Moiya Harab, 25 miles east of the Little Bitter Lake, being occupied by 6,000 Ottoman troops. Reports from elsewhere were received indicating that advanced parties had exchanged fire with the enemy. Reserves began to be brought up to the rear areas all along the canal. Royal Navy vessels HMS *Swiftsure, Clio, Minerva*, and *Ocean*, the Royal Indian Marine vessel *Hardinge*, and French ships *D'Entrecasteaux, Prosperine*, and *Requin* all took up places along the canal and its lakes along with other smaller craft. The canal was now closed each night and re-opened each morning.[53]

The Ottoman Army command was supplemented with a series of German officers, chief amongst these was General Liman von Sanders. Sanders had had misgivings about the Ottoman attack at Sarikamish, but his advice was not heeded by Enver Pasha. Sanders felt that the expedition against the Suez Canal was equally doomed to failure given the limited number of men available to Djemal for the offensive.[54] Djemal had a German staff of six officers at his disposal for the offensive, including, as his chief of staff, Colonel Freiherr Kress von Kressenstein. It was he who organised the expedition and should be credited with the successful transporting of the men and materials across the Sinai. Kress von Kressenstein was, according to the official history, the soul of the offensive. The Ottomans made their crossing of the desert in just seven days, moving only by night, and staying well clear of the coastline which was guarded by British and French ships. The largest problem for Kress von Kressenstein and his fellow German staff officers was keeping a good supply of water. This was left in the hands of German Major Fischer, who had a train of 5,000 camels carrying water. Fischer's task was helped by the fact that the season had been wetter than usual, leaving wells quite full. Through German efficiency and a stroke of luck there was never a shortage of water.[55]

Observations from the night of 30 January showed General Wilson where to expect the Turkish attack. The greatest build-up of troops was nine miles east of the canal at Bir Habeita, almost opposite Serapeum. For Wilson the Turkish intentions were obvious, they intended to attack the central sector of his canal defences.[56] The Turks began to make a number of probing attacks to gage the strength of the defences. They clashed with Indian patrols all along the front. These probes left the British command in some doubt as to which part of the central sector would have to bear the brunt of the Turkish attack.[57] As sophisticated as the RFC's aerial reconnaissance system was

---

53 MacMunn & Falls, *Military Operations Egypt and Palestine* pp. 29-30; Weekes, *History of the 5th Royal Gurkha Rifles* p. 209; TNA CAB 37/125/15 Defence of the Suez Canal. Narrative of events, January 25 to February 8, 1915.
54 Sanders, *Five Years in Turkey* pp. 37-44.
55 MacMunn & Falls, *Military Operations Egypt & Palestine* pp. 34-6; Sanders, *Five Years in Turkey* pp. 43-4.
56 MacMunn & Falls, *Military Operations Egypt and Palestine* p. 31.
57 Hadaway, *Pyramids and Fleshpots* p. 60.

it was of little use at night; the Turks had moved across the Sinai at night and were likely to move into position to attack at night, if not launch the attack itself under the cover of darkness. To remedy this dogs were left chained at intervals on the Asian side of the canal. These traditional guard dogs would bark at any approaching men.[58]

The central sector between the Great Bitter Lake and Lake Timsah was manned by 22nd Infantry Brigade, consisting of 62nd and 92nd Punjabis and 2/10th Gurkhas, with 2nd Queen Victoria's Own Rajputs also. Supporting them was four 15 pound field guns of the Lancashire territorials and four mountain guns of the Egyptian Artillery. On the east bank, two companies of the 92nd were stationed each at Tussum and Serapeum, and two companies of Gurkhas at Deversoir. On the west bank there was eleven posts of two platoons each; each of which had a frontage of six hundred yards. Sentries were set every two hundred yards.[59]

Djemal launched his attack after nightfall on the evening of 2 February. The advance of the Turks was held up by a strong and unexpected sandstorm. At around 3:25am, on 3 February, Punjabi sentries at Tussum could hear movement and voices to the south-east of their post. When loud chanting broke out Major T.R. Maclachlan, lead out a half platoon and a machine gun to the post and fired in the general direction of the vague figures and shouting. Fire was returned but the fighting petered out in the darkness. The chanting is likely to have been Arab soldiers undertaking a pre-battle ritual against orders.[60]

The Turks had carried or dragged on wheels a large number of boats with which they intended to cross the canal. These craft, made in Constantinople, were made of galvanised steel. They were twenty four feet long and five feet across. They could hold between twenty and thirty men. Pontoons had also been brought across the desert by the Turks but these were for use after the defenders had been forced back and the canal taken. These were found abandoned about a mile to the east of the canal.[61] As the sandstorm died away and clouds lifted, the moonlight revealed the Turkish forces. The Egyptian battery was placed on a high point on the west bank and was able to rain shells onto the now illuminated Turkish masses. The Turks had managed to launch a number of the steel boats across the canal. Three reached the western bank. One of these craft landed in vicinity of Auchinleck's 62nd Punjabis. He recalled 'our men charged down the bank and put a bayonet into them'. A number of the Turks were killed or captured. Around twenty of the crossing party hid under the west bank and were later rounded up by the Rajputs in daylight.[62] For the most part however,

---

58 Rogan, *The Fall of the Ottomans* p. 120.
59 MacMunn & Falls, *Military Operations Egypt and Palestine* pp. 38-9.
60 MacMunn & Falls, *Military Operations Egypt and Palestine* p. 39; Hadaway, *Pyramids and Fleshpots* p. 60.
61 TNA CAB 37/125/15 Defence of the Suez Canal. Narrative of events, January 25 to February 8, 1915.
62 MacMunn & Falls, *Military Operations Egypt and Palestine* p. 40; Warner, *Auchinleck* pp. 22-3.

these boats were destroyed in the crossing process. Torpedo Boat No. 043 and the *Mansoura*, an armoured tug boat commanded by a Lieutenant of the Royal Indian Marine, were despatched from Ismailia to attack the Turks as they punted across the canal. The official narrative notes that this was accomplished satisfactorily using gun fire and explosives.[63]

Morning light revealed the Turkish crossing party in disarray. Boats and pontoons abandoned. The men of the Ottoman 73rd and 75th Regiments, which had attempted the crossing, were scattered. Many were sheltered opposite Tussum in trenches on the eastern bank which had been abandoned by the Indians overnight. Several counter-attacks were launched by the 92nd Punjabis to clear these. Fighting continued until the afternoon. Eventually seven Ottoman officers and 280 other ranks were led away as prisoners. Confident that no attack was coming to the south of Serapeum, Brigadier General S. Geoghegan, commander of 22nd Brigade, collected men to cross the canal and advance up the east bank toward Tussum. He hoped to force the Turks to withdraw or push them onto the guns of the defenders at Tussum. This did not work out. Two platoons of Rajputs and two companies of the 92nd crossed the canal but were met by a strong contingent of Turks, supported by two batteries of artillery, with their own objective. This Ottoman force began to advance towards Serapeum. Their own advance checked, the Punjabis and Rajputs moved to face the Ottomans. Joined by six platoons of the 2/10th Gurkhas and supported by fire from the *Requin* and *D'Entrecasteaux* this small Indian force managed to hold the Turkish advance towards Serapeum about 1,200 yards from the canal.[64]

The Turks also made diversionary attacks but these were ineffectual. In the far south a half-hearted attack at El Kubri was easily forced back. At Ismailia, at the Northern end of Lake Timsah, an attack was made after first light but was held off with machine gun and small arms fire. RIMS *Hardinge* engaged in a long range artillery duel with an Ottoman howitzer battery. Fire initially fell short of the *Hardinge*, but eventually the Turkish artillerymen found their range. High explosive shells hit both of the *Hardinge's* funnels and another exploded on the foredeck causing casualties. The *Hardinge* had to make its way into Lake Timsah to avoid being sunk by the Ottoman heavy artillery. The *Reguin* moved up to fill the gap left by the *Hardinge*. The French ship ultimately silenced the howitzer battery. HMS *Clio* had a similar duel further north at El Ferdan.[65] These faint attacks were not made with enough vigour to fool Wilson into believing larger attacks were commencing elsewhere.

The use of naval vessels as artillery support would not have been a new concept to the Indian Army. During the Third Anglo-Burmese War a naval brigade, led by the

---

63 TNA CAB 37/125/15 Defence of the Suez Canal. Narrative of events, January 25 to February 8, 1915.
64 MacMunn & Falls, *Military Operations Egypt and Palestine* p. 41-2.
65 Ibid. p. 43; TNA, CAB 37/125/15 Defence of the Suez Canal. Narrative of events, January 25 to February 8, 1915.

armed steamers *Irradwady* and *Kathleen*, travelled up the Irrawady River in support of the infantry. The brigade knocked out a number of Burmese artillery batteries and forts on the river bank. The official report called this a 'unique campaign'. Just as on the Suez Canal in 1915, the brigade in 1885 was accompanied by torpedo boats to clear any obstacles in the river.[66] Though none of the battalions in 22nd Brigade, which took the brunt of Djemal's attack, had fought in the Third Anglo-Burmese War, a number of other battalions defending the canal had played some part in the conflict and the majority of regular officers of the Indian Army would have been aware of the campaign; it featured in an article published in the *Journal of the United Services Institute of India* for example.[67]

A small number of skirmishes took place during the night of 3 February but by morning light on 4 it was clear that the attack not only failed but been halted. Detachments of Indian troops were despatched to the Asian side of the canal to clear out the remaining Ottoman soldiers. A number of firefights ensued, but each time the Indians overcame the Turkish resistance, killing or capturing them. Imperial Service Cavalry followed the retreating Turks and there was a number of clashes with the Turkish rearguard. Wilson wisely decided against launching a large offensive against Djemal's retreating force. There was no convoy or transport system in place to get water and supplies across the Sinai for a counteroffensive to be effected. The RFC was able to bomb the retreating force, however.[68] With their characteristic thoroughness and efficiency Djemal's German Staff had provided for everything in advance. From prisoners taken during the attack the British intelligence staff were able to learn that the officers already had a hotel picked out in Cairo where they were to dine after a successful attack; some prisoners even suggested that the menu had been prepared.[69]

Conclusion

Callwell's assertion that the Indian soldiers defending the Suez Canal were wholly qualified to take part as they were trained regular soldiers is not strictly true. Pre-war regulars these men may have been but the Indian Army had no experience of fighting against regular soldiers, armed with rifles and artillery of similar calibre to their own. Most of the troops in Egypt had only experienced warfare on the North West Frontier. Some, such as Auchinleck and his unit, had no experience of battle. Considerable time was either lost through transport problems or given over to labouring on the earthwork defences. These regulars had to work with less experienced territorial and Egyptian artillery and were assisted by a patchwork air force, which was still a fledging military

---

66 TNA, ADM 127/17 The Burma War.
67 Brigadier-General Prothesoe, 'Burma 1885-87 (Military Operations)' in *Journal of the United Services Institute of India* Vol. XXI No. 100 (Simla; Cotton and Morris, 1892).
68 MacMunn & Falls, *Military Operations Egypt and Palestine* pp. 47-9.
69 G. Wyman-Bury, *Pan-Islam* (London: Macmillan, 1919) p. 27.

arm in 1915. As with other campaigns of the First World War the Indian Soldiers, who were used to their every religious and caste requirement being met, provided a stout defence of the Suez Canal despite having to abandon their spiritual and class sensibilities. Despite such handicaps and upheavals the men of 10th and 11th Indian Divisions applied their learning and development techniques, taken from the North West Frontier, with a successful outcome.

The Indian contribution to the war on the Western Front in 1914 and 1915 has been well documented and given much publication since the commemorations for the centenary of the Great War began in 2014. In France and Flanders in 1914 the soldiers of 3rd Meerut and 7th Lahore Divisions first saw action when they were required to plug a gap in the Allied line. In Egypt in late 1914 and early 1915 just such a gap appeared - a gap in the British imperial defensive line. The cause of which was the demand for men and resources to fight the Germans in Europe. Had Djemal's force managed to take a portion of the canal, even for a short period, it would have had a detrimental effect on the British Empire's war effort.

6

The Dark Shadow of the Dardanelles: Churchill's *World Crisis* and his Portrayal of the Indian Army at Gallipoli[1]

Cat Wilson

Winston Churchill's wife, Clementine, recalled how the disastrous Dardanelles campaign had affected him – it 'haunted him for the rest of his life'. Even though he had 'always believed' in the strategy, she thought he 'would never get over' it and might even 'die of grief'.[2] This 'sharpest' and 'deepest wound' certainly lingered.[3] Already a seasoned war correspondent and journalist, Churchill knew that writing about his part in the campaign (let alone the origins, course, and aftermath of the First World War), might alleviate not just the pain he clearly continued to feel, but the somewhat misplaced and excessive blame he encountered for the failure of the strategy to force British imperial and Allied troops through the Straits to Constantinople. A contract with the publishing house Thornton Butterworth, brokered by Churchill's representative (Andrew Dakers) at the literary agents Curtis Brown, was duly signed, and resulted in the five-volume work, *The World Crisis*.[4] Reviews ranged from 'an elastic strength of an enthralling narrative,' to the former Prime Minister Arthur J. Balfour's

---

1 The term Indian Army refers to the British-led Indian Army which comprised British officers, Indian VCOs (Viceroy Commissioned Officers), and Indian file.
2 Clementine Churchill to Martin Gilbert in Martin Gilbert, *Winston S. Churchill, Volume 3, 1914–1916* (London: Heinemann, 1971), p. 473.
3 Violet Bonham Carter, *Winston Churchill: As I Knew Him* (London: Eyre & Spottiswoode, 1965; Reprint Society Ltd, 1966), p. 407.
4 CHAR 8/38/37: Andrew H. Dakers (Director of Curtis Brown) to Winston Churchill, 1 November 1920; CHAR 8/38/39–41: Churchill to Messrs Curtis Brown confirming his official acceptance of them acting as his literary agents regarding his proposed memoirs of the First World War. Within little over a week, Thornton Butterworth, of the self-named publishing house, was writing to Churchill and claiming that 'if at any time' Churchill decided to 'write a new book' it would be a 'great favour if' Churchill would allow him 'the privilege of publishing it', CCAC CHAR 8/38/43: Thornton Butterworth to Churchill, 9

rather pithy, but no less relevant, quip that *The World Crisis* was little more than 'Winston's brilliant Autobiography, disguised as a history of the universe'.[5] Written as a vindication of his role in the planning and execution of the campaign, Churchill's undoubted skill as a writer helped to situate his version of events before the public and his peers. Although the Dardanelles Commission exonerated Churchill from total culpability for the campaign's failure, he nonetheless decided to commit to paper his reasoning for, and justification of, the campaign within his *World Crisis*.[6]

Of the 469,000 British and Commonwealth combatants (and non-combatants) who served in the Gallipoli campaign, the Indian force (both combatant and non-combatant) approximated 16,000.[7] The total losses of British and Commonwealth troops throughout the Dardanelles venture is staggering – 31,389 killed, 78,749 wounded and 9,708 missing.[8] Indian losses amounted to 900 killed or died, and 3137 wounded.[9] Historians who research the Indian Army frequently lament upon how the history of Indian troops under the *Raj*, particularly their role within the First and Second World Wars, has been side-lined or, worse still, ignored. With regards to the contribution that the Indian Army made to the Great War in France and Belgium, the tide has begun to turn. Although in no way as voluminous as the body of work on the battles of the Somme, Passchendaele, or even Mons, 'there now exists a sufficient corpus of secondary material' from which 'nuanced and sophisticated analyses' can be drawn.[10] The importance of such secondary sources should not be overlooked, as

November 1920. Winston S. Churchill, *The World Crisis, Volumes 1–5* (London: Thornton Butterworth, 1923–31).

5 J. L. Garvin, 'Winston and War, *The World Crisis*', *The Observer*, 6 March 1927; Balfour cited in David Reynolds, *In Command of History: Churchill Fighting and Writing the Second World War* (London: Allen Lane, 2004), p.5; referenced also by Peter Clarke, *Mr Churchill's Profession: The Statesman as Author and the Book That Defined the 'Special Relationship'* (London: Bloomsbury, 2012), p. xiv.

6 The Dardanelles Commission was set up in August 1916 to investigate the reasons behind the campaign's failure. Following an interim report (published on 9 March 1917), the Commission's final report concluded that 'from the outset the risks of failure…outweighed its chances of success', Tim Coates (series ed.), *Defeat at Gallipoli: The Dardanelles Part II, 1915–16* (London: Stationery Office, 2000), p. 287.

7 Figures extrapolated from Peter Stanley, *Die in Battle, Do Not Despair: The Indians on Gallipoli, 1915* (Solihull: Helion & Company Ltd, 2015), Appendix V, pp. 311–14.

8 L. A. Carlyon, *Gallipoli* (London: Doubleday, 2002), p. 531, put the total losses for the British (no distinction being made between British or Indian troops) at 73,485, including 21,255 dead. Ashley Ekins (ed.), *Gallipoli, A ridge too far* (Wollombi: Exisle Publishing, 2013; 2015 edition), p. 18, cites the same British total and also Indian losses total: 1,358 died, 3,421 wounded. See Stanley, *Die in Battle, Do Not Despair*, for a comprehensive assessment of 'strengths, reinforcements and losses' in Appendix V, pp. 311–14.

9 Stanley, *Die in Battle, Do Not Despair*, Appendix V, pp. 311–14. The Commonwealth War Graves Commission puts the figure at 1516 commemorated on the peninsula (Helles Memorial).

10 Chandar S. Sundaram, "Arriving in the Nick of Time': The Indian Corps in France, 1914–15', *Journal of Defence Studies*, 9/4 (2015), p. 73.

it is the comparative paucity of primary sources from the Indians themselves which, although understandable, sometimes makes for a limited study.[11]

This chapter focuses upon a hitherto under-researched and still little known episode of the Indian Army's role in the First World War – that in Gallipoli – an historical event that Churchill not only participated in, but also wrote about.[12] Furthermore, Churchill's complex relationship with India, the India Army, and his fervent belief in the British Empire (particularly the longevity of the *Raj*), make his portrayal of the Indian Army at Gallipoli even more nuanced. This chapter analyses Churchill's portrayal of the Indian Army's undertaking in the Dardanelles, particularly the challenging scramble for Sari Bair of August 1915, and explores the extent to which vindicating his own role in the Dardanelles campaign, as well as the far wider implication of the future security of the *Raj*, may have impacted upon his portrayal of the Indian Army.

With the Ottoman Empire aligning itself with Germany on 2 August 1914, there were far-reaching consequences for the Allies – other than the Dardanelles campaign – as the Ottoman-German alliance led to theatres of war opening up in Egypt, Palestine, Macedonia and Mesopotamia.[13] The British question of how best to defeat the Ottoman Empire was raised early on in the war.[14] Distracting Turkish forces, thereby enabling Russian forces to recover and then push back onto the German Eastern front, was thought to be central to Allied success on the Western Front. Maintaining British access to the Suez Canal was of paramount importance as it kept

11 See David Omissi, *Indian Voices of the Great War: Soldiers' Letters, 1914–18* (Basingstoke: Palgrave Macmillan, 1999). Apart from Omissi's work on Indian letters/censorship, there remains little evidence in the way of letters from sepoys to family and friends, and the associated replies, when compared to British soldiers in the trenches writing back home, because of a far lower rate of literacy amongst Indian soldiers.
12 The exceptions to this statement are Stanley, *Die in Battle, Do Not Despair*, and Rana Chhina 'Their mercenary calling: The Indian army on Gallipoli, 1915', in Ekins (ed.), *Gallipoli*, pp. 232–53. While the Australian and New Zealand Commonwealth troops have had their role in Gallipoli laid down not only in history, but also further-framed through the medium of film such as Peter Weir's *Gallipoli* (1981), other troops, not just those of the Indian units, have remained on the periphery – the role that French troops played has arguably not been given fair representation either.
13 The Ottoman Empire did not fully enter the war until 29 October 1914 when the Turkish fleet, under the German Admiral Souchon, bombarded the Russian-held port of Odessa. Russia could from then on, be supplied by the Allies only via Archangel or Vladivostok.
14 A full-scale naval attack on the Dardanelles, the objective being to push British forces through to Constantinople, had been considered since 1880 when a War Office report deemed that, if the element of surprise were not present, a successful outcome was not guaranteed. The plan was reviewed in 1904, again in 1906, and later still in 1911. At no time was it thought to be a plan which would yield a definitely successful outcome. As Admiral Sir John Fisher, the First Sea Lord who had been in charge of the 1904 review, would later relate to the Dardanelles Commission of Enquiry, the success of the outcome, 'even with military co-operation', was nothing less than 'mightily hazardous'. The National Archives, Kew, CAB 19/29.

open imperial troop movement with India, Australia and New Zealand, as well as the freedom to move troops to Egypt, Palestine, Macedonia and Mesopotamia. Of equal importance was the prospect of maintaining the oil supply from Persia – necessary for the newly commissioned oil-fired, rather than coal-fired, British Dreadnought battleships. By the end of 1914, the stalemate which occurred on the Western Front made such a plan even more attractive and necessary; not only to keep Britain's shipping-related vested interests secure, but also to help concentrate Allied success and strategy. For the British War Cabinet, the failure of the Dardanelles campaign highlighted the difference between expectation and achievable reality.[15] There was however, a wider implication and one that had the potential to impact on the stability of the *Raj*. Would fighting for a freedom which they themselves did not have, politicise the Indian Army? Would the Indian Army's loyal wartime service, be used by political India to secure their post-war expectation of Dominion status?

Churchill first entered the Commons in 1900 at the tender age of twenty six. His first profession however, was that of a writer which pre-dated his life in politics by several years.[16] Beginning as a war correspondent in 1895, he quickly became a prolific author and commentator.[17] By November 1920, when Curtis Brown agreed to act as the 'exclusive agents for the negotiation and sale of the publication rights throughout the world' for his *World Crisis*, Churchill had already earnt a considerable sum from his literary career.[18] Churchill was adamant that his work, originally planned as a two-volume set, would be 'a broad account of the war in its naval, military and

---

15 While the objective of the Dardanelles campaign was not achieved by the Allied forces, neither were the Ottoman attempts to comprehensively defeat them. There were some Allied successes (such as the action at Gully Ravine on 28 June), but the stalemate and the eventual evacuation of Allied troops in December 1915 led to the campaign being called an outright failure and the worst defeat Britain had ever suffered.
16 See Reynolds, *In Command of History*, and Clarke, *Mr Churchill's Profession*.
17 Churchill's literary career began when he became a war correspondent in Cuba in 1895; a year later he covered the Siege of Malakand in British India's North West Frontier Provence, and then the Boer War in South Africa. See Simon Read, *Winston Churchill Reporting: Adventures of a Young War Correspondent* (Philadelphia: Da Capo Press, 2015), and Frederick Woods (ed.), *Young Winston's Wars: The Original Despatches of Winston S. Churchill, War Correspondent, 1897–1900* (New York: Cooper, 1972). Churchill first experienced the power that historical writing held when he attempted to silence his late father's detractors by means of writing his biography: Winston S. Churchill, *Lord Randolph Churchill: Volumes 1–2* (London: Macmillan, 1906).
18 CHAR 8/38/37: Andrew H. Dakers (Director of Curtis Brown) to Churchill, 1 November 1920. Money was 'a prime motive' behind all of Churchill's literary works, and he 'probably made more in real terms than any non-fiction author in the twentieth century', Robert Blake, 'Winston Churchill as Historian', in Wm. Roger Louis (ed.), *Adventures with Britannia: Personalities, Politics and Culture in Britain* (Austin: University of Texas Press, 1996), p. 44. See also Martin Gilbert, *Churchill: The Power of Words* (London: Bantam, 2012), pp. vii–ix; and David Lough, *No More Champagne: Churchill and his Money* (London: Head of Zeus, 2015), pp. 49–76.

political aspects as viewed and experienced' by him.[19] He planned to adopt 'the style of personal narrative', and while his work was 'not intended to be a complete history', it would be 'a contribution to that history from the standpoint of one who was in a position to know in regard to every important matter what happened, how it happened and why it happened'.[20] In the first volume, which he claimed would be 'solidly supported by authentic documents and letters' throughout, Churchill proposed to detail the precipitating conditions for war as well as the outbreak of hostilities.[21] At the planning stage, in 1920, he intended to include 'the convoying of the troops and contingents from all parts of the British Empire and from India'.[22] The second volume would concern itself mainly with the Dardanelles, 'the genesis and story of which' would be 'most fully and searchingly described' from Churchill's point of view, and he would argue how the campaign could have been a success. His plans for the second volume intended to illustrate how his 'further efforts as a member of the Cabinet and War Council' were an attempt to 'carry' the Dardanelles to 'a successful conclusion'.[23]

The first Indian troops to land on Gallipoli, alongside the Anzacs on 25 April, were the 21st Kohat (Sikh) and the 26th Jacob's (Punjabi Muslim) Mountain Batteries – collectively known as the 7th Indian Mountain Artillery Brigade.[24] Three Indian Field Ambulance teams and the Indian Mule Cart Train proved to be vital elements on Gallipoli. The 29th Indian Infantry Brigade, of the 10th Indian Division, landed

19   CHAR 8/38/27: 'Strictly Confidential, Summary of Mr. Churchill's design and plans for the book', 18 Dec. 1920; see also CHAR 8/41/23: Thornton Butterworth reiterating original two–volume set outline to Churchill, 2 Feb. 1922; and CHAR 8/41/24–28: copy of 'Strictly Confidential, Summary of Mr. Churchill's design and plans for the book'. Churchill relied upon the services of several advisers when writing his *World Crisis*, such as Maurice Hankey (appointed Secretary to the War Cabinet in 1916); Lord Maxwell ['Max'] Beaverbrook (appointed Minister of Information in 1916); James Wycliffe Headlam (later Sir Headlam-Morley), a classicist and Government advisor, appointed as Churchill's 'historical advisor' (see CHAR 8/41/16: Tyrell to Churchill, 19 Jan. 1922); Brigadier General Sir James Edward Edmonds who, after a successful military career, became Officer in charge of Military Branch, Historical Section, Committee of Imperial Defence, 1919–49; and the ex-Commander-in-Chief Sir Douglas Haig (although Haig's role was more of a proof reader and commentator rather than an adviser in the strictest sense).
20   CHAR 8/38/29–30: 'Strictly Confidential, Summary of Mr. Churchill's design and plans for the book', 18 Dec. 1920. Churchill echoed this sentiment, that his writing was a 'contribution to history', in the preface to his memoir of the Second World War: Winston S. Churchill, *The Second World War: Volume 1, The Gathering Storm* (London: Cassell, 1948), p. vii.
21   CHAR 8/38/30: 'Strictly Confidential, Summary of Mr. Churchill's design and plans for the book', 18 Dec. 1920.
22   CHAR 8/38/28: 'Strictly Confidential, Summary of Mr. Churchill's design and plans for the book', 18 Dec. 1920.
23   CHAR 8/38/30: 'Strictly Confidential, Summary of Mr. Churchill's design and plans for the book', 18 Dec. 1920.
24   Stanley, *Die in Battle, Do Not Despair*, p. 47.

on Gallipoli on 30 April and 'held the left of the line at Helles', and after a brief period of respite and reorganisation at Imbros returned to Gallipoli.[25] While at Imbros reinforcements for the 29th were sought, and eventually two double companies of the Patiala Imperial Service Infantry arrived and became attached to the 14th King's Own Ferozepore Sikhs. After the 69th and 89th Punjabis had been packed off to Mesopotamia, they were replaced by the 1/5th and 2/10th Gurkha Rifles who fought alongside the 14th Sikhs, and the 1/6th Gurkha Rifles.[26]

The assault on Sari Bair ridge was to be made by a Right and a Left Assaulting Column. It commenced at night, on 6 August, under the command of Major General H.V. Cox, The Right Assaulting Column, which consisted of Francis Johnston's New Zealand Brigade and one battery of Indian mountain artillery, was to move out from Anzac Cove, turn inland, go up Rhododendron Spur and take Chunuk Bair. An intense and exhausting steep march covering approximately one and a half miles. The Left Assaulting Column consisted of John Monash's 4th Australian Brigade and the 29th Indian Brigade, along with the second Indian mountain artillery. With the 4th and 29th marching in echelon, their remit was to move out from Anzac Cove, hug the coast line for two miles and then turn inland. After a further two to three miles of marching inland, also along inhospitable terrain and hazardous inclines, the Left Assault Column would split: the 4th Australian were to take Koja Chemen Tepe (Hill 971), whereas the 29th Indian Infantry were to scale up to the central height of the Sari Bair ridge and take Hill Q. In capturing these three main points along the ridge (Chunuk Bair, Hill Q, and Koja Chemen Tepe), the 'Turkish forces to the south would be cut off, the Dardanelles forts taken from the rear and the campaign as good as won'.[27]

It was a potentially perilous trek – hampered by miscommunicated instructions, extreme geological and topographical difficulties (which exacerbated the confusion of command and prevented cohesive attacks) and, of course, enemy fire. Peter Stanley vividly describes the assault as one where 'men hauled themselves up by grabbling roots and bushes, gasping for breath in the heat, often under fire from Turks on adjacent hills'.[28] On 9 August, the 1/6th Gurkha Rifles (led by their CO, Major C.J.L. Allanson) almost achieved their objective – they got within 100 feet of the top of the ridge and, once the artillery bombardment had ceased, they took the crest of the

---

25 Charles Chenevix Trench, *The Indian Army and the King's Enemies, 1900–1947* (London: Thames and Hudson, 1988), p. 50. See also Chhina, 'Their mercenary calling', pp. 232–53.
26 See also Chhina, 'Their mercenary calling', pp. 234–5; 242–3. Chhina gives the clearest breakdown of the composition of the Indian troops (designated as the Indian Expeditionary Force (IEF) 'G') who fought in the August offensive, pp. 245–6.
27 Trench, *The Indian Army*, p. 54. A point which Chhina also makes, 'Their mercenary calling', p. 253.
28 Stanley, *Die in Battle, Do Not Despair*, p. 202.

ridge and advanced on the retreating Turks.[29] Despite his 'excitable and unreliable' nature, Allanson's words, albeit written after the event, relayed the disorganisation and confusion.[30] 'There was a feeling of panic', he wrote, 'and doubt in the air as to where we were and where we were going; it was a pitch black night'.[31] Irrespective of the chaos and uncertainty, and how 'blood was flying about like spray from a hairwash bottle', the 1/6th Gurkhas made a 'most perfect advance' on Hill Q. Allanson described himself as a 'very proud man', because the 'key to the whole peninsula war was ours'.[32] Within hours, the Turks counter-attacked and as Allanson's promised reinforcements failed to arrive, the ridge was lost to Turkish forces until the end of the war. Judged as a failure, the blame was not laid at the feet of the Indian troops, rather 'solely to the dislocation caused by the breakdown of a too ambitious scheme'.[33]

True to his word, Churchill highlighted how Britain's imperial troops answered the call to arms in August 1914. He first described how, alongside the six Regular Infantry divisions, the one Cavalry division, and the additional 7th and 8th Infantry divisions, it had been decided to further 'employ two divisions, half British and half native, from India'. Standing behind these trained forces (which Churchill defined as being 'unquestionably of a very high order'), were four Indian divisions that had set sail for Europe across the *Kala Pani* (the 'black waters' – the forbidden sea) and were disembarking in Marseilles.[34]

When narrating the April landings on Gallipoli, Churchill made no distinction between British and Indian soldiers. A strict word limit meant that he had neither

---

29 In the interest of parity it must be noted that men from the 6th South Lancashires and the 9th Warwickshires also fought alongside Allanson's 1/6th Gurkhas on their way to the summit of Hill Q.
30 Stanley, *Die in Battle, Do Not Despair*, p. 209. It was General Alexander Godley, William Birdwood and Cox who, writes Stanley, described Allanson as such. Allanson was adamant that he and the 1/6th Gurkha Rifles had come under friendly fire from British naval ships when on the ridge on 9 August. What now transpires is that it was a previously arranged, but either uncommunicated or miscommunicated attack made by New Zealand howitzers which revealed that both Cox and Allanson 'clearly did not know what the Allied fire plan was'. Chhina citing Major A.C. Temperley of the New Zealand Brigade as quoted in Tim Travers, *Gallipoli 1915* (Stroud: Tempus, 2002), p. 247.
31 Allanson cited in Trench, *The Indian Army*, p. 54.
32 Allanson cited in Trench, *The Indian Army*, p. 66.
33 Anonymous, War Diary, 1/5th Gurkhas, Aug. 1915, cited in Stanley, *Die in Battle, Do Not Despair*, p. 215.
34 Winston Churchill, *The World Crisis, Volume 1, 1911–1914* (London: Thornton-Butterworth, 1923; Folio Society, 2007), p. 231. For detail of their journeys, and the almost rapturous welcome from the French in Marseilles see: Shrabani Basu, *For King and Another Country: Indian Soldiers on the Western Front 1914–18* (New Delhi: Bloomsbury, 2015), pp. 31–37; Gordon Corrigan, *Sepoys in the Trenches: The Indian Corps on the Western Front 1914–1915* (Stroud: Spellmount, 2006), pp. 39–41; DeWitt C. Ellinwood, 'The Indian Soldier, The Indian Army and Change' in DeWitt C. Ellinwood and S. D. Pradhan (eds), *India and the First World War* (Columbia, Montana: South Asia Books, 1978), pp. 201–03.

the space nor time to narrate 'the feat of arms which signalized the day'– to do justice to the events, he explained, would entail 'each Beach' deserving a chapter, 'each battalion a page'.[35] He did, however, name the British 29th Division, the Australian and New Zealand Corps, the French troops landing near Troy as a diversionary tactic, the Royal Naval Division feigning a landing at Bulair, and, for parity, the Turkish divisions witnessing all of this.[36] Churchill's narrative of the 'Battle of the Beaches', the landings at 'V', 'W', 'X' and 'Y' beaches, is still a fluid, absorbing, and evocative account. He describes the actions of the Dublin and Munster Fusiliers, the Hampshire Regiment, the Lancashire Fusiliers, the Worcesters, the Royal Fusiliers, the Inniskillings and Border Regiments, and the opposing Turkish forces.[37] His account of the Anzac landings, half a mile north of Gaba Tepe, contained Churchill's first mention of the 'two batteries of Indian mounted artillery' who landed alongside their fellow imperial soldiers.[38]

Stylistically, Churchill favoured presenting counterfactual history, the 'what ifs..?' of history, and he used it to his advantage. One of his most earnest post-war concerns was with illustrating how the Dardanelles campaign could have been a success. Churchill was adamant that had 'two or three fresh divisions of French, British or Indian troops' been deployed after the initial landings, had these fresh divisions been made readily available on the 28th or 29th April, then the Turkish defence would have been broken and 'the decisive positions would have fallen into our hands'.[39] The first mention of the 29th Indian Brigade occurs in this context, and illustrates how, in Churchill's mind, these troops could have made the difference between pressing on with the campaign at this initial stage instead of the 'complete equipoise' between Turk and Allied invader occurring.[40] Towards the end of his 'Battle for the Beaches' chapter, the implication that lies in the language Churchill used reveals how he saw no separate distinction between British and Indian troops: 'all the available British reserves, including the Indian Brigade...had been thrown in and largely consumed after their opportunity had passed'. He may have viewed, as did many of his contemporaries, the British, Australian, New Zealand and Indian troops in a hierarchical manner, but the Indian troops were designated as part and parcel of the British forces.[41] It was the delay in

---

35 Winston Churchill, *The World Crisis, Volume 2, 1915* (London: Thornton Butterworth, 1923; Folio Society, 2007), p. 247.
36 Churchill, *The World Crisis, 1915*, p. 247.
37 Churchill, *The World Crisis, 1915*, pp. 248–51.
38 Churchill, *The World Crisis, 1915*, p. 252.
39 Churchill, *The World Crisis, 1915*, p. 255.
40 Churchill, *The World Crisis, 1915*, p. 255.
41 Churchill was not the only man to think in such terms. At a meeting of the War Council on 24 February, when the question of whether troops would be necessary to aid the naval bombardment and defeat of Turkish defences in the Dardanelles plan, Asquith questioned whether, if such troops could be made available, 'the Australian and New Zealanders 'were good enough' for an important operation of war' to which Kitchener replied 'that they were good enough if a cruise in the Sea of Marmara was all that was contemplated".

sending the Egyptian garrison troops, namely the Yeomanry and the 29th Indian Brigade, as soon as possible to Gallipoli, which meant that 'a long and costly struggle' would ensue and 'far greater efforts would…certainly be required'.[42]

Churchill referred to the Battle of Suvla Bay as a 'heart-breaking episode' where the 'only hope' for success lay in the 'devotion of the troops and the skill of their leaders'.[43] Describing the action to take the 'fateful summits of Sari Bair', he deemed it a 'great attack… by the two Australasian divisions, reinforced by the 13th New Army and one British and one Indian brigade'.[44] Until this point in his narrative, Indian troops had always been the last to be listed but this does not mean that he did this either deliberately or with malice; he was merely reflecting the British imperial normative view. Churchill viewed all native troops as inferior to British troops; he even viewed them as inferior to both the Australian and New Zealand soldiers whom he thought were, in turn, below the standard of the British troops. In his memoirs of the Second World War, he would go so far as to state that 'native' troops were to be mixed together 'so that one lot can be used to keep the other in discipline'.[45] There was a hierarchy of troops in Churchill's mind in the first two volumes of *The Second World War*, and without exception, Churchill intimated that Indian troops were not to be trusted.[46] When he was writing his memoirs of the Second World War, however, Churchill was grinding a different axe to that which he was sharpening by way of his *World Crisis*. In his *Second World War*, Churchill was securing his place in history, attempting to acquire a further tenure at 10 Downing Street, trying to fix Britain's position as one of the three most powerful forces (alongside America and Russia) in the post-war world, and, to some extent, lamenting the advent of Indian independence. Arguably, Churchill was well aware of the potentially fragile nature of 'political' India when he was writing his *World Crisis*. Being a so-called 'die-hard' imperialist (albeit an image which he used only when it suited his motives), he did not, in the case of his *World Crisis*, appear to allow his imperial prejudices influence his narrative of the achievements on the Indian army during the First World War.

In his narrative of the attempt to take Sari Bair, Churchill listed those troops who were to undertake the push for the top of the ridge: 'the line of Ghurkas [sic], British and Anzacs lay across the mountain slopes' waiting for the right conditions to

---

Martin Gilbert, 'Churchill and Gallipoli', in Jenny Macleod (ed.), *Gallipoli: Making History* (London: Cass, 2004), p. 35.
42 Churchill, *The World Crisis, 1915*, p. 256–7. Churchill referenced the argument between Lord Kitchener and Sir Ian Hamilton upon this very issue, see p. 339.
43 Churchill, *The World Crisis, 1915*, p. 341; 343.
44 Churchill, *The World Crisis, 1915*, p. 345; 343.
45 Winston S. Churchill, *The Second World War, Volume 3, The Grand Alliance* (London: Cassell, 1950), Churchill to Chief of Staff Committee, 17 Feb. 1941, in Appendix C, p. 653.
46 Churchill, *The Gathering Storm*; and *The Second World War, Volume 2, Their Finest Hour* (London: Cassell, 1949).

attack. He relied heavily upon Allanson's description of events, and emphasised how 'darkness, boulders, scrub and the enemy's outposts' made such an enterprise seemingly impossible.[47] Exhausted and ill-supplied troops who were not 'leap-frogged...by a wave of fresh reinforcements' was the 'cardinal fatality'.[48] Interspersing his brief account of the attack on Hill Q with the battle for Suvla Bay, allowed Churchill to build his case for his damning indictment as to why the venture failed.[49] Listing the catalogue of errors enabled Churchill to reach his almost inevitable conclusion, that it was not the troops who failed – 'it was not upon the Gallipoli Peninsula' that the battle of Suvla Bay and the attempt to take the Sari Bair ridge was lost – but it was 'the mistakes which were committed', not by himself, but by those 'in Downing Street and Whitehall' which meant that the Allied troops 'emerged unsuccessful'.[50]

In a writer's revisions not only are mistakes rectified, but also meaning and detail is cut or expanded upon – this being no less true of memoirists than of historians. In Churchill's case, the sheer volume of proof marked pages (for each of his written works) has left clear evidence of his many revisions, and the proofs for the chapter entitled 'The Battle of Suvla Bay' shed further light on his portrayal.[51] Originally positioned as the nineteenth chapter in Churchill's second volume, his account of the battle for Suvla Bay was ultimately arranged as Chapter 21. Such an occurrence was not rare for Churchill's work, and chapters were often juggled about to either incorporate more text, to allow for further research and select evidence to be inserted, or simply to enable his chronological tale to flow better. The sub-headings for the chapter changed little, especially when compared to other chapters, with only four differences between the proofed and published versions.[52] 'A Fatal Episode' was changed to 'A Fatal Mischance'. Had Churchill left the original 'episode' unchanged, his grinding axe – the claim that the failure of the Dardanelles campaign was due to 'the extremes of valiant skill and of incompetence, of effort and inertia' – would

---

47   Churchill, *The World Crisis, 1915*, p. 345.
48   Churchill, *The World Crisis, 1915*, p. 345.
49   Understandably brief due to the sheer size and scope which he wanted to achieve for his *World Crisis*.
50   Churchill, *The World Crisis, 1915*, p. 358.
51   CHAR 8 is the class of Churchill's literary papers which contains correspondence with publishers, editors, printers, researchers, historians and advisors connected with his literary work both and pre- and post-publication. Contained within this category of papers, which totals 823 sub-classes, are the notes, drafts, and page proofs of Churchill's literary outputs. The classes CHAR 8/44–265 deal with each volume of *The World Crisis* as well as business correspondence with Curtis Brown and Thornton Butterworth. Of equal value is the correspondence with the general public which has been carefully preserved as these reveal not just deference to Churchill the writer but also how he dealt with criticism and accommodated it as and when deemed necessary. CHAR 8/91/1–62: Literary: The World Crisis, Volume 2, 'The Battle for Suvla Bay' (1923).
52   CHAR 8/91/1: Sub-headings page for 'The Battle for Suvla Bay'.

possibly have been dulled.⁵³ Changing the rather benign word 'episode' to the more loaded 'mischance' had far more impact, and continued the tone of Churchill's argument. As 'Colonel Aspinall's Account' did not appear in the proofed version, it suggests that it was another instance of inserting anticipated research which had either not been made available to him at the time of proofing, or it had previously been placed elsewhere within the text. For Churchill's purpose, it had a greater impact in this arrangement. Correcting 'Action of the 15th and 21st' to 'Actions of the 15th and 21st' revealed Churchill's keen proof-reading eye. The fourth variation between the proofed and published version was also another instance where only one letter was added, but its impact was arguably powerful: Churchill changed 'The True Cause of Failure', to 'The True Cause<u>s</u> of Failure'.⁵⁴ The campaign had failed for a myriad of reasons, so to blame one man – Churchill – was wrong.

Changing the original text of 'we cannot here attempt more than a general survey of this lamentable event' to, 'the tale has been often told so no more than a general survey can here be attempted' revealed that he was, like the majority of writers, ever aware of his word limit and eager to avoid repetition of detail which his reader would probably already know.⁵⁵ Compared to other proof chapters for the second volume of *The World Crisis*, such as 'The Darkening Scene', Churchill made fewer revisions to the proofed text than expected.⁵⁶ His keenness to ensure that the correct number of men taking part in the attack, both the Allied and Turkish divisions, was clearly of paramount importance to him as these figures underwent several revisions.⁵⁷ By highlighting the relatively evenly matched numbers of opposing troops, his argument as to why the attempt to take 'the key to the Narrows' failed, and how it was a 'mischance', would have more sway.⁵⁸

Aware that his fragile war-time reputation needed to be steadied in the immediate post-war era, Churchill seemingly took care to eradicate any possible language or turn of phrase which might offend his readers. If he could add weight to his reasons for why the campaign had failed it was a bonus. He achieved both aims in the following example. Instead of leaving these two sentences unchanged, 'Night closed with the troops much wearied, with their units intermingled, and with only their earliest objectives obtained. Only about a thousand casualties had been sustained…', he altered them to, 'Night closed with the troops much wearied, with their units intermingled, their water supply in confusion, and with only their earliest objectives obtained. About a thousand casualties…'. Such a revision enabled Churchill to highlight how poor planning, especially of such a basic commodity as water had contributed to the failure.

---

53   Churchill, *The World Crisis: 1915*, p. 341; CHAR 8/91/2.
54   CHAR 8/91/1: Sub-headings page for 'The Battle for Suvla Bay'.
55   CHAR 8/91/2: proof of 'The Battle for Suvla Bay'.
56   CHAR 8/90/1–17: proof of 'The Darkening Scene' (1923).
57   CHAR 8/91/4: proof of 'The Battle for Suvla Bay'.
58   CHAR 8/91/4: proof of 'The Battle for Suvla Bay'; Churchill, *The World Crisis: 1915*, p. 343.

Deleting 'only' from the start of the second sentence revealed his humanity (without doubt he felt the loss of troops keenly especially after witnessing the horror of modern warfare in the trenches), and his wish to not negate such a loss and to neither upset nor antagonise his readers.[59]

Nowhere within the proofs for this chapter has any reference to the Indian troops or Gurkhas been revised. Their mentions within the original text remained unchanged, and were published as intended. At first glance, this indicates that Churchill was content with how their actions had been originally recorded (as set-out in the proof) and, being limited by a word count, was unable to embellish further. The August offensive proof read: 'On the afternoon of August 6 the great battle began with the British attack on about 1200 yards of the Turkish front at Helles'. Churchill's distinctive hand altered this to read: 'On the afternoon of August 6 the great battle began with the attack of the Lancashire and Lowland Territorial Divisions on about 1200 yards of the Turkish line at Helles' – which made the final publication.[60] As he was already limited by a strict word count (the proofed chapter totalled 7200 words), and had frequently used the word 'British' instead of mentioning the specific names of Divisions up till now, it appears incongruous as to why he would change the proofed copy. While he would have realised early-on that his narrative of this event in the Dardanelles campaign would be Anzac-heavy simply due to the troops involved, perhaps mentioning specific British Divisions by name would enable him to balance out the necessarily numerous references to Anzac troops.

'This is the Day' beckoned one of the first of Thornton Butterworth's adverts for Churchill's first volume of *the World Crisis*. Those eager to read Churchill's work were urged to pre-order their copies as 'the large 1st Edition' had 'already been oversubscribed' by booksellers and libraries. This was a marketing ploy to encourage pre-orders but, when compared to other such adverts in the press, it remains striking.[61] In an advert for the second volume which covered the Dardanelles campaign, Thornton Butterworth quoted from the *British Weekly*: "The World Crisis, 1915' has caused a sensation that is by no means false. For it is a very big book; it is history. To anyone who knows the problem of making an accurate and detailed study of war tactics live and have being [come alive], Chapter VI is nothing less than a masterpiece'.[62] By February 1924, only a few months after its publication, the total number of copies sold of the second volume of his Great War memoirs came to 9,900.[63] Five years later, and once the first four volumes had come on the market, Churchill enquired as to what

---

59   CHAR 8/91/13: proof of 'The Battle for Suvla Bay'.
60   CHAR 8/91/6: proof of 'The Battle for Suvla Bay'.
61   Advert by Thornton Butterworth for 'Mr Winston Churchill's Book, 'The World Crisis'', *The Times*, 8 April 1923.
62   Advert placed by Thornton Butterworth, *The Times*, 16 Nov. 1923.
63   CHAR 8/199/5: Thornton Butterworth to Churchill, 22 Feb. 1924. CHAR 8/199/9: Thornton Butterworth to Churchill, 29 May 1924: three months later the total number of copies sold was 10,074. By June 1929, the total number of sales upon which royalties were

royalties he would receive for the total number of sales for his *World Crisis*. Thornton Butterworth confirmed that, with regards to Churchill's second volume, the total number sold was 12,670 copies.[64] A month later the total sold had risen by another 482 copies.[65] In all the folios of correspondence to Churchill on the subject of his *World Crisis*, not one letter mentions the absence of the Indian troops from his account of the Gallipoli campaign.

Praise for Churchill's volumes came from all quarters. One avid reader wrote that the first and second volume had proved, in her mind at least, to be 'the most wonderful and illuminating history' that she had ever read.[66] Another reader, a Scottish solicitor from Castle Douglas, offered his 'warm thanks' and 'appreciation of' Churchill's second volume, and described it not only as a 'brilliant and convincing book', but also as a vehicle for alleviating the 'stupid and partisan prejudice' which doggedly followed Churchill.[67] The 'clarity of expression' was only equalled by the 'beauty' of Churchill's writing, according to Francis Lloyd who had been the London District Commanding Officer.[68] Each of these three readers, a small number of the many who personally wrote to Churchill to express their admiration for his *World Crisis*, wanted to see Churchill back in Parliament; one went so far as to say that he would prefer Churchill to be on the Conservative benches, but it did not really matter just as long as he was there![69]

What is startling is the profound effect that Churchill's vindicatory volumes had on some readers. One in particular wrote that before the First World War, he had thought Winston to be a typical Churchill: 'all the Churchill's have had brains, but none have ever had morals. They all play for power and popularity irrespective of truth, consistency or fidelity to principle'. As the writer himself stated, not a 'flattering' image of Churchill at all but, upon reading the 'two vindicatory volumes', his perception of Winston 'vastly improved'. So much so, that he deemed that Churchill had been 'fundamentally correct from the start – Gallipoli was the key to the war position from the beginning', and that had it not been for 'smaller minds' the course of the war may have been altered, the length of the war shortened by two years, and 'God knows how many lives and millions upon millions of treasure saved'.[70] While the author of this

      paid to Churchill (for volume 2) were 12,972: CHAR 8/226/69: Thornton Butterworth to Churchill, 15 Nov. 1929.
64 CHAR 8/226/69: Thornton Butterworth to Churchill, 15 Nov. 1929. This letter also included total sales figures for Volume 1, 3 and 4 (*The Aftermath*).
65 CHAR 8/226/70: W. H. Bland (Thornton Butterworth's accountant) to Churchill, 12 Dec. 1929.
66 CHAR 8/197/6: Charlotte Villiers to Churchill, 20 Jan. 1924.
67 CHAR 8/197/7: Patrick Gifford to Churchill, 22 Jan. 1924.
68 CHAR 8/197/9: Francis Lloyd to Churchill, 10 Feb. 1924.
69 CHAR 8/197/9: Francis Lloyd to Churchill, 10 Feb. 1924.
70 CHAR 8/197/12–16: 'Philosophical Scotchman' (a General Manager in Johannesburg) to Churchill, 10 Mar. 1924. Dignitaries such as Major Braithwaite Wallis, the Envoy Extraordinary and Minister Plenipotentiary in Panama, also wrote to congratulate

letter, who signed himself 'philosophical Scotchman', may have been too optimistic regarding the potential shortening of the war by two years if the Dardanelles campaign had been successful, it suggests that Churchill's vindication of his strategy was quite successful. All expressed their agreement with the premise behind the Dardanelles campaign, and nearly all expressed (in some way or another) how history would further vindicate both Churchill's role and the potential for glory the campaign actually had held. None of these admirers mentioned the Indian troops. Churchill's *World Crisis* faced criticism from some. The Chartwell papers contain, for example, correspondence between Churchill and Sir Charles Oman,[71] the distinguished military historian, who disputed the veracity of the figure Churchill used regarding German losses during the Battle of the Somme.[72] Others wished to draw Churchill's attention to the discrepancy between the sizes of an American division when compared to an Allied division.[73] Once again, not one piece of correspondence from the files draws Churchill's attention to the lack of coverage given to the Indian troops.

According to General Archibald Percival Wavell, Churchill had developed a 'curious complex' about India when he had been a subaltern in the Queen's Hussars, stationed in Bangalore, from 1896 to 1899.[74] Throughout his time in India, Churchill had been more concerned with the prestige this position offered, and how it could lead to a political career, rather than what he could learn about India, or the Indian Army itself. His refusal to learn Hindi, which he deemed 'quite unnecessary', meant that he could not understand the 'thoughts and feelings' of the Indian troops which he encountered.[75] Although this attitude was prevalent among the British officers in his cantonment, it did not stop Churchill from writing of the *sepoys* he encountered that 'there was no doubt they liked having a white officer among them, when fighting ... they watched him carefully to see how things were going. If you grinned, they

---

Churchill on his *World Crisis* and stated that the responsibilities that Churchill had born, and his 'magnificent work at the Admiralty' would be seen by future generations as 'landmarks in the history' of their 'beloved country': CHAR 8/197/22–23: Major C. Braithwaite Wallis to Churchill, 17 Apr. 1924

71 Paddy Griffith, 'Oman, Sir Charles William Chadwick (1860–1946)', *Oxford Dictionary of National Biography*, Oxford University Press, 2004; online edn, Oct 2009; [http://www.oxforddnb.com/view/article/35312], accessed 18 Nov. 2015.

72 CHAR 8/209/56–69: Drafts of Churchill's reply to Sir Charles Oman's criticism addressed to the Editor of *The Times*, 25 May 1927.

73 CHAR 8/209/42: Edward Marsh (on behalf of Churchill) to Mr Bruce Lancaster, 30 June 1927; CHAR 8/209/43: Mr Bruce Lancaster to Churchill, 19 June 1927.

74 Penderel Moon (ed.), *Wavell: The Viceroy's Journal* (Karachi: OUP, 1974), Wavell diary entry, 24 June 1943, p. 3. Although stationed in Bangalore for three years, Churchill spent a total of no more than 12 months in India. While this was not usual for any British serving officer, Churchill was unusual in that he interspersed his post with various sorties as a war correspondent (in Cuba, Egypt, and the Sudan), and with several trips back to London. He resigned his commission in May 1899.

75 Winston S. Churchill, *My Early Life, A Roving Commission* (London: Thornton Butterworth, 1930), p. 164.

grinned. So I grinned industriously'.[76] It was not only fellow officers, however, who shared Churchill's view of the Indian troops.[77]

Almost two decades later, Violet Asquith (later Bonham Carter), the daughter of Herbert Asquith (Prime Minister from 1908–16), prodigious diarist and one of Churchill's closest female friends, illustrated how this attitude had morphed into one where the Indian soldiers, who fought alongside the Australian and New Zealander troops at Gallipoli, did not require especial mention. Visiting Alexandria, as the Gallipoli campaign was in full swing and, in order to set-up the Admiralty Information Bureau and visit various hospitals to divine how the injured troops were being treated, she remarked upon the Australian troops she encountered. They had an 'élan vital' that 'knew no bounds', and although coarse, insolent and lacking discipline, the Australians nonetheless fought with a 'heroic dash and courage, advancing irresistibly…without any order like a football scrum'.[78] Casting her gaze over New Zealanders, Violet came to much the same conclusion. Yet having spent four weeks in Egypt, and having written that she had, in some very small way, shared the 'discomforts, trials, triumphs, [and] setbacks' of the wounded returning from Cape Helles, Achi Baba, and Sari Bair, she made no mention of the Indian troops. This is not indicative of any inherent racism, but more that the presence of the Indian soldier was natural – taken for granted even – and did not require comment.

The First World War was an imperial war; in terms of how it was managed, who fought, and where.[79] The protection of the British Empire's interests – 'the destruction of the German and Ottoman empires would quite naturally lead to much more red on the map' – was one of the reasons why Britain fought the Dardanelles campaign.[80] When coupled with the reality that war is a catalyst for change, there were many in Britain who both foresaw and feared the impact such a catalyst would have upon the British Empire, especially the Raj. By the end of the Great War, political India

---

76 Churchill, *My Early Life*, p. 164. Churchill would certainly not have been alone in his refusal to learn Hindi. His unit in Bangalore would not have included any Indian other ranks, so the learning of Hindi 'would not have been an urgent matter'. Furthermore, the languages spoken within the cantonment itself would not have been Hindi, but either Kannada or Tamil, and 'the lingua franca of the colonial Indian Army was not Hindi, but Urdu'. Private correspondence between the author and Dr. Chandar S. Sundaram.
77 Even Major C. J. L. Allanson believed that while 'everyone is unanimous that the Indian Brigade has done well…nothing can compete with the disastrous effect of the loss of BOs. It appears to paralyse a unit completely'. Allanson cited in Trench, *The Indian Army*, p. 53.
78 Bonham Carter, *Churchill: As I Knew Him*, p. 410; Mark Pottle (ed.), *Champion Redoubtable: The Diaries and Letters of Violet Bonham Carter 1914–45* (London: Weidenfeld & Nicolson, 1998), Violet, diary entry, 2 June 1915.
79 The British War Cabinet, and Whitehall staff, consisted of men who, if not so-called die-hard imperialists like Churchill, held significant interest in the longevity and prestige of the British Empire: Curzon, Amery, and Balfour.
80 Ashley Jackson, 'The British Empire and the First World War', *BBC History Magazine*, 9:11 (2008).

was a tinderbox which had 'on the whole trusted and waited, believing that India's contribution must be recognized when the war was won, that India would take a place among the nations beside Canada, Australia and New Zealand'. India was to be, so the historian Philip Mason continued, 'bitterly disappointed'.[81] Introduced to curtail any increase in Indian moves towards independence and as a way of maintaining India's war effort, Britain had dangled the tantalising carrot of partial self-government (the Montagu Declaration of August 1917), and confirmed that the issue of self-government would be considered only after the Great War.[82] The declaration confirmed that the objective of British rule in India was the 'increasing association of Indians in every branch of the administration, and the gradual development of self-governing institutions, with a view to the progressive realisation of responsible government in India as an integral part of the British Empire'.[83] A large proportion of those who fought on Gallipoli, especially those who battled at Suvla Bay, were Anzacs – Dominion troops. The Australian prime minister, William Morris Hughes, sat on the 1917 Imperial War Cabinet and so had direct access to and some say, or at least some representation, regarding the war's progress. There were two Indian members: Ganga Singh, Maharajah of Bikaner and James Meston, Lieutenant Governor of the United Provinces of Agra and Oudh but Indian leaders of the National Congress were excluded from such discussions. With little say in the progress of war it was clear, as Curzon would later write, that the soldiers of the Indian Army were 'not fighting for their own country or people. They were not even engaged in a quarrel of their own making'.[84]

Alongside the usual regimental censorship of all correspondence from soldiers, an extra layer of filtration was applied to correspondence both to and from Indian soldiers in the trenches. Originally this 'systematic examination' was implemented in order to 'prevent seditious literature reaching the troops'; but it quickly became a way of gauging the morale of both the Indian soldiers and the mood of those whom they had left back home.[85] The Raj was clearly worried about the loyalty and morale of the Indian Army not simply during the war, but whether there would be dire consequences

81 Philip Mason, *A Matter of Honour: An Account of the Indian Army, its Officers and Men* (London: Jonathan Cape, 1974; Papermac, 1986), p. 411.
82 See Judith M. Brown, *Modern India : The Origins of an Asian Democracy* (Oxford, OUP, 1985), pp. 188–202; David Low (ed.), *Congress and the Raj: Facets of the Indian Struggle, 1917–1947* (2nd edn, New Delhi: OUP, 2004), pp. 1–46; Budheswar Pati, *India and the First World War 1914–1918* (New Delhi: Atlantic, 1996), pp. 136–241; and Sir Algernon Rumbold, *Watershed in India, 1914–1922* (London: Athlone Press, 1979), pp. 1–126.
83 Edwin S. Montagu, Secretary of State for India, 20 Aug. 1917, *Parl Deb (Commons)*, 5th Series, 97 (1917), 1695–6.
84 The Rt. Hon. Earl Curzon of Kedlestone, Oct. 1917, 'Introduction' to Lt-Colonel J.W.B. Merewether & The Rt. Hon. Sir Frederick Smith, *The Indian Corps in France* (London: John Murray, 1917), p. x.
85 Omissi, *Indian Voices of the Great War*, p. 6; Appendix IV, pp. 369–72.

and fall-out when the soldiers sailed back across the 'black waters'.[86] There is only one mention of the Dardanelles within David Omissi's edited collection:

> There is a country belonging to the Turks too which they call Dadarnes [Dardanelles]. There has been fighting there with the Turks, about which I cannot tell you. There France, Italy, England, and another, four Kings, had their armies. The Turk smashed and bashed the whole lot, and the losses were heavy. The Turks are the bravest of all. We are ever praying that the victory may be granted to our King, the King of peace.[87]

While the Indian soldiers on Gallipoli were fighting the 'bravest of all' soldiers, the Turks, and upholding *izzat*, they were also living and fighting alongside other non-British troops who had answered the motherland's call to arms. 'The Empire Needs Men!'– screamed the recruitment poster, and men from 'Australia, Canada, India and New Zealand' were encouraged to 'answer the call' and enlist so that, 'helped by the Young Lions, the Old Lion' would be able to defy his foes.[88] What effect such colonial encounters had on the Indian troops, not only during their time in Europe but also upon their return to India, is an area which needs further research in order to discern to what extent, if any, Indian soldiers acknowledged how their status was so very different to that of their Dominion imperial relatives.

The inscription on the medal that was awarded to the families of those who had died during the war read, 'He Died For Freedom And For Honour'. Whether the irony of 'freedom' was felt by the Indian soldier remains a pertinent question, but the 'honour' part surely did not as *izzat* had been duly served.[89] There was an inherent contradiction between loyalty to the Empire and *izzat*. War was, and still is, a catalyst

---

86 During the course of the Second World War, Churchill would privately disparage the Indian Army as inept and disloyal. He even went as far as saying that Wavell had created a monster akin to Frankenstein's as he had put 'modern weapons in the hands of sepoys'. Moon (ed.), *Wavell*, Wavell diary entry, 24 June 1943, p. 3.
87 Omissi, *Indian Voices of the Great War*, p. 92, citing India Office Records (IOR) L/MIL/5/825/797: Ghulam Abbas Ali Khan, Guide's cavalry (France), Jullundur Brigade Staff, to Risaldar Muhammad Sarwar Khan, in Mardan (Peshawar District) in Urdu and Punjabi, 31 August 1915.
88 'The Empire Needs Men!', Parliamentary Recruiting Committee Poster No.58. WT.W 13275, Arthur Wardle (artist), produced Mar. 1915, Imperial War Museum (London) catalogue number: Art IWM PST 5110, http://www.iwm.org.uk/collections/item/object/37297, accessed 11 Nov. 2015.
89 The obvious exception to this was the 'Singapore Mutiny' of February 1915. The events in Singapore was a rebellion, no matter how small in comparative terms, of some Indian Army soldiers who, being 'disturbed by the thought of being at war with the Muslims of the Ottoman Empire', set 300 German POWs free. Jackson, 'The British Empire and the First World War'. See also Ian F. W. Beckett, 'The Singapore Mutiny of February, 1915', *Journal of the Society for Army Historical Research*, 62/3 (1984), pp. 132–53; and 'The Mutiny at Singapore', *The Times*, 14 April 1915.

for change. Upon returning to India some soldiers voiced how 'we came to know that the British had no respect for the Indians. They regarded us as their servants. The British soldiers used to get four times more than our salary. Their sepoy did not salute our subedar-major or any NCO'.[90] Another noted how, although he had 'previously [been] satisfied with the existing circumstances' he had begun to protest 'against the disparities which the British had created'.[91] Such 'disparities' became even more defined with the passing of the Rowlatt Acts, in March 1919. These acts were a direct result of the Raj's fear of the growing number of violent expressions of political unrest by Indian nationalists; arguably General Dyer's actions in the Jallianwallah Bagh at Amritsar (on 13 April 1919) were a direct manifestation of these fears.[92] Although Churchill would later be called upon to justify the Government's reluctance to punish Dyer, it was a task which Churchill turned to his advantage as he used it to illustrate his notion of the moral dimension of empire—the duty to protect the weak and vulnerable. This also revealed Churchill's longstanding inability to separate the Indian Army from political India.

In a file marked 'Regimental Colours & Appointments, Honorary Distinctions & Titles for Regiments', is a list of First World War battle honours awarded to certain units of the Indian Army (as well as Indian State Forces). Ranging in date from 1919 to 1927, the file mainly contains additional applications and the subsequent granting of battle honour awards. For example, a claim was made on behalf of Holkar's Transport Corps (formerly Indore Transport Corps) for their part in the 'landing at Suvla', and 'Gallipoli 1915' (as well as other actions).[93] Verifying a unit's claim was made using the relevant war diaries but certain requisite conditions had to be met: 'a claim can only be based on the presence of Headquarters and 50% of the Regiment within the defined area and dates'.[94] Even though the King had already granted Holkar's Transport Corps battle honours for their role in Mesopotamia (1915–16), on Christmas Eve 1925, this

---

90 Sepoy Ralk Singh of the 45th Sikh Infantry cited by S. D. Prahan, 'The Sikh Soldier in the First World War', in DeWitt C. Ellinwood and S. D. Prahan (eds), *India and World War I* (Columbia, Mo: South Asia Books, 1978), p. 224.
91 Lance Naik Khela Singh of the Patiala State Force cited by Prahan, 'The Sikh Soldier in the First World War', p. 224.
92 See Tim Coates (ed.), *The Amritsar Massacre: General Dyer in the Punjab, 1919* (London: HMSO, 1920; Stationery Office edn, 2000); Nigel Collett, *The Butcher of Amritsar: General Reginald Dyer* (2nd edn, London: Hambledon Continuum, 2007); V.N. Datta and S. Settar (eds), *Jallianwala Bagh Massacre* (New Delhi: Pragati, 2000); Nick Lloyd, *The Amritsar Massacre: The Untold Story of one Fateful Day* (London: I.B. Tauris, 2011); and Derek Sayer, 'British reaction to the Amritsar Massacre, 1919–1920', *Past and Present*, 131 (1991).
93 IOR/ L/MIL/7/10765: E.W. Daniel (Assistant Secretary to the Government of India), to the India Office, London, 20 Jan. 1927.
94 IOR/ L/MIL/7/10765: War Office, Medal Branch, A.G. 10., general communication 4492, 7 Mar. 1927; see also IOR/ L/MIL/7/10765: Appendix 19 Army Instruction (India) 141 of 1919 para 5 (f), and in annexure to India Army Order No. 792 of 1924.

did not prevent further battle honours being made as previously bestowed honours were not allowed to 'prejudice claims being considered later should the unit, or units, produce documents to substantiate them'.[95]

The question of whether special field allowances should be made to Indian and Imperial Service troops was asked during the war as there appeared 'to be some case for a special allowance' to be paid although 'the grant of double pay would appear to constitute an undesirable precedent'.[96] A member of the India Office's Military Department answered this question: Stewart wrote that, the War Office were 'disposed to accept...that some concession to the Indians' was 'necessary on political grounds'. But the approved allowances 'were based rather on the hardships of the troops' rather than on Indian campaigning and so were deemed 'not very relevant'. Assuming a 'departure from the present rates' it seemed prudent, Stewart continued, 'to stop short of...double pay and...put these 18 men on an equality with the Egyptian troops alongside of whom they are serving'. He stipulated that 'of course, if any large number of Indian troops should be employed in the Hedjaz the whole question would have to be reconsidered. Double pay would then be out of the question, but in that case I suppose the political consideration ...would not apply'.[97] In a draft letter emanating from the India Office, it had been agreed that Indian soldiers serving in Europe should be awarded a pay increase of some 25 percent (Indian Army Routine Order No. 436, 11 March 1915); this concession had already been 'confirmed for troops and followers serving in the Dardanelles' and was then similarly extended to apply to those who were serving in the Balkan Peninsula, Egypt and Malta.[98] It was later clarified that

---

95 IOR/L/MIL/7/10765: E.W. Daniel (Assistant Secretary to the Government of India), to the India Office, London, 20 Jan. 1927; IOR/ L/MIL/7/10765: Colonel Clive Wigram (Assistant Private Secretary to H.M. the King) to General Sir Alexander Cobbe, 24 Dec. 1925. For example, a claim was made on behalf of the 3rd Sikh Pioneers for the award of additional battle honours following their services in Aden, Egypt (1916–17), La Basse (1914), Armentieres (1914), Aubers, Festubert (1915), Loos, and Kut (1917). These additional battle honours were not previously claimed 'through an omission'. See IOR/L/MIL/7/10765: E.W. Daniel (Assistant Secretary to the Government of India), to the India Office, London, 5 May 1927.
96 IOR/L/MIL/7/17420: Watherstone (War Office, London) to S.F. Stewart (Military Dept. India Office), 8 Oct. 1917.
97 IOR/L/MIL/7/17420: S. F. Stewart (Military Dept. India Office) to Watherstone (War Office, London), 9 Oct. 1917. IOR/L/MIL/7/17420: Sir Francis Reginald Wingate wrote that he strongly recommended that double pay be awarded as he was 'anxious on political grounds to better the position of the India Machine Gun detachment in [the] Hedjaz... which has done excellent work and which compares unfavourably with the Egyptian Army detachment all ranks of which receive double pay in Hedjaz'. Wingate to War Office, London, 25 Sept. 1917.
98 IOR/L/MIL/7/17420: Draft letter, 'H.1863, 12 March 1916'. It ought to be noted that while the War Office were willing to grant such service allowances to Indian troops, it was adamant that 'the whole matter with reasons for fixing new rates will be explained to G.O.C., Force 'D' but we consider it most undesirable to communicate these reasons

'these rates will not in any case be in excess of 25% or 12.5% of the pay (in Europe, or Egypt, Mesopotamia, East Africa, etc., respectively) drawn by these officers, and that the pay as increased will fall short of that of British Officers of corresponding rank'.[99] All of which revealed the extent to which Whitehall was pre-empting potential unrest within an army that it relied upon.

Having been shown the Admiralty door and, for a short time, assigned the Duchy of Lancaster (the 'Cabinet waste-paper basket'), Churchill chose to go the trenches in France.[100] He may have been uncertain as to what his immediate future held but, as his scorn for Kitchener intensified, he wrote that if Gallipoli were evacuated, 'all the facts shall come out. They will be incredible to the world. The reckoning will be heavy & I shall make sure it is exacted'.[101] In July 1915, he had appointed his wife as his 'sole literary executor'. Should he die in the trenches, Churchill wrote that Clementine would be helped to 'secure' all that was 'necessary for a complete record' as 'someday', he wanted 'the truth to be known'.[102] Churchill was very clear in his letters to his wife that it had been the 'damnable mismanagement wh[ich] has ruined the Dardanelles enterprise & squandered vainly so much life'. He continued that if the opportunity arose, especially as the situation cried 'aloud for retribution', the day would come when he would claim said retribution publicly.[103] The day after he wrote this letter, the last British and Indian troops were evacuated from Gallipoli. His ever increasing anger with the Dardanelles situation was evident. He wrote that if he were to take his place in Parliament after the war, he would 'endeavour to procure the dismissal of Asquith & Kitchener'. In the same letter, he wrote that these 'wretched

---

to troops themselves or to give any explanation to them as this would inevitably lead to discussion'. IOR/L/MIL/7/17420: No. H. 971, telegram from Viceroy, 7 Feb. 1916. Finally, on the matter of service pay increase awards, such an increase was not granted to those Indian troops who served in West Africa, China, Singapore, Ceylon or Mauritius, 'unless present conditions change, or in Aden and Persia which are to be considered as part of India for this purpose': IOR/L/MIL/7/17420: 121/Finance/558 (F.2) War Office to Under Secretary of State for India, 21 Jan. 1916.

99 IOR/L/MIL/7/17420: 121/Finance/698. (F.2), War Office, London, directive 7 Aug. 1916.
100 Bonham Carter, *Churchill: As I Knew Him*, p. 408.
101 Mary Soames (ed.), *Speaking for Themselves: The Personal Letters of Winston and Clementine Churchill* (London: Black Swan, 1999), Churchill to Clementine, 8 Dec. 1915, p. 129.
102 Soames (ed.), *Speaking for Themselves*, Churchill to Clementine, 17 July 1915, p. 111. In early July 1915, Lord Kitchener asked Churchill to visit the Dardanelles so he could pass on an accurate assessment. Because of opposition from fellow Tories, the visit only reached the planning stage and was never carried out. The envelope of this letter was marked 'To be sent to Mrs Churchill in the event of my death'. In a later letter, Clementine encouraged Churchill not to stay any longer than necessary in the trenches because 'if you were killed and you had over-exposed yourself the world might think that you had sought death out of grief for your share in the Dardanelles'. Soames (ed.), *Speaking for Themselves*, Clementine to Churchill, 28 Nov. 1915, p. 121.
103 Soames (ed.), *Speaking for Themselves*, Churchill to Clementine, 10 Jan. 1916, p. 150.

men have nearly wrecked our chances. It may fall to me to strike the blow. I shall do it without compunction'.[104] Clementine proved herself to be a worthy sounding-board for her husband. Hers may not always have been a voice of caution but she was shrewd – especially with regards to the blame which was directed at Churchill over the Dardanelles. When his frustrations seemed to peak, and he became increasingly keen to have the relevant papers published during wartime, Clementine wrote that she was 'very anxious' that he 'should not blunt this precious weapon prematurely'.[105] Churchill heeded her words and waited until he could publish them himself in the form of his *World Crisis*.

Churchill wrote *The World Crisis* between 1919 and 1926. During this time his political career regained some of its pre-Dardanelles vigour: he had been Secretary of State for War and Minister of Air (15 January 1919–14 February 1921 and 1 April 1921 respectively), Secretary of State for the Colonies (14 February 1921–October 1922), out of office for almost two years, and then Chancellor of the Exchequer (7 November 1924–30 May 1929). When he had fallen from favour over the Dardanelles, one newspaper observed that there was no place for Churchill at the Admiralty; there was 'no place for a civilian Minister who usurps the functions of his Board' and 'takes the wheel out of the sailor's hand'. 'In this great war', so the piece continued, 'which is a matter of life and death for the British Empire we dare not take such risks'.[106] Tipping his hat at those soldiers who had fought for a freedom they themselves did not have, especially when it complemented his argument that the Dardanelles had been viable, was Churchill's way of not upsetting a precariously poised imperial apple-cart. His narrative merely reflected the general opinion of the time. Some British officers may have held the Indian soldiers in high regard, but they 'never for one instant' imagined them to be the 'equals of the British soldier'.[107] The Indian Army was British-officered and that was how it should stay.

The battle for Sari Bair remains poignant for several reasons. Had the plan succeeded, had the ridge been maintained by the Allies, they stood a chance of forcing themselves further inland and breaking out from their all too static and entrenched positions. Holding the ridge would have gone some way to gaining 'the objectives which the April landing had failed to approach'.[108] The battle for the ridge vindicated those who had been supporters of the Indian troops, as well as the troops themselves – whether Sikh, Punjabi, Gurkha, or from a princely state (the Patiala Imperial Service

---

104 Soames (ed.), *Speaking for Themselves*, Churchill to Clementine, 15 Dec. 1915, p. 132.
105 Soames (ed.), *Speaking for Themselves*, Clementine to Churchill, 11 Jan. 1916, p. 151.
106 *Morning Post*, 23 Apr. 1915.
107 Rozina Visram, *Asians in Britain: 400 Years of History* (London: Pluto Press, 2002), p. 180, citing V.G Kiernan, *European Empires from Conquest to Collapse, 1815–1960* (London: Fontana Paperbacks, 1982), pp.185–6.
108 Stanley, *Die in Battle, Do Not Despair*, p. 193.

Infantry) – as their gallantry and verve for battle was visible to all.[109] Whitehall and the War Cabinet knew of their deeds, but so now did other troops of Empire, the Anzacs, with whom the Indian soldiers had prolonged contact on Gallipoli. The question is whether they were affected by the Dominion outlook? Did some think that the shared horrors of service on Gallipoli (endured by most for the King, and by some for the material conditions – *rizzat*), should hold a more tangible reward than that of *izzat*, of honour for regiment, family, community? Perhaps for country? In 1939, the Indian Army answered the call to arms again. They became the largest volunteer force ever amassed, and were an essential component of the British and Allied success – especially in Africa and the Far East. Once more they fought for, and on behalf of, the Empire; and for a freedom they themselves did not have. As soon as the British electorate, in July 1945, voted Churchill out of Downing Street, he waited only a few months before starting to write his memoir of his time as Britain's wartime prime minister. He wrote the six volumes of *The Second World War* during the period when the declaration of post-war Indian Independence was a painful and bloody reality. Instead of tipping his hat 'To All Who Tried', Churchill's expectations, much like the Dardanelles campaign, did not match the reality, and his pen struck a definite blow against the Indian Army.[110]

---

109 This is not to say that the troops which comprised the 29th Indian Infantry Brigade had to prove their worth on Gallipoli. As Stanley writes, 'several of the regiments' which served on Gallipoli, 'already commanded a respect verging on adulation, even among those who knew the Indian Army well'. Stanley, *Die in Battle, Do Not Despair*, p. 36. Punjabi Muslims are omitted here as they only remained on Gallipoli for two weeks as discussed earlier.

110 Churchill, *The World Crisis, 1915*, dedication. For an examination of Churchill's portrayal of the Indian Army during the Second World War, see Cat Wilson, *Churchill on the Far East in 'The Second World War'* (Basingstoke: Palgrave Macmillan, 2014), especially pp. 90–137.

7

'The Greatest Muslim Power in the World': Islam, the Indian Army and the Grand Strategy of British India, 1914–1916[1]

David Omissi

I. Introduction

In 1916, John Buchan, a British author and future Governor-General of Canada, published his thriller *Greenmantle*.[2] The novel is about espionage, and it features a German plot to bring down the British Empire in the East by exploiting Islam to subvert British rule. In the novel, the hero, Richard Hannay, is briefed by Sir Walter Bullivant, who says:

> There is a dry wind blowing through the East, and the parched grasses wait the spark. And the wind is blowing towards the Indian border. ... We have laughed at the Holy War, the Jehad that old von der Goltz prophesied. But I believe that stupid old man with the big spectacles was right. There is a Jehad preparing.[3]

---

1   Except where otherwise stated, all documentary references are to the records of the Military Department of the India Office (L/MIL) and to the European Manuscripts (Mss Eur) held in the African and Asian Collections at the British Library in London; to the records of the War Office (WO), held at The National Archives in Kew; or to the records of the Home Department of the Government of India, held at the National Archives of India (NAI) in New Delhi.
2   On Buchan see H. C. G. Matthew, 'Buchan, John, first Baron Tweedsmuir (1875–1940)', *Oxford Dictionary of National Biography* (Oxford: Oxford University Press, online edn, accessed 11 April 2016).
3   John Buchan, *Greenmantle* (Harmondsworth: Penguin, 1997 [1916]), pp. 19–20, also quoted in H. Strachan, *The First World War: A New Illustrated History* (London: Simon and Schuster, 2003), p. 123 and in T. L. Hughes, 'The German Mission to Afghanistan, 1914–1918', *German Studies Review*, 25/3 (2002), p. 454.

At the time of writing, Buchan was working in intelligence and propaganda. Sir Hew Strachan has correctly observed that, in this case, 'fact and fiction were closely intertwined'.[4] 'Old von der Goltz' was a real person – a Prussian general with a long association with the Ottoman Army, stretching from the 1880s until his death in Mesopotamia in 1916.[5]

This chapter is about the fact behind the fiction: it examines the relationship between Islam, the Indian Army and the grand strategy of British India in the 21-month period from the European crisis of late July 1914 to the British-Indian capitulation at Kut al-Amara in April 1916. The purpose of the paper is not to examine in detail the military operations that led to the siege and surrender of Kut al-Amara. That has been ably done elsewhere.[6] The aim of this chapter is rather to situate the British strategy that led to the disaster within the wider context of British strategic thinking about the Islamic world, particularly in relation to the security of British India.

The chapter will address several core questions. How did the contending powers try to manipulate Muslim opinion, and with what degree of success? How significant were concerns about Islam to the security of British India? To what extent did the loyalty of India's Muslims to the global community of Islam over-ride loyalty to the British Raj? How effectively did the British Indian authorities deal with any resulting problems of military discipline? Why did British policy makers come to conclude, in the autumn of 1915, that the capture of Baghdad was politically imperative?

The chapter will draw on a range of sources, including vice-regal correspondence, the fortnightly reports by British provincial governors in India (which helped to underpin vice-regal policy) and on British intelligence reports on the Indian vernacular press, which give some sense of Indian 'opinion' – at least as permitted by the authorities during wartime.[7]

---

4   Strachan, *The First World War*, p. 123.
5   Colmar von der Goltz (1843–1916), Prussian Field Marshal and respected military writer. Helped reorganize the Ottoman Army, 1883–1895; military aide to Sultan Mehmed V, 1915; in command of Ottoman forces at Battle of Ctesiphon, November 1915.
6   See, for example, Nikolas Gardner, *The Siege of Kut al-Amara: At War in Mesopotamia, 1915–1916* (Bloomington: Indiana University Press, 2014), and Charles Townshend, *When God Made Hell: The British Invasion of Mesopotamia and the Creation of Iraq, 1914–21* (London: Faber and Faber, 2010).
7   For excerpts from the Punjabi press during the war see the excellent anthology edited by Andrew Tait Jarboe, *War News in India: The Punjabi Press during World War I* (London: I. B. Tauris, 2016). The original reports on the Indian press, catalogued by province and by year, can be found in the British Library, London, in India Office Records class L/R/5, and on open shelves in the National Archives of India. On the Calcutta Urdu weekly *al-Hilal* (closed by the authorities in November 1914), and its short-lived successor *al-Balagh*, see Ian Henderson Douglas, *Abul Kalam Azad: An Intellectual and Religious Biography* (Delhi: Oxford University Press, 1993), Ch. 2. For a discussion of the Indian vernacular press more generally see David Omissi, 'India: Some Perceptions of Race and Empire' in David Omissi and Andrew S. Thompson (eds), *The Impact of the South African War* (Basingstoke: Macmillan, 2002), pp. 215–32.

II. Context

To understand the context of British-Indian strategy, one must first consider some basic facts of demography. In 1914, only 30 million of the world's 270 million Muslims actually lived under Muslim rule.[8] Some 20 million lived in the French Empire, mainly in North and equatorial Africa, and another 20 million were subjects of the Tsar in Russian Asia. The British Empire had about 100 million Muslim subjects in Egypt, the Gulf States and (above all) India.[9] Of India's 300 million people, about 20 per cent were Muslims. There were therefore more Muslims in the Indian Empire than there were in the Ottoman Empire.[10]

The capital of the Indian Empire had been moved from Calcutta to Delhi (the former Mughal capital) in 1911.[11] There was therefore some truth to the claim, that the First Lord of the Admiralty, Winston Churchill (among others) was fond of repeating, that the British Empire was 'the greatest' Muslim power 'in the world'.[12] What were the implications of this demography for the grand strategy of British India?

Most importantly from a military perspective, Muslims formed a significant proportion of the Indian Army. In January 1904, Muslims were 35.3 per cent of the Army, a proportion which had hardly changed by 1914.[13] The single Indian province of the Punjab provided around half of all recruits to the Indian Army, and Punjabi Muslims were the single most numerous 'class' of recruits to the Indian Army, with 136,126 enlisting during the war.[14] There were few all-Muslim regiments, however, and most Muslims served in 'class company' regiments alongside Hindus and Sikhs.

If the British Empire had the numbers, the Ottoman Empire had the spiritual authority. The Ottoman Empire was, along with Afghanistan, one of the few surviving independent Muslim polities.[15] The Sultan claimed to speak for Islam in his capacity as Caliph and protector of all Muslims inside the Ottoman Empire and beyond.[16] The most important Holy places of Islam (Mecca, Medina and Jerusalem among them) all lay within the Sultan's domains.

---

8 Strachan, *First World War*, p. 97.
9 Sean McMeekin, *The Berlin-Baghdad Express: The Ottoman Empire and Germany's Bid for World Power, 1898–1918* (Allan Lane, 2010), pp. 65–6.
10 Warren Dockter, *Churchill and the Islamic World: Orientalism, Empire and Diplomacy in the Middle East* (London: I. B. Tauris, 2015), pp. 9, 303–4.
11 Algernon Rumbold, *Watershed in India, 1914–1922* (London: Athlone Press, 1979), p. 12.
12 Dockter, *Churchill and the Islamic World*, p. 60. See also pp. 9, 59, 91, 93, 102, 110 and 137.
13 Muslims numbered 53,968 of 152,846 Indian troops. See David Omissi, *The Sepoy and the Raj: The Indian Army, 1860–1914* (Basingstoke: Macmillan, 1994), p. 20. David French gives a figure of 35 per cent for 1914: David French, 'The Dardanelles, Mecca and Kut: Prestige as a Factor in British Strategy, 1914–1916', *War and Society*, 5/1 (1987), p. 48.
14 See the figures in David Omissi (ed.), *Indian Voices of the Great War: Soldiers' Letters, 1914–1918*, (Basingstoke: Macmillan, 1999) Appendix III.
15 Rumbold, *Watershed in India*, p. 22.
16 Hughes, 'German Mission', p. 450; French, 'The Dardanelles, Mecca and Kut', p. 48.

Both India and Islam occupied a key place in German strategic thinking from at least the 1890s. Kaiser Wilhelm II cultivated the Ottoman world. In 1896, he sent a birthday card to Sultan Abdul-Hamid II, then out of favour in most of Europe.[17] The Kaiser visited Jerusalem and Damascus in 1898.[18] In Constantinople, he proclaimed that the '300 million' Muslims across the world who revered the Sultan as their Caliph could rest assured that the German Emperor was their friend for all time.[19] The Germans saw Islam as a potential weak link in the Entente, and 'entertained great hopes of provoking a large-scale revolution in India' in the event of war.[20] Even before the outbreak of war, there were rumours that the Kaiser had embraced Islam, and that he had earned the title 'Haji' Wilhelm after secretly making the pilgrimage to Mecca.[21]

These German ideas might seem rather fanciful today, because the global and religious perspectives easily available at the time to strategists on both sides have subsequently been lost in the popular Eurocentric and secular narrative of the war.[22] From the perspective of British India's Viceregal Lodge in 1914–15 it was, however, another matter. The Viceroy of India, Lord Hardinge, was painfully aware of the vulnerability of British rule in India to a pan-Islamic movement, in the many forms such a movement could assume. Germany could plausibly aim to help bring about any or all of the following: a war between the British Empire and Ottoman Turkey, and a declaration of *Jihād*; a war between British India and either Afghanistan or Persia, or both; a rising on India's North-West frontier, then unrest amongst British India's Muslim population; and mutinies among the Muslim troops who made up a substantial minority of the Indian Army.[23] Any one of these problems would be serious, but containable; more than one would be a major challenge; all together they could spell disaster for British India.[24]

---

17   Dockter, *Churchill and the Islamic World*, p. 62.
18   Strachan, *First World War*, pp. 98–9.
19   Dockter, *Churchill and the Islamic World*, pp. 62–3.
20   Fritz Fischer, *Germany's Aims in the First World War* (London: Chatto and Windus, 1967), p. 126.
21   Dockter, *Churchill and the Islamic World*, p. 304.
22   For some countervailing trends see John H. Morrow, *The Great War: An Imperial History* (Routledge, 2004), David Olusoga, *The World's War* (London: Head of Zeus, 2014), and Hew Strachan, *The First World War*, Vol. 1, *To Arms* (Oxford: Oxford University Press, 2001), Chs 6–9.
23   D. Goold, 'Lord Hardinge and the Mesopotamia Expedition and Enquiry, 1914–1917', *The Historical Journal*, 19/4 (1976), pp. 925–5; French, 'Dardanelles, Mecca and Kut', pp. 48–9, 52, 55.
24   Rumbold, *Watershed in India*, p. 21.

III. The First Phase of the War

The British declaration of war on Germany was followed by expressions of loyalty throughout India, even in nationalist circles.[25] The Council of the Muslim League passed a resolution of loyalty, and 'only a handful of ulema worked secretly against the British'.[26] Britain's efforts to mediate during the July crisis were seen to have placed Germany in the wrong, and the German violation of Belgian neutrality was regarded as a legitimate *casus belli*.[27] The leading Urdu newspaper in the Punjab, the daily *Zamindar*, exhorted Muslims 'as Britishers' to 'give their whole-hearted support to Great Britain ... at this critical juncture in the affairs of the Empire'.[28]

India was to feature in German strategy from the very outbreak of the war. When the Kaiser heard of Britain's warnings to Germany on 30 July 1914, he wrote:

> Our consuls in Turkey and India [and] our agents ... must rouse the whole Muslim world into wild rebellion against this hateful, mendacious, unprincipled nation of shopkeepers; if we are to shed our blood, England must at least lose India.[29]

On the very same day, *Zamindar* accurately predicted that the 'war will not be confined to Austria and Serbia, but will be a universal war in which all the great Empires of Europe will be involved'.[30] On 2 August, Helmuth von Moltke (1848–1916), the Chief of the German General Staff, wrote to the German Foreign Ministry calling for revolution in India and in Egypt.[31] On 5 August, 'embittered by' Britain's declaration of war, he reiterated the point: 'Revolution in India and Egypt ... is of the highest importance. The treaty with Turkey will make it possible for the Foreign Office to realise this idea, and to awaken the fanaticism of Islam'.[32] In September, the German Chancellor, Theobald von Bethmann-Hollweg (1856–1921), sanctioned a campaign

---

25 Rumbold, *Watershed in India*, p. 20.
26 French, 'Dardanelles, Mecca and Kut', p. 52.
27 For one Indian press reaction to British mediation see Jarboe (ed.), *War News in India*, Doc. 6.
28 *Zamindar* (Urdu, Lahore, 15,000 daily), 18 Aug. 1914, quoted in Jarboe (ed.), *War News in India*, Doc. 11; see also Appendix. As the war developed, matters took a different turn. *Zamindar*'s editor, Zafar Ali, was interned and the paper closed; see Douglas, *Abdul Kalam Azad*, pp. 98–101. *Zamindar* was founded as a weekly in 1903, becoming a daily in 1912.
29 Strachan, *First World War*, pp. 98–9 and French, 'Dardanelles, Mecca and Kut', p. 51. See also Dockter, *Churchill and the Islamic World*, p. 72.
30 Jarboe (ed.), *War News in India*, Doc. 1.
31 Strachan, *First World War*, p. 99.
32 Fisher, *Germany's Aims*, p. 126. See also Peter Hopkirk, *On Secret Service East of Constantinople: The Plot to Bring Down the British Empire* (London: John Murray, 1994), p. 54.

of subversion in the British Empire.³³ The Germans set up an agency to distribute propaganda to Indian and other colonial soldiers.

German hopes of exploiting Islam were, however, initially misplaced. At the end of October 1914, the Muslim League suspended its annual sessions to avoid embarrassing the Government of India. The Viceroy repeatedly emphasized the importance of not antagonizing India's Muslims by provoking hostilities with the Ottoman Empire.³⁴ The Secretary of State for India, Lord Crewe, and the Secretary of State for War, Lord Kitchener, were also against any action which could be interpreted as 'taking the initiative against Turkey', and hence alienating Muslim opinion in India and Egypt.³⁵ By 21 October, Hardinge was confident enough to write that he was 'not even afraid of the attitude of the Mahomedans in the event of war with Turkey'.³⁶

His confidence was soon put to the test. The stakes were raised when Turkey did in fact enter the war. Despite German involvement, this development, it should be stressed, was a Turkish, not a German, initiative.³⁷ On 29 October 1914, the Turkish fleet, including two ships transferred from the German flag, attacked Russian Black Sea ports.³⁸ A British declaration of war on Turkey followed on 5 November 1914. The British and French had immediate concerns about possible rebellions amongst their Muslim colonial subjects.³⁹

British anxieties were increased when, on 14 November 1914, *fatwās* signed by the Shaikh ul-Islam proclaimed *Jihād* against the Entente powers.⁴⁰ Muslims living under British, French or Russian rule would 'merit the fire of hell' if they fought against the soldiers of Islam; they would 'merit painful torment' if they took up arms against

---

33 Strachan, *First World War*, pp. 98–9.
34 S. A. Cohen, 'The Genesis of the British Campaign in Mesopotamia', *Middle Eastern Studies*, 12/2 (1976), pp. 120–2; Goold, 'Lord Hardinge', p. 925. See also French, 'The Dardanelles, Mecca and Kut', pp. 48, 50 and V. H. Rothwell, 'Mesopotamia in British War Aims, 1914–1918', *Historical Journal*, 13/2 (1970) pp. 288–9.
35 Asquith to Venetia Stanley, 17 Aug. 1914, in Michael and Eleanor Brock (eds), *H. H. Asquith: Letters to Venetia Stanley* (Oxford: Oxford University Press, 1982), Doc. 123. See also Dockter, *Churchill and the Islamic World*, p. 67.
36 Hardinge to Holderness, quoted in Francis Robinson, *Separatism among Indian Muslims: The Politics of the United Provinces' Muslims, 1860–1923* (Delhi: Oxford University Press, 1993), p. 240.
37 For a useful discussion see Efraim Karsh, 'Holding the Balance of Power: Turkey's Complicated Relationship with Europe during the First World War and Since', *Times Literary Supplement*, 5908, 24 June 2016.
38 Strachan, *First World War*, p. 107; Cohen, 'Genesis of the British Campaign', p. 119.
39 McMeekin, *Berlin–Baghdad Express*, p. 101.
40 Geoffrey Lewis, 'The Ottoman Proclamation of Jihād in 1914' in *Arabic and Islamic Garland: Historical, Educational and Literary Papers presented to Abdul-Latif Tibawi* (London: The Islamic Cultural Centre, 1977), p. 159; see also Strachan, *First World War*, p. 97.

Turkey's allies Germany and Austria. The German Foreign Office predicted an anti-British revolt in India.[41]

The *fatwās* placed the loyalty of India's Muslims to the Sultan as Caliph into potential conflict with their obligations to the British Raj.[42] After the proclamation, the British issued a counter-proclamation, blaming Turkey for the outbreak of war.[43] Great Britain, it was promised, would respect the sanctity of the Holy Places of Islam, and they would remain in Muslim, if not Turkish, hands.[44] The Governor of Punjab, Sir Michael O'Dwyer (1864–1940), was still concerned that the Punjab's Muslims would not come forward to fight in a war against Turkey, particularly in lands which had been under Turkish rule and which contained the Holy Places of Islam.[45]

'All these pessimistic anticipations were speedily falsified' recalled Sir Michael, slightly inaccurately.[46] In November, Urdu newspapers in Punjab lamented Turkey's decision to enter the war, and argued that Turkey had been tricked into joining the war by German intrigue.[47] In Lahore, for example, the Urdu weekly *Parkash* noted that Germany had drawn the Ottoman Empire into the war with the aim of stirring up Muslim feeling throughout the world. 'We trust her sinister designs will be frustrated', the paper continued. 'The present war is ... not a war between Muhammadans and Christians; hence it is the duty of all Muhammadans in this country to refuse help to Turkey'.[48] Reactions, for the most part, were similar in the Indian Army itself. For example, one Indian Muslim officer wrote in December 1914:

> What better occasion can I find than this to prove the loyalty of my family to the British Government. Turkey, it is true, is a Muslim power, but what has it to do with us. Turkey is nothing at all to us?[49]

This response was, however, just one point along a spectrum of Indian Muslim soldiers' responses, which ranged from loyalty to outright mutiny.

Most Muslim soldiers occupied a typical middle ground of loyal endurance, with an undercurrent of some religious misgiving. There were, however, immediately some problems in the Indian Army in the Middle East. There were some desertions from the 69th Punjabis, 126th Baluchis and the 128th Pioneers. Some deserters were

---

41 Hughes, 'German Mission', p. 450.
42 Rumbold, *Watershed in India*, p. 31.
43 French, 'Dardanelles, Mecca and Kut', p. 51.
44 Goold, 'Lord Hardinge', p. 925.
45 Michael O'Dwyer, *India as I Knew It, 1885–1925* (London: Constable, 1925), p. 215.
46 O'Dwyer, *India as I Knew It*, p. 215. In fact, there were several mutinies in Muslim units of the Indian Army.
47 Jarboe, *War News in India*, p. 8.
48 *Parkash* (Urdu, Lahore, 3,500 weekly), 8 Nov. 1914, quoted in Jarboe, *War News in India*, Doc. 75. See also Docs 86, 97 and 202.
49 A Muslim officer to his brother (Central India), Dec. 1914 (Urdu), in Omissi (ed.), *Indian Voices of the Great War*, p. 25.

executed when recaptured. The desertions were prompted, according to one British official, by the proximity of Mecca and the suspicion that the British wanted the men to fight against 'the Arab gendarmes of the Holy Places'.[50] Typically, most of the deserters were Baluchis and Pathans – men from the almost entirely Muslim areas of the far West and North of India's frontier provinces.[51] There were also some desertions among Pathans from the Indian Army in Mesopotamia.[52] The prominent pro-British Muslims the Aga Khan and Sir Abbas Ali Beg were sent to Egypt to encourage loyalism among Indian and Egyptian Muslim troops.[53]

German missionaries in India, and their associates, were another potential source of anti-British feeling. 'Wherever we trace German influence', reported Austen Chamberlain (who replaced Lord Crewe as Secretary of State for India in May 1915), 'it is persistently used to stir up ill-will against British rule' in India, and 'to undermine British influence'.[54] Many German-speaking missionaries in India were interned, or confined to their homes, as a precaution, even when there was little direct evidence that they had sponsored anti-British agitation. German missionaries who had left India on the outbreak of war could also be a problem. One German, named only as 'Schultze', formerly a missionary in the Nellore District of Madras, wrote from Florida, USA, to a Muslim of the area in which he had been active in India. After abusing the British he wrote:

> Oh! Would you not wish that the glorious times of Shah Jehan, Aurangzeb and the Grand Mughals would come back and drive the perfidious English from beloved India. They have long enough sucked the life blood out of you and fattened on your land and kept you in bondage. Would to God another Nana Sahib would rise and drive the English out of India. As much as I love peace I would love to come over again and help you Indians in this glorious work.[55]

The recipient, a prudent loyalist, handed over the letter to the authorities. Elsewhere in Madras, the rumours that the Kaiser had converted to Islam had gained some currency, as had the notion that the King-Emperor George V had been carried away by a German Zeppelin.[56]

---

50 French, 'Dardanelles, Mecca and Kut', p. 52
51 Peter Stanley, *Die in Battle, Do Not Despair: The Indians on Gallipoli, 1915* (Solihull: Helion, 2015), p. 56.
52 Gardner, *Siege of Kut al-Amara*, p. 12.
53 French, 'Dardanelles, Mecca and Kut', p. 52.
54 BL, Mss Eur 473/1, Chamberlain to Hardinge, 2 July 1915.
55 NAI, Home, Political, Deposit, Jan. 1915, 43, Report on the Madras Presidency for the Period Ending 10 Dec. 1914, A. Butterworth (Acting Chief Secretary to the Government of Madras) to H. Wheeler (Secretary to the Government of India, Home Department).
56 Ibid.

In 1915, British India faced a perfect storm of Islam-related anxieties, particularly in the few weeks from January to early March. In late January and early February there was a German-sponsored Turkish attack on the Suez Canal; in the same months there were two mutinies among the Indian Army's Muslim troops, including one, at Singapore, involving violence against British officers and European civilians; in February, the Allies began their naval assault on the Turkish forts at Gallipoli; and in March there was an incident of desertion among Indian Muslim troops on the Western Front. The weakness of India's defences compounded these anxieties. India had been drained of the cream of its armed forces and left with 'a bare minimum of the troops required to maintain internal order and to defend the Frontier'.[57] The British garrison of India relied on half-trained and ill-equipped Territorials.[58]

In a memorandum to the German Chancellor on 18 August 1914, Max von Oppenheim (1860–1946), head of the German Intelligence Bureau of the East, had suggested that 'it will not be until the Turks enter Egypt and the fires of revolt flame up in India that England will be ripe for destruction'.[59] Egypt was a critical post of the empire, and the Suez Canal was the shortest sea route between India and Europe.[60] Light Turkish attacks began on 26 and 27 January 1915, and a major attack followed from 3 February.[61] The Germans hoped for a mortal blow against Britain's position, and for a revolt in Egypt.[62] The assault was, however, easily repulsed.[63] A key waterway on the route to India was held, and the threat of Islamic revolution in Egypt was contained.[64] From the outbreak of war most of the canal's defenders were from the Indian Army.[65] Despite a few desertions, Muslim troops in Egypt, it has been argued, 'performed perfectly well against their co-religionists'.[66]

Elsewhere the picture was significantly different. In January 1915, three Pathan companies of the 130th Baluchis mutinied at Rangoon in Burma, when they learned that their regiment was destined for Mesopotamia to fight the Turks.[67] Even more serious was a mutiny at Singapore, which began on 15 February 1915. Around 400 Muslim troops of the 5th Light Infantry murdered their British officers and any local British civilians they could find. The men feared that they were to be sent to fight the

---

57 IOR, L/MIL/17/5/2401, E. G. Barrow, Military Situation in India Consequent on the War, 6 June 1915.
58 Rumbold, *Watershed in India*, pp. 23–5; French, 'Dardanelles, Mecca and Kut', p. 53.
59 Fischer, *Germany's Aims*, p. 126, fn. 1.
60 McMeekin, *Berlin-Baghdad Express*, p. 223.
61 McMeekin, *Berlin-Baghdad Express*, pp. 174–6.
62 Fischer, *Germany's Aims*, pp. 127–8.
63 David French, 'The Origins of the Dardanelles Campaign Reconsidered', *History*, 68/223 (1983), p. 217.
64 Strachan, *First World War*, p. 124.
65 Stanley, *Die in Battle*, p. 58.
66 Stanley, *Die in Battle*, p. 66.
67 Omissi, *Sepoy and the Raj*, pp. 136, 140.

Turks, and a preacher at a local mosque had urged them not to do so. Unusually for the Indian Army, the regiment was an all-Muslim unit.[68]

IV. Gallipoli and India

On 1 January 1915 the Russians appealed to the Allies for a diversionary operation against the Turks to relieve pressure on the Caucasus front.[69] The British and French developed a plan to force the Dardanelles with old battleships. The assault would, it was hoped, persuade Italy and the Christian neutrals in the Balkans to join the Entente, open a supply route to Russia, and prompt a coup d'etat in Constantinople that would take Turkey out of the war.[70] The bombardment of the outer forts on the Gallipoli peninsula began on 19 February 1915.

Shortly afterwards, on the night of 3–4 March, an Indian officer in France, Jemadar Mir Mast, deserted to the Germans. He took with him around 22 followers of his unit, the 58th (Vaughan's) Rifles.[71] The officer and all the men were Pathans. The remaining 120 Pathans of the battalion were immediately disarmed and placed under British guard.[72]

Coming so soon after the Singapore mutiny, this collective act of desertion caused grave concern among the British high command. General Douglas Haig (1861–1928), commanding the First Army of the British Expeditionary Force, speculated that the attack on the Dardanelles had been exploited by German agents, leading Muslim soldiers to believe that Britain was attacking Islam more generally.[73] The incident underlined the potential fragility of the Indian Army's Muslim components. On 4 March 1915, Haig discussed the matter with General Sir James Willcocks, the commander of the Indian Corps France. Haig noted in his diary:

> I told him to consider the question, and let me know tomorrow, whether the Indian Corps is fit to attack on Wednesday or not. If he has any doubts about their advancing I won't employ them. Incidentally he expressed his sorrow at having wasted so much of his life with such a wretched lot as the Indians! And much more in the same vein. It is a serious matter for the future of the Native Army, if the Imperial Commanders judge the regiments here unfit for offensive operations.[74]

---

68 Mason, *Matter of Honour*, p. 426.
69 Strachan, *First World War*, pp. 113–16.
70 French, 'Dardanelles, Mecca and Kut', pp. 50, 53, and 'Origins of the Dardanelles Campaign', p. 218.
71 TNA, WO 33/739, French to War Office, 11 April 1915.
72 TNA, WO 33/739, French to War Office, 5 and 6 March 1915.
73 Entry for 4 March 1915 in Gary Sheffield and John Bourne, *Douglas Haig: War Diaries and Letters, 1914–1918* (London: Weidenfeld and Nicholson, 2005), p. 107.
74 Ibid.

There was, therefore some relief when Indian troops fought well at the Battle of Neuve Chapelle on 10–12 March.[75]

After the landings at Gallipoli, Indian troops, including Muslims, served directly against the Ottomans, the Indians mainly in the 29th Indian Brigade. There was, however, some reluctance to use Muslim troops in the front line, and the Muslim companies of the 69th and 89th Punjabis were sometimes used to unload stores rather than serve in battle.[76] When asked to do so, the Indians fought well, but the 69th and 89th Punjabis were withdrawn in May 1915 because of doubts about the reliability of their Muslim companies.[77] The two battalions were sent to France instead, where they arrived in June 1915.[78] They were replaced by two Gurkha battalions, so the 29th Indian Brigade ended up composed of one battalion of Sikhs and three of Gurkhas.[79]

The 89th Punjabis, one of the regiments sent to France, was a fairly typical Indian Army 'class company' regiment, with three companies of Sikhs, one of Brahmans, one of Rajputs and three of Punjabi Muslims.[80] Like many Indian Army units it served in several theatres of war.[81] The wartime history of the battalion illustrates the fact that the Indian Army was fighting a global war. It was doing so not just in the sense that there were Indian troops in places as far apart as Europe and Hong Kong, but also that there were flows of information through letters and exchanges of military personnel between all theatres. Indian troops were being cross-posted from regiments in India to regiments serving overseas, and whole regiments were being transferred between theatres. Muslim troops could therefore easily exchange ideas about the significance of the war for their faith.

On 19 March, Crewe forwarded to Hardinge a general survey of Indian Muslim opinion composed by Sir Theodore Morison (1863–1936), a member of the Council of India, and a former principal of the Muslim College at Aligarh.[82] Morison made the case that Islamic law enjoined India's Muslims to be 'loyal and obedient subjects' of the Government of India.[83] Allegiance to the Government of India therefore legally 'precluded allegiance to any other Power'. On the other hand, he observed, Indian Muslims had 'a passionate sympathy for the Turks', and there was 'some

---

75 TNA, WO 33/739, French to War Office, 14 and 19 March 1915. See also Jeffrey Greenhut, 'The Imperial Reserve: The Indian Corps on the Western Front, 1914–15', *Journal of Imperial and Commonwealth History*, 12/1 (1983), p. 65.
76 Stanley, *Die in Battle*, p. 122.
77 Stanley, *Die in Battle*, pp. 123–4.
78 Omissi (ed.), *Indian Voices of the Great War*, p. 359–62.
79 Stanley, *Die in Battle*, pp. 122–4.
80 Omissi (ed.), *Indian Voices of the Great War*, p. 363.
81 Stanley, *Die in Battle*, pp. 50, 65–6.
82 On Morison see G. R. Batho, 'Morison, Sir Theodore (1863–1936)', *Oxford Dictionary of National Biography* (Oxford: Oxford University Press, online edn, accessed 1 July 2016).
83 BL, Mss Eur 473/1, Crewe to Hardinge, 19 March 1915, Enclosure by Morison. See also Keith Jeffery, *1916: A Global History* (London: Bloomsbury, 2015), p. 195, citing, *inter alia*, Peter Hardy, *The Muslims of British India* (Cambridge, 1972), pp. 185–7.

danger' that this might 'sweep all other considerations aside'. Muslims wished the British government to conclude a separate peace with Turkey, and to guarantee her independence and territorial integrity. The best alternative would be the creation of an Arab kingdom which would include Arabia, Syria and Mesopotamia.

Indian opinion was also being collected in India on a province-by-province basis. In late April 1915, J. T. Marten (the Chief Secretary to the Government of the United Provinces), reported that Muslim opinion in the Central Provinces on the operations against Turkey in the Dardanelles was 'unsettled and conflicting'. So far, he continued, 'leading opinion seems to be on our side'.[84] In Punjab – more significant from a military perspective – there was evidence in late July of 'some sympathy' among Muslims for the Turks, and there were reports of money being collected being made on behalf of Turkey. Even when 'quite loyal to Government', thought A. B. Kettlewell of the Indian Civil Service, Punjabi Muslim opinion was inclined to regard Russian defeats 'with satisfaction'.[85] In late August 1915, the Commissioner of Jullundur Division in the Punjab suspected that there was a 'good deal of secret satisfaction' among Muslims at the continued retreat of the Russians, and a tendency 'among the less enlightened of them to attribute it to the prowess of Turkey'.[86] Punjabi newspapers reported rumours that the Kaiser had embraced Islam, but editors were sceptical about claims that he had made the pilgrimage to Mecca, or that Germany was the friend of Muslims everywhere.[87]

War with Turkey led to concern that India's neighbours Afghanistan and Persia might enter the war against British India.[88] In November 1914, the Foreign Office discovered that four German missions had been sent through Turkey to Persia and Afghanistan. The signal for revolution in India was to be given by an invasion of India by Afghanistan.[89] In late February 1915 Hardinge reported that the Amir of Afghanistan was 'resisting all temptations to Jihad' and was behaving in a friendly

---

84 NAI, Home, Political, Deposit, May 1915, 49, Fortnightly Report on the Internal Political Situation in the Central Provinces for the Second Half of April 1915, Marten to H. Wheeler (Secretary to the Government of India, Home Department), 1 May 1915.
85 NAI, Home, Political, Deposit, Aug. 1915, 28, Report on the Internal Political Situation in Punjab ... for the Half-monthly Period Ending 31 July 1915, A. B. Kettlewell (Additional Secretary to the Government of the Punjab) to H. Wheeler (Secretary to the Government of India, Home Department), 7 Aug. 1915.
86 NAI, Home, Political, Deposit, Sept. 1915, 57, Report on the Internal Political Situation in the Punjab ... for the Half-monthly Period Ending 23 Aug. 1915, A. B. Kettlewell (Additional Secretary to the Government of the Punjab) to H. Wheeler (Secretary to the Government of India, Home Department), 7 Sept. 1915. The same report confirmed the existence of sympathy for the Turks among the Muslims of Karnal District, and the collection of money on their behalf.
87 Jarboe, *War News in India*, Docs 130, 234 and 245.
88 French, 'The Dardanelles, Mecca and Kut', pp. 52–3.
89 Fisher, *Germany's Aims*, p. 126.

manner'.⁹⁰ But the Viceroy was worried about reports from the North-West Frontier Province that the German embrace of Islam 'was attracting widespread credibility among the generally pro-Turkish tribes'.⁹¹ On 8 July Chamberlain confessed that he was 'a good deal concerned about German activities in Persia, and the approach of armed Germans towards the frontiers of Afghanistan and Baluchistan'.⁹²

By early August 1915, as one German party neared Afghanistan, it had become clear that the Gallipoli operation had failed to break the Turkish lines. British planners had seriously underestimated the Turkish Army's powers of resistance.⁹³ Chamberlain had already concluded that 'the enterprise was based on a serious miscalculation'.⁹⁴ The question of whether or not to withdraw from the Gallipoli peninsula would come to dominate British strategic discussion in the following weeks. In 1906 the British General Staff had studied the problem of forcing the Dardanelles. The conclusion was that 'there would be a grave risk of a reverse, which would have a serious effect on the Mohammaden world'.⁹⁵ The repulse of a British landing 'might be followed by a general uprising against British authority throughout the East'.⁹⁶

This concern over Muslim opinion seems to have become particularly prominent in the last months of 1915, as the possibility of withdrawal was discussed.⁹⁷ As early as July 1915, Hardinge had argued that defeat in the Dardanelles 'would be absolutely fatal' in India, 'since the Mahomedens would then undoubtedly turn their eyes to Turkey far more than towards us, and Pan-Islamism would become a very serious danger'.⁹⁸ In November he opposed withdrawal, arguing that 'from an Indian point of view, our policy should be to hang on to our positions at the Dardanelles even if there is no likelihood of being able to push forward'.⁹⁹ In the event, the Cabinet approved a partial withdrawal on 7 December, then the position at Helles was evacuated in January 1916.

In the meantime, the Germans had reached Afghanistan. In August 1915, a German party, with the deserter Mir Mast, and accompanied by Indian revolutionaries, arrived in Herat. They reached Kabul in October.¹⁰⁰ They intended to persuade Amir Habibullah of Afghanistan to declare war on Britain, tempting him with German recognition of Afghan independence, and the cession of Indian territory as far as

90   BL, Mss Eur 473/2, Hardinge to Crewe, 25 Feb. 1915.
91   Hughes, 'German Mission', p. 459.
92   BL, Mss Eur 473/1, Chamberlain to Hardinge, 8 July 1915.
93   French, 'Origins of the Dardanelles Campaign', *passim*.
94   BL, Mss Eur 473/1, Chamberlain to Hardinge, 16 July 1915.
95   Strachan, *First World War*, p. 113. See also French, 'Origins of the Dardanelles Campaign', p. 211.
96   French, 'The Dardanelles, Mecca and Kut', p. 50.
97   Strachan, *First World War*, p. 121.
98   French, 'The Dardanelles, Mecca and Kut', p. 54.
99   BL, Mss Eur 473/2 Hardinge to Chamberlain, 12 Nov. 1915.
100 Hughes, 'German Mission', pp. 463–4. See also Rumbold, *Watershed in India*, p. 23.

Bombay, once Germany had won the war.[101] Their blandishments were mostly unsuccessful. Habibullah was in no hurry to make up his mind. He did not wish to end up on the losing side, and was aware that the 1907 Anglo-Russian convention placed him in a weak bargaining position.[102] British intelligence was also astute. By September, the British had deciphered a codebook captured from the German mission, and were reading German wireless traffic.[103] The Allies also intercepted some German written correspondence, and were able to inform the Amir of German plots to assassinate him if he did not co-operate with them.[104]

Over the next few weeks, matters were finely balanced. In late September, Hardinge reported that the Amir was behaving 'really too splendidly'.[105] As a reward, Hardinge asked King George V to write an autograph letter to Habibullah, which he could then show to his people. Such a letter was duly sent.[106] The Germans, however, presented a similar letter from the Kaiser in October, although the Amir was not impressed by the fact that it had been written on a typewriter.[107] In October 1915 Colmar von der Goltz was ordered to prepare for an independent war against India, leading a force of German-officered Persian volunteers.[108] On 5 November 1915 Chamberlain reported that the attitude of the Amir was 'most satisfactory'.[109] In January 1916, however, a draft treaty of friendship between Germany and Afghanistan was signed; but the cautious Amir kept raising his demands for entering the war, and in February he publicly reaffirmed his neutrality.[110] In March 1916, the prospect of war was 'about evens' according to the Chief Commissioner of the North-West Frontier Province, Sir George Roos-Keppel (1866–1921).[111] His view turned out to be alarmist. In May 1916 the German mission, disappointed, withdrew from Afghanistan.[112]

V. The Lure of Baghdad

The military operation to capture Baghdad was conceived in the summer and autumn of 1915 in this context of failure at the Dardanelles, and anxiety about global Muslim opinion. What was so appealing about the prospect of taking Baghdad?

---

101 Hughes, 'German Mission', pp. 466–7.
102 French, 'The Dardanelles, Mecca and Kut', p. 57.
103 Hughes, 'German Mission', p. 463.
104 Hughes, 'German Mission', p. 468; Rumbold, 'Watershed in India', p. 26.
105 BL, Mss Eur 473/2, Hardinge to Holderness, 24 Sept. 1915.
106 BL, Mss Eur 473/2, Hardinge to Chamberlain, 30 Sept. 1915.
107 Hughes, 'German Mission', pp. 466–8.
108 Strachan, *First World War*, p. 123; Hughes 'German Mission', p. 472.
109 BL, Mss Eur 473/1, Chamberlain to Hardinge.
110 Hughes, 'German Mission', pp. 470–1.
111 Rumbold, *Watershed in India*, p. 26.
112 Hughes, 'German Mission', p. 472.

The Government of India was attracted to the idea of controlling Mesopotamia as part of British India's 'near abroad' to secure India's defences.[113] Two months before the war with Turkey, Hardinge told Crewe that he wished to 'quietly annex' the province of Basra.[114] In September 1915 Hardinge mooted the possibility that the whole of Mesopotamia might become a province of British India after the war.[115] In November 1915, Hardinge even argued that India was fighting for Mesopotamia.

In May 1915, Austen Chamberlain replaced Crewe at the India Office. He initially wanted to continue a cautious approach in Mesopotamia. Amara was captured in early June, however, and the GOC Mesopotamia Expedition, General Sir John Nixon (1857–1921), wanted to push on to Kut al-Amara. Hardinge persuaded Chamberlain to approve the advance in July.[116] On 28 September Charles Townshend, in command of the 6th Indian Division in Mesopotamia, had attacked Ottoman forces downriver from Kut al-Amara.[117] Kut was captured on 29 September.[118] British and Indian forces were now only 100 miles from Baghdad.[119] The capture of Kut al-Amara was to be the last major British success in Mesopotamia before the decision was taken to march on Baghdad.[120] Despite the victory, Townshend felt that his troops had did not displayed the elan they had shown before. They were enervated by the heat and would need a rest in India even if they were to press on and take Baghdad.[121] Reinforcements were needed and his men were succumbing to 'every imaginable disease'. Nevertheless, on 3 October Nixon telegraphed to say that Townshend's force was 'strong enough to open [the] road to Baghdad'.[122]

The main reason for pressing on to Baghdad was concern about the possible impact of a withdrawal from Gallipoli on Muslim opinion in the East. Baghdad had been the capital of the Abbasid Caliphate, the third of the Muslim caliphates to succeed the Prophet, and was one of the great cities of the Islamic world. Its capture would reverberate throughout the East. The dominant motive for the advance on Baghdad was therefore political, not strategic.[123] As early as November 1914, Sir Percy Cox (1864–1937), the political officer attached to the Mesopotamia expeditionary force, had suggested that the capture of Baghdad might tilt Muslim populations

---

113 Strachan, *First World War*, p. 121; Rothwell, 'Mesopotamia in British War Aims', pp. 275, 280–1, 285.
114 Goold, 'Lord Hardinge', p. 929. He reaffirmed these sentiments in November 1915; see Rothwell, 'Mesopotamia in British War Aims', pp. 274–5.
115 BL, Mss Eur 473/2, Hardinge to Chamberlain, 10 Sept. 1915.
116 Goold, 'Lord Hardinge', pp. 928–9.
117 Gardner, *Siege of Kut al-Amara*, pp. 27–8.
118 Goold, 'Lord Hardinge', p. 932.
119 French, 'Dardanelles, Mecca and Kut', p. 55
120 Goold, 'Lord Hardinge', p. 927.
121 John S. Galbraith, 'No Man's Child: The Campaign in Mesopotamia, 1914–1916', *The International History Review*, 6/2 (1984), p. 371.
122 Goold, 'Lord Hardinge', p. 932; Gardner, *Siege of Kut al-Amara*, p. 30.
123 Galbraith, 'No Man's Child', p. 371.

throughout the Middle East towards Britain.[124] Hardinge put the issue very clearly in mid-September 1915. He wrote:

> Although the fall of the Dardanelles would have an immense effect in the Balkans and the Near East, the fall of Baghdad would certainly have an equal effect in the Middle East. There are few things that will impress the Afghans or the Persians and Arabs so much as the fall of Baghdad. It would be a fine stroke and would create an immense impression in this part of the world.[125]

He was also thinking of the potential impact on India's Muslims who were 'in a rather sulky frame of mind owing to our war with Turkey'.[126]

The authorities in London were also coming round to the idea of a more aggressive policy in Mesopotamia. On 8 October Chamberlain told Hardinge that the Cabinet had been 'greatly impressed with the political (and even military) advantages' throughout the East which would follow the capture of Baghdad.[127] He also reported that 'the failure to make progress in the Dardanelles' was 'producing a very bad effect in Egypt'. A week later, Hardinge wrote that 'the effect of the capture of Baghdad will be very great in the Near East, and have important consequences in Persia and Afghanistan'. It would also 'assist the general situation in India, which ... is difficult, and likely to become so more and more'.[128]

To bring focus to the discussions, the Prime Minister appointed an inter-departmental committee, representing the India Office, the Foreign Office, the War Office and the Admiralty. It was presided over by Sir Thomas Holderness (1849–1924), the Under-Secretary of State for India.[129] The committee's brief was 'to consider the question of an early advance on Baghdad'. The committee was anxious to see Baghdad in British hands, 'if the necessary reinforcements could be found', not least because it would help 'with the Persian difficulty. There ought then to be an end to the Germans overrunning that country.' To the committee it seemed almost as if the Germans in Persia had 'captured the Persian Government' and made 'the country their tool as they had made the Turks and Bulgarians'.[130] On 21 October a meeting of the War Council

---

124 Galbraith, 'No Man's Child', p. 365.
125 BL, Mss Eur 473/2, Hardinge to Chamberlain, 17 Sept. 1915. See also Goold, 'Lord Hardinge', p. 932.
126 BL, Mss Eur 473/2, Hardinge to Chamberlain, 30 Sept. 1915.
127 BL, Mss Eur 473/1, Chamberlain to Hardinge, 8 Oct. 1915. See also Galbraith, 'No Man's Child', p. 369.
128 BL, Mss Eur 473/2, Hardinge to Chamberlain, 15 Oct. 1915.
129 On Holderness see J. O. Miller, rev. Takehiko Honda, 'Holderness, Sir Thomas William, First Baronet (1849–1924)', *Oxford Dictionary of National Biography* (Oxford: Oxford University Press; online edn, accessed 1 July 2016).
130 BL, Mss Eur 473/1, Holderness to Hardinge, 22 Oct. 1915.

approved the attempt to capture Baghdad because the 'political advantages' of doing so seemed to them 'immense'.[131]

On 23 October, Hardinge sanctioned an advance on Baghdad without delay.[132] The staffs in London worried that the Turks might send reinforcements of up to 60,000 men to Baghdad by January 1916.[133] Hardinge, on the contrary, believed that it would be 'almost impossible' for them to do so, 'as they could only come down the Euphrates and Tigris on rafts and would have absolutely no means of ever getting back again except on foot'.[134] It would be very difficult to keep these troops supplied, and the Allies could keep the Turks fully occupied on other fronts, making it difficult to spare such a large force.

In this context, the news that the High Commissioner for Egypt, Sir Henry McMahon (1862–1949), had surrendered practically the whole of Mesopotamia to a proposed Arab state, in his famous letter to Sharif Hussein of 24 October 1915, accordingly came as 'a very severe shock' to Hardinge.[135] The Viceroy was furious that McMahon had denied India the fruit of her 'hard earned victories' in Mesopotamia. The India Office shared his dismay.[136]

The Government of India had agreed to the advance on Baghdad only on the understanding that the Indian Army in the Middle East would be reinforced by at least one of the two Indian infantry divisions then in France.[137] Kitchener, however, was initially very reluctant to part with them.[138] The two divisions on the Western Front were nevertheless withdrawn, and sent to Egypt to refit, before being redeployed in Mesopotamia. As it turned out, they did not join a triumphal march on Baghdad, but were to lose heavily in the failed attempts to relieve the beleaguered force at Kut al-Amara.

On 3 November Townshend announced that he intended to attack Ctesiphon and occupy Baghdad within ten days.[139] He believed, wrongly as it turned out, that he could defeat an equal or superior Ottoman force.[140] On 22–5 November his men inflicted heavy casualties on the Turks at Ctesiphon, but did not achieve a breakthrough.

---

131 BL, Mss Eur 473/1, Chamberlain to Hardinge, 22 Oct. 1915.
132 Goold, 'Lord Hardinge', p. 934; Galbraith, 'No Man's Child', p. 369.
133 Townshend, *When God Made Hell*, p. 140.
134 BL, Mss Eur 473/2, Hardinge to Chamberlain, 29 Oct. 1915. See also Goold, 'Lord Hardinge', p. 934.
135 BL, Mss Eur 473/2, Hardinge to Chamberlain, 5 Nov. 1915. See also Rothwell, 'Mesopotamia in British War Aims', p. 278.
136 Goold, 'Lord Hardinge', p. 931, fn 80.
137 BL, Mss Eur 473/2, Hardinge to Chamberlain, 29 Oct. 1915. French, 'The Dardanelles, Mecca and Kut', p. 55. The two infantry divisions were the 3rd (Lahore) and the 7th (Meerut). Two Indian cavalry divisions remained in France until early 1918.
138 BL, Mss Eur 473/1, Chamberlain to Hardinge, 7 Oct. 2015.
139 Gardner, *Siege of Kut al-Amara*, p. 30.
140 Ibid, p. 42.

His 14,000-strong force lost around 4600 men.[141] Townshend then withdrew from Ctesiphon on the evening of 25 November. On 2 December, on hearing of 'another reverse in Mesopotamia', Maurice Hankey (1877-1963), Secretary of the Committee of Imperial Defence, wrote in his diary that 'our whole eastern empire, which depends on prestige and bluff, is most seriously threatened'.[142] Townshend's division reached Kut at-Amara on 3 December 1915. Ottoman troops surrounded Kut on 7 December, and the siege began.[143] Chamberlain recognized that Townshend's 'enforced retreat', along with the failures at Gallipoli and Salonika, had 'altered the whole situation for the worse'.[144] Hardinge, however, remained confident that Townshend could break out.[145]

In February 1916 responsibility for operations in Mesopotamia was transferred from the Government of India to the War Office.[146] Henceforth, the Commander-in-Chief in India was to receive orders on military operations in Mesopotamia and Persia from the Chief of the Imperial General Staff.[147] These new arrangements proved unable to save Townshend's force. Of around 15,000 soldiers and followers under his command, nearly 4,000 became casualties during the siege. His men faced starvation and deficiency diseases such as scurvy, exacerbated by the reluctance of many Indian soldiers, particularly Muslims, to eat horse meat.[148] More than 23,000 soldiers were killed or wounded in unsuccessful attempts to relieve the division. Relief efforts were suspended in late April 1916, and Townshend surrendered his force on 29 April. Thousands of his men would subsequently die in Turkish captivity.

Islamist concerns also affected the relief forces. On 23 February 1916 the 15th Lancers were ordered to march up the Tigris to join the forces at the front. The men peacefully refused to do so.[149] They expressed 'very strong religious scruples against fighting in the vicinity of the holy places of Baghdad and Kerbela'.[150] The regiment, which had previously served with distinction on the Western Front, was composed of four squadrons of Muslims (two of Multani Pathans, and two of Muslims of

---

141 Goold, 'Lord Hardinge', p. 935.
142 French, 'The Dardanelles, Mecca and Kut', p. 45.
143 Gardner, *Siege of Kut al-Amara*, p. 63. See also Goold, 'Lord Hardinge', p. 935.
144 BL, Mss Eur 473/1, Hardinge to Chamberlain, 10 Dec. 1915.
145 Goold, 'Lord Hardinge', p. 937. See also Andrew Syk (ed.), *The Military Papers of Lieutenant-General Sir Frederick Stanley Maude, 1914–1917* (Stroud: The History Press for the Army Records Society, 2012), p. 122.
146 Goold, 'Lord Hardinge', p. 939.
147 Lord Hankey, *The Supreme Command, 1914–1918* (London: George Allen and Unwin, 1961), ii, p. 500.
148 Gardner, *Siege of Kut al-Amara*, pp. 123–5.
149 Jeffery, *1916: A Global History*, p. 204; Syk (ed.), *The Military Papers of Lt-Gen. Maude*, diary entry for 28 Feb. 1916, p. 129.
150 IOR, L/MIL/7/18327, Notes from War Diaries, Special Series, Force 'D', Army Headquarters, India, April 1917.

the Derajat and Cis-Indus).¹⁵¹ The 429 mutineers were sentenced to long terms of imprisonment or transportation.

Indian troops in other theatres quickly became aware of the mutiny, for example through letters. On hearing the news, one Punjabi Muslim wrote a saddened reply from France:

> When I read about the behaviour of the regiment, I was overwhelmed with grief. ... This is the time to show loyalty and give help to the Government and not be false to one's salt. It was to work for government and not for disobedience that they girded their loins and left their nearest and dearest. ... I feel sure that you will remember our hereditary services and show yourself worthy of our family traditions. ... Remember our duty is loyalty and bravery. I again say I am deeply grieved and hurt by the behaviour of our people.¹⁵²

Nearly all the mutineers were released on the King's birthday (which fell on 3 June) in 1917.¹⁵³ Perhaps significantly, their release happened three months after Baghdad had finally fallen.

In March 1917, at the time of the fall of Baghdad, the India Office looked back at the early stages of the Mesopotamia campaign. In a memorandum to the War Cabinet, officials justified the campaign on the plausible grounds that it had:

> probably arrested a pan-Islamic movement on a large scale throughout Mesopotamia, Persia and Afghanistan, which might easily have developed into jehad on the Indian frontier. It may justly be asserted that this timely offensive stroke saved India from being involved in a great war on her own borders, the consequences of which would have been a serious strain on the vital resources of the whole British Empire.¹⁵⁴

VI. Conclusions

The First World War has often been seen as a European civil war. It was, however, also a war which exposed significant fractures within global Islam, with millions of Muslims being swept up in the conflict, on all sides, across three continents. The 'Islamic factor'

---

151 IOR, L/MIL/7/18327, Extract from para. 41 of an (Army) Despatch from the Government of India, 14 Dec. 1917.
152 Susan VanKoski, 'Letters Home, 1915–16: Punjabi Soldiers Reflect on War and Life in Europe and their Meanings for Home and Self', *International Journal of Punjab Studies*, 2/1 (1995), p. 47.
153 Omissi, *Sepoy and the Raj*, p. 146.
154 India Office memo for the Imperial War Cabinet, 11 March 1917, quoted in Rumbold, *Watershed in India*, p. 27.

was an important part of German global strategy, and in the counter-strategy of British India. The differences between the British 'Westerners' and 'Easterners' partly reflected the fact that the British Empire maintained two great military establishments – the British Army and the Indian Army – 'which saw the world from very different viewpoints'.[155] They involved different perceptions of the Islamic world, and of its relationship to the British Empire. The war was partly a struggle for Muslim hearts and minds, and it is worth emphasizing the sheer range and variety of Muslim responses – actual and potential – to the war. The possible Islamic revolt in the British Empire was one of the great 'what ifs' of the First World War. Muslim troops of the Indian Army were fighting in many theatres of war, and there was interaction between them, on many levels. An appeal to Islam could have overturned their imperial loyalties, but it mostly failed to do so.[156] Why was this? In the first place, 'Haji Wilhelm' was a rather unconvincing champion of Islam; and Britain had better claims than Germany to be the protector of Muslims.[157] Grandiose German plans to bring about a global Islamic revolution lacked the means and personnel to do so.[158] Nor should one discount the effectiveness of British intelligence.[159] German strategy was, therefore, a 'gamble that failed'.[160] It was, however, not a reckless or foolish gamble; the Germans knew what they were doing. Just because Afghanistan and Persia did not enter the war, and the Islamic revolt in British India did not take place, did not mean that British anxieties about the loyalty of the Empire's Muslim subjects were misplaced or unimportant. In early February 1919, Amir Habibullah demanded British recognition of full Afghan sovereignty as a reward for Afghanistan's wartime neutrality. He was rebuffed, and was told that Britain would continue to regulate Afghanistan's external affairs. Two weeks later, he was murdered. His successor took up arms, and the resulting Third Afghan War forced Britain to recognize Afghan independence. It has been argued that 'if the unknown assailant who killed Habibullah in February 1919 had committed his deed three years earlier while the German mission was there, developments would have been dramatically different'.[161]

In July 1916, British Prime Minister Herbert Asquith reluctantly conceded an enquiry into the Mesopotamia fiasco.[162] The subsequent Mesopotamia Commission, which reported in June 1917, attributed blame to many British individuals, and

---

155 Galbraith, 'No Man's Child', p. 375.
156 Strachan, *First World War*, 98.
157 For similar German attempts in the Second World War see David Motadel, 'Muslims in Hitler's War', *History Today*, 65/9 (2015), pp. 19–25.
158 Fischer, *Germany's Aims*, p. 131.
159 French, 'Dardanelles, Mecca and Kut', p. 57.
160 Hughes, 'German Mission', p. 474.
161 Hughes, 'German Mission', p. 473.
162 Rumbold, *Watershed in India*, p. 27. For Hankey's argument against an enquiry see French, 'Origins of the Dardanelles Campaign', p. 210.

the memory of the campaign turned into a 'cemetery of reputations'.[163] The most prominent political casualty was Austen Chamberlain, who announced his resignation as Secretary of State for India in the House of Commons on 12 July 1917.[164] Others shared responsibility. The advance on Baghdad, and the subsequent failure at Kut al-Amara, have often been attributed to British over-confidence, and, in particular, to Hardinge's 'excessive optimism'.[165] Both Hardinge and Nixon overestimated Townshend's chances of taking the city, and the 6th Indian Division certainly did not have enough troops to do so.[166] The Indian Army was unprepared for a major war.[167] The supply system was inadequate, and the medical arrangements deplorable.[168] The issues at stake, however, were not just military and logistical; they were also religious. As the disaster at Gallipoli unfolded, anxiety – even desperation – about the prospect of a structural failure in the delicate scaffolding of the British Empire's relations with its Muslim subjects and neighbours became a dominant concern. Between 1914 and 1916, the grand strategy of British India was driven, to a significant extent, by the fact that the British Empire was 'the greatest' Muslim power 'in the world'.

163 Galbraith, 'No Man's Child', pp. 374–5.
164 Robert C. Self (ed.), *The Austen Chamberlain Diary Letters* (Cambridge: Cambridge University Press, 1995), pp. 47–8.
165 Goold, 'Lord Hardinge', p. 937.
166 Galbraith, 'No Man's Child', p. 385.
167 Syk (ed.), *The Military Papers of Lt-Gen. Maude*, pp. 17, 122–3.
168 Galbraith, 'No Man's Child', p. 364.

8

The Expansion of the Indian Army Officer Corps during the First World War

Alan Jeffreys

The historian Christopher Atkinson, who served as a captain in the Oxford University Officer Training Corps during the First World War and authored a number of First World War formation and regimental histories, stated that the difficulties of raising, recruiting, training and equipping the Indian Army in the last two years of the war 'will be seen to rank high among great administrative achievements' of the war.[1] However no official histories of the Indian Army during the Great War were commissioned and thus there is no equivalent to the Second World War official history, *Expansion of the Armed Forces and Defence Organisation 1939-1945*.[2] This chapter partially attempts to rectify this by looking at the expansion of the officer corps of the Indian Army during the First World War.[3]

At the beginning of the First World War, the Army in India despatched six Expeditionary Forces lettered A to F to France and Flanders, East Africa, Mesopotamia, Egypt and the Mediterranean, Force G was created in mid-1915 for Gallipoli after Indian troops had been sent there. One of the major problems for the

---

1   C. T. Atkinson, 'The Expansion of the Indian Army' in Sir Charles Lucas (editor), *The Empire at War* (London: Humphrey Milford & Oxford University Press, 1926), p. 201.
2   See Sri Nandan Prasad, *Expansion of the Armed Forces and Defence Organisation 1939-45* (New Delhi: Pentagon Press, 2012). This volume of the official history of the Indian Armed Forces in the Second World War was originally published in 1956.
3   See F. W. Perry, *The Commonwealth Armies: Manpower and organisation in two World* Wars (Manchester: Manchester University Press, 1988), pp. 91-96; I. D. Leask, 'The Expansion of the Indian Army during the Great War' (University of London: unpublished MPhil thesis, 1989) and Brian D. N. Stevens, 'The Expansion of the Indian Army during World War I', *Journal of the Society for Army Historical Research*, Vol. LXXVI, No. 305, Spring 1998, pp. 34-42.

Indian Army was to find replacements for these forces and in particular officers.⁴ As an official memorandum remarked:

> The provision of British officers for Indian units has been one of the most difficult problems of the war. In the first place, the small British community in India, being engaged for the most part in government service or in the industries of national importance, offers very limited scope as a source of recruitment; and secondly, the pre-war organisation of the Army in India having been based on the requirements of the frontier campaign only, had made no provision, even within the limits available, for a reserve of officers to replace casualties on a large scale or to fill the junior commissioned ranks of newly raised units.⁵

By the end of 1916 the army needed 15,250 replacements a month. Thus Army Headquarters (AHQ) India found it increasingly difficult to recruit, train and replace personnel for units fighting overseas. Prior to 1914 there were 138 infantry regiments, 39 cavalry regiments and 12 mountain batteries in the Indian Army. In addition, the Army in India incorporated the British Army and Imperial Service forces which meant that there were an additional 52 British Army infantry battalions, 9 cavalry regiments and 64 artillery batteries as well as 10 Imperial Service battalions and 2 Imperial Service mountain batteries. In numerical terms the Army in India numbered 236,000 with 155, 423 of these being Indian Army.⁶ Of these there were actually only 2586 officers. By 1919 the Indian Army had recruited 877, 068 combatants with 9,583 officers being commissioned during the war, 5,653 of which were trained in India.⁷

In 1886 single infantry battalion regiments had been linked together in groups of two to five units with one regimental centre responsible for recruitment, training and reinforcements but as a 1924 history of the organization of the Indian Army stated:

> It had the obvious disadvantage that, in practice, the units of the group could only be reinforced by depleting the strength of the unit which happened to be located at the regimental centre. As there were 43 of these centres it followed that, in cases of grave emergency, the system would have to be abandoned or 43

---

4   See Dennis Showalter, 'The Indianization of the Egyptian Expeditionary Force, 1917-18: An Imperial Turning Point', in Kaushik Roy (ed.), *The Indian Army in the Two World Wars* (Leiden: Brill, 2012), p. 148 and Perry, *Commonwealth Armies*, p. 92.
5   IOR, L/MIL/17/5/2381, Memorandum on India's contribution to the war in men, material and money, p. 7.
6   See S. D. Pradhan, *Indian Army in East Africa 1914-1918* (New Delhi: National Book Organisation, 1991), pp. 1-18.
7   IOR, L/MIL/17/5/2381, Memorandum on India's contribution to the war in men, material, and money, pp. 7-9. See also *Statistics of the Military Effort of the British Empire during the Great War 1914-1920* (London: HMSO, 1922), p. 777.

battalions, all fully trained, that is to say, one-third of the strength of the Indian Infantry, would not be available for active service.[8]

Thus, the system broke down during the First World War and the 115 battalions serving overseas had their own individual depots that were all trying to recruit, train and reinforce their battalions in isolation.[9] For the first few years of the war, new units were created to eventually form six extra infantry divisions by 1918. In 1917 for example, 55 new battalions were raised. These units were then posted into British Army Divisions, such as the 53rd Welsh Division in Palestine, as the British units were broken up and British Army personnel were sent to the Western Front, a process called 'Indianization'. This expansion of the Indian Army in Palestine was further increased by the removal of companies from regiments in Egypt and Mesopotamia to form new battalions. The shortfall was made up by partially trained men from the depots in India and, as James Kitchen has pointed out, officered by British and Indian officers who had experience of active service.[10] He has clearly shown that in the period 1917-18, as in 1914-15 on the Western Front, the Indian Army acted as the imperial reserve by providing troops for Palestine and also Salonica in order to free up British troops for the Western Front showing 'the all-encompassing and global nature of the 'totalizing logic' of the First World War'.[11] By the end of the war there were 10 Indian Divisions overseas and four in India.

Traditionally officers of the Honourable East India Company were trained at the East India Company military seminary at Addiscombe in Surrey but when the Company came under government control in 1858 officer cadets like their British Army counterparts attended the Royal Military College at Sandhurst where they underwent eighteen months training (or RMA Woolwich for Sapper & Miners who went straight to their units and were commanding sub-units after a few months

---

8   *The Army in India and its Evolution* (Calcutta: Superintendent Government Printing, India, 1924), p. 99.
9   See for example Captain Roly Grimshaw, *Indian Cavalry Officer 1914-15* (Tunbridge Wells: D. J. Costello Publishers, 1986), in particular the section 'A Day at an Indian Cavalry War Depot', pp. 183-197.
10 BL, Mss Eur E420/18-24, Papers of General Sir Charles Monro, Despatch by H.E. General Sir C. C. Monro GCB, GCMG, C-in-C India, on the part played by India, including Indian States, in the prosecution of the War, 9 April 1919, p.11. See also James E. Kitchen, 'The Indianization of the Egyptian Expeditionary Force: Palestine 1918' in Kaushik Roy (ed.), *The Indian Army in the Two World Wars* (Leiden: Brill, 2012), pp. 173-4 and James E. Kitchen, *The British Imperial Army in the Middle East: Morale and Military Identity in the Sinai and Palestine Campaigns, 1916-18* (London: Bloomsbury, 2014), pp. 190-203.
11 Kitchen, *British Imperial Army in the Middle East*, p. 196. See also George Morton Jack, 'The Indian Army on the Western Front, 1914-1915: A Portrait of Collaboration' *War in History*, Vol. 13, No. 3, 2006, pp. 329-362.

probation) and then were put on the unattached list.[12] They would spend a year with British unit commanding at platoon level, acclimatising to India and learning the language before joining an Indian Army unit usually at company level.

In 1903 Lord Curzon attempted to organize officer training in the largely politically inspired Imperial Cadet Corps (ICC) for Indian gentry and nobility. The aristocratic graduates were granted commissions in His Majesty's Native Land Forces but they were subordinate to the most junior British officer. Their role, if they remained in the Indian Army rather than the States Forces, was for ceremonial purposes at the various Durbars and acting as aides-de-camp (ADC) on the staffs of senior officers. For instance Amar Singh, who graduated from the ICC in 1905 and was ADC to General O'Moore Creagh until 1914, was eventually commissioned as a King's Commissioned Officer into the Indian Army along with eight fellow ICC graduates in 1917. This was due to increasing political pressure but with a date of seniority dating from 1917, rather than 1905. Captain Amar Singh did see active service in the Waziristan campaign after the First World War and commanded his regiment for a short period in 1920. However, he only found fulfilment when he formed and commanded the Jaipur Lancers in 1923 becoming Commander of all the Jaipur States forces and retiring as a Major-General in 1936.[13]

At the outbreak of the war the War Office commandeered all Indian Army officers who were on leave in the UK amounting to 253 officers in order to help raise the Kitchener Army Battalions.[14] Francis Yeats-Brown was on leave in Ireland at the time when he was ordered first to report to his regiment, the Bengal Lancers (17th Cavalry) in India and then a second telegram arrived, ordering him to a Cavalry Depot near Aldershot.[15] For each British division 598 officers were needed. In the 38th Welsh Division, there were five Indian Army officers, either retired officers or those who were in the UK in 1914, then attached to the War Office.[16] In addition

---

12 See J. M. Bourne, 'The East India Company's military seminary, Addiscombe, 1809-1858', *Journal of the Society for Army Historical Research*, Vol. LVII, No. 323, Winter 1979, pp. 206-22. See also H. M. Vibart, *Addiscombe: Its Heroes and Men of Note* (London, 1894).

13 See Chandar Sundaram, "Treated with Scant Attention": The Imperial Cadet Corps, Indian Nobles, and Anglo-Indian Policy, 1897-1917', *Journal of Military History*, Vol. 77, January 2013, pp. 41-70. See also S. H. Rudoplh, L. I. Rudolph with Mohan Singh Kanota, *Reversing the Gaze: Amar Singh's Diary, A Colonial Subject's Narrative of Imperial India* (Boulder, Colorado: Westview Press, 2002); DeWitt C. Ellinwood, Jr., *Between Two Worlds: A Rajput Officer in the Indian Army, 1905-1921: Based on the Diary of Amar Singh of Jaipur* (Lanham, Maryland: Hamilton Books, 2005) and Michael Creese, 'Swords Trembling in their Scabbards': The Changing Status of Indian Officers within the Indian Army, 1757-1947 (Solihull: Helion, 2014).

14 IOR, L/MIL/17/5/2381, Memorandum on India's contribution to the war in men, material, and money, p. 7.

15 See F. Yeats-Brown, *Bengal Lancer* (London: Anthony Mott, 1984), p. 118.

16 Namely Major General Sir Ivor Philipps, Brigadier General Sir Henry Edward ap Rhys Pryce who went on to be the first Indian Army officer to hold the post of Master General Ordnance, Brigadier General Gwyn Thomas, Lieutenant Colonel R. C. Bell

there were five Indian Army officers commanding Kitchener Army Divisions.[17] Although their service was not particularly highly regarded by all as retired officers were nicknamed 'dugouts' and the regulars from the Indian Army and the colonies were called 'backwoodsmen'.[18] In addition, four officers were taken from each British Army infantry and cavalry unit in India. Even Indian Army officers sent to Britain for convalescence were seconded to the British Army with the result that wounded officers in Force B in East Africa were sent back to India so that they could return to the Indian Army on recovery rather than be commandeered by the British Army. At the same time, all officers commissioned from Sandhurst would now join the British Army with an overall result that there was a dearth of trained officers in India. This was intended to be made up through the Indian Army Reserve of Officers (IARO), however this actually only amounted to 39 officers in 1914, 11 cavalry and 28 infantry, who were mainly retired Indian Army officers. The IARO were members of the Volunteer Corps and undertook two weeks annual training. According to Major Walter Crum of the Calcutta Light Horse writing in the *Journal of the United Service Institution of India (JUSII)*:

> Before the war the knowledge of the very existence of an Indian Army Reserve was confined to a few enthusiastic members of that Reserve and their friends. The regulations dealing with the subject were comprised in three pages of an Appendix to Army Regulations Volume II.
>
> No serious attempt was ever made to recruit for the Reserve, the only standard of military knowledge required was that the Officer should obtain a certificate of proficiency such as is granted to a Captain of Volunteer forces in India, and only in the case of cavalry was a yearly training of 14 days insisted on.[19]

From this inauspicious start, the plan was to expand the IARO by 800-900. By 1915 500 applicants had been accepted by raising the age limit to 35 for Europeans in India with no experience of military service and no age limit for those serving in Volunteer units who numbered about 30,000 and had had some training. Initially IARO were

and Lieutenant Colonel James R. Gaussen. I'm grateful to Peter Robinson for this information.

17 The Divisional Commanders of Kitchener's New Armies were: Major General Alexander Wallace – 15th (Scottish) Division; Major General Charles G. Mansell Fasken – 19th (Western) Division; Major General Sir John G. Ramsey – 24th Division; Major General Sir Edward C. W. Mackenzie-Kennedy – 26th Division; Brigadier General John G. Hunter – 35th Division; Major General Sir Charles Herbert Powell – 36th (Ulster) Division and Major General Sir Ivor Philipps – 38th (Welsh) Division.

18 See Captain A. V. Gompertz, ' A Divisional School for officers in the field in 1915-1916' *Journal of the United Service Institution of India*, Vol. XLVII, No. 210, January 1918, p. 29.

19 Major W. E. Crum, 'The Indian Army Reserve of Officers' *Journal of the United Service Institution of India*, Vol. XLV, 1916, p. 282. Major Crum was President of the Bengal Chamber of Commerce, a member of the Legislative Council and knighted in 1920.

sent to a British Army unit in India in accordance with the pre-war practice. They underwent about six weeks training consisting of lectures, physical drill, rifle training, drill, entrenching and minor tactics. Training would be based on the War Office publications *Field Service Regulations Part 1* and *Infantry Training* and some exercises such as night operations. As an article in the *JUSII* in 1916 by Major Hardman of the Somerset Light Infantry stated it might:

> ...also prove of some interest to others who wonder how the not inconsiderable number of very passable and tolerably efficient officers of the Indian Army Reserve have been moulded (practically from the raw material) into what they are now, namely able to do their bit, and of great assistance to the Indian Army in this time of stress.[20]

Major George Molesworth, who was the adjutant with the Somerset Light Infantry at the same time, wrote in his memoir, *Curfew on Olympus*, that he stayed up all night preparing a six week training programme for seventeen new recruits from the Indian Civil Service, tea plantations and firms in Calcutta and Bombay who he regarded as excellent material.[21] Molesworth transferred to the 15th Punjab Regiment in 1928 and ended up as Deputy Chief of the Imperial General Staff at General Headquarters India during the Second World War.

IARO officers were sent out to France as replacements in 1915 with General Willcocks, the Indian Corps Commander, praising their quality.[22] Although Generals Nixon and Townshend in Mesopotamia were not quite so complimentary.[23] According to I.D. Leask's thesis on the expansion of the Indian Army during the First World War the IARO was expanded by volunteers from both the UK and India but depended on two criteria from the UK. Firstly they had to be 'socially acceptable' which he described as 'a rather vague assessment of leadership qualities determined at interview' and secondly they had to be proficient in an Indian language. John Morris, who joined the Indian Army during the war, noted that in 1916 pamphlets were circulated inviting junior British Army officers to apply for regular commissions in the Indian Army. He wrote:

> The brochure was designed like an advertisement for foreign travel, and it gave the impression that life in India was one long holiday. There were facilities for every kind of game; even polo cost next to nothing, and it was apparently possible

---

20 Major H. F. Hardman, 'The Training of Officers of the Indian Army Reserve' *JUSII*, Vol. XLV, 1916, p. 371.
21 See Lieutenant General G. N. Molesworth, *Curfew on Olympus* (London: Asia Publishing House, 1965), p. 17.
22 See Leask, Expansion of the Indian Army during World War I, p. 169.
23 See Edwin Latter, 'The Indian Army in Mesopotamia 1914-1918' Part II, *Journal of the Society for Army Historical Research*, 1994, p. 172.

to shoot a tiger from the bungalow veranda as one lay sipping one's morning tea. Strangely, there was no mention of the Indian peoples; so far as the pamphlet was concerned they did not exist.[24]

Whereas in India prospective officers just needed to be 'socially acceptable' with volunteers coming from the business communities and the ranks of Territorial Army sent out India who were often middle class and had undergone some military training.[25] Captain Winn was posted to the IARO in 1914 joining the South Lancashire Regiment at Quetta for training. He noted that there were only five regular officers in the battalion with the rest of the officers from the IARO. He commented that 'The majority are planters and they are a fairly rough set – still they know how to behave like gentlemen on occasion'.[26] The officers were also recruited from the Indian Police Service, the Indian Civil Service and the Public Works Department. It would seem that the existing Indian Army officers were keen to maintain the middle class basis of the officer class that had been the mainstay of the Indian Army since the beginning of the nineteenth century.[27]

The volunteer forces were also reorganised at the beginning of the war. For instance, the 1st Battalion, Calcutta Volunteer Rifles were divided into 11 companies recruited from different communities in Calcutta: A company was recruited from the Calcutta Free School Cadets; B1 company from the Anglo-Indian Jewish Community; B2 form the Anglo-Indian Trades; C company from the La Martiniere College Cadets; D company from the Medical College; F company from Europeans working in various trades; G company form the Calcutta Boys School Cadets; H company from the Kidderpore Docks; I company from the mercantile community; J company from mercantile veterans and K company from the Armenian community. The second battalion, the Port Defence Volunteers and the Calcutta Scottish were organised along similar lines. The Calcutta Light Horse (CLH) were recruited from mercantile firms and the professions with men from the same firm being posted together. During the 1913-14 season the CLH had a reasonable turnout rate in comparison to most Volunteer forces as over 40% attended over 40 drills.[28]

The IARO did expand, in August 1916 it numbered 2,100 increasing to 3,500 by April 1917 and by 1918 5,300 commissions had been granted. The majority were recruited from civilians, the Volunteer Forces and the British Army Territorial units, all based in India rather than from the UK. From 1917 onwards a quota system was put into practice where each Territorial battalion had to provide two officer candidates

---

24 John Morris, *Hired to Kill* (London: Rupert Hart-Davis, 1960), pp. 47-48.
25 See Leask, Expansion, pp. 166-170.
26 IWM, 97/18/1, Documents.6508, Papers of Captain H. E. Winn.
27 See P. E. Razzell, 'Social Origins of Officers in the Indian and British Home Army: 1748-1962', *The British Journal of Sociology*, Vol. 14, No. 3, September 1963, pp. 248-280.
28 See Major W. E. Crum, 'The Improvement in strength and efficiency of the Volunteer Force in India', *JUSII*, Vol. XLVI, No. 206, January 1917, pp. 11, 13.

a month and an artillery unit providing one, amounting to at least 60 recruits per month with all units encouraged to do so.[29] These recruits then attended one of four temporary officer schools at Ambala, Sabathu, Bangalore and Nasik, who combined trained 3,620 officers in India during the war. Ambala and Sabathu were set up as officers' schools of instruction to train IARO infantry officers taking 300 officers for four months, whereas Bangalore took cavalry officers as well. Nasik was formed to train British service officers in the duties of a platoon commander with a slightly shorter course of three months.[30]

From April 1915 officer cadets were trained for six months at Quetta with a hundred cadets coming out to India having passed the examination. The other officers' school was at Wellington but only Europeans or Anglo-Indians were allowed to attend. However the Quetta and Wellington courses were for those officer cadets who wanted to become regular Indian Army officers and as a result only 1,312 cadets passed out of these two colleges during the war.[31] For example Stanley Jepson, who later became editor of *The Illustrated Weekly of India*, passed the Civil Service Army Entrance Exam in 1914 and was selected to join the new military college at Quetta and later joined the 40th Pathans.[32] Later in the war, once perspective regular Indian Army cadets had passed the entrance examination or been nominated for a commission, Quetta and Wellington took 150 and 120 cadets per year respectively where they undertook a twelve month course of which three would be spent with an officer cadet battalion in the UK.[33] Dermot Killingley spent his three months with a battalion in Newmarket just before the armistice and then spent a year in Wellington where he 'enjoyed the course very much' before joining the 37th Lancers.[34] Training at all these schools and colleges were along similar lines to War Office establishments in the British Army. Sandhurst provided officers for the Indian Army from 1915 onwards up until a limit of 40. By the end of the war 221 officers came out from Sandhurst. In addition, in 1917 all officers below the rank of General Staff Officer (Grade 2) who had been originally commandeered by the War Office in 1914 could now return to Indian service. AHQ could apply for their return to command the new units being formed in India. This was in line with official policy that India needed to raise more troops in order to free up British troops for service on the Western Front.

29 See Major General Nigel Woodyatt, *Under Ten Viceroys: The Reminiscences of a Gurkha* (London: Herbert Jenkins, 1922), p. 258.
30 IOR, L/MIL/7/19018, Military Training Pamphlet No. G.S. 33: Schools and Specialist Courses for the Training of officers, NCOs and men of the Army in India, instruction at which is carried out under the guidance of General Staff, pp. 4-15.
31 IOR, L/MIL/17/5/2274 Standing Orders of the Cadet College, Wellington, January 1917. L/MIL/17/5/2275 Standing Orders of the Cadet College, Quetta, February 1918.
32 See Khushwant Singh, *Sahibs who loved India* (New Delhi: Penguin, 2010), p. 16.
33 IOR, L/MIL/7/19018, Military Training Pamphlet No. G.S. 33, pp, 23, 32.
34 D. M. Killingley, *Farewell the Plumed Troop: A Memoir of the Indian Calvary 1919-1945* (Newcastle: Grevatt & Grevatt, 1990), pp. 9, 12-13.

A number of schools of instruction were set up during the First World War such as an artillery school at Quetta, three musketry schools at Pachmarhi, Satara and Rawalpindi, four schools of physical and bayonet training at Ambala, Kasauli, Quetta and Poona, a machine gun training school, signalling schools, a Central Bombing and Stokes Trench Howitzer School at Mhow and a Staff School at Saugor.[35] As well as the Mountain Warfare School set up in 1916 at Abottabad that historian Tim Moreman has recognised began to bear dividends as early as 1917.[36] However, some courses of instruction were behind the standards of training in the UK at the same time. Captain Pepperall who transferred from the West Somerset Yeomanry to the Indian Army in 1918 noted that at the musketry course at Quetta he 'was now required to assimilate a course which was quite out of date by English standards' but realised that it was essential to have systems of training in the interests of standardized across the Indian Army.[37] However, at the Officer Training School at Indore training was based on *Field Service Regulations Part 1* as well as the Stationary Service (SS) pamphlet series.[38] The Jhansi Brigade was trained by Brigadier General R. M. Poore, who was seen as an inspirational trainer, based on guidance from AHQ, as Major General Woodyatt commented in his memoir:

> He was the first man I knew to see that we must prevent training getting *dull*, and must do all possible to increase the interest and intelligence of the Indian recruit. His system included the novel and most successful experiment of 'recruit teaching recruit,' which at Jhansi reached a high standard of excellence. Whenever it proved a failure elsewhere, the system was at once blamed, whereas it was not the system that was at fault at all, but the method of supervision.[39]

Indeed in the campaign theatres the training was very current, with Indian troops in Palestine training along the lines of the latest lessons learnt on the Western Front, as well as learning through combat. Training Manuals from the Western Front such as SS 143: *The Training and Employment of a Platoon, 1918* and SS 135: *Training and Employment of Divisions, 1918* were distributed in the Indianized Divisions.[40]

---

35   IOR, L/MIL/7/19018, Military Training Pamphlet No. G. S. 33, pp. 1-3, 50-71.
36   See Tim Moreman, *The Army in India and the Development of Frontier Warfare, 1849-1947* (Basingstoke, Macmillan, 1998), pp. 99-103.
37   IWM, 08/42/1, Documents.16108, Captain R. A. Pepperall, 'From Bridgewater to Baghdad via Bullecourt and Passchendaele' (Unpublished memoir), p. 100.
38   IOR, L/MIL/7/19018, Commissions for Indians – Disposals of Reports on Indian cadets at Indore.
39   Woodyatt, *Under Ten Viceroys*, p. 240.
40   See Kitchen, *British Imperial Army in the Middle East*, p. 203. For the importance of these training pamphlets see Jim Beach, 'The Division in the Attack – 1918: SS 135 in *The Strategic and Combat Studies Institute Occasional*, No. 53, 2008 and Paddy Griffith, *Battle Tactics of the Western Front: the British Army's Art of Attack, 1916-18* (New Haven, Yale University Press, 1994).

At the beginning of the war the only Indian officers in the Indian Army were in the Indian Medical Service (IMS). For example Lieutenant Cursetjee nicknamed Charlie Curstjee had been educated in India, Cambridge University and at a London hospital. He joined the Indian Medical Service in 1912 and was attached to the 14th Sikhs in Gallipoli and was twice mentioned in despatches and badly wounded. He then served in Mesopotamia and was awarded the Distinguished Service Order. During the Second World War he was promoted to Major General; his last post was as Deputy Director Medical Services for the North-Western Army in 1943-45. Lieutenant General Thapar who served with the IMS for forty years left a rather damning opinion of the IMS during the First World War:

> During the Great War the two medical organisations, the British and the Indian, functioned side by side in almost all theatres of war where troops were engaged in action. The British service, the RAMC, being a properly organised and unified corps stood the test under most conditions of warfare, whereas the Indian service succumbed in many situations unless it was supported by the RAMC. This was largely due to the fact that having no established set-up of a military nature of its own it had no recognised standing in the Army hierarchy. The main policy was decided upon, at the top, by the British service but its interpretation and execution was left to senior IMS officers, from the civil, who were inexperience in appreciating medical situtsions and incapable of demanding the necessary personnel, equipment and stores. This resulted in a series of muddles, inefficiency and a lack of esprit de corps. Having little morale in its own ranks reflected poorly on the troops.[41]

The IMS numbered 213 Lieutenant Colonels., 266 Majors and 244 captains in 1914. This remained fairly static throughout the war with 733 permanent officers in 1918 and the 675 new officers were only given temporary commissions.

In 1917 due to political pressure and the contribution of the Indian Army throughout the war, nine Indian officers under the ICC Corps scheme were granted King's Commissions and in 1918 Indian cadets were admitted to Sandhurst for the first time. Ten officers were allowed to attend for King's Commissions for the duration of war with all fees exempted. Although Lieutenant Colonel Sharma in his *Nationalisation of the Indian Army* stated that: '...selection for these was restricted to leading families of martial races and of high social standing'.[42] In 1918 a temporary school of Indian cadets was formed at Daly College, Indore. The first batch comprised 42 cadets out of 70 applications who trained for a year with 39 qualifying on 1 December 1919 and 33

---

41 Lt Gen. D. R. Thapar, *The Morale Builders: Forty Years with the Military Medical Services of India* (Bombay, 1965), p. 39.
42 Lt. Col. Gautam Sharma, *Nationalisation of the Indian Army* (New Delhi: Allied Publishers, 1996), p. 52.

granted a King's Commission on 17 July 1920. This first batch included future Indian Army leaders like Field Marshal Cariappa and General Rudra. Rudra served with the British Army during the First World War. He passed the selection board in 1918 but was informed that no more commissions would be granted as there were too many regular British Army officers left over from the war. He was then sent to Indore where he commented in his memoir transcribed to Major General Palit:

> I found the cadets a very motley collection. The authorities had made selections on the basis of 'two of each' – from various regions and classes of India: two Jats; two Coorgis, two Bengalis; two Christians – and so on, by what yardstick the individuals were chosen I could not imagine. There were a number of 'rankers' from the Army; and here, as I later found out. Commanding officers did not always scruple to send the best men as cadets to Indore (or later, to Sandhurst or the IMA). Many preferred to reward loyal 'yes-men' rather than select good officers material. Some even sent unsuitable prospective cadets in the hope that they would thus undermine 'Indianisation' scheme.[43]

Rudra thought very few of the candidates had had the advantage of attending boarding schools that fostered self-reliance and as a result found it difficult to fit into the officers' mess or 'Cantonment Culture'. Much to his annoyance in 1922, 700 British officers from cadet schools in India, Australia and Canada were given seniority of one day over the Indore cadets. This affected Rudra later when at the rank of major, he was second in command of the 1st/15th Punjab Regiment and remained so for a long period to an officer who had been given the one day seniority.[44] In his final report the Commandant at Indore, Brigadier General W. C. Black, wrote of Rudra, who passed out 31st, that he 'gives promise of holding his own in regimental life' and had been much impressed that he had previously served in the British Army. Whereas Cariappa, who passed out 7th, who apparently had a tendency to 'show off' but 'should develop into a competent and useful officer' who had 'won the mile in the Athletic Sports in fine style'.[45]

Thus at the end of the First World War there were four avenues of King's Commissions for Indian officers: ten cadets attending Sandhurst; a maximum of twenty officers who were commissioned for distinguished service during the First World War; temporary commissions through Indore and honorary commissions for maharajahs and princes up to a maximum of 200.[46] These very limited concessions

---

43   Major General D. K. Palit, *Major General A. A. Rudra: His Service in Three Armies and Two World Wars* (New Delhi: Reliance Publishing House, 1997), pp. 54-55.
44   See ibid., pp. 55, 65-66.
45   IOR, L/MIL/7/19018, Commissions for Indians – Disposal of Reports on Indian Cadets at Indore.
46   See for example Hugh Purcell, *The Maharaja of Bikaner* (New Delhi: Rupa Publications, 2010), pp. 33-34.

did not assuage public opinion after the sacrifice of the Indian Army during the First World War.

The administrative changes in India that were brought in the last two years of war that included the further expansion of the officer corps were largely the responsibility of the new Commander-in-Chief (C-in-C) India, General Charles Monro, appointed on 1 October 1916. According to a recent study by Kristian Coates Ulrichsen he: 'gathered around him a group of talented administrative officers with recent military experience in Egypt and at the Dardanelles, in a prime example of cross-campaign absorption of lessons learned'.[47] Colonel (later Brigadier General) William Villiers-Stuart who was Commandant of the Mountain Warfare School from 1917-1918 was more forthright in his views of the British service generals who were Inspectors General of Infantry before he was in October 1918:

> General Christian, British Service, had recently been made Inspector General of Infantry and as such had to tour the country and report on the standards of various units and assist them to improve where necessary. He was useless. He did not know anything of the Indian Army or the Gurkha Service; knew no detailed work at all, and despised the Territorials. So after a time he was persuaded to resign from the work…
>
> That none of this occurred to AHQ India was not surprising as they merely thought that all kinds of troops were the same except that of course the British troops must be the best. In their eyes all was well.[48]

In the *Indian Army List* for January 1917, out of the senior positions at AHQ in Delhi, only the Director of Military Operations, Brigadier General Andrew Skeen, was Indian Army, The C-in-C, India, the Chief of the General Staff, the Director of Staff Duties and the Inspector of Infantry were all British service, presumably Monro was instrumental in this predominance of British service officers in his General Staff. Indeed as John Bourne has suggested this was one of the reasons that Monro was appointed C-in-C and gathered round himself a staff that were not 'old India hands'.[49] As the war progressed, some Indian Army officers were advanced in AHQ, Brigadier General Gerald Christian did not resign as Villiers-Stuart suggests but the post of Inspector of Infantry was divided into two due to the difficulties of finding officers and also those capable of instructing them, with Christian covering the North of

---

47 Kristian Coates Ulrichsen, *The First World War in the Middle East* (London: Hurst, 2014), p. 138.
48 R. M. Maxwell, *Villiers-Stuart goes to War* (Edinburgh, Pentland Press, 1990), pp. 193-194. Monro was also a proven trainer of soldiers, see Ian Beckett, Timothy Bowman and Mark Connelly, *The British Army and the First World War* (Cambridge: Cambridge University Press, 2017), p. 81.
49 See John Bourne, 'Charles Monro', in Ian F. W. Beckett & Steven J. Corvi, *Haig's Generals* (Barnsley: Pen & Sword, 2006), p. 136.

India and the south was covered by Major General Nigel Woodyatt, a Gurkha officer, in October 1917 and Villiers-Stuart was appointed Inspector of Infantry, North in September 1918.[50] The exception was the 'old India hand' Lieutenant General Havelock Hudson who as Adjutant General oversaw the successful recruitment campaign during the war.

The expansion of the Indian Army was essential in 1919 when the army was involved in the Third Afghan War and the campaign in Waziristan as well as providing internal security and occupation forces in Egypt, Turkey, Palestine and Mesopotamia.[51] As the official memorandum on India's contribution to the war remarked: 'The number of British officers added to the Indian Army and the Indian Army Reserve between 1 August 1914 and 31st October 1918 was nearly four times the number on the strength of the Indian Army at the outbreak of war'.[52] Indeed the expansion of the officer corps compares very favourably with the example of the Second World War. A similar organisation of Officer Training Schools were set up in India and an institutionalized training framework developed from the First World War onwards, although the numbers involved were far greater as 15,540 Indian officers, for example, were commissioned by the end of the Second World War.[53]

---

50 See *Indian Army Lists* for October 1917 and November 1918. See also Woodyatt, *Under Ten Viceroys*, pp. 235-236.
51 See Perry, *Commonwealth Armies*, p. 97.
52 IOR, L/MIL/17/5/2381, Memorandum on India's contribution to the wat in men, material, and money, pp. 7-8.
53 See Alan Jeffreys, *Approach to Battle: Training the Indian Army during the Second World War* (Solihull: Helion, 2017). See also Prasad, *Expansion of the Armed Forces*, pp. 99-104 and Kitchen, *British Imperial Army in the Middle East*, p. 219.

9

The Sikh Experience[1]

David Omissi

When King George V, the Emperor of India, declared war on Germany in August 1914 the whole empire, including India, was deemed to be at war.[2] The war would become a test of loyalty for all communities in India. British efforts to win the war and to mobilize India's resources were to make major inroads into Indian life. Taxes and prices, especially of staple food grains and imported goods, rose dramatically.[3] The strains of war were felt especially in the Punjab, which was the main recruiting ground for the Indian Army.[4] The pressures were particularly important among those communities, like the Sikhs, who had strong military connections.

This chapter will address several questions. Why were Sikhs recruited into the Indian Army, and what role did they play? What difference did the war make to one of the Indian Army's most important 'martial races'? How was the war 'received' in the Sikh recruiting districts of Punjab? How much Sikh opposition was there to the war, and how effective was it? What were the main legacies of the war for the British-Sikh military relationship? This chapter will not confine its attention to Sikhs serving in the Indian Army, but will also address those who, for personal, political or institutional reasons, were proximate to the Army – the military families in the recruiting grounds;

---

1 Documentary references are to the National Archives of India (NAI) in New Delhi; and to the Hardinge Papers in the collection of European Manuscripts (Mss Eur) and the records of the Military Department of the India Office (L/MIL), both in the Asian and African Collections of the British Library (BL) in London. Material in square brackets in the footnotes indicates editorial conjecture.
2 A. J. Stockwell, 'The War and the British Empire' in John Turner (ed.), *Britain and the First World War* (London: Unwin Hyman, 1988), p. 37.
3 Judith Brown, *Modern India: The Making of an Asian Democracy* (second edition, Oxford: Oxford University Press, 1994), pp. 194–6.
4 Tan Tai-Yong, 'An Imperial Home-Front: Punjab and the First World War', *Journal of Military History*, 64 (2000), pp. 371–410, passim.

British and Indian recruiting officers; and Sikh revolutionary agents attempting to subvert the discipline of their military co-religionists.

II

The military ethos of the Sikh religion long predated the intrusion of the East India Company into Northern India. A key date was the foundation of the Khalsa (Elect) brotherhood in 1699 by the tenth Guru, Gobind Singh (1666–1708). The Khalsa was an order of religious warriors, all of whom adopted the name Singh or 'Lion'.[5] They were baptized in water stirred with a sword, and they wore the five markers of the Sikh religion, one of which was a dagger.[6] The toughness and military spirit of the Sikhs in the Sikh Wars of the 1840s had impressed the British, and the recruitment of Sikh soldiers by the East India Company began in this period.[7]

During the 1857 rebellion, Sikh chieftans had responded to John Lawrence's call for recruits, raising their own armed men.[8] Nearly one-third of the 60,000 men recruited from the Punjab in 1857–58 were Sikhs of the Khalsa.[9] After the mutiny, it became fashionable to enlist Sikhs, and Sikh soldiers became an 'essential girder in the new structure' of the reconstructed Indian Army.[10] Sikhs served not only as soldiers. After the annexation of Upper Burma in 1886, many Sikhs served as police in the new province, and some went on to work as bank guards and watchmen in Shanghai, Hong Kong and Singapore.[11]

By 1914, the Indian Army had been recruited for several decades according to the theory of the 'martial races' which contended that only a minority of Indian communities were naturally warlike, and hence suitable for recruitment. The theory had emerged in the context of the Russian threat to India in the 1880s, and had been vigorously promoted by Lord Roberts (1832–1914), the Commander-in-Chief in India from 1885 to 1893.[12] Roberts believed that for war against Russia, India should have an army 'drawn from the best fighting races'. He advised getting rid 'of

---

5   T. A. Heathcote, *The Indian Army: The Garrison of British Imperial India, 1822–1922* (David and Charles, 1974), p. 102.
6   Hugh McLeod, *The Evolution of the Sikh Community* (Oxford: Oxford University Press, 1976), pp. 14–15. The other four symbols were uncut hair, a bracelet, a comb, and breeches.
7   Heathcote, *Indian Army*, p. 103.
8   Tan, 'Imperial Home-Front', p. 400.
9   J. S. Grewal, *The Sikhs of the Punjab* (Cambridge: Cambridge University Press, 1990), p. 136.
10 Philip Mason, *A Matter of Honour: An Account of the Indian Army, its Officers and Men* (London: Jonathan Cape, 1974), p. 234.
11 T. G. Fraser, 'The Sikh Problem in Canada and its Political Consequences, 1905–1921', *Journal of Imperial and Commonwealth History*, 7 (1978), p. 37.
12 On the theory of the 'martial races' see Heather Streets, *Martial Races: The Military, Race and Masculinity in British Imperial Culture, 1857–1914* (Manchester: Manchester University Press, 2004); Lionel Caplan, *Warrior Gentlemen: 'Gurkhas' in the Western*

every sepoy not required for local purposes' from the Madras and Bombay Armies, and 'replacing them with soldiers of the most warlike races'.¹³ From the 1880s and 1890s recruitment to the Indian Army gradually turned towards Northern India, and especially the Punjab. By 1914, around half of the Indian Army was recruited from the Punjab.¹⁴

Like most of the martial races, the Sikh population was overwhelmingly rural. According to the Census of India over 70 per cent of all Sikhs were agriculturalists.¹⁵ The Sikhs numbered only around 2 per cent of the Indian population. In 1904, however, of the 152,846 Indian soldiers in the Indian Army, 30,975 (or 20.3 per cent) were Sikhs.¹⁶ Sikhs were therefore over-represented in the Army by a factor of just over ten. (It should, however, be noted that Punjabi Muslims were the most numerous of the Indian Army's martial races in both world wars.)

There had been a long debate within the Indian Army about how best to deal with issue of ethnic and religious difference in the organization of the Indian Army's regiments. By 1914, there were two main systems in use: the 'class company' regiment and the 'class' regiment. In a 'class company' regiment, each company was recruited from a single community, but the eight companies that made up a battalion were typically recruited from three or four different communities. In a 'class' regiment, all eight companies were recruited from a single community. Because of their ethnic homogeneity – which implied loyalty and trust – class regiments were sometimes seen as the elite of the Indian Army; the ten all-Gurkha regiments, for example, were regarded in some circles as the Indian Army's equivalent of the British Army's Brigade of Guards.¹⁷

The Indian Army contained some all-Sikh units – a sign of the Sikhs' high status as a martial race. Examples included the 14th Ferozepore Sikhs, the 15th Ludhiana Sikhs, and the 47th Sikhs – all of whom were to serve with distinction in the Great War. But divisions between Sikh units reflected Sikh social hierarchies. The middle-peasant Jat Sikhs normally served in infantry units. Mazbi and Ramdasia Sikhs, whose social origins lay in the ranks of outcaste Hindus, normally served separately

---

Imagination (Providence, RI: Berghan, 1995); and David Omissi, *The Sepoy and the Raj: The Indian Army, 1860–1940* (Basingstoke: Macmillan, 1994), Ch. 1.

13 'Note on the Necessity for Increasing the Efficiency of the Native Army', 25 Sept. 1886, in Brian Robson (ed.), *Roberts in India: The Military Papers of Field Marshal Lord Roberts, 1876–1893* (Dover: Alan Sutton for the Army Records Society, 1993), p. 352.

14 Michael O'Dwyer, *India as I Knew It, 1885–1925* (London: Constable, 1925), p. 214; George Morton Jack, 'The Indian Army on the Western Front, 1914–1915: A Portrait of Collaboration' *War in History*, 13/3 (2006), p. 333.

15 Grewal, *Sikhs of the Punjab*, p. 139.

16 Omissi, *The Sepoy and the Raj*, p. 20, Table 1.4. The Sikh total included 23,108 Jat Sikhs and 7,867 'other' Sikhs.

17 Raymond Callahan, 'The Great Sepoy Mutiny' in Daniel Marston and Chander S. Sundaram (eds), *A Military History of India and South Asia* (Westport, Conn.: Praeger, 2007), p. 33.

in Pioneer regiments, such as the 34th Sikh Pioneers.[18] Despite the language of the 'martial races', Sikhs were strictly speaking not a 'race', but a cluster of religious communities, collectively referred to as the *Panth*.[19] The markers of the Sikh religion were carefully fostered by British officers and by the Indian Army more generally.[20] Indeed, it has even been argued that service in the Indian Army prevented Sikhs from being reabsorbed into the Hindu mainstream.[21]

III

Britain's declaration of war was greeted with enthusiasm in India – not least because the cause was seen as just – and with a desire for British success.[22] This enthusiasm greatly increased when it became clear that the Indian Army was to participate in the struggle in Europe.[23] The Lieutenant Governor of the Punjab, Michael O'Dwyer (1864–1940), later recalled that:

> The Legislative Council of the Punjab, at its first meeting after war was declared, unanimously passed a resolution assuring the King-Emperor of the devotion of the people of the Province and of their determination to serve His Majesty, in every form in which their help might be required, against the enemies of his Empire.[24]

Among the hundreds of letters, telegrams and resolutions pledging support, was a message from the Khalsa Diwan, the 'national synod of the Sikhs'.[25] A *Punch* cartoon, 'India for the King', from September 1914, showing two Sikh soldiers and a Gurka, reflected the enthusiasm in India and in the Indian Army for the war.[26] The cartoon also captures the popular British perception that the Indian Army consisted almost exclusively of Sikhs and Gurkhas. German calculations about India's ripeness for anti-British subversion were upset by these expressions of Indian loyalty.[27]

---

18   David Omissi (ed.), *Indian Voices of the Great War: Soldiers' Letters, 1914–1918* (Basingstoke: Macmillan, 1999), p. 363.
19   On the development of the *Panth* see McLeod, *Evolution of the Sikh Community*, pp. 5–19.
20   Heathcote, *Indian Army*, p. 103.
21   Mason, *Matter of Honour*, p. 352.
22   Mason, *Matter of Honour*, p. 408.
23   BL, Mss Eur 473/2, Hardinge to Robertson (USS India), 8 April 1915. See also O'Dwyer, *India as I Knew It*, p. 216.
24   O'Dwyer, *India as I Knew It*, p. 213.
25   Mason, *Matter of Honour*, p. 408.
26   Chandrika Kaul, *Reporting the Raj: The British Press and India, c.1880–1922* (Manchester: Manchester University Press, 2003), p. 121.
27   Mason, *Matter of Honour*, p. 109. On German attempts at subversion see Thomas G. Fraser, 'Germany and Indian Revolution, 1914–18', *Journal of Contemporary History*, 12 (1977), pp. 255–72.

The primary function of the Indian Army in 1914 was not to fight a first-class power overseas, but to defend India's NorthWest Frontier, to fight minor colonial wars, and to maintain internal security.[28] In August 1914, however, two Indian infantry divisions and a cavalry brigade were despatched to France to fight on the Western Front. This was done principally because India was the only part of the empire that could provide an immediate source of trained soldiers.[29] Indian units, including Sikhs, saw action at all the main battles of the British Expeditionary Force on the Western Front in 1914 and 1915.

The first Indian soldiers arrived in France in late September and early October 1914. They landed at Marseilles, then went by train to Orleans. At the front they were thrown into the battles around Ypres in October and November 1914.[30] They suffered very heavy losses, but proved themselves to be invaluable soldiers.

Conditions in the improvised, and often flooded, trenches were terrible. One British eye-witness, Captain 'Roly' Grimshaw of the 34th Poona Horse, left a graphic description of the casualties. He wrote in his diary that:

> The state of the wounded beggars all description. Little Gurkhas slopping through the freezing mud barefooted; Tommies with no caps and plastered in blood and mud from head to foot; Sikhs with their hair all down and looking more wild and weird than I have ever seen them; Pathans more dirty and untidy than usual – all limping or reeling along like drunken men, some helping an almost foundered comrade, in most cases misery depicted on their faces.[31]

Given the conditions and the losses, morale was understandably poor by late 1914. There is evidence that some Indian troops tried to escape the trenches by means of self-inflicted wounds.[32] According to one report, this practice was a particular problem amongst Sikhs.[33] Some men, across all faiths, wrote letters home, urging friends and relatives not to enlist. Isar Singh, a Sikh sepoy lying wounded in hospital in Brighton, told a friend in India that the battle was 'being carried on very bitterly. ... Thousands of men die daily.' He advised his friend, also a soldier 'so far as is in your power

---

28   Mason, *Matter of Honour*, p. 410; Morton Jack, 'Indian Army', p. 334–5, 338; Algernon Rumbold, *Watershed in India, 1914–1922* (London: Athlone Press, 1979), p. 24; John S. Galbraith, 'No Man's Child: The Campaign in Mesopotamia, 1914–1916', *International History Review*, 6/3 (1984), pp. 376–7.
29   Rumbold, *Watershed in India*, p. 23; Fraser, 'Germany and Indian Revolution', p. 256.
30   Morton Jack, 'Indian Army', pp. 338–9.
31   Diary entry for 20 Dec. 1914 in J. Wakefield and J. M. Weippert (eds), *Indian Cavalry Officer: Captain Roly Grimshaw* (Tunbridge Wells: Costello, 1986), p. 54 [punctuation added].
32   Jeffrey Greenhut, 'The Imperial Reserve: The Indian Corps on the Western Front, 1914-15', *Journal of Imperial and Commonwealth History*, 12 (1983), p. 57; Morton Jack, 'Indian Army', p. 340.
33   Greenhut, 'Imperial Reserve', p. 57.

do not come here'.³⁴ In Amritsar District, one of the core Sikh recruiting grounds, wives and mothers did all they could to prevent their menfolk from enlisting; and in November 1914 some women even followed recruiting parties for miles in the hope of luring their men away.³⁵ In August 1915, the Secretary of State for India, Austen Chamberlain (1863–1937) noted that the commander of the Indian Corps, General Sir James Willcocks (1857–1926) 'spoke highly of the Gurkhas, who, he said, had entirely recovered from their earlier demoralization. The troops of whom he spoke with least favour were the Sikhs, especially those who were formed in pure Sikh battalions.'³⁶

It was decided to treat the Indian wounded in hospitals specially created for them in towns on the South coast of England.³⁷ After the 1857 Indian Mutiny – which was widely understood by contemporaries as a war of race and religion – the authorities in India had taken great care not to offend the religious feelings of Indian troops.³⁸ The religious provision for Sikhs in hospitals in Britain was accordingly excellent. There were separate kitchens for Muslims, for meat-eating Hindus and Sikhs, and for vegetarians.³⁹ A tented *gurdwara* was constructed in the grounds of Brighton hospital grounds. A Sikh soldier wrote home to India:

> They take great care of us here such as no one else would take except a man's mother, not even his wife. If a man falls sick at home and remains ill for a month the whole household grows weary of his illness, but these people do not grow weary. The arrangements for our food are very good, because men have been selected from the regiments to look after it and every man is served by his caste fellows.⁴⁰

Convalescent soldiers could make sight-seeing journeys once they were well enough. On 23 December 1914, for example, the Khalsa Jatha (Sikh Association) of the British Isles celebrated the 248th birthday of Guru Gobind Singh at Caxton Hall, Westminster. A party of 25 Sikh officer and soldiers were present. The men were convalescent from their wounds, and had travelled from the hospital at Barton-on-Sea, near Milton, in the New Forest.⁴¹

---

34 Isar Singh, Sikh, 59th Rifles, Brighton, to a friend, 50th Punjabis, India [Gurmukhi], 1 May 1915, quoted in Omissi (ed.), *Indian Voices of the Great War*, p. 59
35 Tan, 'Imperial Home Front', p. 383 and fn. 45.
36 BL, Mss Eur 473/1, Chamberlain to Hardinge, 13 Aug. 1915.
37 For which see Alan Lester, 'British India on Trial: Brighton Military Hospitals and the Politics of Empire in World War I', *Journal of Historical Geography*, 38/1 (2012), pp. 18–34.
38 Morton Jack, 'Indian Army', p. 335.
39 Morton Jack, 'Indian Army', p. 357.
40 Bir Singh, 55th Rifles, to Gunga Singh, 55th Rifles, Kohat, NWFP [Gurmukhi], 17 July 1915, quoted in Omissi (ed.), *Indian Voices of the Great War*, p. 79.
41 'Sikhs in London', *India: A Journal for the Discussion of Indian Affairs*, 1 Jan. 1915.

An important charity, the Indian Soldiers' Fund, was set up shortly after the outbreak of war. Its purpose was originally to provide warm clothes to the Indian soldiers serving in France and Belgium, but its remit later extended to providing all sorts of comforts such as sweets and cigarettes. The Committee was chaired by Lady Willcocks, the wife of Sir James, and Lord Curzon lent his London home as a headquarters. Money came in from many sources, including British and Indian royalty, and from cities with strong links to India, such as Dundee.[42]

When the British military censors noted complaints in Sikh soldiers' letters about the shortage of Sikh religious artefacts, for example, the Indian Soldiers' Fund commissioned a cutlery firm in Sheffield to make steel daggers, bracelets and combs for Sikhs to an approved pattern.[43] Indian princes also got in on the act. In July 1915, the Maharaja of Jind presented 10,000 combs for Sikh soldiers of the Indian Expeditionary Force, and 1,000 Sikh prayer books for the wounded in Europe, Egypt and East Africa.[44] Letters from Sikh soldiers showed their appreciation of these acts of charity. On learning of the donation of a Granth, sowar Mohan Singh wrote home that the donor had 'conferred a great favour on us, since we can have worship celebrated during our sojourn in a foreign land'.[45]

On 10–12 March 1915 the two Indian infantry divisions in France took part in the Allied attack at Neuve Chapelle. The attack was successful, and several lines of German trenches were overrun.[46] The losses, however, were very heavy: of the 12,811 British and Commonwealth casualties, 4,233 occurred in the Indian Corps.[47] The 47th Sikhs lost 80 per cent of their strength in two days.[48] Reinforcements for the regiments in France were drawn from many different units, leading to a loss of regimental cohesion. For example, by June 1915 the 15th Sikhs was composed of men who had originally belonged to nine different units.[49]

Faced with casualties on this scale, there is clear evidence that religion motivated Sikh soldiers in action. Sikhs frequently evoked the Guru, or the warrior traditions of Sikhism, in letters urging bravery in battle. British officers were aware of their men's beliefs, and would play on them to motivate their troops. A wounded Sikh soldier conveyed this relationship in a letter home describing the death of a Sikh officer:

---

42 BL, Mss Eur. F.120/7, Second Report of the Indian Soldiers' Fund, 1 April to 20 Nov. 1915.
43 Morton Jack, 'Indian Army', p. 337.
44 NAI, Foreign and Political, Internal-B, Aug. 1915, 279, Inspector General, Imperial Service Troops, to Political Secretary to GI Foreign and Political Department, 17 July 1915.
45 Mohan Singh, 6th Cavalry, France, to Sirdani Bishan Devi, Lyallpur District, Punjab, 25 Feb. 1916 [Urdu], quoted in Omissi (ed.), *Indian Voices of the Great War*, p. 156.
46 Greenhut, 'Imperial Reserve', p. 65.
47 J. W. B. Merewether and Frederick Smith, *The Indian Corps in France* (London: John Murray, 1919), p. 268.
48 Greenhut, 'Imperial Reserve', p. 65.
49 Morton Jack, 'Indian Army', pp. 358–9.

The 47th Sikhs were charging. [The] Sahib [British Officer] said 'Chur Singh, you are not a Sikh of Guru Gobind Singh, [you] who sits in fear inside the trench!' Chur Singh was very angry. Chur Singh gave [the] order to his company to charge. He drew his sword and went forward. A bullet came from the enemy and hit him in the mouth. So did our brother Chur Singh become a martyr.[50]

Sikh soldiers in particular valued the outward marks of their religion. For example, they associated the wearing of *pagris* (turbans) with the Sikh religion.[51] There was therefore initially some reluctance among Sikhs to adopt protective steel helmets when they were introduced in 1916.[52] Helmets eventually found some limited acceptance among Sikhs. By the 1930s, as the Indian Army slowly began to modernize, those Sikhs who had decided to shave off their beards, cut their hair, and wear helmets had become known in Indian Army parlance as 'mechanized Sikhs'.[53]

The two Indian infantry divisions left France for the Middle East at the end of 1915. The two Indian cavalry divisions, however, remained until early 1918. During their long stay, what did Sikh soldiers make of France and of the French? Sikh soldiers' letters illuminate their attitudes to French religion, food and gender relations. One Sikh commented on the beauty of the French women, noting that 'the sight of them delights us, but we are ashamed to touch them lest we lose caste. The men and women of this place', he continued, 'treat us very lovingly'.[54] Another man wrote:

> If you look at the condition of things in this country you cannot but see that all men here are considered equal in the sight of God. ... They eat everthing donkey, dog, horse, pig, cow – they abstain from nothing. They do all kinds of work themselves, even to the cleaning of the WC. They are fixed in their manners and customs, but they worship idols.[55]

---

50 A sepoy of the 47th Sikhs, a hospital, Brighton, to a friend in India [Gurmukhi], 14 Dec. 1915, quoted in Omissi (ed.), *Indian Voices of the Great War*, p. 126. See also VanKoski, Susan, 'Letters Home, 1915–16: Punjabi Soldiers Reflect on War and Life in Europe and their Meanings for Home and Self', *International Journal of Punjab Studies*, 2/1 (1995), p. 45.
51 Heathcote, *Indian Army*, p. 103.
52 Abdul Alim, 6th Cavalry, France, to Dafadar Majat Ali Khan, 6th Cavalry, Rohtak, Punjab [Urdu], 30 June 1916, quoted in Omissi (ed.), *Indian Voices of the Great War*, pp. 198–9.
53 Heathcote, *Indian Army*, p. 103.
54 A Sikh sepoy [probably of the 47th Sikhs, France] to Gurun Ditta Mal of the 47th Sikhs' Depot, Fatehgarh, Farrukhabad District, UP [Gurmukhi], 12 May 1915, quoted in Omissi (ed.), *Indian Voices of the Great War*, p. 60.
55 Tara Singh to Sirdar Karbar Singh, Teacher, Rawalpindi District, Punjab [Gurmukhi], 17 July 1916, quoted in Omissi (ed.), *Indian Voices of the Great War*, p. 208.

His mixture of admiration and religious concern was a fairly typical reaction. The soldiers were surprised that all French people, even women and children, could read and write.[56]

Relations between French men and women elicited a more mixed response. The soldiers admired the bravery and hard work of French women, and their stoicism in the face of loss.[57] They were struck by the easy familiarity between the sexes, and the apparent happiness of French marriages. 'The very best custom in this country is that a man chooses his own wife, and a woman her own husband, and there are no disagreements and troubles after marriage', remarked Teja Singh, a Sikh sowar.[58] Others, however, thought French women to be 'shameless' because they mixed so freely with men.

To travel is to see home in a different light, and perhaps to reflect critically on home.[59] Indian soldiers in France began to reconsider everyday Indian customs that they might previously have accepted without much reflection. In particular, India's poverty was brought into stark relief by the relative affluence of France. 'If you were to see the general conditions of life, you would be astounded' wrote one Sikh soldier. 'The man whom God wishes to punish is born in India'.[60] Soldiers advised their families at home not to spend so much on wedding ceremonies, especially if they were from a cultivating caste such as Jats. Several men urged their families to emulate the French and send their children to school.

Relations with French civilians were not always so harmonious. One Sikh officer wrote a letter in October 1915 lamenting that 'Asil Singh Jat and Harbans have done a vile thing. They forcibly violated a French girl, nineteen years of age. It is a matter of great humiliation and regret that the good name of the 31st Lancers should have been sullied in this way.'[61] It is notable that, in commenting on this case, – an isolated one – the officer's chief concern was for the reputation of his regiment. The two men were each sentenced to 17 years' rigorous imprisonment.[62]

---

56 VanKoski, 'Letters Home', p. 53.
57 VanKoski, 'Letters Home', p. 52.
58 Teja Singh, 2nd Lancers, France, to Ganga Singh, Sialkot District, Punjab, [Gurmukhi], 6 March 1918, quoted in Omissi (ed.), *Indian Voices of the Great War*, p. 357.
59 Nigel Rapport and Andrew Dawson (eds), *Migrants of Identity: Perceptions of Home in a World of Movement* (Oxford: Berg, 1998), *passim*.
60 Quoted in Omissi, David, 'Europe Through Indian Eyes: Indian Soldiers Encounter England and France, 1914–1918', *English Historical Review*, 122/496 (2007), p. 390.
61 Ressaidar Kabul Singh, 31st Lancers, attached 29th Lancers, France, to Risaldar Sirdar Bahadur Mohinddin Sahib, ADC to HE the Viceroy, Remount Base Depot, Marseilles [Urdu], 29 Oct. 1915, quoted in Omissi (ed.), *Indian Voices of the Great War*, p. 115.
62 Morton Jack, 'Indian Army', p. 361. He gives the men's names as Anil Singh and Harbans Singh.

IV

There was another side to this picture of Indian and especially Sikh loyalty.[63] There were serious troubles in Punjab, particularly in early 1915. In 1912, the German General von Bernhardi had suggested turning pan-Islamic and Bengali revolutionary sentiment to German advantage in the event of war with Britain. On 4 September 1914, the German Chancellor Bethmann-Hollweg (1856–1921) sanctioned a campaign of subversion in India and Egypt.[64] The Germans were aware that they probably could not overthrow British rule in India, but they thought that they could create sufficient disturbance to keep troops in India that might otherwise have been used elsewhere.[65] The most promising ploy was to exploit pan-Islamic sentiment once the Ottoman Empire had joined the war on the side of the Central Powers.[66] The most relevant to Sikhs, however, was the Ghadr (or 'Mutiny') movement based principally in North America.

Much of the political trouble among the Sikh population of Punjab in this period was associated with immigrant grievances in Canada, and with returning Sikh emigrants.[67] Sikh migration to Canada began when other opportunities had closed down, notably the settlement of the canal colonies in Punjab. Anti-British sentiment amongst Sikhs in Canada resulted from poor treatment, and from the racism of white Americans and Canadians.[68] This Canadian hostility to Sikh immigrants needs to be understood in the context of earlier Chinese and Japanese immigration to British Columbia, which had aroused anti-Asian feeling more generally.[69] Indeed, so great was the white antipathy to Asian migration that there were fears that British Columbia might secede from the Canadian Confederation over the issue.[70] Their encounter with racial prejudice created a backlash among the Sikhs against the white-dominated British Empire in general.

Feelings were inflamed by an incident which began in May 1914, when the *Komagata Maru*, a Japanese ship carrying Indian migrants, reached Vancouver. Most of the 376 Punjabi passengers were Sikhs, mainly Jats from the central Punjab districts.[71] The ship was refused permission to dock, on the grounds that it had not come directly from the passengers' country of origin.[72] After much argument, the ship was sent

---

63 Fraser, 'Sikh Problem', pp. 36, 51.
64 Fraser, 'Germany and Indian Revolution', p. 256.
65 Fraser, 'Germany and Indian Revolution', p. 261.
66 Galbraith, 'No Man's Child', pp. 376–7.
67 Fraser, 'Sikh Problem', p. 36.
68 Fraser, 'Germany and Indian Revolution', pp. 257–8. See also Grewal, *Sikhs of the Punjab*, pp. 153–4.
69 BL, Mss Eur 473/1, Chamberlain to Hardinge, 13 Aug. 1915; Fraser, 'Sikh Problem', pp. 38–9, 51.
70 Fraser, 'Sikh Problem', p. 40.
71 Fraser, 'Sikh Problem', p. 46.
72 Grewal, *Sikhs of the Punjab*, p. 154.

back to India and was at sea when war broke out. No passengers were allowed to disembark before the ship berthed at Calcutta. When the ship docked, the passengers were ordered to board special trains to take them to the Punjab.[73] Many refused, and a riot broke out. The police opened fire, killing 18 men and wounding 25 others.[74]

The military significance of the Gadhrite movement lay not in the absolute number of Sikh immigrants in Canada, for far larger numbers of Indians had migrated elsewhere in the empire. (See Table X.1.)

Table X.1. Indian Migrant Population in Selected Areas of the British Empire, 1907

Mauritius		264 000
Caribbean		
British Guiana	127 000	
Trinidad	103 000	
Jamaica	13 000	
Caribbean Total		243 000
Africa		
Natal	115 000	
East Africa	28 000	
Africa Total		143 000
Fiji		31 000
Canada		5 000
Total (Selected Areas Only)		686 000

Source: Adapted from Fraser, 'Sikh Problem', p. 36.

The importance to the Indian Army of the disaffection among Indians in Canada rested on the fact that most of them were Jat Sikhs from the central Punjab. As an India Office memorandum of August 1915 put it:

> The seriousness of the question, as regards the British empire in India, is that the people of the Punjab, the chief recruiting ground for the Indian Army, are the class of Indians practically affected, and the grievances of the Sikhs as regards Canada have been very skilfully utilised by agitators to excite discontent in the Punjab. ... The classes of Indians who go to South Africa are of no military

---

73 Fraser, 'Sikh Problem', p. 48.
74 Tan, 'Imperial Home Front', p. 388.

importance, but the Sikhs, ever since the Indian Mutiny, have been a most important element [of the Indian Army], and the attempts to tamper with them have been closely connected with immigrant grievances.[75]

The Indians who had migrated elsewhere in the empire were either indentured labourers or were from the mercantile and professional classes, and hence had few military connections.[76]

The Ghadrites were coming to India not only from Canada and the US, but also from Hong Kong and Shanghai.[77] They returned believing India to be in a state of unrest, and they intended to bring about a revolution.[78] They planned to send emissaries though villages – especially Sikh villages – to 'raise the people to a feeling that the moment to strike had come'.[79] This attempt to raise rebellion among Sikh civilians had little immediate impact, however.

Having failed with the civilians, the Ghadrites turned their attention to the Sikhs in the Indian Army, making attempts to subvert Army units at Lahore, Ferozepore and Meerut.[80] They planned a concerted rising and raids on military armouries for 21 February 1915.[81] The police, however, had penetrated the organization, and the movement was easily forestalled.[82] In March, reported Hardinge, a 'revolutionary emissary' was caught with 12 bombs in the lines of the 12th Cavalry at Meerut. Some soldiers, 'probably Sikhs', he speculated, were in on the conspiracy.[83] Once the conspiracy had been scotched, the Ghadrites were put on trial. In all 42 Ghadrites were executed, 114 were transported for life, and 93 were sentenced to various terms of imprisonment.[84]

The Ghadrites also attempted subversion in South East Asia. In October 1914, they decided to make Siam (Thailand) one base of operations, believing that they could infiltrate agents into British territories in the region. The Ghadrites made attempts to subvert the Burma Military Police, a paramilitary body of about 15,000 men. In January 1915, these plans were discussed with Germany's eastern expert Max von Oppenheim in Berlin.[85] The Germans agreed to support these efforts, which had some

---

75 Fraser, 'Sikh Problem', p. 36. See also the appeal by Chamberlain mentioned in Fraser, 'Sikh Problem', p. 50.
76 Fraser, 'Sikh Problem', p. 37.
77 Grewal, *Sikhs of the Punjab*, p. 154; Fraser, 'Germany and Indian Revolution', p. 260.
78 Tan, 'Imperial Home-Front', p. 387.
79 NAI, Home, Political, Deposit, Jan. 1915, 43, Fortnightly Report on Internal Situation in Punjab for period ending 16 Dec. 1914.
80 Grewal, *Sikhs of the Punjab*, p. 155.
81 Rumbold, *Watershed in India*, p. 32. The date was brought forward to 19 February.
82 Fraser, 'Sikh Problem', pp. 48–9.
83 BL, Mss Eur, 473/2, Hardinge to Crewe, 1/2 April 1915.
84 Lawrence James, *Mutiny in the British and Commonwealth Forces, 1797–1956* (London: Buchan and Enright, 1987), p. 219; Grewal, *Sikhs of the Punjab*, p. 155.
85 Fraser, 'Germany and Indian Revolution', p. 266–7.

success. In July 1915 Hardinge noted that Sikhs in the military police in Burma had been 'tampered with' by Sikhs from America who had returned to India via Siam and Burma.[86] Hardinge had reason to be nervous, as the number of British regular troops in India had been seriously depleted by mid-1915, to be replaced by indifferently armed and trained Territorials.[87] An Indian agent penetrated the Ghadrite organization, however, leading to the arrest of Ghadrites in Burma and Thailand.[88]

There was also a countervailing movement of loyalty in which the Sikh elites played a major role. For example, on 27 February 1915 leading Sikh gentlemen gathered in Lahore to help advise the Government of India. Sikh religious leaders declared that the Ghadrites were apostates, and politicians repudiated their revolutionary aims.[89] In Ludhiana, a Sikh Committee was formed in March 1915, and in April published a loyalist manifesto denouncing the Ghadrites. On 16 July a deputation of leading Sikhs from Amritsar District met the Deputy Commissioner 'with the object of devising means to remove the stigma which had been brought upon the name of the Sikhs by the conduct of a few returned emigrants', wrote A. B. Kettlewell of the Indian Civil Service.[90] 'Their action', he continued, 'is reported to have been entirely spontaneous and indicates a realisation of their responsibilities towards Government in the present juncture'.

By May, Hardinge was able to report that things in India were 'now well in hand'; and in early June, he told Chamberlain that the Punjab was 'fairly quiet'.[91] O'Dwyer later recalled that 'there was no serious cause for anxiety' in the province from September 1915 until the last year of the war.[92]

V

From the outset the First World War was a wider war – a global war in a world of empires.[93] Accordingly, by the end of 1914, Indian troops had been sent not only to Europe but to East Africa, Egypt, Hong Kong, Basra and Abadan.[94]

---

86 BL, Mss Eur 473/2, Hardinge to Chamberlain, 2 July 1915.
87 IOR, L/MIL/17/5/2401, Military Situation in India Consequent on the War, 6 June 1915. See also Rumbold, *Watershed in India*, pp. 23, 25 and Brown, *Modern India*, p. 197.
88 Fraser, 'Germany and Indian Revolution', pp. 267–8.
89 Tan, 'Imperial Home-Front', pp. 398–9.
90 NAI, Home, Political, Deposit, Aug. 1915, 28, Report on the Internal Political Situation in the Punjab in special reference to the European War for the ... period ending 31 July 1915.
91 BL, Mss Eur 473/2, Hardinge to Chamberlain, 27 May and 10 June 1915.
92 O'Dwyer, *India as I Knew It*, p. 217. See also Tan, 'Imperial Home Front', p. 399.
93 John H. Morrow, *The First World War: An Imperial History* (London: Routledge, 2004), *passim*.
94 Mason, *Matter of Honour*, p. 411; Galbraith, 'No Man's Child', pp. 364–5, 377; Tan, 'Imperial Home Front', pp. 375–6.

Sikh troops served in small numbers with the Indian Army at Gallipoli, alongside British, French and ANZAC soldiers.[95] Two batteries of Indian mountain gunners, about half of whom were Sikhs, went ashore with the ANZACs on 25 April 1915. Later on, the 29th Indian Brigade formed part of the reinforcements sent from Egypt after the initial landings did not succeed. The Brigade had four battalions, including the 14th (Duke of Connaught's Own) Ferozepore Sikhs. Sikhs also made up about a quarter of the 69th and 89th Punjabis, although these battalions were subsequently withdrawn after concern that their Muslim companies might not wish to fight against the Turks. They were later replaced by three Gurkha battalions.

The Brigade landed at Cape Helles in early May 1915. At the Third Battle of Krithia on 4 June the Brigade was attached to the British 29th Division. During the battle, the 14th Sikhs attacked with 15 British officers, 14 Indian officers and 514 Indian other ranks.[96] The Sikhs suffered badly from Turkish machine-gun fire at Gully Ravine.[97] Twelve British officers, 11 Indian officers and 371 sepoys were killed or wounded.

Sir Ian Hamilton's despatch to the Commander-in-Chief in India describing the 'magnificent' action of the 14th Sikhs on the Dardanelles was 'received with much enthusiasm by the Sikhs generally as showing that they are true to their military traditions of pluck and dash'.[98] Recruitment among Sikhs significantly improved after the publication of the despatch.[99] In July and August 1915 thousands of people gathered at the Golden Temple in Amritsar to express 'satisfaction' at the heroic deeds of the 14th Sikhs at Gallipoli. In Rawalpindi a Sikh meeting on the war's first anniversary included a sermon urging every Sikh 'to place everything at the disposal of the benign British government which has shown so many favours to the Khalsa'.[100]

From late 1915 until the end of the war the main Indian Army war effort was in the Middle East. Indian troops took part in the successful defence of the Suez Canal against Turkish attacks in early 1915. Most Indian troops were to serve in Mesopotamia and Palestine. Apart from oil, the main significance of the campaign in Mesopotamia lay in the prospect of knocking the Ottoman Empire out of the war.[101] The humiliating surrender at Kut al-Amara in April 1916 was avenged the following March with the capture of Baghdad. On 1 November 1918, of the 13 Indian Army divisions serving overseas, eight (two cavalry and six infantry) were in Palestine and

---

95 For which see the excellent book by Peter Stanley, *Die in Battle, do not Despair: The Indians on Gallipoli, 1915* (Solihull: Helion, 2015).
96 Stanley, *Die in Battle*, p. 134.
97 Travers, *Gallipoli*, p. 135.
98 NAI, Home, Political, Deposit, Aug. 1915, 28, Report on the Internal Situation in the Punjab in special reference to the European War for the ... period ending 31 July 1915. See also 'The Sikhs', *The Times*, 18 Aug. 1915.
99 Stanley, *Die in Battle*, p. 142.
100 Stanley, *Die in Battle*, p. 187.
101 Galbraith, 'No Man's Child', pp. 384–5.

five (one cavalry and four infantry) were in Mesopotamia.[102] As a significant element of the Indian Army in the Middle East, Sikhs therefore played an important role in the military destruction of the Ottoman Empire.[103]

The campaign in Mesopotamia was clearly of religious significance for the Indian Muslim troops, because it presented them with the problem of whether or not to fight against their fellow-Muslims in lands under Turkish rule.[104] This problem had been compounded by the Ottoman declaration of Jihad in 1914.[105] There were, indeed, several mutinies by Muslim soldiers – at Rangoon, Bombay and Basra – when they knew or suspected that they were going to be sent to fight against the Turks.[106] The most important of these mutinies occurred at Singapore in February 1915, when about 400 Muslims of the 5th Light Infantry shot their British officers, and any local Europeans they could find. One might think that Mesopotamia would not have had the same religious resonance for Sikhs and Hindus as it did for Muslims. In July 1915, however, the Deputy Commissioner for Rohtak District noted that the number of Jats enlisting the District was 'still satisfactory'. He had been told that the Jats were 'showing the greatest keenness to enlist in regiments fighting the Turks'.[107] He regarded their 'innate hostility' to Muslims as 'the cause of their loyalty, and as being likely to ensure its continuance'.

Sir Frederick Stanley Maude (1864–1917), who took over as Commander-in-Chief in Mesopotamia in July 1916, spoke highly of his Sikh regiments. In 'severe' fighting on the right bank of the Tigris in January 1917, for example, he reported that the 47th Sikhs (along with other Indian Army regiments) had done 'extremely well'.[108]

---

102 Robert Holland, 'The British Empire and the Great War', in Judith M. Brown and Wm Roger Louis (eds), *The Oxford History of the British Empire*, Vol. IV, *The Twentieth Century* (Oxford: Oxford University Press, 1999), p. 136.
103 On the Indian Army's role see Rumbold, *Watershed in India*, p. 29.
104 O'Dwyer, *India as I Knew It*, p. 215.
105 For which see Geoffrey Lewis, 'The Ottoman Proclamation of Jihād in 1914' in *Arabic and Islamic Garland: Essays Presented to Abdul-Latif Tibawi* (London: The Islamic Cultural Centre, 1977), pp. 159–65.
106 Omissi, *Sepoy and the Raj*, Ch. 4, *passim*.
107 NAI, Home, Political. Deposit, 28, Report on the Internal Situation in the Punjab in Special Reference to the European War for the Half-Monthly Period ending 31 July 1915. As he was referring to Rohtak District, these Jats were probably Hindu, but Sikh Jats may well have shared their anti-Turkish sentiments. On recruitment in Rohtak District see Tan, 'Imperial Home Front', p. 396.
108 Maude to Whigham, 15 Jan. 1917, in Andrew Syk (ed.), *The Military Papers of Lieutenant-General Sir Frederick Stanley Maude, 1914–1917* (Stroud: The History Press for The Army Records Society, 2012), pp. 195–6. For a discussion of the date of the handover see Galbraith, 'No Man's Child', p. 384 and fn. 102.

VI

Between August 1914 and November 1918, of the 683,149 Indian combat troops recruited, no fewer than 349,688 (or 51 per cent) came from the single province of Punjab.[109] Of the total recruits 88,925 were Sikhs, almost all from the Punjab. The war brought about a very close relationship between the province's civilian administration and the needs of the Indian military.[110] By 1917 the whole administrative machinery of the province had been converted to a highly-effective recruiting machine.[111]

Recruitment methods were to change drastically over the course of the war. Before the war, recruits went to a recruiting centre for their 'class', of which there were four in the Punjab. All Sikhs wishing to enlist, for example, had to go to the centre in Amritsar.[112] Sikhs from Rawalpindi could not enlist in the centre in Rawalpindi, which was reserved for Muslims.[113] Furthermore, there was little co-ordination between different regimental recruiting parties. This system worked well enough in peacetime – or during short, colonial campaigns – but proved too restrictive when recruiting had to be expanded to meet the needs of a prolonged world war.

By mid-1916, it had become clear that peacetime methods would no longer suffice.[114] New incentives were introduced. The 'most effective of all inducements to the Punjab peasant', considered O'Dwyer, were the 180,000 acres of canal-irrigated land which he put at the disposal of the Commander-in-Chief in India for distribution to Indian soldiers 'who had served with special distinction in the field'.[115] From 1 January 1917, free rations replaced a 'rather inadequate' messing allowance; and pay and pensions were also increased.[116] An enlistment bonus of 50 rupees was offered to every recruit from mid-1917.[117] More far-reaching methods were also needed. The Government of India, if it were to take a full part in raising manpower, had to fully engage the 'whole machinery and influence' of the Goverment's civil administration.[118] In May 1917, the Government of India appointed a Central Recruiting Board.[119] The Board fixed a quota of combatants and non-combatant recruits for each province.[120] In June 1917, a Provincial Recruiting Board was set up in Lahore to direct a Punjab-wide recruiting campaign.[121] O'Dwyer chaired the Board, and incorporated the province's landed

---

109 Tan, 'Imperial Home-Front', p. 374; Omissi (ed.), *Indian Voices of the Great War*, pp. 366–7.
110 Tan, 'Imperial Home Front', pp. 408–09.
111 O'Dwyer, *India as I Knew It*, p. 219; Tan, 'Imperial Home Front', pp. 374–5.
112 O'Dwyer, *India as I Knew It*, p. 219.
113 Tan, 'Imperial Home-Front', p. 379–81.
114 Tan, 'Imperial Home-Front', p. 383.
115 O'Dwyer, *India as I Knew It*, p. 216; Tan, 'Imperial Home- Front', p. 395.
116 O'Dwyer, *India as I Knew It*, p. 222.
117 O'Dwyer, *India as I Knew It*, p. 222; Tan, 'Imperial Home-Front', p. 396.
118 O'Dwyer, *India as I Knew It*, p. 218.
119 O'Dwyer, *India as I Knew It*, p. 220.
120 Tan, 'Imperial Home Front', p. 390.
121 Tan, 'Imperial Home-Front', pp. 391, 397.

elites to serve upon it.¹²² The Board decided how the burden of recruiting should be shared across Punjab's districts. The Governor toured the districts, but it was Indian officials who were made responsible for obtaining the recruits.

Even within Punjab there was a very uneven pattern of recruitment by district for all religions. Muslim recruitment was particularly strong in Jhelum and Rawalpindi Districts, in what is now Pakistan. Communities of Hindu Rajputs of Kangra and Hoshiapur Districts and Hindu Jats of Rohtak and Gurgaon were among those who were 'foremost both in the proportion of men raised and in their fighting value'.¹²³ Among Sikhs, recruitment was strong in Amritsar, Ludhiana and part of Ferozepore Districts. In Lahore, Lyallpur, and Gujranwala, however, rural prosperity and highly-developed agriculture deterred enlistment.¹²⁴

Recruitment was often dependent on the energy and enthusiasm of local officers, and on rural leaders and notables.¹²⁵ Sikh social structure was generally more egalitarian than in the Muslim-majority areas of Western Punjab, and it was therefore harder to find such notables in the Sikh areas of central Punjab. Recruitment came to rely heavily on a handful of families who possessed influence within the Sikh community by virtue of being descendents of the former Sikh aristocracy, and on Sikh *mahants* of Gurdwaras.¹²⁶ In Ludhiana District, prominent Sikhs on the board helped to recruit Sikhs, and to assure the welfare of soldiers.¹²⁷ In Jullundur District, however, one recruiting officer lamented that the District 'lacked born leaders', and hence did not produce as many recruits as Ludhiana, Ferozepore and Amritsar.¹²⁸

Once the Punjab government had sought the support of the rural notables in the enlistment campaign, the notables realized that they could turn the government's need into an opportunity to entrench their position.¹²⁹ Rewards were generous. Notable families received Landed Gentry Grants in the canal colonies. Prominent recruiters received honours and had their names entered into the official guide to *Chiefs and Families of Note in the Punjab*, ensuring access to government patronage. Similar forces were at work in the Punjab's princely states. The Maharaja of Patiala, for example, urged his subjects to volunteer for military service.¹³⁰

The most striking difference in recruitment, however, was between the urban and rural populations.¹³¹ The urban-rural divide had, of course, been a feature of the

---

122 O'Dwyer, *India as I Knew It*, p. 227; Tan, 'Imperial Home-Front', pp. 391, 397.
123 O'Dwyer, *India as I Knew It*, p. 226.
124 O'Dwyer, *India as I Knew It*, pp. 226–7.
125 O'Dwyer, *India as I Knew It*, p. 227.
126 Tan, 'Imperial Home Front', p. 402; Ian Talbot, *Punjab and the Raj, 1849–1947* (New Delhi: Manohar, 1988), pp. 44–5.
127 Tan, 'Imperial Home-Front', p. 395.
128 Tan, 'Imperial Home-Front', p. 404.
129 Tan, 'Imperial Home-Front', pp. 403–4.
130 Stanley, *Die in Battle*, p. 190.
131 O'Dwyer, *India as I Knew It*, pp. 227–8.

pre-war Indian Army, which drew almost all its recruits from rural areas. But the efforts to broaden wartime recruitment to the cities of Punjab mostly failed, all across the religious divide.

As the war intensified, so did nationalist activity. The Hindu press in Punjab stepped up its agitation in favour of Home Rule for India. This campaign had made 'no appeal to the people at large', reported one British official in August 1917. 'Among the rural classes, the Sikhs and [Hindu] Jats who go into the Army', he observed, 'it has found no response whatever. Recruiting activity has been maintained throughout the province.'[132]

By then, the war had lasted for three years. After prolonged separation, families in the Punjab started writing letters to Sikh (and other) soldiers, begging them to come home. The troops generally wrote very patient replies to these pleas, explaining that they could not return home until the King had won a victory.[133]

By the Spring of 1918, the Russian Revolution, Russia's subsequent exit from the war, and the German offensives in the West had made the Allied manpower situation critical. In April, the British Prime Minister, David Lloyd George (1863-1945), made a public appeal to the people of India to redouble their efforts.[134] The Government of India promised to find 500,000 more recruits. Of these, Punjab was to supply 180,000 combatants and 20,000 non-combatants, putting the administration of the Punjab under tremendous pressure. In June, the Provincial Recruiting Board discussed, and recommended, the introduction of conscription. This idea was rejected by the Viceroy on the advice of the Central Recruiting Board, because it was feared that it might lead to unrest and distrust.[135]

VII

Following India's efforts in the war, some political change in India was inevitable after Edwin Montagu's famous declaration in the House of Commons in August 1917 that the goal of British policy towards India was now to be 'the progressive realisation of responsible government as an integral part of the British Empire'.[136] In November 1917 a Sikh deputation met the Viceroy, Lord Chelmsford (1868–1933), to plead for a separate electorate for Sikhs on the basis of their 'unique position' – meaning their status in pre-annexation Punjab and their services to the British Empire.[137] The July 1918 Montagu-Chelmsford Report proposed reforms to enact the August 1917

---

132 NAI, Home, Political, Sept. 1917, 6, Report on the Political Situation in the Punjab for the Period Ending 31 Aug. 1917.
133 VanKoski, 'Letters Home', pp. 48–9.
134 Rumbold, *Watershed in India*, p. 25.
135 Tan, 'Imperial Home Front', pp. 406–7.
136 Rumbold, *Watershed in India*, p. 89; Brown, *Modern India*, p. 204; Robin J. Moore, 'Curzon and Indian Reform', *Modern Asian Studies*, 27/4 (1993), pp. 719–40.
137 Grewal, *Sikhs of the Punjab*, p. 152.

Declaration.[138] The Report recommended that 'to the Sikhs ... therefore, and to them alone, we propose to extend the system [of a separate electorate] already adopted in the case of Muhammadans.'[139]

The resulting 1919 Government of India Act conferred a limited degree of self government to the provinces of British India. Under the terms of the Act, all ex-soldiers were enfranchised – a move which favoured the Sikhs with their strong connections to the Indian Army. Punjabi Sikhs were only 11.1 per cent of the province's population, but ended up as 24.1 per cent of the voters.[140] The Punjab Government also strongly recommended a separate electorate and constituencies for the Sikhs. A separate electorate was indeed awarded, although the Sikh electorate was not given the weighting that it felt it deserved.[141] Sikhs had hoped to gain 30 per cent of the provincial council of the Punjab; in the event they obtained only 10 out of 58 seats. There were protests about this outcome from the Sikh delegation in London, who claimed 'subterfuge' on the part of the Government of India.[142]

A turning point came on 13 April 1919 at Amritsar, the city at the heart of the Sikh religion. After significant disturbances in the city, General Dyer (1864–1927) ordered his Indian troops to fire on a crowd, killing 379 persons, according to official estimates. After the massacre, Dyer was made an 'honorary Sikh' by Arur Singh, the government-appointed custodian of the Golden Temple in Amritsar.[143] Dyer alluded to this fact during his testimony in response to the Hunter Committee, which investigated the massacre.[144] Sir William Joynson-Hicks even claimed in the House of Commons on 8 July 1920 that Dyer was beloved of the Sikh nation.[145] Strenuous objections to these claims came from the Sikh delegation in the UK. The massacre, and the British reaction to it, helped to kick-start the Akali Sikh movement in the 1920s, which raised doubts about the continuing loyalty of Sikhs. The Akalis became a 'major thorn in the flesh' of the Indian Army generally.[146] Despite Dyer's honour, the Hunter Committee identified the Ghadr movement, and its associated grievances, as a major cause of dissent in the Punjab.[147]

In this context, an analysis by the head of India's Northern Command, General Sir William Birdwood (1865–1951), of the changing relationship between the

---

138 Brown, *Modern India*, p. 205.
139 Grewal, *Sikhs of the Punjab*, p. 152.
140 Brown, *Modern India*, pp. 205–7.
141 Grewal, *The Sikhs of the Punjab*, p. 152.
142 'Indian Legislature', *The Times*, 17 Aug. 1920.
143 Sayer, 'British Reaction', pp. 143–4.
144 Army: Disturbances in the Punjab: Statement by Brig. General R. E. H. Dyer, CB, Cmd 771 (1920).
145 Sayer, 'British Reaction', p. 131.
146 Mark Jacobson (ed.), *Rawlinson in India* (Stroud: Sutton for the Army Records Society, 2002), p. xxii. See also pp. 34, 74 and 128 of the same volume.
147 Fraser, 'Sikh Problem', p. 49.

Government of India and the Sikhs in the early 1920s is worth quoting at length. In September 1923 he wrote to the Earl of Derby:

> I have served with Sikhs for over thirty-five years, and know them well. I count, among them, some of my best friends – men whom I would trust, knowing that they would give their lives and all they possessed for one at any time. I know them though ... to be a sullen, vindictive, land-grabbing, and ... hard-hitting race of men. Excessive prosperity, far beyond their dreams – the result of our wonderful canal systems in the Punjab, which has turned miles of desert country into smiling fields of grain and cotton – has entirely turned their heads, and made them swell enormously. They now talk of the rights of their nationhood, and a great many of them aim at ruling the Punjab, as old Ranjit Singh did.[148]

Sikhs continued to serve loyally, and in significant numbers, in the Indian Army, but the Sikh relationship to the Government of India became a more uneasy one from the 1920s than it had been before 1914.[149] Matters occasionally turned violent. On 13 March 1940, Michael O'Dwyer, the former governor of the Punjab, was shot dead in London by Udham Singh, a Sikh who had been at Jallianwala Bagh on the day of the Amritsar massacre. The assassin was tried and hanged. Because it was wartime, Singh's 'statement to the jury was suppressed under the Emergency Powers (Defence) Act of 1939'.[150]

---

148 Birdwood to the Earl of Derby, Sept. 1923, in Jacobsen (ed.), *Rawlinson in India*, p. 166 [punctuation added].
149 Fraser, 'Sikh Problem', p. 49.
150 Sayer, 'British Reaction', p. 164.

10

Indian Prisoners of War in Germany during First World War

Andrew Jarboe

> When we at last get back to our homeland, and tell our tribesmen about our experiences in Germany and tell them how good we were treated in Germany and that we did not have to cover any of the expense of traveling to Constantinople so that we could fight for our faith, who knows if they will believe us. If we could show them a medal or document from the government, then no one would dare to doubt our story, and all would believe that Germany is not just the friend of Muslims, but of Afridis as well.

Sepoys of the 58th Rifles to their German captors, August 1915

Captivity was a central part of the war experience for millions of human beings during World War I, yet the topic remains among the most understudied aspects of the war. European armies interned between seven and nine million people between 1914 and 1918.[1] None of the combatant states were prepared in August 1914 for such a flood of prisoners. By one estimate, Germany held 586,000 prisoners of war at the end of 1914: 310,000 Russians, 220,000 French, 40,000 Belgian, and 16,000 British. A little more than a month later, Germany held 700,000 captured enemy soldiers – about one percent of its prewar population.[2] The conflict also marked a watershed in the way European states and their militaries treated captured civilians and soldiers.

---

1 Niall Ferguson, *The Pity of War* (London: Pengiun, 1998), p. 369.
2 TNA, FO 383/39, Senator Beveridge, Report on Prisoners' Camp in Germany, February 1915. Beveridge later republished the report in a book, *What is Back of the War* (Indianapolis: Bobbs-Merrill, 1916).

At the turn of the century, Spanish General Valeriano Weyler invented internment camps during the brutal war he waged in Cuba from 1896 – 97. During the South African War, the British used crude concentration camps to segregate and supervise the Boers. World War I marked the first time Europeans deployed these colonial practices in Europe.[3] The majority of soldiers who fought in the war had been civilians prior to August 1914 and in the age of mass armies any civilian could just as readily become a soldier. Therefore, the military powers fighting in Europe deposited both in vast and complex labyrinths of concentration camps, prisoner of war camps, and forced labor battalions. All the major powers, Germany included, made some nominal effort to honor their prewar commitment to the liberal tradition and the stipulations of the 1899 and 1907 Hague Conventions.[4] But any lingering 'benevolent captivity interpretation' fails to take into account the widespread brutalities and systematic violence forced upon combatant prisoners of war.[5] One recent study found that as many as one million soldiers died in prisoner of war camps.

This chapter investigates the policies that shaped the daily lives of Indian soldiers captured on the Western Front between 1914 and 1918. As German soldiers fought the global armies of the combined British and French empires on the Western Front, prison camps in Germany worked to 'convert' captured Indian and African soldiers. Some of the converts, the Germans hoped, might freely re-enlist in the Ottoman Army. Others – like captured Indian sepoys - might themselves serve as the vanguards of nationalist or pan-Islamic revolution in British India. They could smuggle guns, money, and revolutionary propaganda across the Middle East and bring the war to gates of India. This was Germany's version of world war on the cheap. How captured Indian soldiers fell into Germany's schemes, why some collaborated, and why most did not, is the subject of our investigation here.

The decentralized nature of Germany's network of prison camps, combined with poor record keeping, makes it nearly impossible to pin down the exact number of Indian soldiers taken prisoner during the war. In all likelihood, the Germans never really knew the actual number.[6] A number of soldiers fell captive to the Germans during the seesaw battles outside Ypres in the closing months of 1914. Havildar Ganga Ram of the 2/2nd Gurkhas told his captors that he and his men had only been at the front eight

---

3   Stephane Audoin-Rouzeau and Annette Becker, *14-18: Understanding the Great War* (London: Profile, 2002), p. 71.
4   Richard B. Speed III, *Prisoners, Diplomats, and the Great War: A Study in the Diplomacy of Captivity* (New York, Westport, London: Greenwood Press, 1990), p. 10.
5   Heather Jones, *Violence Against Prisoners of War in the First World War: Britain, France and Germany, 1914-1920* (Cambridge: Cambridge University Press, 2011).
6   Wilhelm Doegen (1921). Doegen made no distinction between British and Indian soldiers in his tables showing the total number of prisoners captured by the Germans, lumping both together under the category 'Engländer.'

days when a hail of German hand grenades forced them to surrender.⁷ Two days of fighting in late December produced roughly 100 fresh Indian prisoners of war from the 129th Baluchis, 59th Rifles, and 125th Napier Rifles.⁸ Taken prisoner at Festubert on 19 December 1914, Subadar Major Sher Singh Rana of the 1/4th Gurkha Rifles spent the remainder of the war in captivity; first at a camp in Lille where 'the Indian soldiers were left behind, but the Gurkhas (who were treated as Europeans) were sent with the Turkish and French prisoners to Cologne'; a brief stint in Cologne; Osnabruck until April 1916; Zossen through August; Clausthal through much of 1917; a punishment camp in Strohen; and finally a hospital in Holland. The Germans repatriated the Subadar Major to England in 1918.⁹ Rana's case is exceptional. The English – and just as likely the Germans – rarely knew the whereabouts of individual soldiers. In August 1915, Field Marshal French complained that the Germans never furnished him with an accurate list of Indian prisoners. The lists he did receive were 'so incomplete in details that hitherto it has been impossible to identify more than sixty per cent of the individuals mentioned.'¹⁰ One list, for example, identified an Indian prisoner only as 'Thapa.' A beleaguered secretary at the Prisoners of War Department in London circled the name and scribbled in the margins, 'In one Gurkha regt alone there are over 100 'Thapas' missing.'¹¹ By November 1915, the Indian Soldiers' Fund had the names of nearly 500 Indian prisoners in Germany to whom it sent care parcels.¹² At that time, 3247 Indian soldiers were still categorized on its rolls as 'missing.'¹³

Families in India and Indian audiences knew much less about the fates of those captured by the Germans on the Western Front. The Germans delivered soldier letters only sporadically. In Lahore, the newspaper *Akhbar-I'-Am* wrote in a February 1915 article, 'We wonder what treatment [the enemy] is meting out to [Indian prisoners]. Some American commission should pay a visit to these poor people also, though they are not Christians.'¹⁴ In early 1915, the Maharaja of Rewa wrote to the Government of India. 'I have read in the papers from time to time with pleasure the arrangements made by the British Government for the Indian soldiers, but I wish to know, if possible,

---

7   Political Archives of the Foreign Officer, Berlin [hereafter PAAA] R19354, report on Zossen, 16 August 1915.
8   Ibid.
9   TNA, FO 383/390, sworn statement of Subadar Major Sher Singh Rana 1/4th Gurkha Rifles.
10 IOR, L/MIL/7/13561, dispatch from Field Marshal French to the War Office, 31 August 1915.
11 IOR. L/MIL/7/13561, list of Indian prisoners of war, received December 15, 1915.
12 J. Merewether and F. E. Smith, *The Indian Corps in France* (London: John Murray, 1918), p. 503.
13 Ibid, p. 459. A century has elapsed and the frustrations of the war's contemporaries have not been settled. Historian Gerhard Höpp counted anywhere between 500 and 600 Indian prisoners of war in Germany. The estimates of other historians are higher, in the range of 1000.
14 IOR, L/R/5/196, *Akhbar-I'-Am*, 26 February 1915, p. 123.

whether the enemy respects scruples of the Hindus with regard to food. For example, a Hindu would rather die than take beef.' The Government of India's political agent in Baghelkand replied that no reports had yet been received concerning Hindu prisoners of war, but that the British army would make enquiries.[15]

Neither side overlooked the profound tactical implications of soldiers surrendering to the enemy in large numbers. On 8 August 1918, the British Army attacked exhausted and badly outnumbered German troops near Amiens. Although the attack stalled out two days later, the German commander, General Erich Ludendorff, called 8 August 'the black day of the German army,' because nearly 30,000 German soldiers surrendered. It was the clearest signal yet that the German army was beaten at long last.[16] Armies recognized that captured enemy soldiers served far greater utility than killed soldiers. Captured soldiers could be used as sources of intelligence, labour, hostages, and even as propaganda: treated well, a prisoner could induce his comrades to surrender.[17] Offered the right combination of carrot and stick, he might even be persuaded to take up arms in the cause of his captors.

Germany's strategy for war in 1914 involved hitting its British, French and Russian enemies where they were weakest – Africa and Asia. Britain may have been more prepared than Germany to fight a global conflict, but Whitehall did not want the Continental war to go intercontinental and the British Empire had the most to lose from a world war. When the Australian government telegraphed on 3 August its willingness to send and finance an expeditionary force, the Army Council in London demurred, preferring instead to feed Australian and New Zealand troops piecemeal into British formations. In short order, British (and French) policy made the war global. But the Germans also had a hand in broadening the scope of things. On 30 July, when it became clear that 'perfidious Albion' would intervene, the Kaiser erupted, 'Our consuls in Turkey and India ... must fire the whole Mohammedan world to fierce rebellion' against England. 'If we are to be bled to death, at least England shall lose India.'[18] On 2 August, the Kaiser's ministers secured Turkey's allegiance and in October, the Ottoman Empire entered the war, offering a seemingly open road to the gates of India. Then on 14 November, the Sheikh-ul-Islam in Constantinople declared an Islamic holy war against the British, French, and Russian empires. Britain was the

---

15 TNA, FO 383/39, copy of a demi-official letter no. 4150 dated 3 December 1914 from Lt-Col. S.H. Godfrey, C.I.E. Political Agent in Baghelkand, to the Hon'ble Mr. O.V. Bosanquet, C.S.I., C.I.E., Agent to the Governor General in Central India.
16 Roger Chickering, *Imperial Germany and the Great War, 1914-1918* (Cambridge: Cambridge University Press, 2004), p. 184.
17 Ferguson, *Pity of War*, p. 371.
18 Quoted in Fritz Fischer, *Germany's Aims in the First World War* (London: Chatto & Windus, 1967), p. 121.

world's foremost 'Muslim Power,' ruling over nearly 100 million Muslim subjects. In India, the Muslim population exceeded 60 million.[19]

For Baron Max von Oppenheim and his agents at the Intelligence Office for the East, Muslim soldiers from the British and French empires captured on the Western Front represented potential recruits for the Sultan's pan-Islamic jihad. The Foreign Office recalled Oppenheim's services on 2 August. An errant orientalist and onetime diplomat, the Baron fronted his own fortune to convert the Foreign Office into a pan-Islamic clearinghouse responsible for distributing anti-Entente pamphlets in every conceivable language. He maintained that captured North Africans 'seriously doubt the prospects of a final victory, and this could spoil their interest in remaining loyal to France.'[20] He planned to 'convert' these soldiers, re-enlist them in the Turkish army, and then re-deploy them to various fronts under Turkish and German leadership. 'The arrival of the first detachment of prisoners in Constantinople will naturally make a great impression.' These soldiers, he hoped, would inspire the masses of the Ottoman Empire and set in motion an unstoppable Turkish army that would conquer Egypt, sweep across Tripoli, and wrest Northwest Africa from the hands of the French.[21] Oppenheim envisioned similar schemes for captured Indian soldiers, Muslim and non-Muslim equally. Upon renouncing their allegiance to Britain, a small number of Indian prisoners might join an expedition to Afghanistan to persuade the Emir to invade India. In the ensuing disorder and general panic, the soldiers would spearhead a general uprising against England in India. A larger battalion of Indian Volunteers would serve in the Emir's army.[22]

By the close of 1914, Oppenheim had outlined a set of general policies for the handling of North African and Indian prisoners of war, stipulating above all that 'they must be treated ... in accordance with their various religions and customs.'[23] Indians, he noted in one memorandum, were 'extremely sensitive. Above all, therefore, avoid anything that might offend their sense of honor.'[24] The British, he learned, were making every accommodation for the Indian troops, 'whom they so desperately need on all of the warfronts.' The Indian Soldiers' Fund had already raised more than two million Marks to provide supplies to the troops in the field while special facilities at the Indian hospitals catered to the religious and dietary needs of the troops. 'In light of these well-designed efforts by the English, the good treatment of Indian prisoners on our part is of the utmost importance.'[25] With winter fast approaching, and Indian

---

19 Tilman Lüdke, *Jihad made in Germany: Ottoman and German Propaganda and Intelligence Operations in the First World War* (LIT Verlag, 2005), p. 33.
20 PAAA, R21244, Foreign Office memo by Baron von Oppenheim, October 1914.
21 PAAA, R21244, Ibid.
22 PAAA, R21244, Telegram from Oppenheim, November 1914.
23 PAAA, R21244, Foreign Office memo from Oppenheim, October 1914.
24 PAAA, R21244, 'Verpflegung und Behandlung der indischen Gefangenen,' 31 December 1914.
25 PAAA, R21244, Oppenheim to the Foreign Office, 31 December 1914.

and North African prisoners scattered across the Reich and occupied territories in France, Oppenheim worried, 'The longer the [Muslim and Indian] prisoners are treated as enemies and left with other prisoners the more difficult it will be to use them later on for our interests.'[26]

From the start of 1915 through the end of the war, the German War Ministry concentrated Muslim and Indian prisoners of war in two camps located 50 kilometers south of Berlin in Zossen: nearly 12,000 Russians lived in the *Tatarenlager* at Zossen-Weinberge, French Muslim prisoners and Indian prisoners were held at Wünsdorf, generally referred to as the *Halbmondlager* (Crescent Moon Camp). The Indians were later confined to their own section, the *Inderlager*, and then transferred to a camp in Romania in April 1917.[27] At its maximum occupancy, Zossen housed approximately 14,000 Russian, African and Indian troops. The Kaiser provided the 45,000 marks required for the construction of a small mosque for the camp's Muslim inhabitants.[28] Muslim soldiers observed the fast of Ramadan.[29] Indian soldiers prepared their own food and baked their own bread. North Africans had access to a coffee stand and gramophone.[30] After a January 1915 visit with a small number of Gurkhas, Rajputs, one Sikh and one Pathan, the Indian Independence Committee reported that the soldiers wanted more bread, butter, rice and vegetables. Tobacco and 'something to read,' the Committee added, would also please the prisoners.[31] 'It will likely serve our own interests to see to it that these small requests are met as soon as possible,' Oppenheim penned.[32] J. B. Jackson of the American Embassy in Berlin visited the Indian prisoners of war camp at Zossen in July 1915 and reported that the troops were satisfied with the arrangements. The soldiers' barracks were not overcrowded, there were no armed German guards in the camp itself, and the non-commissioned officers who attended to its administration were 'very considerate of the feelings of the Indians and do not go into their kitchens or the prayer section of the Mahommedan barracks.' The health of the camp appeared satisfactory and 'all in the camp seemed to be in good spirits.'[33]

The propaganda campaign was relentless. 'Everything should be done to impress upon the prisoners that we are not their enemies,' Oppenheim stressed, 'and that it is only because of circumstance that we find ourselves opposite one another.' Captured

---

26   PAAA, R21244, Oppenheim to Zimmermann, 13 November 1914.
27   Gerhard Höpp, *Muslime in der Mark* (Berlin: Das Arabische Buch, 1997), pp. 44-5.
28   PAAA, R21245, Nadolny to the Foreign Office, 27 March 1915.
29   PAAA, R21250, Report on the observance of Ramadan at the Halbmondlager, 25 July 1915.
30   PAAA, R21246, undated, untitled document.
31   PAAA, R21244, Report on 4 January 1915 visit to Zossen by members of the Indian Independence Committee.
32   PAAA, R21244, Oppenheim to the Foreign Office, 4 February 1915.
33   TNA, PRO 383/65, Report by Mr. Jackson on Visit to Indian Prisoners of War Camp at Wünsdorf (Zossen).

in November 1914, sepoy Mahomed Arifan later recalled, 'the camp [Zossen] was overrun with Mahommedan propagandists, Turks, Fakirs, and what not, who tried by every means to influence the Indian soldiers to break their allegiance to the British Empire.' Intelligence Office revolutionaries and Ottoman officials combined the appeals of nationalism and pan-Islamic jihad interchangeably. 'It is in our interests to develop Muslim and Hindu elements together,' Oppenheim instructed. 'If handled delicately, cultivating both elements is possible.'[34] Ottoman officials and religious leaders delivered frequent lectures focused on the glory of the former Islamic Empire, the history of various Islamic peoples, exchange and interaction between the Orient and the Occident, the political, economic, and intellectual strength of Germany, and wartime relationships between Germany and Muslim territories. In November 1915, a member of the Indian Committee delivered a lecture at Zossen for the Indian troops on the 'political geography' of India, concluding on the subject, 'The people of India, their essential unity in spite of apparent diversity of races and creeds.' In September 1915, the Germans took a group of prisoners on a tour of Berlin to impress the men with German 'order, authority, and power.'[35] The Indian Committee published a newspaper in Urdu and Hindi for Indian prisoners called *Hindustan*. One edition of the paper touched on anything from 'English misrule in India' and a general uprising in India, to actions taken by Indian soldiers to carry out the jihad.[36] Cheaply and quickly printed leaflets reinforced the message. 'Never forget about your oppression by the English,' ran the headline of one. 'The time for revenge is now.'[37]

The Germans also hoped their activities at Zossen might win them converts among the Indian soldiers still stationed in frontline trenches. In December 1914, Paul Walter asked that a few captured Indians be allowed to work with him in Lille where he saw to the needs of recently captured sepoys. 'It is important to try and influence new arrivals from the very outset,' he told Oppenheim. 'Then when they are ready, they will return to their tribal brethren in the enemy lines at night, or in some other suitable way.'[38] Airships and balloons dropped leaflets and propaganda over the lines occupied by Muslim troops.[39] At the Censors' Office, E. B. Howell worried that German activities at Zossen might have some effect on troops at the front. Letters and postcards written by Indian prisoners of war in Germany revealed that the Germans were 'anxious to impress upon the Indian troops in the field the good treatment which their fellows who have been taken prisoner are receiving in Germany.' He also warned, '[The Germans] have lately been distributing over that part of the line held by Indian troops leaflets with pictures of the Indian prisoners'

---

34 PAAA, R21245, plan for the handling of Muslim and Indian prisoners, 27 February 1915.
35 Höpp, *Muslime in der Mark*, p. 55.
36 PAAA, R21256, report on contents of *Hindustan*, n.d.
37 PAAA, R21245, 'Never forget about your oppression by the English,' n.d.
38 PAAA, R21244, Walter to Oppenheim, 12 December 1914.
39 PAAA, R21244, Foreign Office memo by Baron von Oppenheim, October 1914.

camps, and information about the number of prisoners, guns taken, and the extent of territory conquered by the German army.'[40]

When at last joint German-Ottoman plans came together in late 1915 to form battalions of 'converted' North African and Indian soldiers, the pressure on prisoners of war to volunteer intensified. At the end of Ramadan on 20 October 1915, the Muslim soldiers in Zossen celebrated the Bairam Feast. As German camp authorities handed out cigarettes, sugar and tea, the Turkish ambassador watched as a procession of the first battalion of 900 North African *Freiwilliger* (Volunteers) for the Holy War marched through the camp to the sound of drums and horns. 'The course of the festival can be described as entirely successful,' observed one German witness. 'It should have a good influence on the mood of the prisoners.'[41] The first detachments of the North African Volunteers left the prison for Constantinople the following month.[42] In January 1916, 1,400 Russian Muslims departed for the Caucasus.[43] The Germans moved the 41 Indians who pledged to join the Indian Battalion to their own barracks, 'resulting from, as anticipated, complications between them and the other Indian Muslims.'[44] Camp authorities also singled-out Indian soldiers who continued to refuse their captors' appeals and sent them away to punishment camps. In mid-1916, the Indian Committee wrote to the Foreign Office, calling attention to

> the baneful influence that is being exercised on the prisoners in Wuensdorf by the Sikh Jamadar Suwai Singh and the Gurkha Subedar-Major Sher Singh Rana. From intimate conversations with the prisoners we are able to show not only that these two men are doing their best to resist the spread of patriot ideas among the soldiers, but that they are secretly carrying on a strong anti-German and pro-English propaganda.[45]

In August 1916, Rana recalled, camp authorities transferred the two soldiers (and others) to Clausthal and thereafter to Strohen, 'owing to our refusal to accept German advances.'[46] In the end, 44 Indians joined the ill-fated Indian Battalion, departing for Constantinople in April 1916.[47]

But there could be just as much pressure on Indians not to enlist in the Volunteer Battalion. For many of the soldiers recruited in India, fighting for Turkey was completely out of the question. 'They come from the British territory of Punjab, their

---

40   IOR, L/MIL/17347, Communication from E.B. Howell, 21 October 1915.
41   PAAA, R21252, report on the Bairam Feast at Zossen, 25 October 1915.
42   PAAA, R21252, letter from von Ramsay to von Lossow, 9 November 1915.
43   PAAA, R21253, Foreign Office internal memo, 20 January 1916.
44   PAAA, R21253, report on the Halbmondlager, 25 December 1915.
45   PAAA, R21258, Indian Independence Committee to the Foreign Office, 21 June 1916.
46   TNA, FO 383/390, sworn statement of Subadar-Major Sher Singh Rana 1/4th Gurkha Rifles.
47   PAAA, R21254, list of Indians sent to Turkey on 3 March 1916.

land and their families are dependent upon [the British], and they want to go back to India once peace has been declared,' camp authorities conceded.[48] Soldiers from Afghanistan and trans-border Pathans also worried that if they were recaptured while fighting for the Turks they would lose their pensions and suffer a lengthy prison sentence.[49] Sikh and Gurkha officers used their position and influence among the men to keep sepoys loyal to the British.[50] 'I did my best to dissuade Indian soldiers from listening to any advances,' Rana recalled. 'In my opinion the sedition propaganda had little effect on them 'going in at one ear and out at the other.'"[51] When persuasion did not work, some Indian prisoners relied on intimidation and violence to keep comrades loyal to the British Empire. On 10 January 1916 a fight broke out in the camp among Sikhs. Three men were badly beaten. 'The Sikh Jemadar and certain other officers (who are all very friendly to the English and opposed to the idea of men leaving for Constantinople or the Indian frontier) hold that the fight was the outcome of some foolish and petty jealousies.' But the Indian Committee investigation revealed,

> About fifteen non-commissioned officers and Mr. Kartaram (whose word cannot be doubted) hold that the fight was brought about by the Sikh Jemadar and his faction to intimidate the patriotic Sikh prisoners, especially Mita Singh, who has been very active in carrying on propaganda among the Sikhs.
>
> Undoubtedly the Sikh Jemadar and the four Mohammadan officers have been using their influence (which is not a negligible quantity) to counteract our work and to dissuade men from participating in our patriotic cause. There is also a rumor that some of the officers are spending money to win people to their side and keep them subservient.[52]

Sepoys interned at Zossen had a choice to make. They could renounce all allegiance to the British Empire, collaborate with their captors and join the Indian Battalion, or they could refuse the overtures of the Germans and Indian Committee and wait out the war in captivity. Either option came with considerable risk. Collaborators risked ostracism or physical violence from a resentful peer group, death on another battlefront, or a lengthy prison sentence if recaptured by the British or if the Germans lost the war. Those who held out against the Germans might be sent to punishment camps, forced to perform life-threatening physical labour, or endure severe physical violence at the hands of vengeful camp guards. In some ways, the lot of the Indian soldiers was unique. France's North African soldiers very likely never had a choice.

---

48   PAAA, R21252, from the commander of Zossen prison camp to the Foreign Office, 18 November 1915.
49   PAAA, R21246, memo, 27 May 1915.
50   PAAA, R21253, report by the commander of the Halbmondlager, 25 January 1916.
51   TNA, FO 383/390, sworn statement of Subadar-Major Sher Singh Rana 1/4th Gurkha Rifles.
52   PAAA, R21253, Indian Independence Committee to the Foreign Office, 14 January 1916.

One Tunisian soldier, captured trying to desert from the Ottoman army, told his captors that he never wanted to fight for the Turks. German documents verify his claim. France's colonial subjects who traveled to Mesopotamia to fight for the Turks were forced to go.[53] Sepoys were not.

The different treatment afforded North Africans and Indians reveals as much about the political priorities of the Germans and their allies as it does a shared, pan-European repertoire of racist attitudes. World War I coincided with the heyday of German (and American) racial science. Racial hygienists combined pseudo-science with social Darwinism, classified and isolated 'desirable' and 'undesirable' racial characteristics, and proscribed plans for improving the biology of the human species.[54] At times, the Germans applied racial stereotypes to Indian and African prisoners of war indiscriminately. When authorities finished construction of the camp mosque in early 1915, the *Berliner Tageblatt* commented on the inauguration of the 'strange looking [building] on the soil of Germany' for 'our oriental enemies fighting for France and England.'[55] In his 1916 book, *Unsere Feinde*, Otto Stiehl provided a number of portrait photographs of the different 'races' interned in German prison camps. 'The mixture of tribes and races mobilized by our enemies from all five continents to fight on the old soil of Europe is outrageous, far surpassing anything ever seen before in world history.'[56] But visitors to the camp just as readily drew sharp distinctions between Indians and Africans. In early 1915, United States Senator Albert Beveridge (R-Indiana) toured Zossen.

> In the barracks occupied by the prisoners from India there is an unusual feature: every Hindou cooks and in every way prepares his own food, for he will not eat anything touched by Christian hands. Many of them were observed at this private and religious culinary occupation. The Gourka sergeant in charge of this barrack, spoke English very well. He and his comrades were treated very well, he said – much better than they expected.
>
> Would he like to get back to India? He would – more than anything.
>
> Why had he come to the war?
>
> 'Orders, sir'
>
> He good-naturedly interpreted for a group of tall, grave-faced Sikhs, statues of dignity and gravity.
>
> Why had they come so far to fight?

---

53   Richard Fogarty, 'Out of North Africa,' in Andrew Jarboe and Richard Fogarty, eds., *Empires in World War I: Shifting Frontiers and Imperial Dynamics in a Global Conflict* (London: I.B. Tauris, 2014), p. 150.
54   Robert Proctor, *Racial Hygiene: Medicine under the Nazis* (Cambridge: Harvard University Press, 1988), pp. 16-18.
55   'Die Moschee im Gefangenenlager,' *Berliner Tageblatt*, 9 July 1915.
56   O. Stiehl, *Unsere Feinde: 96 Characterkoepfe aus deutschen Kriegsgefangenenlagern* (Stuttgart: Verlag Julius Hoffman, 1916), p. 5.

> 'The service' was the answer; and the Gourkha sergeant tried to make their meaning clear by such expressions as 'their duty' [']their profession', 'their business'. As to wanting to go home, we gathered that they were quite indifferent, that it was all the same to them, and that they took things as they happened.⁵⁷

The 'gravity' and 'dignity' of the sepoys stood in stark contrast to the North African prisoners the Senator visited next.

> In the barracks where the Turcos lived, came the one disagreeable, even shocking surprise of the day. It is impossible to imagine more villainous looking creatures. Nearly all of them are small men, and most of them have viciousness stamped on every feature. Their evil eyes follow you expressionless, unblinking, like those of a serpent. Some of these men undoubtedly are criminals – the forehead, jaw, mouth, back head, and above all the merciless, soulless eyes spell depravity. The Sikhs and Gourkas from India, many of whom have fine and even noble features, and infinitely superior to this scum of Northern Africa; for such at least most of these particular Turcos must be. There are some faces among them that are not bad; but, most of them justify the harshest description. It is not thinkable that these are fair samples of the inhabitants of northern Africa.⁵⁸

The Germans' Ottoman allies showed considerably less interest in forming an Indian battalion.⁵⁹ India had never been part of the Ottoman Empire as North Africa had. Indians had never been Ottoman subjects. After the small detachment of Indian Volunteers departed for Constantinople in April 1916, camp authorities gave up recruiting efforts entirely. 'Future propaganda efforts ... are unlikely to win over any more Muslims because the remaining are Punjabis who have little interest in the Holy War,' read one camp report.⁶⁰ And try as they might, the Indian Committee never convinced the Germans to do more in Zossen to cultivate Indian nationalism alongside pan-Islamism. Hindu prisoners of war told members of the Indian Committee that while they might be willing to fight for India, they did not want to take up arms for Turkey or Germany.⁶¹ 'We are, of course, aware that the Mohammedans are impatient to go to Turkey,' offered one Indian Committee report, 'but our object in our propaganda among the prisoners has been to get them to accept the idea of fighting their way through Persia to India.'⁶² By mid-1915, with Indians deployed in large numbers against the Turks in the Middle East, the Indian Committee argued that

---

57 TNA, FO 383/39, Senator Beveridge, Report on Prisoners' Camp in Germany, February 1915.
58 Ibid.
59 PAAA, R21255, Report from Zossen, 14 March 1916.
60 PAAA, R21253, report by the commander of the Halbmondlager, 25 January 1916.
61 PAAA, R21253, Indian Independence Committee to the Foreign Office, 9 January 1915.
62 Ibid.

the only hope for convincing Indians to join the Volunteer Battalion was to cultivate national sentiment.

> From the Lager authorities I have come to know that they have instructions from the General Staff to carry on propaganda only among the Mohamedans, so as to make them willingly leave for Turkey. About the Rajputs, Sikhs and Gurkhas the Lager authorities are instructed to carry on such propaganda that these people will feel friendly to Germany and speak well of the German Government and people when they return to India.
>
> If we mean seriously to organize an Indian Corps (composed of these prisoners and other Indians available in Turkey and Persia) which will march towards the Indian frontier through Persia, and if the German Government sees the feasibility and immense political and moral value of the scheme, then the Lager authorities should be asked to carry on propaganda in co-operation with the representatives of the Indian National Party, among the Sikhs, Rajputs and Gurkhas also, so that these people will volunteer for our cause.[63]

But there is little to suggest that patriotic or nationalistic propaganda would have carried much sway among Indian prisoners of war either. When asked by one member of the Indian Committee if he thought about Indian autonomy, Sher Singh Rana replied that he was a Gurkha of Nepal and 'refused to listen to any such talk.'[64] Nepalese soldiers made up a considerable percentage of the inmate population. Not one joined the Indian Battalion. Punjabis hailed from rural and agricultural communities. Members of the Indian Committee – Taraknath Das, Virendranath Chattopadhaya, Maharaj Narayan Kaul – were college educated and cosmopolitan. This class divide remained difficult for the Indian Committee to bridge as is evidenced after the war by how repatriated sepoys described Committee members: 'One was from Baroda, probably a Mahratta'; 'a Sikh of Hoshiapur, but his hair and his beard clipped'; 'a regular 'Company' of Bengalis.'[65]

It is not even altogether clear that the sepoys who did join the Indian Battalion harboured any fiery commitment to pan-Islamism, much less anti-imperialism. Granted, one group of recently captured soldiers told the Indian Committee that they 'felt betrayed by the English,' that upon reaching the Western Front 'they were placed at the forefront of the battle and ruthlessly sacrificed.'[66] Another group of Afridi Volunteers proclaimed they were 'ready to be the champions of their religion

---

63   PAAA, R21253, Indian Independence Committee to the Foreign Office, 14 January 1916.
64   TNA, FO 383/390, statement of Subadar Major Sher Singh Rana, 1918.
65   Andrew Jarboe, 'Indian Soldiers in Hospital and Prison, 1914-18,' in *Empires in World War I* (2014).
66   PAAA, R21244, Report on 4 January 1915 visit to Zossen by members of the Indian Independence Committee.

and their land in order to end British rule in India.'⁶⁷ But these were most likely the words of soldiers trying to make something out of nothing, to secure some modicum of advantage for themselves (to minimize their disadvantage) when no one else in the world was looking out for their best interests. The Germans seemed to be promising them a one-way ticket home. And there were simple, household economics to consider. The Germans guaranteed Indian Volunteers regular pay and a pension. Every single one of the 24 soldiers who deserted from the 58th Rifles in March 1915 joined the Battalion. By leaving their trenches, each had forfeited any and all pay, pension, and social status guaranteed by the British, '& this ruined their future prospects entirely,' read one Indian Committee report.⁶⁸ Three Sikhs of the Punjab also joined the battalion. Of these, Mita Singh deserted his post at the front, and Hardas Singh shot his British officer and then deserted. The third, Shemir Singh, only told his captors that he feared what the British might do to him if he ever fell back into their hands.⁶⁹ One group of recently captured sepoys admitted to the Indian Committee, 'They fought for England because of the money, and would, for the same reason, be willing to fight for the Germans.'⁷⁰ Meanwhile, the Committee suspected that many of the Afghan 'converts' had no intention of bringing revolution and jihad all the way to the gates of India. 'Unless [the Indians] were all persuaded to take part in a general patriotic scheme, the Mohammadans would merely wish to go to settle down in Turkey, which is not good for them and is not what we desire.'⁷¹ Settling in Constantinople is exactly what many of them did, disappearing into the city, from German-Ottoman authorities, and from the archival record.

The example of one soldier reveals how adept some of the sepoys must have been at manipulating their captors even without stretching the truth considerably. Sepoy Mahomed Arifan convinced the Germans and Indian Committee beyond any reasonable doubt that as a 'devout Muslim,' he would 'be pleased to fight with the Turks against their enemies.'⁷² A native of Peshawar, near the Khyber Pass, Arifan joined the Indian Army 14 years prior to the outbreak of World War I and served in the 127th Baluchis. He was a veteran of an operation in Somaliland where he had been wounded. Shot through the knees and captured on the Western Front in late 1914, Arifan assured the Germans that Afghan soldiers had no particular fondness for the British Empire and joined the ranks of the Indian Army because it provided a reliable source of income. 'The Indian Army is able to recruit a lot of Afghans,' he told a German interrogator, 'because they are paid well.' At the Battle of La Bassée, he said, many of his fellow countrymen ran when they spotted the Germans, 'because they

---

67 PAAA, R21250, Graetsch to the Foreign Office, 9 August 1915.
68 PAAA, R21246, Indian Independence Committee to the Foreign Office, 29 May 1915.
69 PAAA, R21253, report on the Halbmondlager, 14 January 1916.
70 PAAA, R21244, Report on 4 January 1915 visit to Zossen by members of the Indian Independence Committee.
71 PAAA, R21253, Indian Independence Committee to the Foreign Office, 9 January 1915.
72 PAAA, R21245, summary of interrogation of Mohamed Arefin, 20 January 1915.

did not want to fight against our friends, the Germans.' He was eager to participate in propagating jihad. 'I am confident that when the Muslim soldiers fighting in the English army learn about the Holy War, they will no longer fight against the Germans but against their true enemies.'[73]

Yet Arifan never joined the Afghan expedition or the Indian Battalion. The severity of his wound must have undone his candidacy considerably. With little to gain from the Germans, Arifan threw his lot back in with the British. In November 1915, the Germans transferred him to Görlitz. 'He was in a wretched state ... and was nothing but a miserable bundle of filthy rage,' recalled Sergeant J.P. Walsh of the 1st Gloucester Regiment. Walsh 'took charge of [Arifan] from the moment of his arrival, and he became devoted to me during the 17 months we were together in Görlitz.' Arifan told Walsh that Germany's attempts to convert the sepoys were a complete failure.

> And as a result the Germans systematically persecuted them by every means, withdrew the sanction hitherto accorded to caste feeling, and finally sent away from Zossen those who stood out firmest, and were most influential among their fellows in preserving loyalty to the King-Emperor.[74]

Arifan 'bore himself well' during his internment alongside Sergeant Walsh, 'and is a credit to the Indian Army.' The British sergeant 'always assured him that the British Government would not forget his loyalty and that of his comrades at Zossen,' adding,

> [Arifan] was intensely proud of being a British subject. He was frequently placed in prison for refusing to work for the Germans, and the last I saw of him was when he was sent away in March 1917 to Königsbruck to look after an elephant, but he told me he would continue to refuse to do any work for the Germans.[75]

Bad health care – like that Arifan received while in German custody – may have done as much as anything else to dissuade sepoys from even collaborating with the Germans. Sick soldiers were certainly in no condition to fight in the armies of their captors. '[The prisoners] cough practically all the time,' read one camp report. 'Most of the diseases [in the camp] are of the lungs. Deaths are almost all causes by pulmonary tuberculosis.'[76] By the close of 1915, there were some 650 Indian prisoners in Zossen. They complained frequently that the camp failed to provide them with warm weather clothing and coal.[77] As repeated outbreaks of tuberculosis ravaged the

---

73 Ibid.
74 TNA, FO 383/390, Treatment of Indian Prisoners at Zossen and Goerlitz, statement of Sergeant J.P. Walsh, 1/Gloucester Regiment, obtained by Major M. Wylie, 1/4 Gurkha Rifles, 6 March 1918.
75 Ibid.
76 PAAA, R21252, report on Zossen to the Ministry of War, 24 November 1915.
77 PAAA, R21252, Indian Independence Committee to Foreign Office, 23 December 1915.

inmate population in 1915 and in 1916, the Germans lost any remaining goodwill they may have earned from propaganda and the 'small requests' they had provided. 'We regret very much to have to say that the prisoners have no faith in the efficacy of the medical treatment they receive,' warned the Indian Committee in 1916. 'The chief reason is undoubtedly the high rate of mortality among the prisoners.'[78] Repatriated to Holland in 1918, Jemadar Suba Sing Gurung of the 2/2nd Gurkha Rifles told a British officer that in addition to a 'persistent campaign of sedition,'

> The main complaint the Jemadar had against the camp… is that the water was bad, and that in consequence large numbers of men became ill, and had to go to hospital. No men were allowed to go with them as orderlies or nurses, and the result was that they rapidly became worse, and a very large percentage died. There were 52 men of the Jemadar's regiment, 2/2nd Gurkha Rifles, taken prisoner, and of these 18 had died by April, 1917, and he states that this was not a remarkable percentage, and that from 33 to 50% of the original prisoners had certainly died. There was a good deal of tuberculosis as well, and one Subadar Prem Sing Thapa, 1/4 Gurkha Rifles, died of the disease.[79]

The Indian Committee tried repeatedly to bring the seriousness of the situation to the attention of the Germans and repair the goodwill they feared had been lost. In February 1916, they advised that camp authorities transfer Gurkha Subadar-Major Prem Singh, 'who has been ill for some time and who in our opinion should be removed as soon as possible to a hospital in or near Berlin. This officer is highly respected and influential among the soldiers, and, if the special consideration that we are now requesting be shown to him, it will have a very good effect among them.' The Committee offered various suggestions to improve health conditions in the camp.

> We desire to produce the belief that the German Government is anxious to do all in its power for the Indian prisoners. If our suggestion [to improve conditions and send sick Indians to recuperate in Switzerland] is carried out, we shall take steps to have the facts published in India and thus counteract to some extent the attempt of the English enemy to undermine India's pro German tendencies.[80]

But conditions deteriorated markedly in mid-1916.

---

78 PAAA, R21255, Indian Independence Committee to the Foreign Office, 23 April 1916.
79 TNA, FO 383/390, Treatment of Indian Prisoners at Zossen and Goerlitz, statement of Jemadar Suba Sing Gurung, obtained by Major M. Wylie, 1/4 Gurkha Rifles, 6 March 1918.
80 PAAA, R21255, Indian Independence Committee to the Foreign Office, 23 April 1916.

Deaths in the Indian Camps

Month	Halbmondlager, Zossen			Romania	
	1915	1916	1917	1917	1918
January	1	7	5		1
February	2	6	9		
March	-	8	12		
April	3	10	7		
May	2	13		16	
June	1	14		7	
July	11	16		1	
August	2	10		2	
September	6	8		3	
October	6	6		2	
November	4	8		6	
December	2	8		1	
Total	40	114		71	1

Source: TNA, FO 383/406 1

Germany's propaganda campaign at Zossen – and the generally poor results it produced among Indian soldiers – is perhaps a perfect illustration of former US House Speaker Tip O'Neill's expression, 'All politics is local.' The fate of the British Empire in India was decided during World War I by the collective actions of people in many localities, and the brutality and racism of one Anglo-Indian camp guard employed by the Germans at Zossen represents but one of innumerable everyday acts that helped 'save' the British Empire from Germany's world ambitions. The man's name has been lost to history. But his behavior was the subject of numerous complaints filed by the Indian Committee. The man first came to the attention of Indian Committee co-founder Bhupendranath Dutt during a December 1915 visit to the camp. Sepoys told Dutt, 'They [the Germans] want us to believe they are good, but they are no better than the English.' Dutt filed a complaint with camp authorities requesting that they transfer the man to another camp. 'The conduct of the officer in question is not conducive to success in our propaganda.'[81] German authorities did nothing. The Indian Committee filed another protest in March 1916.

---

81   PAAA, R21252, Indian Independence Committee to Foreign Office, 23 December 1915.

We find that [the guard] has in no way changed his brutal conduct nor his ... language in dealings with the sepoys and even with the officers. The following are some specimens of the highly insulting language used by him without any sort of provocation: -

'Badmâsh' (You scoundrel), 'Jangli' (You savage), 'Suar ka bachcha' (You son of a pig), 'Sala' (Fellow whose sister I have ravished), 'Mâdarchôd', 'Bahanchôd' (You fellow who have committed incest with your mother, with your sister).

We beg to express our desire that this Anglo-Indian be immediately removed from the Lager, and replaced by Mr. Walter who is much liked by the soldiers by reason of his gentlemanly and sympathetic treatment of them.[82]

By April, things reached the breaking point. Pending the man's removal, Dutt wrote, it would be useless for the Committee to continue its work in the camp to 'try to do anything among the prisoners to make them believe that the Germans are really more gentlemanly and more humane than the English.'[83]

The British carried out a limited counterpropaganda campaign of their own in Germany's prison camps. In June 1915, representatives from the India Office, Foreign Office, War Office, Indian Soldiers' Fund and the Prisoners of War Help Committee met informally at the India Office to consider various questions in connection with Indian prisoners of war in Germany. At the top of the agenda were questions concerning where the Germans interned Indian prisoners, whether they confined Indian troops with their British officers, if they kept and might provide complete lists of Indian prisoners, whether they allowed Indian prisoners to communicate with their friends, and if the British Government could ask the American Embassy to make a special report on the condition and wants of Indian prisoners.[84] The Indian Soldiers' Fund (ISF), an organization set up shortly after the outbreak of the war, sent large dispatches of food, clothing and other comforts to Indian prisoners.[85] 'The packages for the English prisoners are not superfluous,' noted the Zossen Kommandant. 'Instead, they are intended to counter the effects of German propaganda.'[86]

A few of the Volunteers who set out for the Indian frontier made it home during the war. Some secured German guns and money and then did nothing to bring revolution

---

82 PAAA, R21254, Indian Independence Committee to Foreign Office, 5 March 1916.
83 PAAA, R21256, Indian Independence Committee to Foreign Office, 28 April 1916.
84 TNA, PRO FO 383/65, Minutes of an informal Conference held at the India Office on 17 June 1915 for the purpose of considering various questions in connection with Indian Officers and other ranks prisoners of War in Germany.
85 See TNA, FO 383/151, the American Embassy in Berlin also acted as an important link between the British Empire and Indian prisoners until the Americans broke off diplomatic relations with Germany in 1917. In January 1916, the Calcutta Office of the Y.M.C.A. sent large supplies of curry powder and 'similar consignments' to Indian prisoners in Germany through the care of the American embassies in London and Berlin.
86 PAAA, R21253, findings of inspection of Zossen, 19 January 1916.

to the Indian frontier. In 1917, British agents captured a number of German, Austrian and Turkish agents during a surprise raid in Shiraz, Persia. Nine sepoys from the 58th Rifles and 2 soldiers formerly belonging to the 20th Punjabis – all of them Kambar Khel Afridis – accompanied the agents. The soldiers told British agents that they had been captured by the Germans and had been forced to accompany their captors, but the British never believed the story. The men carried identical purses and each had £100 in his possession. A Civil Intelligence Officer in Kabul concluded, 'It is an established fact ... that the deserters of the 58th Rifles were employed as secret agents of the enemy when arrested ... all were equipped and commissioned as secret agents by the same authority.'[87] Instead of going home, the captured sepoys spent the remainder of the war in a prison in Karachi.

The eventual repatriation of Indian prisoners of war interned in Germany (and Turkey) was not a matter British authorities wished to leave to hasty improvisation. With very little information forthcoming on the activities of the German, Ottoman and Indian sedition agents in prisoner of war camps – beyond vague reports that Indians received 'special treatment' at the hands of their captors - the British believed they could not take for granted the loyalty of the Empire's interned subjects. A 7 May 1915 telegram from the Government of India to the Foreign Office read:

> Reliable information has been received by Criminal Intelligence Department that German newspaper invited some Indians in Europe to go to Germany where they will be well paid for talking to captured Indian soldiers. Those prisoners most amenable to the talk will be the first selected for exchange if and when exchange of prisoners with England begins. Germans intend that after exchange these men should do their best to persuade other soldiers to revolt against the British. It is known for a fact that some Indians are employed by German Government. In the event of exchange becoming practical question or of Indian prisoners being permitted to escape, mental attitude of such Indians will require consideration.[88]

British concern for the stability of India – and for the 'mental attitude' of Indian prisoners of war – intensified as the war dragged on. In mid-1915, a German expedition led by Lieutenant Oskar Ritter von Niedermayer reached Kabul, Afghanistan where it tried to convince the Emir to abandon neutrality and invade Northwest India.[89] A handful of Indian sepoys – soldiers belonging to the 58th Rifles who deserted from their posts on the Western Front in March of that year – accompanied the team.

---

87 IOR, L/PS/11/129, 4700, Civil Intelligence Officer, Karachi, 23 July 1917.
88 TNA, FO 383/62, telegram from the Government of India to the Foreign Office, 7 May 1915.
89 Oskar Ritter von Niedermayer, *Im Weltkrieg vor Indiens Toren: Dier Wüstenzug der deutschen Expedition nach Persien und Afganistan* (Hamburg: Hanseatische Verlagsanstalt, 1936).

The British, alerted to the expedition and its intentions, bought the Emir's continued neutrality by increasing his annual stipend by £25,000. The Secretary of State for India, Austen Chamberlain, estimated a year earlier that there were still some 700 Indian soldiers interned in German prison camps. These men, he worried, had been exposed to 'strongly hostile influences' and might contribute to growing unrest in India after the war.

> There would seem to be a risk that some of these men when they return to their homes may become the willing tools of extremist and anarchist factions in India; and the possible influence in Nepal of men whose minds may have been poisoned against the British connection will not be overlooked.[90]

Intelligence smuggled out of the prisoner of war camps to British authorities appeared to validate the Secretary's concerns. Subadar Major Mala Khan spent most of the war in captivity after his capture on the Western Front in late 1914. During his time as an internee at Zossen in 1916, he compiled a list of 35 Indian sepoys from the 129th Baluchis, the 127th Baluchis, and the 58th Rifles who had 'gone over to the enemy.' He also created a list of Indian soldiers who were actively collaborating with the Germans in the camps, trying to spread sedition within the Indian ranks. He smuggled his lists out of the camp to the British, hiding them in the clothes of a sick Indian the German authorities had agreed to repatriate via England.[91] Other sepoys, sick from an outbreak of tuberculosis and repatriated to England prior to the end of the war, divulged additional names from the comfort of their hospital beds. Cross-referencing these testimonies with the lists provided by Mala Khan, by October 1918 the British finalized a master list of 92 Indian prisoners of war who they believed had deserted to the enemy or given information or assistance to the enemy after their capture in France.[92] The India Office took this information and formulated an elaborate plan for handling the repatriation of Indian prisoners of war at the end of hostilities. Soldiers released on the Western Front would congregate at Marseilles. Those released by way of ports on the North Sea through neutral Holland passed first through London before rejoining their compatriots in southern France. At both sites, the British separated the soldiers into four categories, based on the information they had gleaned earlier: (a) genuine prisoners of war; (b) declared deserters to the enemy; (c) those among (a) who were known to have taken up arms against the British or to have accepted service with the enemy; and (d) those among (a) who were believed to have been armed and equipped by propaganda and required watching in India.

90 IOR, L/MIL/7/18501, Secret memo from Austen Chamberlain to the Governor General of India, 11 August 1916.
91 IOR, L/MIL/7/18501, Statements of repatriated Indian Prisoners of War, December 16, 1918.
92 IOR, L/MIL/7/18501, Statements of repatriated Indian Prisoners of War, December 16, 1918.

Protocol stipulated: for (a) and (d), repatriation to India where on arrival special arrangements would be made for (d); for (b), returned to unit for trial or to India in custody to await trial on return of unit from overseas, or dispatched to unit overseas if more convenient and evidence unobtainable in India; and (c) returned to India in custody pending collection of evidence against them.[93]

After the 1918 Armistice, the victorious powers faced tremendous pressure to demobilize as quickly as possible. Audiences in Britain, France, and Europe's colonies wanted their soldiers to come home. Soldiers no less greeted the end of the war with relief. They considered a speedy return home their long-overdue right. Demobilizing India's soldiers presented a considerable logistical challenge, however. By the end of the war, the Indian Army had enlisted close to 1.4 million men. Between 1914 - 1918, they had been deployed across much of the earth's land and water surfaces. Most of Britain's South Asian soldiers were in Mesopotamia. Other units remained in Palestine, Egypt, and East Africa. To facilitate the return of so many men to India, the Government of India set up Indian Soldier Boards in all the provinces of India (except for Bengal), as well as District Soldier Boards to help reintegrate demobilized soldiers back into society by offering employment and financial subsidies on top of land and other service rewards.[94]

But it was not so much the operational logistics of returning men home that concerned the British as it was the political volatility of the regions to which many of the men would return. Far from welding 'the strongest link' in the chain of the British Empire, British attitudes and wartime policy had set the stage for the political disputes, disappointments, and violence of the postwar decades.[95] The war had galvanized India's nationalist movement. Edwin Montagu hoped his August 1917 announcement that 'self-governing institutions' and 'responsible government in India as an integral part of the British Empire' might usher in an age of cooperation and goodwill between Britain and India after the war. But in March 1919, Britain passed a series of laws called the Rowlatt Bills which extended the Defence of India Act of 1915 into peacetime, permitting the detention (without trial) of those suspected of political crimes. These sparked Gandhi's first nationwide campaign of *satyagraha*, a coordinated series of non-violent protests, strikes, and fasts that did not abate until

---

93   IOR, L/MIL/7/18501, Paraphrase of a cipher telegram from War Section, A.H.Q., Simla, India to the D.A.G., 3rd Echelon, G.H.Q., Indian Section, Rouen, France, November 15, 1918.
94   Daniel Marston, *The Indian Army and the End of the Raj* (Cambridge: Cambridge University Press, 2014), p. 18.
95   Historian Robert McLain has recently argued that the April 1919 killings in Amritsar at the hands of Gurkha soldiers under the command of General Reginald Dyer ought not be viewed as the beginning of India's march to independence, but as a tragic coda to 'the accelerating social and political anxieties that wracked late-Victorian and Edwardian imperial and domestic public spheres' in the decades leading up to World War I. See Robert McLain, *Gender and violence in British India: the road to Amritsar, 1914 – 1919* (New York: Palgrave Macmillan, 2014), p. 1.

1922. In April 1919, Delhi and the Punjab exploded in widespread civil unrest, the most serious threat to British rule since the 1857 rebellion. At the Jallianwala Bagh in Amritsar, on 13 April, Brigadier General Reginald Dyer, commander of the Jullunder Brigade, ordered a detachment of sepoys under his command (90 total, 50 of whom were armed) to fire into a crowd of 20,000 people, murdering 379 and wounding over 1,000. Though some of his superiors condemned the act, the British subsequently imposed martial law. Then in May 1919, the long-anticipated Third Afghan War broke out along the Indian frontier.[96]

With India seemingly coming undone, the British hoped sepoys might buy them some goodwill among the Empire's South Asian subjects. Prior to the November 1918 armistice, the Indian Soldiers' Fund worked to ensure the regular shipment of care parcels to former Indian prisoners of war as they slowly trickled across Western Europe to hospitals in London. 'It is a matter of real importance that Indian prisoners of war should not return to their own country with any ground for regarding themselves as neglected by this Department.'[97] In October, 45 Indian prisoners of war arrived in England, all of them sick with tuberculosis.

> These men have been in captivity for several years, and from a political point of view it seems to us that proper arrangements should be made to meet them and look after them when they come to England, and we venture to think that the India Office would be only too glad to do this and to see that the men are properly looked after. It may make a very bad impression in India when these men get back if they do not carry away with them a good impression of the way in which they have been treated in England, and we are sure that the India Office would not wish this.[98]

But failure on the part of the British to implement efficiently their own repatriation policy did leave some soldiers with lingering feelings that they had been mistreated by their imperial hosts after the war. Havildar Abdul Aziz Khan, an Afghan from Peshawar, enlisted in the Indian Army at the outbreak of the war, serving on the Western Front with the 9th Hodson's Horse. Captured by the Germans sometime in 1914 or early 1915, he spent the remainder of the war interned in Germany. At the end of the conflict, he was repatriated to London where he lived in a YMCA. with a number of former Indian prisoners of war until 1919 when he finally received his ticket home to India. As far as the soldier was concerned, the war was over for him. But upon arriving in Bombay, Khan was arrested by the local authorities, suspected

---

96 Nick Lloyd, 'The Indian Army and Civil Disorder: 1919-22,' in Kaushik Roy, *The Indian Army in the Two World Wars* (Leiden: Brill, 2012).
97 IOR, L/MIL/7/18502, letter from India Office to J.I. Macpherson, M.P., 31 October 1918.
98 IOR, L/MIL/7/18502, letter from the Indian Soldiers' Fund to the India Office, 28 October 1918.

of having fed information to the Germans during the war. Khan wrote to a friend in England, 'On 3rd May I landed in Bombay. Immediately I and another man, who also has come with me from England and is my countryman were put under arrest. I tried to know the reason of the sudden calamity and failed. Even till today nothing can I know but what I have gathered is that the government suspect me, why and how rests with the government.'[99] Decisions concerning the repatriation of Indian prisoners of war were made on-the-spot. In the case of Havildar Khan, paranoia and circumstances on the ground in postwar India shaped policy more than any concrete evidence of Khan's wartime activities. A confidential memo from the Government of India to the India Office suggests that the British bungled the implementation of their own recommendations. It read: 'The Government of India had been warned in regard to the possibility that the Germans had taken steps to tutor Indian prisoners of war for propaganda purposes' and that 'they could not afford to run the risk of setting suspects at liberty, particularly at a time of internal disturbance and with trouble on the frontier of India.' The Chief Commissioner and Agent to the Governor General of the North-West Province, within whose jurisdiction Abdul Aziz Khan's home was situated, 'was unwilling to allow men suspected of contamination to return to the North-West Frontier Province at [this] juncture.'[100]

Khan's frustrations with the authorities in India appear warranted. His letter to an English friend prompted this letter, addressed by Mary Cruikshank to the War Office in August 1919:

> I beg to invite your attention to the enclosed true copy of a letter just received by a friend of mine from an Indian non-commissioned officer of the 9th Hodson's Horse. This man, Abdul Aziz Khan, who is of good family (his brother being Khan of Zaida near Peshawar) is an Afghan. He enlisted in the Indian Army for the war, & was for some time a prisoner of war in Germany. He was released & came to England in December or January of the last winter, & remained in London staying at a Y.M.C.A. hostel with other released Indian soldiers until April 1st when he left England with two other Indian soldiers & proceeded overland to Taranto, whence he sailed for India. During his stay in England, he was not, to my knowledge, under any suspicion, he appeared free to go anywhere he wished in London. He also paid a short visit to my friend in Leicestershire. Some weeks ago I saw a letter from him dated about June 25th in which he said he had been arrested on arrival at Bombay: the officer who arrested him refused to give any reason.[101]

---

99 IOR, L/MIL/7/18501, letter from Havildar Khan to Ms. Fisher.
100 IOR, L/MIL/7/18501, confidential memo from the Government of India to the Secretary, Military Department, India Office, October 23, 1919.
101 IOR, L/MIL/7/18501, letter from Mrs. Mary Cruikshank to the War Office, 10 August 1919.

Not long after Mrs. Cruikshank wrote to the War Office, Indian authorities released the Havildar. 'It has now been decided that it would not be in the interests of the service to retain Dafadar Abdul Aziz Khan and he has accordingly been discharged,' noted a secret memo from the Government of India.[102]

Some Indian prisoners of war who collaborated with the Germans chose to remain in Germany after the war rather than risk further internment in Indian or British prisons. Guli Jan deserted to the German trenches in March 1915 and served with Oppenheim's Indian Battalion in Constantinople before returning to Zossen towards the end of the war. In December 1918, he and nine other Indian prisoners of war secured funding from German agents formerly employed by Oppenheim's Intelligence Office and secured housing and work in Berlin.[103] In June 1920, two of the soldiers, Mir Baz Khan and Mir Zamir, walked into the offices of the British Passport Control Officer in Berlin, requesting a written pardon from the British government and permission to return home to South Asia.

> We have the honour to beg you that we are Afghan Afridis of Khyber. We were since a long time in British India Army 57th Regiment. At the beginning of the Great War we were sent with other Indian troops to West Front France to fight against Germany. We were engaged for about 2 years in the West Front & fought faithfully for our King Emperor against the enemy, but unfortunately again we were sent to Egypt to fight against our Religious fellows, the Turks, & our Khalifa. It was impossible according to our religion to fight against our religion. Our religion forbids us to fight against a Muslim ... We have done nothing against our Govt. only that we did not fight against our Khalifa & it was our religious duty to do so. During this long time we remained neutral & did not serve the British enemy. We have served our Govt & our nations the Afridis also helped the British Govt during the Great War. Now we are starving we have nothing to live with. We hope you would be kindly enough to send for our Amnesty & feed us till we leave for our country. For this act of kindness we should pray for your long & prosperity.

The Passport Officer recommended that authorities grant the soldiers' request. 'It is thought that under proper treatment they might be of use to Indian Intelligence, but in the hands of unscrupulous people in Berlin they might become a possible danger to the Empire.'[104] But the India Office did not agree. An internal memo noted, 'The suggestion that the men who deserted to the enemy in the war should be pardoned, because of 'the possible danger to the Empire' involved in their stay in Germany,

---

102 IOR, L/MIL/7/18501, confidential memo from the Government of India to the Secretary, Military Department, India Office, 23 October 1919.
103 PAAA, R21262, letter from Graetsch to the Foreign Office, 11 December 1918.
104 IOR, L/MIL/7/18899, letter from Passport Control Officer, Berlin, 25 June 1920.

seems thoroughly unsound from the point of view of the effect produced on the men who did not desert.'[105] Mir Baz Khan and Mir Zamir remained in Berlin.

Other sepoys found their own way home, navigating the politically volatile Eurasian landscape. Guli Jan returned to Afghanistan safely in 1921 by way of civil war torn Russia and central Asia. That he did so with a German wife and their infant in tow makes his story all the more exceptional. The Indian soldier vanishes almost entirely from the British archives after March 1915 when he deserted to the German trenches. In October 1923, his wife walked into the British Legation in Kabul and asked for permission to travel through India on her way to Europe by ship. She and Guli Jan met shortly after the war and lived together in Danzig until November 1920. They made their way to Afghanistan by way of Riga, Moscow, Tashkent, Kushk, Herat and Kandahar. They reached Kabul on foot in March 1921.[106]

---

105 IOR, L/MIL/7/18899, India Office, internal memo, 1920.
106 IOR, L/PS/11/237, P4421/1923. The Government of India refused her request.

11

The Indian Cavalry in Palestine 1917-19

Michael Creese

The campaign fought in Palestine in 1918 by the Indian cavalry which, together with their Australian and New Zealand allies, formed the Desert Mounted Corps, must rank among the most successful cavalry actions in military history. Philip Mason ranks the battle of Megiddo as one of the most complete victories of the First World War, even more decisive than Tannenburg in East Prussia or Caporetto in Italy.[1] It was in some ways a precursor of the *blitzkrieg* tactics of the Second World War with an initial rapid break-through followed by a ruthless and rapid exploitation. In their advance the Desert Mounted Corps covered nearly 400 miles in thirty-eight days, capturing 83,700 prisoners and about 160 guns. Colonel Maunsell of the Scinde Horse makes an interesting comparison between the victory of the Corps and the pursuit by the French cavalry led by Marshal Murat of the defeated Prussians after the twin battles of Jena/Auerstadt in 1806. On that occasion the French cavalry covered 425 miles in 23 days. However, the Colonel points out that the loss in horses in the Indian cavalry (21%) was significantly less than that in the French units due to the superior horse management of the sowars.[2] A Sikh squadron of the 19th Lancers reached Damascus with every one of its horses fit for further action.[3] Sadly this magnificent exploit has been largely overlooked, coming as it did when the War was ending and there was, as always, a greater concentration upon events on the Western Front. This Chapter will seek to consider the effectiveness of the Indian cavalry in this campaign and the reasons for it.

---

1   See Philip Mason, *A Matter of Honour*, (pbk, London, Macmillan, 1986), p 441.
2   Col. E. B. Maunsell, *The Prince of Wales Own, The Scinde Horse* (London, Butler and Tanner, 1926), p. 237.
3   Marquess of Anglesey, *A History of British Cavalry 1816-1919, Vol V*, (London, Leo Cooper, 1994), p. 331.

Turkey, spurred on by offers of cash and military support from Germany, declared war on Great Britain and France in October 1914. The Turks hoped to end their diplomatic isolation and, with German aid, to regain the territories that they had lost in the Balkans. The Germans, meanwhile, had dreams of a sphere of influence extending through the Balkans and Turkey and into Persia.[4] Turkey controlled both Palestine and Syria and the entry of Turkey into the war threatened the Suez Canal, a vital trade route connecting Great Britain with India and beyond. The Egyptian Expeditionary Force (EEF), charged with the defence of the Canal was initially commanded by General Sir Archibald Murray. However, after the failure of his troops at the First and Second Battles of Gaza, he was succeeded in June 1917 by General Sir Edmund Allenby (nicknamed The Bull) who had been serving on the Western Front. James Kitchen suggests that Allenby's achievements have been somewhat overrated by writers such as Wavell and T. E. Lawrence, while Murray's contribution to victory, especially in terms of the vital logistics, have been undervalued.[5] However, Kitchen admits that Allenby brought an increased professionalism to the campaign and had a significant effect in raising the morale of the troops.[6] The Marquess Anglesey suggests that it was his single-minded dedication that earned him the dedication of his staff.[7] When Allenby arrived in Palestine, the Turkish line ran from Gaza to Beersheba and he immediately adopted more aggressive tactics than those of his predecessor. Allenby attacked in October 1917, Beersheba falling on October 31st and Gaza on November 7th. He went on to capture Jerusalem, entering on foot at the head of his victorious troops on Christmas Day 1917. The Turks counter-attacked but were unable to retake the city and Jericho was captured by the British in February.[8]

The battleground over which the Indian cavalry would fight in 1917-18 is a relatively narrow strip of land, some 100 miles in width and roughly 450 mile in length, squeezed between the Mediterranean Sea and the inhospitable Syrian Desert. It stretches like a finger southward from Aleppo the capital of Syria down to the Gulf of Aqabar on the Red Sea. From Jerusalem to Aleppo is about 300 miles. The main Hedjaz railway line runs north-south to the east of the River Jordan from Aleppo to Aqabar. An important branch line ran east-west from the main line at Deraa through Beisan and Afuleh to Haifa on the coast. The coastal plain varies in width from fifteen miles down to between only one mile at Mount Carmel. The central range of mountains, the Hills of Samaria, rises to 3,000 feet and is cut roughly at right angles by the Plain

---

4   See Mason, *Matter of Honour*, p. 428.
5   James Kitchen, *The British Imperial Army in the Middle East*, (London, Bloomsbury Academic, 2014), p. 102 et seq.
6   Ibid, pp. 219-220.
7   Anglesey, *History of British Cavalry 1816-1919, Vol V*, p. 123.
8   See Gurchan Singh Sandhu, Major-General, *The Indian Cavalry: History of the Indian Armoured Corps till 1940*, (New Delhi, Vision Books, 1981*)*, p. 344.

of Esdraelon.⁹ The Jordan rises seven feet below sea level to the west of Damascus then runs southwards towards the Red Sea through the Sea of Galilee and the Dead Sea. The atmosphere in the valley is oppressive and humid.¹⁰ The regimental historian of the 19th Lancers referred to the 'dust-devils' in which the dry dust is thrown into choking clouds.¹¹ Colonel Maunsell of The Scinde Horse appeared as a lone voice in stating that the horrors of life in the Valley were greatly exaggerated.¹² The summers in Palestine were dry and hot with temperatures up to 55 degrees Centigrade. The rainy season is between November and March and major operations were impossible during this period. However, the change of scene was a welcome one for the Indian cavalry after the mud and constant bombardments of Flanders. Captain Whitworth of the 2nd Lancers comments that the prospect of being used purely as cavalry where there were no trenches or barbed wire was much appreciated.¹³ At last their horses would have a chance to 'stretch their legs'.

Unfortunately, in order to meet the major German offensive in France in March 1918, two complete Divisions together with other units including Australian and British infantry regiments and some British yeomanry units were transferred to France from the EEF which lost a total of about 60,000 front-line troops.¹⁴ They were replaced in Palestine by newly raised Indian infantry regiments from India as well as men from Mesopotamia including the Lahore and Meerut Divisions which had fought in France. In addition, thirteen Indian cavalry regiments were transferred from France to Palestine, of which only three had been seriously engaged in France.¹⁵ German U-boats were very active in the Mediterranean at this time but fortunately the only loss involved one Yeomanry regiment travelling to France. The Indian cavalry regiments which had transferred were brigaded with British Yeomanry regiments, each of the four brigades consisting of two Indian regiments and one Yeomanry regiment.¹⁶

When the Indian troops arrived in Palestine, gas-masks and steel helmets were withdrawn, the first as unnecessary, the second as being uncomfortable in the hot sun.¹⁷ Early experience gained in cavalry patrols showed that Turkish soldiers

9   General Sir H Hudson, *History of the 19th King George's Own Lancers, 1858-1921*, (Aldershot, Gale and Polden, 1937), p. 206.
10 Gurchan Singh Sandhu, Major-General, *The Indian Cavalry: History of the Indian Armoured Corps till 1940*, p. 345.
11 Hudson, General Sir H., *History of the 19th King George's Own Lancers, 1858-1921*, p. 214.
12 Maunsell, *Scinde Horse* , p. 194.
13 Cspt. E. E. Whitworth, *A History of the 2nd Lancers, Gardner's Horse) from 1809 to 1927*, (London, Sifton Praed and Co, 1924), p. 117.
14 Anglesey, *History of British Cavalry 1816-1919, Vol V*, p. 220.
15 Maunsell, *Scinde Horse*, p. 194.
16 Major General Gurchan Singh Sandhu, *The Indian Cavalry: History of the Indian Armoured Corps till 1940*, pp. 344-5.
17 Whitworth, Capt. D. E., *A History of the 2nd Lancers, (Gardner's Horse) from 1809 to 1927*, p. 119.

were rarely killed with the sword as they either surrendered or got into a trench or under a bush where they could not be reached. It was therefore decided to re-arm as many of the cavalry as possible with lances. However, Jacob's Horse continued as a sabre regiment due to a shortage of lances.[18] Colonel Maunsell argued that as a far as mounted fighting is concerned, the lance is definitely the better weapon as it gives an extra reach of a yard over the sword as well as having a greater moral effect.[19] The regimental historian of the Deccan Horse, Lt. Colonel Tennant, was of the same opinion, stating that one of the lessons learnt in Palestine was that for mounted cavalry, the lance was immeasurably superior to the sword.[20] Of course, neither of the writers realised just how quickly both weapons would become obsolete on the battlefield. According to Colonel Maunsell, the Indian cavalry were prepared to charge the Turks at night – a tactic which the latter deplored.[21] By May 1918 two Brigades from the 4th and 5th Divisions, now re-armed with lances, were stationed in the Jordan Valley where they were involved in a number of successful patrol actions. Brigades were rotated through the Valley as conditions were most unpleasant with a multitude of flies and scorpions as well as malarial mosquitos. There was no grass or corn available which meant that all of the supplies necessary for the troops stationed there had to be brought by lorry.[22] Regiments were relieved after about three weeks before going into the divisional reserve for ten days.[23] The Indian 6th and 8th Cavalry Brigades spent the longest period in the valley and accordingly their regiments later suffered the greatest losses in men and horses.[24]

In January 1918, the Turkish army in Palestine, consisting of 32,000 infantry and 4,000 cavalry together with 400 guns, held two sectors separated by the River Jordan.[25] The Turkish Seventh and Eighth Armies were deployed between the coast and the Jordan while their Fourth Army lay to the east of the Jordan, between the river and the desert. While the Fourth Army defended the Hedjaz railway, the line of communication for Seventh and Eight Armies was the east-west railway line which ran from Deraa to Haifa.[26] The Hedjaz line was being sabotaged by Colonel T. E. Lawrence and the Arabs. The British and Indian forces possessed a very considerable superiority with 57,000 infantry, 12,000 cavalry and 540 guns.[27] The Allied front line extended from a point on the coast some ten miles north of Jaffa roughly

18   Sandhu, *Indian Cavalry*, p. 349.
19   See Maunsell, *Scinde Horse*, p. 209
20   Lt-Col E. Tennant, *The Royal Deccan Horse in the Great War*, Appendix E, p 107.
21   Maunsell, *Scinde Horse*, p. 200.
22   Ibid, p. 193
23   Major General Gurchan Singh Sandhu, *I Serve: The Eighteenth Cavalry*, (New Delhi, Lancer International, 1991), p. 84.
24   Sandhu, *Indian Cavalry*, p. 351
25   Ibid, p. 345.
26   Sandhu, *I Serve: The Eighteenth Cavalry*, p 83.
27   Hudson, *History of the 19th King George's Own Lancers, 1858-1921*, p. 222.

south-eastwards towards the Jordan before turning south along the river and ending on the Dead Sea.[28] The defence system consisted of a chain of strong points which were linked by communication trenches. A continuous belt of barbed wire lay on the Turkish side of the trenches.[29] There were also three bridgeheads over the Jordan, each strongly held by infantry with a squadron of cavalry for reconnaissance. Their purpose was to guard against a possible Turkish attacks towards Jerusalem by their Fourth Army.

When a regiment was based in the Jordan Valley, the squadrons took it in turns to find the outposts for the day. At sundown, another squadron put out picquets in front of the infantry trenches in order to prevent a surprise attack by the Turks.[30] Patrols were constantly sent out both by day and by night. The Turks sometimes attempted to ambush the Indian patrols and, not infrequently, the latter met enemy patrols who were always attacked. For instance, a patrol of the 2nd Lancers charged a Turkish patrol, killing three of them and capturing the rest. On another occasion, Lieutenant Hearsey of the regiment was awarded the Military Cross for rescuing a trooper whose horse had been shot under him.[31] In July a night patrol of The Poona Horse took an enemy company by surprise, killing 15 Turks and capturing five for the loss of one Indian officer and seven men killed.[32] In August 1918 the Central India Horse was in the valley and learning that the Turks were concentrating in the Hills of Moab with a view to making a reconnaissance of the bridgeheads, the regiment sent out two squadrons daily. On September 6th the patrol encountered a strong Turkish force consisting of a mixed brigade together with a battery of artillery. The patrol was compelled to withdraw in the face of this superior force though the Turks withdrew having fired a few shells at the regimental headquarters.[33] The constant pattern of patrolling kept the Turks on the alert and helped to convince them that the main threat would come across the Jordan on their left flank.

There was a swing bridge across the Jordan at the El Henu bridgehead and in another action of this period, a standing patrol of the Jodhpur Lancers were attacked by the advance guard of the 2nd Turkish Caucasian Cavalry Brigade on July 7th 1917.[34] A full squadron of Lancers came to the aid of the patrol but themselves came under heavy fire. The Jodhpurs attempted to push southwards while the Turks moved northwards

---

28   C. Chevenix-Trench, *The Indian Army and the King's Enemies*, (London: Thames and Hudson, 1988), p.91.
29   Anon, History of the Guides 1846-1922, (No details of publisher), p. 229.
30   Whitworth, *A History of the 2nd Lancers*, p. 12.
31   Ibid, p. 123.
32   TNA, WO 95/4519, War Diary of the Poona Horse, Entry for 28/7/18.
33   Major General W. A. Watson, *King George V's Own Central India Horse*, (Edinburgh, Blackwood and Sons, 1930), pp. 389-390.
34   TNA WO 95/4519, War Diary of the Jodhpur Lancers, July 1918 to Dec 1919, Entry for 14/7/18. IOR, L/MIL/17677, Major General Sir H. Watson, *A short History of the Services rendered by the Imperial Service Troops in the Great War*.

with a view to getting behind the squadron and cutting them off. As the enemy came out of the hills to the east at 1200 yards range they were brought under heavy fire from the Lancers using both rifles and Hotchkiss machine-guns. By 8 am it was realised that the squadron had at least 300 of the enemy in front of them from the 9th and 11th Turkish Cavalry Regiments with the 7th Cavalry Regiment in reserve. Pushing out patrols, the Lancers were able to locate the whole of the enemy's position over a frontage of two miles held by a total of around 1,200 Turks with a number of machine guns.[35] Two squadrons of the Lancers were ordered to assemble, cross the Jordan at Henu and roll up the enemy position from south to north. The two squadrons moved steadily south eastwards, taking advantage of a dry valley as cover. Once in position, they turned north and galloped straight over the first objective. Seeing the advance of the Lancers, three troops of Turkish cavalry on the extreme right flank immediately made off to the east. The Lancer's leading troop thundered on towards their second objective, killing all of the enemy there. Meanwhile the remainder of the Lancers made for the next ridge further east which was covered with Turkish troops. It was here that the stiffest fighting took place and there were many individual acts of bravery. Major Dalpat Singh, leading the charge and accompanied only by his trumpet-major, went full-tilt for an enemy machine gun, killing the gunners and capturing the gun. He later captured the Commandant of the 11th Turkish Regiment. He was awarded the Military Cross for his leadership and courage on that day - one of the first Indian officers to be so honoured.[36] Fearing a counter-attack from the large number of Turks still in the field, the regiment fell back towards the river. 100 enemy had been killed or wounded and seventy prisoners taken for the loss of two Indian officers killed and one wounded, 13 sowars killed, 7 wounded and 5 missing. In addition to Major Dalpat Singh's immediate award of a Military Cross, six Indian Orders of Merit (2nd Class) and seven Indian Distinguished Service Medals were distributed among the Lancers.[37] The Brigade History commented that the success gained was mainly due to the spirited action, dash and able leadership displayed in the mounted attack by five troops of the Jodhpur Lancers. The author also remarked on the offensive spirit of the junior Indian officers, typically exhibited by Risaldar Shaitan Singh, who outpaced his troop and galloped alone into a troop of enemy.[38] General Allenby, who visited the Brigade on the 27th, wrote that 'The day's operations would live on as one of the great feats of the war!'[39] The general was perhaps a little previous in his congratulations as the Jodhpur Lancers would accomplish an even greater feat a few weeks later.

35 TNA, WO 95/4519, War Diary of the Jodhpur Lancers, July 1918-December 1919, entry for 14/7/18.
36 Ibid
37 TNA, WO 95/4519, War Diary, The Jodhpur Lancers, entry for 234/9/17.
38 *History of the 15th (IS) Cavalry Brigade during the Great War 1914-18*, (London, HMSO, 1920), p. 437
39 TNA, WO 95/4519, War Diary of the Jodhpur Lancers, July 1918 to Dec 1919, Entry for 14/7/18.

In August there was some re-organisation of the Indian cavalry regiments before the final offensive which was planned for September and whose aim was to destroy the Turkish forces in Palestine, Syria and Lebanon. They now, together with the Australian and Australian/New Zealand Mounted Divisions formed the Desert Mounted Corps.[40] The order of battle of the Indian cavalry in September 1918 was therefore as follows:-

4th Cavalry Division

10th Cavalry Brigade
Dorset Yeomanry, 2nd Lancers, Central India Horse, 10th Cavalry Brigade Signal Troop RE and 17th Machine Gun Squadron
11th Cavalry Brigade
1st County of London Yeomanry, 29th Lancers, Jacob's Horse, 11th Cavalry Brigade Signal Troop RE and 21st Machine Gun Squadron.
12th Cavalry Brigade
Staffordshire Yeomanry, 6th Cavalry, 19th Lancers, 12th Cavalry Brigade Signal Troop RE and 18thMachine Gun Squadron

5th Cavalry Division

13th Cavalry Brigade
Gloucestershire Yeomanry, Hodson's Horse, 18th Lancers, 13th Cavalry Brigade Signal Troop RE and 19th Machine Gun Squadron.
14th Cavalry Brigade
Sherwood Rangers, Deccan Horse, Poona Horse, 14th Cavalry Brigade Signal Troop RE and 20th Machine Gun Squadron.
15th (Imperial Service) Cavalry Brigade
Jodhpur Lancers, Mysore Lancers, Hyderabad Lancers, Kathiawar Signal Troop, Imperial Service Machine Gun Squadron.

Both Divisions had, in addition, an Artillery Brigade, Signal and RE Field squadrons, Ammunition and RASC trains and three mobile veterinary sections.

N.B. The Indian cavalry was reorganised in 1922, with regiments being amalgamated and renumbered/titled. The titles and numbers given above are correct for 1918.

There was a strong emphasis on training and the period of training followed was particularly important for the 18th and 19th Lancers which had sent experienced men to India to assist in the formation of two new regiments and had received raw

40   Maunsell, *Scinde Horse*, p187.

recruits in return.⁴¹ For example, the week-long training programme for the Jodhpur Lancers in August consisted of practical work in the morning commencing at 7 am. This was followed by a lecture at noon and a second practical session commencing at 3 pm.⁴² There was a strong emphasis on musketry, together with instruction on the Hotchkiss machine-gun. The week of troop and squadron based training was followed by a regimental tactical scheme, a brigade staff ride, a regimental staff ride and finally a divisional tactical exercise in which the Hyderabad Lancers acted as the 'enemy'.⁴³ The three State Force regiments (from Hyderabad, Jodhpur and Mysore) were officered almost entirely by Indians with only one or two English 'advisers' and the training programmes included specific training for the Indian officers.⁴⁴ Kitchen points out that the patrol work undertaken by the cavalry whilst in the Jordan valley also provided excellent practical training.⁴⁵ The 1918 offensive had originally been planned using British forces. However, as Colonel Maunsell of the Scinde Horse points out, the Indian Cavalry coming from France, 'had nothing whatever to learn from any of the mounted troops (in Palestine) and in dash the sowar (trooper) from France could show the way to most.'⁴⁶

Allenby's plan was to use his infantry to break through the Turkish defenses near the coast and then pass the cavalry immediately through the gap. The order for the operation stated that 'The army, pivoting on its positions in the Jordan Valley, will attack on the high ground east of El Mugheir and the sea, with the object of inflicting a decisive defeat on the enemy and driving him from the line Nablus - Tul Keram – Caesarea.'⁴⁷ Major Cardew of Hodson's Horse suggested that only a commander thoroughly imbued with the cavalry spirit, such as Allenby, could have conceived such a plan.⁴⁸ The whole of the Mounted Corps was to move secretly from Jordan valley to the coast without the enemy becoming aware of the move.⁴⁹ After the breakout, the 5th Cavalry Division was to ride north along the coast for about twenty miles before swinging north-east to capture Nazareth. The 4th Division, nearer the Jordan, was to head first for the key railway junction at Afuleh before turning east to Beisan in the Jordan valley.⁵⁰ Capture of these two towns would cut the Turkish supply lines. Between and slightly to the rear of the two Indian Divisions was the Australian Mounted Division.

41 Hudson, *History of the 19th King George's Own Lancers, 1858-1921*, p. 221.
42 TNA, WO 95/4519, War Diary of the Jodhpur Lancers, August 27th to the 31st 1917.
43 TNA, WO 95/4519, War Diary of the Hyderabad Lancers, September 14th, 1917.
44 Ibid, September 1917.
45 Kitchen, *The British Imperial Army in the Middle East*, pp. 206-7.
46 Maunsell, *Scinde Horse*, p. 188.
47 Quoted in *History of the Guides*, p.234.
48 Major F. G. Cardew, *Hodson's Horse* (Edinburgh and London, Blackwood and Sons, 1928), p. 198.
49 Sandhu, *Indian Cavalry*, p. 354.
50 Chevenix-Trench, *The Indian Army and the King's Enemies*, p. 92.

As with Operation Fortitude linked to the D-Day landings in June 1944, deception was a crucial element in planning the assault, so that the enemy was convinced that the real attack would come at a point where in fact there would only be a feint. The real attack would come where a feint was expected and a gap would be made by the infantry in the Turkish defenses through which the cavalry would pour. Dummy roads and camps were set up and tents were erected along the Jordan on the Turkish left flank. Dummy horses made of straw and sandbags were set up in order to deceive observation from the air. Horses dragged bushes about so that clouds of dust were raised. Troops were marched in daylight from the direction of the coast towards the Allied right flank. Those troops were then carried in lorries back again during the night and they repeated the eastward march the next day.[51] Last's Hotel was requisitioned in Jerusalem and laid out as an impressive headquarters – never to be used.[52] In order to preserve secrecy, Brigade and Divisional commanders only received their orders from Allenby himself only two or three days before the assault was launched.[53]

Meanwhile, three cavalry divisions and two infantry divisions were moved discreetly to the coast, marching by night and taking cover during the day. The move was covered by British aircraft which prevented Turkish planes from observing what was happening.[54] The cavalry finally moved forward in preparation for the attack on the night of the September 18th into carefully concealed positions in orange groves south east of Jaffa. No fires were allowed and horses were only to be watered at fixed times when the Air Force was overhead.[55] As a result of experience gained in France, the cavalry were positioned close behind the infantry who were to make the gaps in the Turkish lines in order to avoid delay in the breakout.[56] They were to advance along a narrow strip of seashore backed by sand dunes beyond which was a wider sandy plain with loose shifting sand and coarse grass. The troopers dumped all their heavy baggage and each man carried a day's iron rations together with two day's emergency rations. The horses each carried 21 pounds of corn or barley.[57]

The Allied barrage began at 4.30 on the morning of September 19th and lifted at 5.15 am.[58] There had been no preliminary bombardment and surprise was total. On the coast the Turkish defences consisted of three lines of trenches among the sandy hillocks. There were many machine guns and a trench mortar manned by a German detachment. The first line of trenches was to be taken by zero plus 10 minutes, the second by zero plus 40 minutes and the third line by zero plus seventy minutes. The Seaforth Highlanders, Black Watch and 1st and 2nd Battalions of the Guides

---

51 See Maunsell, *Scinde Horse*, p. 211.
52 Sandhu, *Indian Cavalry*, p. 356.
53 Hudson, *History of the 19th King George's Own Lancers*, p. 225.
54 Whitcroft, *A History of the 2nd Lancers*, p. 131.
55 Hudson, *History of the 19th King George's Own Lancers*, p. 226.
56 Byron Farwell, *Armies of the Raj* (London: Viking, 1989), p. 93.
57 Sandhu, *Indian Cavalry*, p. 356.
58 Chevenix-Trench, *The Indian Army and the King's Enemies*, p. 94.

Infantry (21st Brigade of the 7th Division), supported by their own trench mortars, were through by a quarter past six.[59] Their Divisional commander congratulated the men on their dash and heroism which enabled the cavalry to get through before the Turks had had time to form a rearguard.[60] General Gurchan Singh Sandhu points out that, although it was Indian infantry which broke through the Turkish lines, it was the cavalry pouring through which turned a retreat into a rout.[61]

Hodson's Horse, acting as the cavalry advance guard of the 5th Division, followed closely behind the infantry and the regiment was through the main enemy defences by 6 am. The countryside consisted of rolling downs, ideal country for the cavalry.[62] Initially the regiment met little opposition, but, as they continued to move forward the leading troop under Risaldar Nur Ahmed came under heavy fire from Turkish cavalry in a strongly entrenched position. A mounted attack by the regiment resulted in the capture of three officers, between fifty and sixty men, two guns and twelve wagons. The regiment continued the advance across an open plain meeting only scattered opposition. At the end of the day the regiment halted, having advanced twenty six miles, the last sixteen of them in action, and captured five hundred prisoners.[63] The pace was so hot that the 18th Lancers, following behind, lost five horses to exhaustion and ten more had to be left behind.[64] The Poona Horse stood to arms at 4.15 am on the 19th and moved off at 7.30. By the end of the next day they had covered 60 miles and captured 250 prisoners. They watered their horses at 7.30 on the 20th for the first time since they started their march. A few days later they were complimented by Allenby on the condition of their mounts.[65] On the 21st of September the Gloucestershire Hussars, advance guard of the Division, raided Nazareth, the German/Turkish Headquarters. Some 12,00 prisoners were taken and the Headquarters totally disorganised. The Turks themselves blew up the wireless station.[66] Although the German commander, General Liman von Sanders, escaped by car in his pyjamas.[67] The Hussars retired but the town was retaken the following day. The 13th Cavalry Brigade of 5th Division captured Acre, which had defied all of Napoleon's efforts to take it over one hundred years previously, on the 23rd. The town was taken and two field guns captured by a patrol of the 18th Lancers led by Jemadar Munshi Singh who was awarded the Indian Order of Merit.[68] Meanwhile the 15th (Imperial Service) Brigade was detached with orders to capture the important port of Haifa.

59 *The History of the Guides*, pp. 235, 246.
60 Ibid, p. 248.
61 Sandhu, *I Serve: The Eighteenth Cavalry*, p. 81.
62 Whitworth, *A History of the 2nd Lancers*, p. 133.
63 See Cardew, *Hodson's Horse*, pp. 200-201.
64 Hudson, *History of the 19th King George's Own Lancers*, p. 227.
65 TNA, WO 95/4519, War Diary, The Poona Horse, entries for 19 and 20/ 9/17.
66 Hudson, *History of the 19th King George's Own Lancers*, p. 232.
67 Byron Farwell, *Armies of the Raj*, p. 98.
68 See Hudson, *History of the 19th King George's Own Lancers*, p. 237.

Unfortunately the attacking infantry were not able to open a gap in the Turkish defences quite so quickly for the 4th Cavalry Division as had been the case for the 5th Division. It was not until nine o'clock that the advance guard formed by Jacob's Horse was through the Turkish front line.[69] However, they then met less opposition than had their comrades of the 5th Division It was important that the heights of El Lejjun (also known as Megiddo) were secured before dawn on September 20th and the village could only to be reached through the very narrow Musmus Pass, fourteen miles long. The 2nd Lancers eventually entered the village without opposition at 3 am on the morning of September 20th. 100 Turks were found sitting around a fire and were easily captured.[70] Moving forward towards El Afuleh the regiment met and in a spirited attack overcame Turkish opposition which consisted of one battalion with three machine guns. Between 40 and 50 Turks were killed and the 470 captured. This particular battalion had been moving up to defend the Musmus Pass where they might have imposed a severe delay upon the advance.[71] The Lancers met little further resistance as they entered the town of El Afuleh with its important rail junction and airfield.[72] Some sixty eight miles had been covered in twenty seven and a half hours.[73] The 4th Division, less one regiment, then turned eastward and pushed on to the key town of Beisan. The 11th Cavalry Brigade came across from a large body of Turks trying to escape across the Jordan. The Turks held an extended position with many machine guns. One squadron of the 29th Lancers moved around the enemy flank and charged from the rear capturing over 1,000 Turks, including a Divisional General, and 18 machine guns. The regiment followed up the enemy as they retired across the river. Overall the regiment captured 3,000 prisoners, including 100 Germans, and twenty-one machine guns.[74] Risaldar Bachan Singh of the Deccan Horse with his troop captured nearly 300 prisoners including 5 officers. He was awarded the Indian Distinguished Service Medal.[75] The only Victoria Cross awarded to an Indian in the campaign was given posthumously to Risaldar Badlu Singh of the 14th Lancers attached to the 29th Lancers. Heavy casualties were being inflicted on his squadron by a group of 200 Turks armed with machine guns who were positioned on a small hill. He charged without hesitation, followed by a group of six sowars, capturing the position. He fell, mortally wounded, at the top of the hill.[76]

---

69 Byron Farwell, *Armies of the Raj*, p. 94.
70 Whitworth, *A History of the 2nd Lancers*, p. 137.
71 Ibid, pp. 43-4.
72 Ibid, p. 138 et seq.
73 Hudson, *History of the 19th King George's Own Lancers*, p. 241.
74 See Tennant, *The Royal Deccan Horse in the Great War*, p 164.
75 TNA, WO 95/4519, War Diary, The Deccan Horse, entry for 20/9/17.
76 See E. Swift, *The Brave and the Prejudiced: Together they won an Empire*, (Chelmsford: Springfield Publishers, 1982), p. 139.

By the evening of 20 September the 4th Division was astride the main communication line between the Turkish 7th and 8th Armies and Damascus.[77] The vital rail junction of Afuleh was strongly held by the Allies and Australian cavalry were also holding Lajjun and Jenin – both important rail and road links. The key positions behind the Turkish forces on the west bank of the Jordan were thus all in Allied hands, trapping the Turkish troops to the south of them. On the morning of 22 September some 3,000 Turkish prisoners surrendered south of Beisan with a further 4,000 being captured later in the day. The Hyderabad Lancers escorted 12,000 prisoners from Lajjun to Kerkur on the same day.[78] British casualties were light. For instance Hodson's Horse lost only two men killed and one officer and eight men wounded.[79] Phase One of the operation had been completed in 36 hours and the 5th Division had advanced 110 km. General Hudson refers to the close co-operation between the cavalry and the Air Force; the Air force harrying the retreating Turks by day and the cavalry pursuing by night.[80]

On 26 September Allenby issued the following order:

> I desire to convey to all ranks and all arms of the force under my command my admiration and thanks for the great deeds of the past week, and my appreciation of their gallantry and determination, which have resulted in the total destruction of the VIIth and VIIIth Turkish Armies opposed to us. Such a complete success has seldom been known in all the history of war.[81]

Allenby now launched the second phase of the campaign whose aim was to capture Aleppo, the capital of Syria. The Fourth Turkish Army was retreating northwards on the east bank of the Jordan via Remte to Deraa and hoping to make a stand at Damascus. Allenby launched his forces in two columns in a pincer movement. The 4th Division was to cross the Jordan and advance via Deraa along the east bank and then join up with the Arab forces to drive the Turks northward. The Australians and the 5th Division were to move northwards directly on Damascus by the Nazareth-Tiberias road.[82] Two Australian Brigades were to block the roads from Damascus to Homs and Beirut.[83]

The 4th Division began its move northwards on 26 September. The 10th Cavalry Brigade were ordered to Irbid while the 12th Brigade covered the bridge across the Jordan at Es Shuni. Meanwhile Divisional Headquarters and the 11th Brigade moved to Jisr-i-Majami.[84] The Dorset Yeomanry acting as the advance guard of the 10th

---

77   Sandhu, *Indian Cavalry*, p. 360.
78   Ibid, p. 361.
79   Cardew, *Hodson's Horse*, p. 205.
80   Hudson, *History of the 19th King George's Own Lancers*, p. 244.
81   Quoted, for instance, in Cardew, *Hodson's Horse*, p. 206.
82   Ibid, p. 207.
83   Tennant, *The Royal Deccan Horse in the Great War*, p. 78.
84   See Sandhu, *Indian Cavalry*, p. 364.

Brigade were followed by the Central India Horse. The village of Remte was strongly held but a white flag was shown as the Yeomanry advanced into it. In spite of the white flag, shots were then fired by the defenders resulting in several British casualties. The leading squadron of the Central India Horse went forward to assist resulting in the capture of 100 men and four machine guns.[85] The Division concentrated at Remte on 27 September for the attack on Deraa. However, as the troops prepared to attack they found that it had already been taken by the Sherifean Arabs who had burnt and looted the town. The remainder of the Division moved on towards Kiswe. Jacob's Horse and the 29th Lancers prepared to attack Turkish troops on high ground short of the town but the attack as called off as it became too dark. This turned out to be the last action of the Division of the war.[86] The Division was within striking distance of Damascus by 1 October but they had been beaten in the race by their comrades of the 5th Division.

The 5th Division followed the Australians along the road to the west of the Sea of Galilee, the 13th Brigade joining from Acre. On 28 September the advance of the 13th Brigade was delayed due to the need to repair the bridge over the Jordan The next day the Corps started to ride the last 40 miles to Damascus with the Australians in the lead followed by the 5th Division. The advance was delayed by Turkish rearguards and by the next morning, the advance guard was still 20 miles from Damascus. However, little resistance was encountered on the next day. A message dropped from an aeroplane reported that a large body of Turks – in fact the head of the retreating Fourth Army – was approaching Kiswe on the Deraa Damascus road. The 13th and 14th Brigades were ordered to intercept this force. The country was cut up by ravines and it was some time before D squadron of Hodson's Horse met up with a group of Turks retiring towards the village whom they immediately charged. Risaldar Nur Ahmad of Hodson's Horse accompanied only by his orderly penetrated Kiswe and reported that the town was full of Turks. Two troops were sent to his assistance and the Turks were taken prisoner. One squadron confronted about one thousand Turks and Risaldar Dost Muhamad Khan was killed. Unfortunately a message asking for reinforcements was not received and the regiment was forced to retire under enemy fire.[87] Meanwhile, The Poona Horse of the 14th Brigade had cut the Homs-Damascus road, one squadron taking 200 prisoners. Moving forward, another squadron came across a party of Hedjaz Arabs whom they mistook for enemy troops. The Arabs fled, leaving a staff car containing a European whom Risaldar Major Hamir Singh tried to arrest as spy before he was identified as none other than Colonel T E Lawrence. The regimental history suggests that this event accounts for Lawrence's strong disapproval of the Indian Army which he expresses in *Revolt in the Desert*.[88] The formidable position of Irbid, where there was a large number

---

85 Watson, *King George V's Own Central India Horse*, p. 402.
86 Sandhu, *Indian Cavalry*, p. 366.
87 See Cardew, *Hodson's Horse*, pp. 208 et seq.
88 Lt-General Hanut Singh, '*Fakhr-i-Hind*', *The Story of the Poona Horse*, (Dehra Dun, Akrim Publishers, 1993), p 72.

of Turks supported by machine guns, was taken by the 2nd Lancers. The regimental historian of the 2nd Lancers fought with the regiment during the campaign and was awarded the Military Cross. In his opinion the Indian cavalry could attack and defeat much larger numbers of the enemy, and that rapid movements around the Turkish flanks always threw them into confusion.[89]

General Chauvel, who commanded the Mounted Corps, entered Damascus on 1 October with a composite squadron consisting of men from every regiment in the Division.[90] This formal and official march was intended as a show of force in order to overawe any malcontents. More than 13,000 Turkish prisoners were captured, making a total of 47,000 for the campaign. However, the Turkish Headquarters was now at Baalbek and the railway junction of Rayak was also strongly held. These towns were easily taken but the Turks withdrew to Homs and it was feared that they might hold out there. This allowed time for defences to be prepared at Aleppo which would enable the Turks to continue to hold Syria.[91] Unfortunately, sickness now became a serious problem for the Corps. Long and trying marches, often by night, had exhausted the horses. The men were worn out with fatigue but also suffered from illness and exposure to the climate. Casualties in the 4th Division were particularly severe, due in part at least to their prolonged stay in the Jordan valley coupled with their unsatisfactory diet. The Indian soldiers lived mainly on tea, biscuits and jam because the tinned bully beef was unacceptable to them for religious reasons.[92] On October 6th an influenza epidemic hit the troops, resulting in over 3,000 hospital admissions. Regiments were down to about 25 troopers in the British regiments and 100 in the Indian regiments.[93]

Byron Farwell suggests that the pursuit to Damascus and beyond differed from most pursuits by the British Army in that it was pressed home.[94] In spite of the risks it was decided that the 5th Division, although reduced to 1,500 men, should carry on alone to Aleppo. If Aleppo could be captured quickly, then the campaign would be over. Such a small force could not be expected to take the city by assault but there was also a large Arab force moving on the town. This force could cover the Indian retreat should it become necessary. Homs was reached without serious incident on October 16th. The decision was then taken to carry on to Aleppo in spite of the fact that there some 20,000 enemy troops in the city. General Allenby believed that as many of the enemy soldiers would be already demoralised, the 5th Division would be equal to the task.[95] The Arabs succeeded in entering the town on the 25th. The Turks fled and the 5th Division was able to enter on the next day.[96] As the 15th (IS) Brigade moved

---

89   See Whitworth, *A History of the 2nd Lancers*, p. 161.
90   Sandhu, *Indian Cavalry*, p. 367.
91   Ibid, p. 367.
92   Sandhu, *I Serve: The Eighteenth Cavalry*, p. 91.
93   Sandhu, *Indian Cavalry*, p. 368.
94   Farwell, *Armies of the Raj*, p. 99.
95   Cardew, *Hodson's Horse*, p. 215.
96   See Tennant, *The Royal Deccan Horse in the Great War*, p. 84.

north of the town, they came across a strong Turkish rearguard posted on a ridge near the village of Haritan. The Brigadier decided that instant action was called for and the Mysore Lancers were ordered to move around the east of the ridge and then charge with the Jodhpur Lancers in support. Unfortunately, the enemy was in greater strength than had been realised and the Mysores fell back before rallying to the rear with the Jodhpurs on their left. The Turks advanced as if to counter-attack but dug in and retired during the night. This turned out to be the last battle of the campaign. An Armistice was signed on the 31st of October.

The town of Haifa was captured by the troopers of the 15th (Imperial Service) Cavalry Brigade. Haifa faces north across a bay and behind the town Mount Carmel rises steeply to height of about 200 feet. Access to the town is along a narrow gap between the mountain ridge and the river Kishon which feeds into the sea. Through this defile runs a road and a railway running north to Acre with a spur into Haifa. The ground around the river was very soft and its banks were very steep, making it impassable for mounted men. The position was naturally formidable with a precipitous hill and an impassable river on either side of a defile. It was held by a well-armed force of about one thousand strong which had not yet been engaged.[97]

As the Brigade moved forward, no enemy were discovered until the advanced guard of the Mysore Lancers reached the village of Beled Esh Sheikh. Here they were shelled by enemy guns on Mount Carmel and fired on by machine guns and snipers to the west of the village. A British aeroplane dropped a message saying that Haifa was strongly held. The Jodhpur Lancers were ordered to make a mounted attack to capture the town while the one squadron of the Mysore Lancers worked along the ridge of Mount Carmel via goat trails until they were behind the town.[98] The Jodhpurs were to attack at two o'clock keeping north of the railway line with fire support from the artillery and two squadrons of Mysore Lancers on the plain. The Sherwood Rangers re-joined the Brigade at a quarter to twelve and one of their squadrons was ordered forward to support the Mysore Lancers on the mountain.[99]

At noon the four squadrons of the Jodhpurs moved off in line of troop columns; they halted briefly at Yajur and patrols, which were fired on by the Turks, were sent out to discover whether it was possible to cross the river. The regiment moved off at the appointed time, shells bursting around them and, as they continued steadily forward, machine guns opened up on them from the lower slopes of Mount Carmel and from a position to the north of the railway. As the Lancers crossed the railway line running northwards to Acre, the regiment changed formation into column of troops. Reaching the river, with its very steep banks, two scouts were swallowed up by quicksand. One squadron moved northwards in a fruitless attempt to find a crossing

---

97   Capt. C. Falls and Major A. F. Becke, *Military Operations in Egypt and Palestine from June 1917 to the end of the War* (London: HMSO, 1930), Part II, Vol 2, p. 538.
98   TNA, WO 95/4519, War Diary of the Mysore Lancers, entry for 23/9/17.
99   *Military Operations in Egypt and Palestine from June 1917 to the end of the War*, p. 535.

while the remainder of the regiment, realising that it was impossible to cross the river at this point, moved forward, increasing their pace and veering slightly to the left. It was here that Major Dalpat Singh MC was mortally wounded.[100]

It was clear that the only way that the advance could continue was first to open up the defile by destroying the machine guns on Mount Carmel and then to clear the position to the north of the railway line leading into the town. 'B' squadron was in the lead at this point and was ordered to attack the position on the hill. This was the critical moment, as concentrated enemy fire was bringing down a number of the Lancers' horses. Without hesitation, the squadron charged, spearing all the machine gunners, scattering the riflemen and capturing two machine guns and two camel guns. This success opened the defile and 'D' squadron, which was following 'B', galloped straight down the road towards the town before swinging half-right to take the position to the north of the railway line. They too were successful, capturing four howitzers and four machine guns though their squadron commander, Anop Singh, had two horses shot from under him. Meanwhile the remaining two squadrons rode at full speed and without hesitation straight through the town. The fight was practically over once the defile was passed though there were occasional shots from the houses and a few Turks were ridden down. Once beyond the town, the regiment reformed. Overall, two German officers were captured, 23 Turkish officers and 664 other ranks. Two six-inch naval guns, ten field guns and ten machine guns were captured.[101] This tremendous success was achieved for the loss of one Indian officer (Major Dalpat Singh) and two sowars killed, five officers and 29 men wounded and 60 horses were killed and 83 wounded. The number of horses killed and wounded gives some idea of the intensity of fire faced by the men in their charge.

There is an interesting footnote to the attack. Men of the 15th Field Troop of the Royal Engineers had been busy removing demolition charges from railway bridges during the Brigade's advance. They chanced to be alongside the Jodhpur Lancers as the latter were ordered to charge. The Lancer's commanding officer invited Sergeant Hearne and his sappers to arm themselves with swords and lances from the wounded men. None of the engineers had ever handled these weapons before but they took their position on the right of the line and it is reported that at least one Turk was killed by them.[102]

By any standards, the capture of Haifa on 23 September 1918 by the Jodhpur Lancers was a magnificent feat of arms and unique in military history. The Official History of the campaign commented that: 'No more remarkable cavalry action of its

---

100 See TNA, WO 95/4519, War Diary of the Jodhpur Lancers, Entry for 23/9.
101 *Military Operations in Egypt and Palestine from June 1917 to the end of the War*, p. 537.
102 Major General H. L. Pritchard, *RE Corps History, Vol VI* (Chatham: RE Institute, 1939), p. 393.

scale was fought in the whole course of the campaign.'[103] The Brigade Major, Major Charles Hervey, wrote to his parents:

> I suppose it is the best example of how cavalry should be used and of their value that there has ever been in history. It was the speed at which we came round that did it. It will make people see what Indian cavalry can do. We galloped it at a place which anyone who saw the ground would have thought impregnable. However, a stout hearted body of men on galloping horses take a lot of stopping and within half an hour from the word go, Haifa was ours.[104]

Writing to a couple in Eastbourne where Dalpat Singh had stayed as a boy, Major Hervey wrote:

> All went well until they got near the town when they were blocked by an impassable river. Colonel Holden, who was leading, shouted to Dalpat to wheel the regiment to the left. At that moment, Dalpat was hit in the spine by a machine gun bullet and fell. The machine gunner did not live long after firing that shot; the leading squadron galloped straight at them and killed them in a second.

Sir Pratap Singh, the Regent of Jodhpur, who had served with the regiment in France and Palestine, was not present at the battle. He had longed to lead his men in a glorious charge, but by a dreadful irony, he had gone down with fever on 20 September and he returned to India shortly afterwards. General Allenby telegraphed him, on 24 September:

> Congratulate you on the brilliant exploit of your regiment the Jodhpur Lancers who on the 23rd September took the town of Haifa at a gallop, killing many Turks with the lance in the streets of the town and capturing seven hundred prisoners. Their gallant Colonel Dalpat Singh fell gloriously at the head of his regiment. He was buried with full military honours this afternoon.[105]

Sadly the Lancers were not awarded a battle honour for Haifa - only the more general honour 'Megiddo'. Their descendants, the 61st Cavalry- the only cavalry regiment remaining in the Indian Army apart from the President's Bodyguard - quite rightly still celebrate Haifa Day as one of the most important days in the regimental calendar. 'Megiddo' was the battle honour awarded to all of the regiments which had taken part in the campaign. It was named after a hill 'Tel el Mutasselim' near the northern end of the Musmus Pass.

---

103 *Military Operations in Egypt and Palestine from June 1917 to the end of the War*, p. 538.
104 Major C. Hervey, *Gallop to Aleppo, JUSII*, 113 (1968), p. 155 et seq.
105 Quoted in Van Wart, *Sir Pratap Singh*, (London: Oxford University Press, 1926), p. 216.

By the end of the campaign three Turkish armies had been destroyed and their resistance in Palestine collapsed. After the fall of Damascus the Allies met little opposition, the Turks being demoralised by the boldness of the advance[106] and Charles Chevenix-Trench points out that the victory was won with remarkably little loss of life on both sides. The Indian cavalry had had very few opportunities for mounted action in France, serving for most of the time as infantry in the trenches. When they had been in action they were defeated by the nature of the ground and the heavy concentrations of machine gun and artillery fire. In Palestine however, the going was much more suitable for cavalry and they rarely if ever, faced the barrage of fire which they had met in France. Once the rout began, the Turkish troops, even when stiffened by German troops, were reluctant to stand against the cavalry onslaught.

By 1918 Indian troops formed the majority of the EEF and there can be no doubt of the effectiveness of the Indian cavalry in this campaign. General Gurshan Singh Sandhu, the regimental historian of the 6th Cavalry, commented that the Palestine campaign confirmed the excellence of his regiment as expert practitioners of offensive cavalry operations.[107] The troops were well trained and well led at all levels; Kitchen rightly drawing attention to the leadership displayed by the Indian officers.[108] Following their frustration in France, the sowars were keen to see mounted action and their morale was high – certainly when compared with that of the Turks.[109] Lt. Colonel Tennant of the Deccan Horse suggested that small bodies of cavalry coul successfully dispose of almost any number of enemy troops with weak morale when surprise was on the side of the attackers.[110] Allenby offered strong leadership, a clear vision, and sound planning and preparation. His use of deception was masterly and once the initial breakthrough had been achieved the Turks were given no chance to re-group. Lt. General Sir Harry Chauvel, who commanded the Desert Mounted Corps, wrote that 'the whole of the operations in Palestine and Syria, were textbook illustrations of the perfect combination of all arms, both in attack and defence.'[111] As the history of the 15th (IS) Brigade in the Palestine campaign records: 'When the squadrons drove in spurs and thundered forward, with the sun glinting upon swords and lance-heads, the moral effect was overwhelming.'[112] Palestine 1918 proved to be the swan song of the *arme blanche*. Never again would cavalry in large numbers play an effective role on the battlefield. The mounted man had become too vulnerable to machine gun and artillery fire and horses would be replaced by armoured vehicles. But if this was the cavalry's swansong, it was a magnificent and fitting performance by the Indian cavalry.

106 Cardew, *Hodson's Horse*, p. 216.
107 Sandhu, *I Serve: The Eighteenth Cavalry*, p. 92.
108 Kitchen, *The British Imperial Army in the Middle East*, p. 209.
109 *History of the 15th (IS) Cavalry Brigade during the Great War 1914-18*, p.645.
110 Tennant, *The Royal Deccan Horse in the Great War*, p. 76.
111 Quoted in Tennant, *The Royal Deccan Horse in the Great War*, p. 106.
112 *History of the 15th (IS) Cavalry Brigade during the Great War 1914-18*, p.645.

12

India and the Mesopotamia Campaign

Kristian Coates Ulrichsen

This chapter examines how the mismanagement of the first stage of the Mesopotamia campaign between October 1914 and April 1916 set in motion a thorough reorganisation of India's contribution to the broader imperial war effort. During the initial eighteen months of fighting in Mesopotamia, the Government of India and the India Office in London retained operational as well administrative responsibility for the breakout from Basra toward Baghdad. The institutional failure among the top echelon of British civilian and military planners in India to anticipate the demands of modern, industrialised warfare against Ottoman forces meant that the campaign was, from the beginning, woefully under-resourced and ill-prepared. Between December 1915 and April 1916, the cathartic siege and eventual surrender of the garrison of British and Indian troops at Kut al-Amara triggered a belated yet wide-ranging re-examination of India's role in the war.

As a result of the changes, the War Office in London assumed operational responsibility for the Mesopotamia campaign and oversaw the successful capture of Baghdad in March 1917 and the extension of British control throughout the three Ottoman provinces in Mesopotamia by November 1918. During this second phase of the Mesopotamia campaign, the focus of British attention shifted away from major combat operations after the fall of Baghdad toward the 'pacification' of occupied territory north and west of Baghdad. Indian resources remained pivotal to the incipient 'state-building' endeavour in Mesopotamia in the form both of combatants and of non-combatant labour units as well as supplies of food and fodder. This was made possible by the great intensification in the mobilisation of Indian resources, which nevertheless came close to breaking down in autumn 1918 under the strain of conditions of near-famine and the influenza pandemic.

There are three sections to this chapter. The opening section provides an overview of the constraints that limited India's contribution to the initial stages of the war effort both in Mesopotamia and in other theatres of operation that involved the deployment of Indian forces. Section two constitutes the major component of the chapter and examines in detail India's in the first phase of the operations in Mesopotamia up until the fall of Kut al-Amara in April 1916. The reason for the lengthy analysis of the opening eighteen months of the campaign is because it was the legacy of this formative period of mismanagement that led to such a far-reaching overhaul of India's subsequent war economy, which forms the basis for the third and final section. The chapter ends by illustrating how close the intricate system of mobilisation came to collapsing in the chaotic final months of the war, which came not a moment too soon for British authorities in Delhi.

I

Britain's campaigns in the Middle East reflected the strategic importance of maintaining its Indian Empire and the arteries of maritime routes and naval stations that sustained it. A wide range of military, economic and political connections that developed during the nineteenth century as the political economy of British India increasingly became linked to strategic developments in the Middle East. By 1914, an array of ideational and also institutional linkages imparted a degree of cohesion to Britain's imperial periphery, and constituted a reservoir of ties that facilitated and regulated the diffusion of ideas between the dispersed sites of empire. The career of Sir Evelyn Baring (later Lord Cromer) is a notable example of this trans-national network of governing mentalities, as his formative career experiences in India profoundly shaped his vision of rule in Egypt as Agent-General from 1883 to 1907.[1] Another was Richard Meinertzhagen, who joined the Staff College at Quetta in 1913 and spent Christmas that year travelling through Mesopotamia. In a diary he published in 1960, he recalled how 'the Government of India asked me to collect information about road and river transport, what boats and animal transport are available, roads etc.' He later gained some fame as an intelligence officer in the Palestine campaign in 1917. Such connections became significant during the Great War as officials and officers from the imperial civil service and military in India (and Egypt) played key roles in conducting and administering the campaigns in Mesopotamia and Palestine respectively.[2]

Between August and December 1914, the Government of India assumed responsibility for raising and dispatching four Indian Expeditionary Forces. These sailed to East Africa, Egypt, and Mesopotamia in addition to France. Their mobilisation was a response to emerging threats to Britain's maritime security as German cruisers interfered with the flow of men and munitions from the Dominions to Britain. In September 1914, three cruisers – the *Emden*, *Konigsberg*, and *Karlsruhe* – played havoc with shipping in the Bay of Bengal, East Africa, and Caribbean respectively, and

---

1   Roger Owen, *Lord Cromer: Victorian Imperialist, Edwardian Proconsul* (Oxford: Oxford University Press, 2004), p.233.
2   Richard Meinertzhagen, *Army Diary 1899-1926* (London: Oliver & Boyd, 1960), p.58.

delayed the transportation of troops from Australia and New Zealand as naval escorts had to be organised at short notice. Thus, the elimination of the network of German coaling and wireless stations in East and West Africa and the Atlantic became a short-term priority. By December 1914 this had been achieved through the hunting and sinking of the cruisers in the Indian Ocean and the defeat of the German Asiatic Squadron at the Battle of the Falkland Islands.[3]

India supplied the bulk of the troops and food supplies for these extra-European contingents. This represented a continuation of the Indian Army's pre-1914 function as a strategic imperial reserve.[4] Its new function became necessary in the autumn of 1914 for two reasons. The most urgent was Britain's reliance on imported foodstuffs which rested on making the sea lanes safe from the threat of disruption. This was related to the second reason, which was to smooth the passage of troops, munitions and supplies from the empire to Britain and the European theatre of war. Crucial to this was safeguarding the security of the Suez Canal following the declaration of war with the Ottoman Empire in November 1914. In this context, the continued control of the Persian Gulf sheikhdoms to safeguard the strategic approaches to India meant that the maintenance of British supremacy in the broader Indian Ocean region became an important imperial objective.[5]

India was the pivot around which revolved the intricate network of supplies of agricultural and railway goods to the extra-European campaigns east of Suez. It supplied the campaign in Salonika in addition to Mesopotamia, and made continuous shipments of foodstuffs to Egypt to supplement local resources and prevent a breakdown in food policy there. Nevertheless, India's capacity to contribute to the war effort was constrained in two significant ways. The first was that the Government of India remained responsible for funding the expansion of the Indian Army and the British Government for the maintenance of the Indian Army deployed overseas. While this spared the British exchequer of additional strain, it meant that military financing was held back by powerful assumptions among British governing elites concerning the need for a light-touch state in India. Tax revenues were kept at a very low rate (accounting for a mere 5-7 percent of national income) and public expenditure also was subjected to the prevailing policy of fiscal conservatism.[6] Importantly, these policies continued into the first two years of the war even as military (and administrative) requirements on India grew exponentially, creating bottlenecks and a

---

3   Kristian Coates Ulrichsen, *The Logistics and Politics of the British Campaigns in the Middle East, 1914-22* (Basingstoke: Palgrave Macmillan, 2011), p.28.
4   Keith Jeffery, "An English Barrack in the Oriental Sea?' India in the Aftermath of the First World War,' *Modern Asian Studies*, Vol. 15, No. 3, 1981, p.369.
5   Benjamin Schwarz, 'Divided Attention: Britain's Perception of a German Threat to her Eastern Frontier in 1918,' *Journal of Contemporary History*, Vol. 28, No. 1, 1993, p.104.
6   Dharma Kumar, 'The Fiscal System,' in Dharma Kumar and Tapan Raychaudhuri (eds.) *The Cambridge Economic History of India, Volume 2: c.1757-c.1970* (Cambridge: Cambridge University Press, 1983), p.921.

diverging gap between policy intent and capability that culminated in the debacle in Mesopotamia in 1916.[7]

This meshed with the second impediment that held back the mobilisation of Indian resources for the British campaigns in the Middle East, which was the legacy of decades of British policies to de-industrialise India before 1914. During this period, India was transformed gradually from being an exporter of manufactured goods, primarily textiles, to being a supplier of primary commodities and an import market for finished consumer goods. Partially done for reasons of 'national security' after the 1857 rebellion shook British rule in India to its core, and partially to protect British commercial enterprise, the net result was that India was denuded of indigenous skilled expertise and industrial capacity, both of which remained almost entirely reliant on British skilled workers for what amounted to the small 'military-industrial' complex that did exist in India in 1914.[8] It was only later in the war, in 1917 and 1918, when military exigency finally led to a sharp change in the structure of taxation and public expenditure in India, belatedly enabling the Government of India to raise and equip the mass armies of soldiers and labourers that formed the backbone of the Mesopotamian Expeditionary Forces and made possible the rapid advances of 1917 and 1918.[9]

During 1916 therefore, the expansion of the military campaigns both in Egypt (with the advance across the Sinai Desert and into Palestine) and Mesopotamia and the decision to utilise local resources to the greatest possible extent transformed the character of India's contribution to the imperial war effort. The logistical requirements of supplying and transporting the Egyptian and Mesopotamian Expeditionary Forces tilted the balance between civil and military resources decisively towards the latter. A pervasive expansion of centralised state powers allowed British officials and their local collaborators to reach deeper into society to organise the collection and extraction of local agricultural goods and manpower. This extension of state control marked a temporary reversal of the dominant views on the political economy of empire, based on indirect collaboration and light taxation, and enabled the authorities to divert civilian patterns of economic and social activity to military use.[10]

For these reasons India became interlinked with the British campaigns in the Middle East in general and with the Mesopotamia campaign in particular. Decisions and events in India had immediate and serious implications for the conduct of the campaign in Mesopotamia, as well as for British military and civilian planners in the territory that came under British control. The wartime processes of mobilisation and extraction of man- and animal-power and local resources required the colonial

---

7   Kristian Coates Ulrichsen, *The First World War in the Middle East* (London: Hurst & Co, 2014), p.124.
8   K.N. Chaudhuri, 'Foreign Trade and Balance of Payments (1757-1947),' in Kumar and Raychaudhuri, *Cambridge Economic History of India*, p.807.
9   Coates Ulrichsen, *Logistics and Politics*, pp.90-91.
10 Ibid.

state in India to hastily expand its political footprint and penetrate much deeper into society, as it also did in British-controlled Egypt. A re-working of state-society relations gradually occurred (in both India and Egypt) as the British civil and military authorities embedded themselves within local social organisation and interfered with existing structures and hierarchies of power.

II

The 16th Indian Brigade of the 6th Division of the Indian Army left Bombay on 16 October 1914 in a convoy headed to Egypt and then on to France to reinforce Indian Expeditionary Force A. However, the Brigade was ordered to detach itself from the convoy and make its way to the British-protected Persian Gulf sheikhdom of Bahrain, where it arrived on 23 October. Once there, it encountered unexpectedly stiff local unease at its presence, which forced the 5000 men and 1200 animals to remain on their cramped troopships in hot and oppressive conditions.[11] They remained there until 31 October. With the declaration of war with the Ottoman Empire imminent, 16th Brigade sailed northward to the Shatt al-Arab at the head of the Persian Gulf and prepared for an attack on the Faw Peninsula south-east of Basra. At 6am in the morning of 6 November 1914, HMS *Odin* fired the first shots of the campaign as it bombarded the local Ottoman fort and landed 600 men on the peninsula. The Brigade proceeded to Abadan (in Persian territory) on 9 November, where it disembarked with some difficulty, owing to a lack of suitable river craft and high winds. Two days later, they beat off an Ottoman counter-attack to confirm their foothold on the peninsula.[12]

16th Brigade (and later the remainder of 6th Division) formed the nucleus of what became Indian Expeditionary Force D in Mesopotamia. Yet it was held in very low esteem by British military officials in London and Delhi, who considered it unfit for fighting in Europe but adequate for colonial-style operations. This reflected the prevalent belief among the top military echelons in the Indian Army and in Force D itself that the operation would amount to nothing more than a traditional exercise in 'gunboat diplomacy.' Indeed, in 1916 (and speaking with the benefit of hindsight), the Principal Maritime Transport Officer responsible for all the water transport arrangements for the force, retrospectively admitted to the Mesopotamia Commission of Inquiry that he envisaged 'some sort of expedition on the beach in the Persian Gulf...I had no conception, no idea whatsoever, that it was going to be up the Shatt al-Arab.'[13] This mentality and the general assumption that Force D would undertake a

---

11 Charles Townsend, *When God Made Hell: The British Invasion of Mesopotamia and the Creation of Iraq, 1914-1921* (London: Faber and Faber, 2010), pp.4-5.
12 IOR, L/MIL/17/88, 'Report by Brigadier General W.S. Delamain on the Operations of Indian Expeditionary Force 'D' up to the 14th November 1914'.
13 TNA, CAB/19/8, Evidence of Commander A. Hamilton to the Mesopotamia Commission, 26 October 1916.

limited frontier-style operation resulted in 16th Brigade leaving India without its land transport of camels and mules, as well as its river craft.[14]

The declaration of war with the Ottoman Empire led the British military authorities in India to rapidly dispatch a second infantry brigade (the 18th) to reinforce 16th Brigade. It arrived at Abadan on 14 November with Force D's commander, General Arthur Barrett, together with a quantity of stores, artillery, and camel transport units. Two days later, the Cabinet in London authorised the capture of Basra on the condition that the Arab political situation and general military conditions were favourable. A sharp engagement took place at Salih on 17 November in a downpour that turned the desert 'into a veritable sea of mud' and claimed nearly 500 British and Indian and over 1000 Ottoman casualties.[15] This relieved the strain on already-scarce river transport resources by making available to Force D a number of craft in the Persian port of Mohammerah, and paved the way for the final advance to Basra. The city was taken on 21 November, one of the first signal British successes in the Great War.[16]

The successful capture of Basra did not lead to a halt in military operations in Mesopotamia. Instead, and largely for reasons of prestige, the campaign expanded rapidly throughout 1915. This left Force D dangerously over-exposed across mutually unsupportable positions and dependent on a supply and transport network that creaked at the seams before breaking down completely early in 1916. The constant extension of operations took place against the backdrop of a lack of adequate oversight as it remained divided between London and Delhi. This reflected and reinforced the pre-1914 division of responsibility for military preparation and the collection of intelligence in the Ottoman sphere between the War Office in London and the Government of India.[17] The result was a fragmented policy-making process that produced gaps in command which severely and negatively impacted the conduct of military operations in Mesopotamia. It also exposed the material and conceptual failings of a Government of India simply not organised, in the words of the outgoing Viceroy, Lord Hardinge, in 1916, 'for war on the present stupendous scale... [where] what does quite well for a six-week war on the frontier will not do at all...'[18]

Particular confusion lay over the physical terrain that any advance into Mesopotamia would cross. The British Government's acquisition of significant oil interests in the Persian Gulf in 1914 was not followed by any clarity over how those interests were to be defended should that become necessary. Nor was there a cadre of political or

---

14   Coates Ulrichsen, *Logistics and Politics*, p.37.
15   Wilfred Nunn, *Tigris Gunboats: The Forgotten War in Iraq 1914-1917* (London: Chatham Publishing, 2007 edition), pp.39-40.
16   'Dalit,' 'The Campaign in Mesopotamia – The First Phase,' *Journal of the Royal United Services Institute*, Vol. 69 (1924), p.520.
17   'Dalit,' Campaign in Mesopotamia, p.520.
18   Cambridge University Library (CUL), Papers of Viscount Hardinge, Volume 102, Letter from Lord Hardinge of Penshurst to Lieutenant-General Sir James Willcocks, 10 February 1916.

intelligence officers in India with sufficient local knowledge of physical, tribal, or social conditions either in Mesopotamia or in Persia.[19] Lack of information-sharing between London and Delhi was matched, after war was declared in November, by inadequate consultation or awareness of the type of operation being envisaged in Mesopotamia. Deficiencies were magnified by the continuous pressure from Delhi and (to a lesser degree) the India Office in London to extend the scope of operations beyond Basra. This flowed from the perceived need to maintain prestige and reflected the lure of a succession of 'easy' military victories that came at comparatively little cost to the attacking Force D during 1915.[20]

The combination of these factors led British officials in the India Office and the Government of India to sanction a series of military offensives which, they argued, were necessary to consolidate control over Basra and a progressively larger hinterland. Furthermore, the potential prize of Baghdad became a tempting source of much-needed prestige as the fighting in Europe became an increasingly bloody stalemate. In this vein, the Political Secretary at the India Office, Sir Arthur Hirtzel, set aside the operational limitations of Force D to argue (as early as 25 November 1914, four days after Basra was taken) that 'the eventual occupation of Baghdad is so desirable as to be practically essential.'[21] Even at this early stage, the idea of an advance toward Baghdad was also supported by Sir Edmund Barrow (the Military Secretary at the India Office) and by Sir Percy Cox, the Chief Political Officer with Force D.[22] The issue of prestige was raised again just three days after Hirtzel's memorandum. On 27 November, Barrow warned against 'a policy of passive inactivity' if 'we are to impress the Arab and Indian world with our ability to defeat all designs against us.' He accordingly proposed that Force D advance to Qurna, a town 50 miles north of Basra located at the confluence of the Tigris and Euphrates.[23]

The advance to Qurna first revealed the extent of the logistical constraints that later crippled Force D. The shortage of suitable river craft was compounded by the fact that it took place when water-levels were at their lowest following the long hot summer months. The first attempt to take Qurna on 4 December had to be abandoned as an absence of pack animals to transport supplies (which could not be borne up-river) forced the advancing party to return to Basra. This failure necessitated a second try which succeeded, albeit in the face of determined Ottoman resistance, in capturing

19 Stephen Longrigg, *Iraq, 1900 to 1950: A Political, Social and Economic History* (London: Oxford University Press, 1953), p.78.
20 Ian Rutledge, *Enemy on the Euphrates: The British Occupation of Iraq and the Great Arab Revolt* (London: Saqi Books, 2014), pp.54-55.
21 TNA, CAB 19/8, Evidence of Sir Arthur Hirtzel to the Mesopotamia Commission, 7 September 1916.
22 TNA, WO 106/54, Note by Sir Edmund Barrow, Military Secretary, India Office, 'Persian Gulf Operations', 27 November 1914.
23 Ibid.

the town on 9 December 1914.[24] Its seizure represented a watershed in the embryonic campaign in Mesopotamia, as from that point on the oversight of operations shifted from the India Office in London, which hitherto had sanctioned all moves, to the political authorities in India and the 'men on the spot' with Force D in Basra.[25]

During 1915, Force D expanded beyond breaking-point as its operational growth far exceeded the capacity of its overstretched supply and transport network. Simultaneous advances occurred on the Tigris and Euphrates but without fitting into any strategic plan. The towns of Amara (on the Tigris) and Nasariya (on the Euphrates) were captured with relative ease in June and July, while a large-scale Ottoman counter-attack had been beaten back at Shaiba on 12 April.[26] By July, this haphazard growth left Force D distributed over five disparate positions in southern Mesopotamia, at Basra, Qurna, Ahwaz, Amara, and Nasariya. Moreover, insufficient intelligence capabilities meant that neither the commander of the new Army Corps, Lieutenant Colonel John Nixon (a 'fighting, pushing kind of general') nor the commander-in-chief of 6th Division, Major General Charles Townshend, was aware of the arrival of significant Ottoman reinforcements as Baghdad grew inexorably closer.[27]

Broader developments in the war and international considerations also contributed to the eagerness of officials in London and Delhi for military successes that would offset the ongoing stalemate at the Dardanelles. With prestige playing an integral part of the 'imperial bluff' that enabled small contingents of civil servants and soldiers to rule vast territories in India (and Egypt), they became anxious for good news that would overcome the failure to break through and decisively defeat the Ottoman forces at Gallipoli.[28] Their concerns were further heightened by the sensitivities of operating against an enemy whose Caliph was the spiritual head of Sunni Islam, and the fact that campaigning in Mesopotamia occurred close to the Shiite holy shrine cities of Najaf and Karbala. Active Ottoman attempts to spread propaganda among Indian troops using leaflets printed both in Hindi and in Urdu called on the soldiers to abandon the 'army of disbelievers.'[29] While the Sunni aspect most closely concerned British authorities in (Sunni-majority) Egypt, its Shiite dimension reared its head early in 1915 when the Viceroy of India, Lord Hardinge, refused to send the 126th

---

24 TNA, WO 106/54, *'Despatch by Lieutenant-General Sir A.A. Barrett, Commanding I.E.F. D, Regarding the Operations Resulting in the Capture of Qurnah, 9th December 1914'* (Simla: Government of India Centre Press, 1915).
25 Coates Ulrichsen, *Logistics and Politics*, p.36.
26 Leila Tarazi Fawaz, *A Land of Aching Hearts: The Middle East in the Great War* (Cambridge, MA: Harvard University Press, 2014), pp.64-65.
27 Eugene Rogan, *The Fall of the Ottomans: The Great War in the Middle East* (New York, NY: Basic Books, 2015), p.203.
28 David French, 'The Dardanelles, Mecca and Kut: Prestige as a Factor in British Eastern Strategy, 1914-1916,' *War and Society*, Vol. 5, No. 1, 1987, pp.54-55.
29 Rogan, *Fall of the Ottomans*, p.232.

Regiment to Mesopotamia because he felt he could not trust the loyalty of two of its (Shiite) Hazara Companies.[30]

In this complex atmosphere of hope, expectation, but also trepidation, the (eventually) successful taking of Basra and Qurna camouflaged the logistical, administrative and operational shortcomings of Force D. As the two brigades expanded into a full infantry division (6th Division under Townshend) it remained chronically short of river-borne and land-based transport. As with the abortive first attempt to take Qurna in December 1914, this rapidly became an issue during the spring flooding in February 1915. This transformed the permeable clay soil around Basra and Qurna into a quagmire that paralysed all forms of land (pack animal and motor) transport. Its paralysing impact was vividly described by Major Hubert Young following his transfer to Mesopotamia from the North-West Frontier of India

> It is difficult for anyone who has not seen the effect of rain upon the flat alluvial desert of the Basra delta to form any idea of the resulting abomination. A particularly glutinous kind of mud is evolved in which it is almost impossible to stand upright, and in which cars and carts stick fast, and horses and camels slide in every direction.[31]

Young recalled how during the 1915 flooding 'our troops at Basra found themselves upon an island, with the Shatt al-Arab on the east and a flooded area ten miles wide on the west…' He also noted how Force D lacked any personnel 'who had any knowledge of local conditions or of the effect of wind, tide, and rain on the water and soil of the Tigris-Euphrates basin.'[32]

As the operational scope of Force D expanded steadily throughout 1915, its lack of sufficient land transport effectively tied the zone of military operations to the rivers. This increased the troops' reliance on the already-overstretched river craft for almost all of their supply and transportation. Furthermore, Force D's growth placed a very great strain on the 'practically non-existent' port facilities at Basra, the only point of entry for the supplies that were necessary to maintain the campaign in the near-absence of locally-procurable alternatives. When it was occupied in 1914 it was only capable of receiving two transports every three weeks, but the Government of India parsimoniously refused to sanction additional expenditure to increase its capacity. As a result, when George MacMunn arrived in the spring of 1916 as Inspector General of Communications he found absolutely 'no conception of what modern transportation

---

30   Townshend, *When God Made Hell*, p.71.
31   Hubert Young, *The Independent Arab* (London: John Murray, 1933), p.44.
32   Ibid. p.47.

required' as nobody 'seemed to grasp what would be required if the force increased or moved up river.'[33]

Set against this disparity between force strength and logistical capabilities, the arrival of additional troops merely increased the logistical requirements. They compounded the congestion and disorganisation in Basra and the lengthening lines of communication and supply. One factor that made the position inexorably worse was the stringent financial constraints imposed on Nixon and Force D by the Government of India. Officials in Delhi, led by the powerful Finance Member, Sir William Meyer, consistently refused to sanction expenditure on the port facilities or other infrastructural works, such as a proposed railway from Basra to Nasariya to take the strain off the river, unless and until it was decided to make the occupation of Mesopotamia permanent.[34] Moreover, the Government of India simply did not comprehend the scale of state intervention and mobilisation required to manage and conduct industrialised warfare against a modern enemy. From the beginning of the war until mid-1916 (when its shortcomings in Mesopotamia could no longer be ignored), Delhi pursued a 'business as usual' strategy that did not depart from the cherished tenets of 'Indian administration,' notably low taxation and laissez faire economic policy.[35] Remarkably, the military budget adopted in March 1915 for the 1915-16 fiscal year remained on an essentially peacetime basis, and the conduct of military operations involving the Indian Army (in Egypt, East Africa and Mesopotamia) was not discussed in the Viceroy's Council before 1916.[36] The impact of this policy continually hindered attempts to expand the scope of the Indian war effort until 1916 even as operational requirements grew rapidly. The Adjutant-General of the Indian Army, Sir Fenton Aylmer, even referred to 'the terrorism created by the Finance Officer' [Meyer]. He concluded pessimistically that 'trying to get anything through at Simla is like a man trying to struggle through quicksand or a bog. He becomes exhausted by opposition on all sides and sinks.'[37]

By the summer of 1915, Indian Expeditionary Force D had successfully captured the pre-1914 *vilayet* of Basra, although physical control remained limited to the major towns and military outposts, and administrative initiatives remained in their infancy. Caught between the scent of military success and an increasingly unsustainable logistical situation, Force D then lurched toward disaster in the autumn of 1915. Following the capture of Amara in July, the remorseless logic of 'mission creep' led its political and military planners to identify the next up-river town of Kut al-Amara as vital to controlling the newly-occupied territory. This was immediately made very

---

33 George MacMunn, *Behind the Scenes in Many Wars* (London: John Murray, 1930), pp.215-16.
34 Coates Ulrichsen, *First World War in the Middle East*, p.128.
35 Ibid.
36 Coates Ulrichsen, *Logistics and Politics*, p.91.
37 Quoted in Paul Davis, 'British-Indian Strategy and Policy in Mesopotamia, November 1914 to April 1916,' PhD dissertation, *University of London* (1981), p.250.

clear, in a telegram from the Viceroy to the Secretary of State for India, when Hardinge stated that the occupation of Kut al-Amara was now 'a strategic necessity, since it commands the lower reaches of both the Tigris and Euphrates' and was necessary 'in order to ensure future tranquillity both at Amara and Nasariya.'[38] Throughout the summer and autumn of 1915, the diverging fortunes of the 'terribly severe' fighting at Gallipoli and the apparently easy seizure of outposts in Mesopotamia, where 'General Nixon has done splendidly and has given the Turks a real good knock' became ever more apparent.[39] Politicians and military leaders in Britain and India thus became anxious for a glittering success – such as the capture of Baghdad – to offset the perceived damage to imperial prestige at Gallipoli.[40]

As 6th Division moved north toward Kut al-Amara in September 1915, its commanders also lacked land transport to take the strain of the river and facilitate the movement of supplies and men. Motorised transport was virtually non-existent before 1916 and was limited to a handful of cars and six ambulances. In its absence, commanders planned to rely on the Indian Army's traditional use of animal transport during the crucial operations between September and November 1915. However, this created its own difficulties, as a contingent of bullocks sent from India to haul the heavy artillery required too much forage than was obtainable from local supplies. By February 1916, the unit had to be withdrawn (and orders given not to send any more from India), as the animals simply could not be fed at the front.[41] As a result, the troops remained heavily over-reliant upon the river for their provisions.

The insufficiency of all forms of river and land transport had immediate consequences for Townshend's march northward. The advance took place in mid-September, when the Tigris was at its lowest following the long summer drought, and unsuitable to most types of river craft. As a result, Force D was unable to supply sufficient quantities of food and forage to the men and animals of the infantry and cavalry divisions at the front. This meant that they could not take advantage of the open spaces of the desert, or conduct operations that required self-sufficiency in food or water. These weaknesses prevented the cavalry from pursuing and destroying the retreating Ottoman units after the first (successful) battle of Kut al-Amara in September 1915. In addition, they necessitated a six-week pause in military operations in order to bring up sufficient supplies to the advanced staging-post at Aziziya. This gave the Ottomans time to regroup and reorganise with significant reinforcements arriving from Baghdad.[42]

Yet, the pause in operations necessitated by the need to reorganise and bring up supplies meant that nearly two months elapsed between the engagement at Kut

38 CUL, Hardinge Papers, Volume 103, Telegram from Viscount Hardinge of Penshurst to Austen Chamberlain, 25 July 1915.
39 CUL, Hardinge Papers, Volume 103, Letter from Viscount Hardinge of Penshurst to Lieutenant-General Sir James Willcocks, 15 June 1915.
40 Townshend, *When God Made Hell*, p.139.
41 Coates Ulrichsen, *Logistics and Politics*, p.48.
42 Majd, *Iraq in World War I*, p.184.

al-Amara on 25 September and the commencement of the battle of Ctesiphon on 22 November. During this period, the Ottoman field commander Nurredin Pasha had ample time to prepare a set of strong and mutually-supportable defensive positions. His four infantry divisions, totalling about 18,000 men, faced Townshend's weary 6th Division, which, by this point, had been on the march for over two months, and were now beset by a combination of poor weather and wet terrain. Furthermore, 2000 transport mules and a large quantity of carts that had been collected in Basra failed to arrive at Aziziya in time for the renewal of the advance northward on 11 November. This was due to the fact that more than half of the river craft were required to transport the bulky comestible items, such as grain, firewood, and fodder, necessary to sustain the front-line troops on a daily basis.[43]

Townshend consequently was prevented from building up a reserve either of troops or of transport. These shortcomings became critical following 6th Division's failure to break through the Ottoman defences at Ctesiphon between 22 and 24 November. Both sides suffered very heavy casualties and became exhausted by the intense yet inconclusive fighting. The lack of a strategic reserve, and the additional strain placed on the existing transport units by the 3500 battle casualties, gave Townshend little option but to retreat to Kut al-Amara, and await reinforcements.[44] 6th Division arrived there on 3 December, and Townshend took the fateful decision to halt there as the town contained ample reserves of stores and supplies. Originally, these had been stockpiled as a reserve to support the advance up-river, but Townshend now lacked the river transport to send them back to Basra. Moreover, his troops were exhausted by weeks of continuous hard fighting. On 4 December, therefore, Townshend decided to stand his ground at Kut al-Amara and turn it into an armed camp while he awaited reinforcements from Basra. Accordingly, he informed Nixon that he had one month's supply of rations for his British troops and 55 days' supplies for the Indian soldiers that made up the majority of 6th Division.[45]

This communication of Townshend's estimate had serious consequences for the subsequent operations to relieve him. Although he did not know it at the time, his men ultimately survived for more than four months on the reserves it had available. Townshend's under-estimation imparted a (false) sense of urgency to British Headquarters in Basra, and contributed to the hasty and disorganised relief operations that were put together without adequate planning or preparation. Indeed, as the two Indian infantry divisions based in France (the 3rd and 7th) rushed to Basra alongside a British division (the 13th), which diverted from the Dardanelles, the haphazard arrival of units and stores brutally exposed Basra's limitations as a port and as a base.

43   Coates Ulrichsen, *Logistics and Politics*, p.48.
44   Nikolas Gardner, *The Siege of Kut al-Amara: At War in Mesopotamia, 1915-1916* (Indiana, IN: Indiana University Press, 2014), p.44.
45   F.J. Moberly, History of the Great War Based on Official Documents. The Campaign in Mesopotamia, 1914-1918 (London: HMSO, 1923), volume II, p.167.

As a result of the Government of India's above-described refusal to sanction any expenditure above the bare essential minimum, the port still did not have any modern facilities for berthing and unloading ships, or for allocating storage for supplies. Consequently, the average discharge rate was two steamers every three weeks, as men and cargoes were unloaded from ocean-going transports onto lighters belonging to local firms, and then re-loaded onto river craft for journey up-river.[46]

The arrival of the three additional infantry divisions with auxiliary units between January and April 1916 thus overwhelmed the makeshift facilities at Basra. This formed one of the major reasons for the progressive breakdown in military operations that culminated in the surrender of Townshend and his 6th Division on 29 April. Basra and its port became heavily congested and disastrously over-extended as reinforcements of men and supplies arrived at a quicker rate than they could be discharged and sent upstream. Neither the base nor its surrounding facilities proved capable of handling the increased traffic in the absence of wharves, insufficient numbers of port lighters and tugs, and lack of labour and dry-land availability on the river-front itself. All of these factors became critical to the backlog that accumulated, and fed off each other in an interlocking manner that created a mutually-reinforcing sense of confusion and chaos at the base.[47]

Back in Basra, Nixon's health had broken down, and he was replaced as commander of Force D by Sir Percy Lake. He took command on 19 January 1916 and immediately advocated an advance owing to 'the uncertainty as to date of arrival of reinforcements and of sufficient river craft for maintaining and supporting them at the front.'[48] At this point, Duff, in India, and Robertson, in London, reversed their enthusiasm for earlier military advances, by cautioning against a premature offensive and urging Aylmer to await the arrival of further reinforcements.[49] However, by this point, the congestion within Basra itself and the strain on its port facilities was so great, that even this cautious proposal was deemed unsuitable in practice. By 15 February, the situation reached breaking-point as Lake informed London that the shortage of transport had become so acute that it would not be possible to transport the 13th Division to the front. He also acknowledged that 'the number of my river craft limits the number of men and animals that can be maintained at the front,' and informed Duff that the dispatch of further numbers up-river would reduce by 10% the amount of supplies which could be transported in the scarce river craft. In short, Force D could either transport supplies, or men, but not both at the same time.[50]

---

46 Coates Ulrichsen, *Logistics and Politics*, pp.48-49.
47 Ibid., p.49.
48 TNA, WO 106/905, Telegram from General Sir Percy Lake to the Chief of the General Staff in India, 8 February 1916.
49 Coates Ulrichsen, *Logistics and Politics*, p.50.
50 TNA, WO 106/905, Telegram from General Sir Percy Lake to the Chief of the General Staff in India, 15 February 1916, London.

A second attempt by Aylmer to relieve Townshend failed on 8 March as the Ottomans repulsed an attack on the Dujaila Redoubt and inflicted severe casualties. Following this setback, Aylmer was himself replaced by Lieutenant General George ('Blood Orange') Gorringe as Commander-in-Chief of Tigris Corps. Once again, Lake informed Indian Army Headquarters in India, on 13 March, that the operations on the Tigris were paralysed owing to the incomplete and late arrival of river craft.[51] Lack of transport meant the 13th Division had to trek to the front and take part in the third attempt to relieve Kut al-Amara, between 5-9 April, without any rest or their complement of land transport. As with the aborted first attempt in January, so too, on this occasion, did heavy rain and severe flooding wreak havoc with the operation, as the battlefield became a 'veritable bog.' In these conditions, the Ottomans managed to stall an exhausted division and repel it from reaching its objective.[52]

A final, desperate attempt to move forward to relieve the 6th Division also ended in failure on 25 April. At this point, Gorringe felt compelled to inform India that that Tigris Corps had reached the absolute limit of its offensive capability. He added that it could go no further without a pause in the operations, as his men had been engaged almost continuously since 5 April and had suffered some 9700 casualties. This constituted roughly one-quarter of its fighting force, yet it remained more than twelve miles away from Kut al-Amara.[53] Yet the besieged garrison was also reaching the limit of its endurance as Townshend's men were close to starvation and afflicted by ever-rising daily incidence of disease. On 24 April, a desperate last-ditch attempt to re-supply Townshend was made by attempting to float a ship loaded with a month's worth of supplies up-river. This, too, was unsuccessful, leaving the Secretary of State for War in London, Lord Kitchener, reluctantly sanctioned Duff to open negotiations for the surrender of Townshend and 6th Division. Their capitulation on 29 April was seen at the time as one of the greatest military humiliations ever suffered by a British army, perhaps equalled only by the fall of Singapore in December 1941, as 277 British officers, 204 Indian officers, 2592 British soldiers, 6988 Indian soldiers, and 3248 Indian non-combatants were marched into captivity.[54] Kitchener himself was in no doubt of the magnitude of the psychological damage that the surrender inflicted on British prestige in its extra-European colonies. Privately, he wrote to Duff shortly before Townshend's surrender to state that 'I sincerely hope that it is fully realised by you and all General Officers under your command that it would forever be a disgrace to our country if Townshend should surrender.'[55]

---

51   Coates Ulrichsen, *Logistics and Politics*, p.51.
52   Majd, *Iraq During World War I*, p.209.
53   TNA, WO 106/905, Telegram from General Sir Percy Lake to the Chief of the General Staff in India, 22 April 1916.
54   Rogan, *Fall of the Ottomans*, p.267.
55   TNA, WO 106/906, Telegram from Field Marshal Lord Kitchener to General Sir Beauchamp Duff, 25 April 1916.

The surrender of Kut al-Amara was the outcome of a chaotic interplay of factors that each built upon and magnified the impact of the others. Individual commanders on the ground and in Delhi were disgraced; Duff committed suicide in January 1918, Nixon was found by the Mesopotamia Commission to be principally responsible for the disaster, while Townshend never overcame the shame of his capture and the differential treatment he received under house arrest in Istanbul while thousands of his soldiers endured terrible privations on forced marches through the Syrian desert and died in disgrace in 1924. The Mesopotamia Commission of Inquiry launched by the British Government produced a report so damaging in its exposure of what went wrong that the government agonised for two months over whether to publish it. It claimed the political scalp of the Secretary of State for India, Austen Chamberlain, when it did see the light of day, as it shed devastating light on the administrative misconduct of the Government of India and its inability to comprehend or undertake modern military operations. However, the report also blamed the duality of control between the India Office in London and the Government of India in Delhi, which contributed to the sense of drift and lack of oversight as the campaign faltered.[56] While no one factor was decisive in condemning the first attempt to capture Baghdad to failure, together they overwhelmed the rudimentary military capabilities of Force D. The cathartic shock of the accumulation of failures triggered a widespread reorganisation of operational control, which was passed to the War Office in London, as well as the systems of administrative, and logistical responsibility, and paved the way for the resumption of the advance after months of soul searching.[57]

III

The scale of the institutional and intellectual change in Indian governing structures after 1916 is fully comprehended when placed in the context of what it superseded. Following the outbreak of war in August 1914, and lasting until the disastrous maladministration of the Mesopotamian campaign became publicly and politically apparent in the middle of 1916, the Government of India pursued a 'business as usual' policy that increasingly diverged from the path of incremental strategic mobilisation in the United Kingdom. Throughout this formative period of the war, the powerful focus on continuing laissez-faire policies, as well as the bureaucratic inertia for which the Government of India was infamous, ensured that steps were not taken to extend state control over the transportation networks or agricultural resources within India. Similarly, no steps were taken to amalgamate the six branches of the army responsible for various dimensions of recruitment into one central organisation until October

---

56 Townshend, *When God Made Hell*, pp.332-335.
57 Coates Ulrichsen, *First World War in the Middle East*, pp. 136-138.

1916.⁵⁸ Recruiting, as with so much else within the Government of India, remained wedded to peacetime lines even as the pillars that supported the Indian Army began to crumble under the impact of fighting prolonged military campaigns on multiple fronts against foes equipped with modern weaponry.⁵⁹

In July 1916, London's decision to develop India as the principal supply base for the campaigns east of Suez coincided with the beginning of the Mesopotamia Commission of Inquiry. These two events heralded a decisive shift in the mind-set of the civil and military echelons in the Indian bureaucracy and an end to the lingering belief that colonial-style frontier campaigning would suffice. Moreover, soldier-administrators with practical experience drawn from the first two years of fighting an industrialised war in the European and Mediterranean theatres arrived to assist in the strategic mobilisation of Indian resources. Men such as the new Commander-in-Chief of the Indian Army, Charles Monro, and Edward Altham, who became Inspector General of Communication, directed radical changes in the Government of India's attitude to the war and the measures necessary to conduct it. They belatedly began to extend the powers of the state both at central and provincial levels, and intervene in society to penetrate and mobilise local resources of manpower and commodities.⁶⁰

This new centralising initiative took off in March and April 1917 when the central state began to exert its powers of organisation and penetration with the creation of the Indian Munitions Board and the Central Recruiting Board respectively. The formation of these two boards was the critical development in the expansion and projection of centralised state control over Indian resources. The new organisations established central control over the two pillars of India's logistical effort, agricultural resources and manpower. The Indian Munitions Board centralised the purchasing departments of the Government of India into an organisation whose mandate was 'the control and development of Indian resources, with particular reference to war requirements.'⁶¹ It identified and extended state control over strategic industries that provided material for the war effort, such as railway track, ordnance factories, textiles, timber and jute manufacturing. The Board also attempted to overcome the constricting limitations of India's pre-war industrial organisation that had left it dependent on the United Kingdom for machinery and skilled workmen.⁶²

The Central Recruiting Board was established to centralise state control over the processes of recruitment to the various combatant and non-combatant branches of the army. It contained both civilian and military members who co-operated in an effort to safeguard vital agricultural districts and strategic industries from being denuded of

58 IOR, L/MIL/17/52398, 'Development of Man Power in India, and its utilization for Imperial Purposes,' Army Headquarters, April 1918.
59 Coates Ulrichsen, *Logistics and Politics*, p.91.
60 Coates Ulrichsen, *Logistics and Politics*, p.91.
61 IOR, L/MIL/17/5/2381, 'Memorandum on India's Contribution to the War in Men, Material and Money, August 1914 to November 1918,' p.20.
62 Ibid. p.21.

local labour.⁶³ This was especially important in the Punjab which, until 1917, provided the majority of recruits for military service and agricultural produce for the war effort. Consequently, the Central Recruiting Board took measures to widen and deepen the field of recruitment and extend the geographical spread of recruits. This was necessary both to lessen the burden of providing manpower on the two 'martial' provinces of the Punjab and the North-West Frontier Province and in order to tap the hitherto-largely neglected reserves of manpower in the 'non-martial' provinces of southern India.⁶⁴

This decision to broaden the sphere of recruitment to include groups that hitherto had lain outside the 'martial races' represented a radical departure from pre-war policy. It required officials to temporarily set aside ethno-racial stereotypes for the duration of the war, although the persistence and strength of such mentalities endured in private remarks and comments. In one such example of the pervasive racism that dominated colonial discourse and mentality, the official eye-witness to the campaign, Edmund Candler described a group of Santals from Bengal as 'like happy, black gollywogs... the expression on their faces is singularly happy and innocent, and endorses everything Rousseau said about primitive content. Evolution has spared them, they have even escaped the unkindness of war.'⁶⁵ Nevertheless, these measures proved a success as the overall number of recruits jumped from 93,000 in 1915 and 104,000 in 1916 to 194,000 in 1917 and 327,000 in 1918. Simultaneously, the proportion of recruits who came from the Punjab fell from 49% in 1915 to 38% in 1918.⁶⁶ This move toward shifting the impact of military requirements for manpower more equitably across India allowed the Indian Army to double in size between January 1917 and November 1918 and meet the King-Emperor and Lloyd George's call for India to 're-double' her war effort in March 1918.⁶⁷

This new administrative machinery presided over a vast increase in the scale and scope of India's contribution to the war effort. It spread the burden of meeting logistical and military requirements more evenly throughout India, although its impact continued to be felt most strongly in the Punjab. This remained the chief recruiting ground for the Indian Army but now was also tapped heavily for exports of grain, both for overseas and to relieve deficit provinces elsewhere in India.⁶⁸ Yet, the new measures extended the horizontal and vertical powers of the state and its

---

63 Michael O'Dwyer, 'India's Man-Power in the War,' *The Army Quarterly*, Vol. II (1921), p.255.
64 Ibid. pp.253-255.
65 Edmund Candler, *The Sepoy* (London: John Murray, 1919), p.218.
66 O'Dwyer, *India's Man-Power*, pp.253-255.
67 F.W. Perry, *The Commonwealth Armies: Manpower and Organization in Two World Wars* (Manchester: Manchester University Press, 1988), p.95.
68 BL, Lord Chelmsford Papers, Mss Eur E264, box 9, Telegram from Lord Chelmsford to Sir Edwin Montagu, 23 January 1918.

penetrative scope into society and amounted to a head-on assault on the powerful pre-war orthodoxy of laissez-faire economic policy in India.[69]

A similar 'revolution' in official attitude took place in the methods by which the Government of India financed these policies. Prior to 1914, the political value and utility attached to keeping taxation and public expenditure low ensured that the Government of India operated on a very constricted revenue base. As described earlier in this chapter, the innate conservatism among British officials in Delhi also acted as a powerful brake on the expansion of Indian fiscal policy after 1914.[70] With the decisions taken from mid-1916 onward to develop and maximise India's role in maintaining the campaigns in the Mediterranean and the Middle East, this fiscal policy underwent an equally sharp change to finance the massive increase in military and related capital expenditure. In 1917-18 this 'temporary revolution' in economic and financial policy identified by Clive Dewey[71] accelerated as the costs of financing the expansion of the Indian Army, enormous military expenditure on capital works such as the improvements to the dockyard facilities at the ports of embarkation in Karachi and Bombay, and the taking over of £100 million worth of British Government War Debt led to a spike in levels of direct and indirect taxation and public borrowing.[72] Particularly significant was the shift in the structure of taxation toward the imposition of import duties on cotton and other goods. This marked the first occasion that London's need for Indian collaboration trumped the vested interests of British trading firms.[73]

The cumulative impact of the measures to centralise and co-ordinate the extraction of resources ensured that the Indian contribution to the imperial war effort expanded steadily in 1917-18 and peaked shortly before the armistice.[74] This differed sharply from the British reserves of manpower and material, which peaked late in 1917 and declined steadily thereafter. Between early 1917 and November 1918, the Indian Army doubled in size and the British military authorities began to 'Indianise' the campaigns in Salonika and Palestine, which in 1918 replaced Mesopotamia as the principal drain on Indian resources.[75] India additionally supplied all railway material for Mesopotamia and East Africa, and substantial amounts of track for Egypt and Palestine. The country made regular shipments of grain to meet shortfalls in the

---

69   Coates Ulrichsen, *Logistics and Politics*, p.166.
70   B.R. Tomlinson, *The Political Economy of the Raj, 1914-1947: The Economics of Decolonization in India* (London: Macmillan, 1979), p.21.
71   Clive Dewey, 'The Government of India's 'New Industrial Policy,' 1900-1925: Formation and Failure,' in Clive Dewey & K.N. Chaudhuri (eds.), *Economy and Society: Essays in Indian Economic and Social History* (New Delhi: Oxford University Press), p.232.
72   Ibid. pp.108-109.
73   Dharma Kumar, 'The Fiscal System,' in Dharma Kumar and Tapan Raychaudhuri (eds.), *The Cambridge Economic History of India. Vol. 2: c.1757-c.1970* (Cambridge: Cambridge University Press, 1983), p.921.
74   Coates Ulrichsen, *Logistics and Politics*, p.166.
75   Perry, *Commonwealth Armies*, p.95.

civilian food supplies in Egypt, Palestine, Mesopotamia and Salonika, and during the year to April 1918, it provided 700,000 tons of grain to the military authorities in Salonika and Egypt alone.[76] These figures illustrate the pivotal importance of India to the maintenance of all the extra-European campaigns undertaken by British and imperial forces during the war.

The problem was that this 'redoubling' of the military effort in 1918 resulted in India raising an army beyond the capacity of its logistical base to sustain. The need to feed, clothe and transport the new mass army strained Indian food resources and transportation to its capacity and caused a near-breakdown, which only the termination of hostilities averted. The system came close to collapse in late-1918, when a sudden increase in civilian demands on the Indian railway network and supplies of foodstuffs for famine relief operations contributed to a near-breakdown in India's logistical effort. As in Egypt, the link between agriculture and railways needed to be finely balanced to meet pre-war policies that had encouraged the concentration and specialisation of particular crops in different areas.[77] Integral to this process and vital to its equilibrium was the development of an extensive railway network that consisted of 'famine lines' that transferred foodstuffs from food-producing regions to food-deficit areas. However, military demands for railway track and rolling stock pared the civilian network to its subsistence minimum by late-1917, when four-fifths of the available rolling stock was in military use.[78]

Diversion of rolling stock to military usage severely dislocated domestic markets and intensified the general rise in prices, which brought an already-impoverished population even closer to the margins of subsistence.[79] This was similar to the Egyptian experience, but in India the impact of railway shortages and the resulting congestion was magnified by their vital role in famine relief works. As early as April 1917, the general shortage in shipping meant that rolling stock was diverted from transporting wheat and grain to carry coal from Bengal to the ports of Bombay and Karachi. This prompted Chelmsford to warn the War Office about the heavy strain being placed on the railways to simultaneously meet civil and military needs.[80] Instead, military demands for rolling stock and track remained high for the remainder of the year, as Allenby extended his rail network into Palestine, and Maude and subsequently Marshall developed their own network around Baghdad. Demands rose steadily in

76 Ibid.
77 George MacMunn, 'The Quarter-Master General's Department and the Administrative Services in India from the Mutiny to the Present Time,' *Journal of the Royal United Services Institution*, Vol. LXV (1925), p.118.
78 Judith Brown, 'War and the Colonial Relationship: Britain, India and the War of 1914-1918,' in M.R.D. Foot (ed.), *War and Society: Historical Essays in Honour and Memory of J.R. Western, 1928-1971* (London: Elek, 1975), p.93.
79 Ibid. p.94.
80 BL, Chelmsford Papers, Mss Eur E264, box 8, Telegram from Lord Chelmsford to Sir Austen Chamberlain, 3 April 1917.

1918 as the new military units and their logistical supplies needed to be transported to the base ports for disembarkation, and the Indian railway authorities issued regular warnings of an imminent breakdown in the entire network.[81]

The delicate balance between civil and military demands for rolling stock and foodstuffs finally broke down in the late-summer and autumn of 1918, when the partial failure of the Arabian Sea monsoon led to poor harvests in central and northern India.[82] The resulting shortages of grain, atta and flour caused prices to rise to famine levels in parts of India, and prompted food riots in Madras.[83] Scarce rolling stock needed to be diverted back to civil usage to dispatch wheat from the Punjab and rice from Burma to deficit provinces. This was urgently necessary to avert localised famine and lower prices to politically acceptable levels. However, it forced the Government of India to finally take measures to reconcile the competing military and civil claims on the railways as the situation became critical.[84]

On 2 October 1918, Chelmsford informed the Secretary of State for India, Edwin Montagu that 'stocks of all food-grains will barely suffice to meet internal demands apart from Mesopotamia.'[85] Nine days later, the Government of India took the decision to end further purchasing of wheat for export overseas other than Mesopotamia, and appointed a Foodstuffs Commissioner to oversee the re-distribution of wheat and rice from food-producing to deficit regions.[86] In London, the War Office reacted by instructing British authorities in Cairo and Salonika to investigate the possibility of substituting locally-produced resources in the occupied regions of the Levant for Indian stocks.[87] A complete breakdown in the intricate network of Indian supplies seemed imminent, and was only averted by the end of the fighting in November 1918. The armistice thus came not a moment too soon for India, which was by this time facing the devastating impact of the influenza pandemic, magnified by the constant moving-about the country of large numbers of men, and which eventually killed more than five million Indians.[88]

---

81 Coates Ulrichsen, *Logistics and Politics*, p.167.
82 BL, Chelmsford Papers, Mss Eur E264, box 9, Telegram from Lord Chelmsford to Sir Edwin Montagu, 21 July 1918.
83 BL, Chelmsford Papers, Mss Eur E264, box 9, Telegram from Lord Chelmsford to Sir Edwin Montagu, 2 October 1918.
84 BL, Chelmsford papers, Mss Eur E264, box 9, Telegram from Lord Chelmsford to Sir Edwin Montagu, 17 December 1918.
85 BL, Chelmsford papers, Mss Eur E264, box 9, Telegram from Lord Chelmsford to Sir Edwin Montagu, 2 October 1918.
86 BL, Chelmsford papers, Mss Eur E264, box 21, Letter from Sir Claude Hill to Lord Chelmsford, 11 October 1918.
87 TNA, WO 33/960, Telegram from the War Office to the Commander-in-Chief of the Egyptian Expeditionary Force.
88 Coates Ulrichsen, *Logistics and Politics*, p.168.

In August 1918, the Viceroy, Lord Chelmsford, felt able to write that 'under pressure from war demands India's economic resources have developed in marked degree.'[89] By the close of the war in November 1918, a total of 3,691,836 tons of supplies had been shipped overseas from India. Moreover, the number of soldiers India was responsible for maintaining had risen from the 75,000 of the British garrison in India in 1914 to over one million, as Army Headquarters assumed responsibility for feeding and clothing its Indian soldiers for the first time.[90] In the final analysis, it was India's role as provider of agricultural raw materials and supplier of foodstuffs to a clientele of consumers in the Mediterranean and the Middle East that enabled these campaigns to be sustained for the duration of the war. The policy of utilising local resources to maintain the campaigns East of Suez successfully met the vast logistical requirements posed by the Egyptian and Mesopotamian Expeditionary Forces and their auxiliary and transport units. In addition, they allowed both forces to undertake major offensive military operations which resulted in the capture of significant swathes of Ottoman territory.

However, by November 1918 the inexorable demands of modern warfare combined with the external shocks to the system to place this network of supplies under extreme duress and throw its continuation into 1919 into doubt. Between mid-1916 and the end of the war, the vast increase in scope and complexity of the Indian war effort extended Indian resources toward their limit and rendered them vulnerable to any external shock to the system such as the partial failure of the Arabian Sea monsoon and the outbreak of the influenza pandemic. Moreover, the shift toward 'total war' involving the mobilisation of all forms of resources not only upset and tested to the limit the delicate equilibrium between civilian and military demands for resources and infrastructural capacity such as railways to transport them within India itself, but also provided a foretaste of similar demands which would be placed on India on a still greater scale during the Second World War.

---

89 BL, Chelmsford Papers, Mss Eur E264, box 9, Telegram from Lord Chelmsford to Sir Edwin Montagu, 4 August 1918.
90 IOR, L/MIL/17/5/2381 'Memorandum on India's Contribution to the War in Men, Material and Money, August 1914 to November 1918'.

13

Terriers in India: a preliminary report

Peter Stanley

It might seem that with a busy military past, rich archives and an active community of amateur and academic researchers interested in the subject, just about every aspect of any consequence in British military history must have been covered, if not dealt with to the point of satiety and repetition. This surmise might apply particularly to Britain's participation in the Great War, which attracts books, journals, magazines, television features, website, organisations such as the Western Front and Gallipoli associations and the attentions of re-enactors, friends of various museums and immense public engagement. What else is there to discover or say, you might ask? Let me suggest that there is more: the experience of fifty-thousand-odd men whose contribution to the Great War has been almost entirely overlooked.

In 2012 and 2013 I was fortunate to spend time exploring the cantonments of the Punjab, the Shimla Hills and Uttar Pradesh – not always an easy matter when 'old British cantonments' remain the home of units of the Indian Army, whose members are wary of anyone with a camera. I was able to spend time investigating the complex but absorbing 'visual archaeology' of cantonment architecture; that is, looking at and photographing buildings. I also spent as much time as I could in cantonment cemeteries. Their memorials and gravestones provided a rich and evocative source on the lives and deaths of India's British garrison from the early nineteenth century to independence.

In cantonment cemeteries at Agra, Delhi, Meerut, Dugshai and Ferozepore I found inscriptions that shed light on the mid-nineteenth century period in which I was particularly interested, in order to complete a novel (set in the first Anglo-Sikh war and published in 2014 as *The Cunning Man*). But in the course of those visits I became aware that India's British cemeteries included graves bearing familiar Commonwealth War Graves Commission badges and stickers, indicating that the commission was in the process of surveying and identifying war graves relating to the world wars and, in the cemeteries I visited, specifically to what I soon realised were, among others, British Territorial units that served in India in the Great War. The Commonwealth War Graves Commission's website disclosed that British war graves from 1914-21 could be found in over sixty cemeteries across India, the majority of which were probably of Territorials (something I now know to be so – indeed, some of the graves I photographed in 2012 turned up in the albums of comrades now in regimental and county collections in Hampshire, Wiltshire and Kent).

As I was also in the final stages of researching and writing a book on the Indian Army's involvement in the Gallipoli campaign of 1915 (published by Helion in 2015 as *Die in Battle, Do not Despair: the Indians on Gallipoli, 1915*) I was open to – and indeed eager to begin – further research on the British military experience of India, I soon nurtured a curiosity about the reasons why cantonment cemeteries came to hold such graves. In 2014, with the Indians on Gallipoli book delivered, I began to investigate what soon became the 'Terriers in India' project. In that I possess the priceless luxury of occupying a Research Professorship, I was soon able to make it my premier academic project, one to be embarked upon once I had completed several books due to be delivered in 2015 and 2016.

The idea of investigating Terriers in India had a great appeal to me as an historian interested in the history of the British army and the British military presence in India. Territorials, I knew, were a quite different sort of soldier to the long-service regulars who had formerly comprised the garrison of British India. These men – the sons of the respectable British clerks, shop-keepers, artisans and small farmers – had joined the new Territorial Force, established by Edward Haldane in 1908 to defend Britain against invasion. Imbued with patriotic fervor, in late 1914 many had elected to accept the invitation to accept 'Imperial Service', inspired by the empire's need to bring its regulars back to fight in France. Many volunteered for overseas service on the assumption (and indeed on the understanding) that they would return to fight in France. While many Territorial units moved on from India to active theatres of war (to Mesopotamia and Palestine especially), many remained in India throughout the entire war. What other troops were available to replace them? Later in the war some seventeen 'Garrison battalions' were despatched to India (whose members were Territorials, regulars, Kitchener and Derby men), but some fifteen Territorial battalions remained in India throughout (including the 1/9th Hampshires, which left for Siberia, of all places, in October 1918, returning via Canada in 1919 and becoming the only British battalion to go around the world in the course of the war).

The Territorials, enthusiastic and idealistic, encountered India anew, and more-or-less at the same time, during the cold weather of 1914-15 – the first transports arrived at Bombay in mid-December. Their experience immediately suggested several promising questions. How did they learn the rules and customs of the cantonment life? How did they react to India; and how did India react to them? What did they do that distinguished them from regulars? What did they bring back with them from their Indian service? India experienced profound political change during the Great War (the nationalist movement changed from naïve co-operation with the Raj to a determination that Congress should make the war India's opportunity): how did

Territorials see and react to the political context of their service? What did they actually do in India? How useful actually were they as part of India's garrison?

The project soon grew to become a major preoccupation of my weekends and evenings – ironically, occupying exactly the same time that I had formerly allocated to military historical research before I became an academic historian, when I worked as the Principal Historian at the Australian War Memorial and later the head of the National Museum of Australia's Research Centre. Embarking on a complex project such as this (dealing with troops from Britain and serving in India, with research undertaken from Australia) is of course much easier in the age of the internet than it would have been a decade or more earlier, and my position and the resources which it affords made such a project highly feasible.

This chapter constitutes a sort of preliminary report, based on the initial six months of serious research, in which I identified the major sources and repositories and have undertaken research on published sources and on some of the actual primary sources in Britain and in India. It outlines the subject, posits some of the major directions and foreshadows some of the probable findings of the project. It fulfils several functions. It alerts readers to the experience of a group of British soldiers in India whose existence has been virtually invisible in the century since they arrived there. It provides an example of how a military-social historian goes about framing and conducting a research project. It advertises the project to the military historical community, constituting a sort of extended 'help wanted' advertisement to any who may know of relevant sources. Finally, it provides some preliminary insights into the substance of the Terriers' experience in India.

Extraordinarily, it soon became reasonably clear that virtually no one had published much on this subject since the early 1920s. References in regimental histories are almost all brief and some practically in passing, with few exceptions, such as George Blick's *The 1/4th Battalion The Wiltshire Regiment 1914-1919*, a brief history compiled in 1933 by several officers after they realised that the battalion's records had been lost. Otherwise there existed only a couple of memoirs (Nigel Woodyatt's lively memoir, *Under Ten Viceroys and* a transcript of his talk to the United Services Club, and Alban Bacon's *The Wanderings of a Temporary Warrior*, all published in 1922). Apart from that, it seemed that no one had written an account of the service of Territorials in India. The only notable recent secondary works, curiously, relate to the Somerset Light Infantry.

C.P. Mills's *A Strange War*, based largely on the diaries of former Quartermaster Sergeant Ed Ewens and the words of Bert Rendall, taken from an oral history interview made for the Imperial War Museum in 1985.[1] Both served in the 2/5th Somerset Light Infantry in Burma and India. Their complementary accounts provide the most detailed coverage of one battalion's experience, full of incidental detail. Two books based on officers' letters were published, both in 1999: John Mackie's *Answering*

---

1 C.P. Mills, *A Strange War* (Gloucester: Alan Sutton, 1988).

the Call: Letters from the Somerset Light Infantry 1914-19 and Ann Noyes's *Engaged in War: the Letters of Stanley Goodland 1914-1919*.[2] Apart from that the only published source is Fred Mundy's informative *A Journal of the 1/4th Battalion Wiltshire Regiment 1914-1918*, published in 2011 by The Rifles, Wardrobe and Museum Trust in 2011.

The field, it seemed was wide open, a thought confirmed when I made contact with Charles Messenger (author of the wonderfully detailed book *Call to Arms: The British Army 1914-1918*), the Territorial Army authority Bill Mitchison and several fellow members of the Western Front Association. (One of the distinguishing features of military history as I have encountered it is the extraordinary generosity offered from overseas colleagues. It is impossible to undertake military historical research at a distance without it, but with it a delight.)

As a starting point I needed to establish which Territorial units had served in India. I knew from Nigel Woodyatt's book and article that the number was large – up to forty or fifty thousand men; but which formations and units had they belonged to and where might their records be? Again, the internet gave me a massive starting boon. The authoritative website dealing with the British Army in the Great War, *The Long, Long Trail* (http://www.1914-1918.net/) provided what became my initial point of departure. It provided summaries of both and formations and units that soon told me that three Territorial divisions had gone to India from late 1914, the 43rd (Wessex), 44th (Home Counties) and 45th (2nd Wessex). (Actually I soon discovered that in fact this was technically not so: the divisions were broken up on arrival in India, and they were numbered only later, in 1915, so in fact the numbers were illusory.)

But *The Long, Long Trail* website gave an invaluable initial guide because it also provided summaries of the service of the constituent battalions (Regular, Militia, Territorial and New Army) of every infantry regiment in the British Army. Much dedicated searching enabled me to build up a provisional list of units. (This work was helped by my boyhood obsession with British Army lineage. For years rather than counting sheep I would run through the order of precedence of line infantry regiments, from the Royal Scots to the Leinster Regiment. Resurrecting this arcane knowledge forty years on proved surprisingly easy: in any case I found myself plunged back into the world of the army of the Haldane reforms, focusing, naturally, on Territorial battalions.

The Long, Long Trail site (checked against regimental and other histories) enabled me to devise a more-or-less complete list of some forty battalions:

1/4th and 1/5th Queen's Own Royal West Surrey
1/4th and 1/5th Buffs
1/4th, 1/5th, 1/6th, 2/4th and 2/5th Devonshire Regiment

---

2   John Mackie (ed.), *Answering the Call: Letters from the Somerset Light Infantry 1914-19* (Eggleston: Raby Books, 1999); Ann Noyes (ed.), *Engaged in War: the Letters of Stanley Goodland 1914-1919* (Guildford: Twiga Books, 1999).

1/4th, 1/5th, 2/4th and 2/5th Somerset Light Infantry
1/1st Brecknockshire Battalion, South Wales Borderers
1/5th and 1/6th East Surrey Regiment
1/4th and 2/4th Duke of Cornwall's Light Infantry
1/4th and 2/4th Border Regiment
2/6th Royal Sussex
1/4th, 1/5th, 1/6th, 1/7th, 1/9th, 2/4th, 2/5th, 2/6th and 2/7th Hampshire Regiment
1/4th and 2/4th Dorsetshire Regiment
1/4th and 1/5th Queen's Own Royal West Kent
1/4th King's Shropshire Light Infantry
1/9th and 1/10th Middlesex Regiment
1/4th and 2/4th Wiltshire Regiment
1/25th London Regiment
Kent Cyclist Battalion[3]

While the Territorial divisions were divested of staff, medical, engineer and service corps units before embarking for India, some 29 batteries of Territorial artillery accompanied the infantry. Equipped with obsolescent guns and inadequate tools, their experience was generally an unhappy one.

Like the infantry, the artillery units hailed from England's southern counties, meaning that, besides the collections of the London institutions (the National Army Museum, the National Archives, UK, the Imperial War Museum and the British Library) virtually all the sources were held in regimental museums and county archives in a compact band stretching from Kent to Cornwall. Moreover, nearly half of the battalions came from just three counties. While the main British primary sources were located over 16,000 kilometres from my home in Canberra, they were relatively accessible within Britain. Research conducted for my book on Indians on Gallipoli in 2014 had also disclosed that the Indian Army's headquarters war diaries, held in the National Archives of India (with copies in the British Library) would also be invaluable; and New Delhi is closer to Canberra than London, and cheaper to visit. It also has the advantage that it is a great deal closer to the cantonments in which the Territorials served, which I knew partly from earlier trips to India, though this would oblige me to visit stations I did not know – the main southern cantonment, Secunderabad; the main Bombay presidency station, Poona; the hill stations of Ootacamund, Dehra Dun and Naini Tal. A further trip to India in December 2015, to launch *Die in Battle*, enabled me to consult all the relevant available records in the National Archives of India, to capture newspapers in the National Library of India, Kolkata, and to visit several stations, such as Lebong, near Darjeeling, where the 1/5th Queen's Own Royal West Kent had been stationed in 1915. As I had demonstrated through my 2008 book,

---

3   Some sources claimed that three 'Territorial' battalions of the Rifle Brigade, the 18th, 23rd and 24th went to India. They did; but not as Territorials.

A Stout Pair of Boots, a guide to battlefield research, I have a firm conviction that historians need to visit the places about which they write. This project had, after all, germinated before Territorials' headstones in cantonment cemeteries.

Initial research offered promising signs. Even working at a distance (and in my spare time while I got on with more pressing commitments) I found that the on-line catalogues of the big London national museums proved rewarding. While Territorial units in India did not maintain war diaries while overseas until entering operational theatres of war (of which more presently) the National Archives and the British Library hold records shedding light on the higher direction of the Territorial Force (for example, through the records of the Army Council and the India Office's files). The Imperial War Museums and the National Army Museum between them hold over a hundred individual collections relating to specific Territorial units with Indian service, and to India in the Great War generally. Correspondence with regimental museums and county archives held out the prospect of a similar magnitude of sources, including many photographic albums, which I believed would disclose insights that written sources might not offer. Fortunately, late in 2014 I obtained a grant from my university that would enable me to spend a month in Britain in 2015, and my university generously allowed me to take up the opportunity to spend several weeks in Britain in 2016, so I could count on having the wherewithal to visit all of the regimental or county museums or archives holding relevant material.[4]

Meanwhile, again by drawing largely on the resources available through the internet, I was able to establish not just that printed primary sources existed, but was able to obtain them directly. The satirical magazine *Punch*, for example, became available digitally just as I began serious research. It soon disclosed not only that a Territorial officer had written a series of articles describing his unit's voyage to India and the first year of its Indian service, but the articles could be printed. Likewise *The Times* Digital Archive gave entrée to many articles that revealed when Territorials in India intruded into the consciousness of Britons. *The Times's* columns dealt not just with official pronouncements (such as in 1915 when the War Office recognised that Indian service entailed unforeseen costs for both officers and men) but also when relatives in Britain lobbied on behalf of men who often felt that they had been duped into signing on for 'Imperial Service' when they were obliged to remain in India, not to serve on the Western Front, as many believed that they had been promised, and were obliged to remain in India long after the war's end. Parliamentary Papers (available on open shelves in the National Library of Australia) provided valuable official records, while the State Library of Victoria held rare Indian items, a relic of the time when a public library in Melbourne aspired – and could afford – to document

---

4 Because most infantry came from the Wessex or Home Counties Divisions, most relevant regimental museums are located across southern England. The exceptions are the South Wales Borderers (Brecon), the King's Shropshire light Infantry (Shrewsbury) and the Border Regiment (Carlisle).

the empire. Their holdings included *Our Indian Empire*, the booklet distributed to troops destined for India to inform them of India, its peoples, religions and customs, including glossaries of useful phrases and a 'what turban is that?' section. Finally, a huge digital data base of 'trench and troopship serials of the Great War' included, fortuitously the regimental magazines of several Territorial battalions in India – *The Braganza* (the Queen's Regiment), *The Londoner* (1/25th Londons), *Invicta* (1/1Kent Cyclists) and the *Royal Sussex Herald* (2/6th Royal Sussex, published in Bangalore). Similar magazines may exist in other regimental collections.

Australian newspapers of the period (which are searchable through the National Library of Australia's 'Trove' data base) disclosed not only occasional reports on Territorials in India, distributed across the empire by wire services, but also the presence in Sydney of at least two detachments of Territorials, of Devons and King's Shropshire Light Infantry. Both were escorting German internees to camps in Australia, but the KSLI company became caught up in the notorious St Valentine's Day protest in 1916, when thousands of Australian Imperial Force recruits objecting to being obliged to train for longer 'working' hours briefly took over Sydney's streets in before order was restored. The Shropshire Territorials stood to but were not called upon to intervene.[5]

By mid-2015 the project seemed to have reached the 'stake-off' stage. A trip to Britain in May-June enabled me to drill a 'test-well', consulting about half of the forty-odd collections it holds relating to Territorials in India. They comprised a great range, from odd letters to substantial memoirs and diaries, to the papers of civilians living in India at the time, taking in both officers and other ranks, from the Royal Artillery and from seven infantry regiments, and some civilians. Exposure to these sources provided both reassurance – the idea of a book on Territorials in India was clearly feasible – and it helped to develop some of the themes, ideas and above all questions that I had begun to formulate. Surveying some of the sources I consulted helped to identify some of the questions and themes I pursued in approaching the over 200 further unofficial sources in other national collections, regimental and county collections that I consulted in 2015.

The 'Indian' Territorials' service outside India remains a matter for consideration in framing both the research and the book. Tracing the service of individual battalions (mainly from regimental histories) it became clear that while a dozen Territorial battalions remained in India for the entire war, most others left for service elsewhere. The elsewhere included mainly Mesopotamia – the first drafts and transfers left in 1915, and most Territorial units, infantry and artillery, ended up there eventually. Some of the first Territorials sent to Mesopotamia were to be captured in the disastrous and tragic fall of Kut-el-Amara; others endured the trials of the miserable winters and hot summers of Mesopotamia. Territorial units also went to Palestine in 1917. Several

---

5   See Peter Stanley, *Bad Characters: Sex, Crime, Mutiny, Murder and the Australia Imperial Force* (Sydney: Murdoch/Pier 9, 2010), pp. 59-60.

served in Aden, including the 1/1st Brecknockshire Battalion (of the South Wales Borderers), the only non-English Territorial unit to serve in India. This process, along with rotation of units going to Aden, continued through 1916, 1917 and 1918.

Some Territorial units had very adventurous wars. The 1/4th King's Shropshire Light Infantry in Rangoon was ordered in January 1915 to disarm an Indian infantry battalion of the local garrison which was threatening mutiny. Soon after, the mutiny among the 5th Light Infantry in Singapore saw the KSLI sent there, and it was this unit that found one of its companies in Sydney, facing further military protest. The most wide-ranging Territorial Force unit sent to India was the 1/9th (Cyclist) Battalion of the Hampshire Regiment, which, though originally destined for East Africa sailed for India in February 1916. (It was some of its graves, in Ferozepore cantonment cemetery, bearing the battalion's 'bicycle wheel' badge that had alerted me to the possibilities offered by the story of Territorials in India.) In October 1918 it went to Vladivostok, travelling by the Trans-Siberian railway 4,500 miles westward as far as west as Ekaterinberg in May 1919 (where the Russian royal family had been murdered the previous July). The battalion re-embarked from Vladivostok in November 1919 and returned to Southampton in December 1919.

A relevant question is: to what extent should this book tell the story of Territorial units that served in India and then went on to other stations and theatres, stories which have largely not been told with an emphasis on the Territorials? While the Mesopotamian debacle is notorious, the later victories, much less the messy aftermath of the war in central Asia, are less familiar, and the particular service of Territorials in Mesopotamia is largely unknown still. Likewise the service of the Aden brigade, which saw low level but arduous service throughout the war. But how much of a book on Territorials in India should be devoted to their contribution elsewhere? This question will need to be solved through encounters with the records, but my provisional decision is to deal with the Mesopotamian, Aden and Siberian aftermath relatively briskly, to complete the story of the 'Indian' Territorials' war.

The Great War did not end neatly with the Armistice. In 1919 several Territorial battalions, most by that time veterans of Indian service, took part in the third Anglo-Afghan war. That episode is certainly part of the story of their 'Imperial Service'. Indeed, it bears out the value of sending Territorial Force units to India. The war saw the involvement of Indian Army units (mostly comprising wartime recruits, the regulars mostly serving in Mesopotamia still), Territorials and some of the eight British regular battalions that remained in India throughout the war. These units, which were regarded as the irreducible minimum to ensure the internal and external security of British India, could be seen as either the most fortunate battalions of the old British army, or the most unlucky, because they were obliged to remain in India while their counterparts were destroyed at Ypres, Gallipoli, the Somme and at Ypres again. Though not Territorials, these battalions are a part of their story, because they provided the experienced men who were drafted to the newcomers' units to introduce them to the Indian Army's ways.[6]

How should such a book be structured? There is, of course, no one ideal structure, but in my experience books emerge from an interplay between the questions around which the enquiry is farmed and exposure to the sources. One influences the other: the more sources an historian locates, the more questions they suggest; but also the more evidence they generate to respond to those starting questions and the more they help to shape the experience into a satisfactory narrative. In the case of the Territorials' service in India, some of the broader organising themes have emerged quite early. The book is clearly going to deal with the task of garrisoning imperial India, the challenge the Great War imposed, the decision to send Territorial troops there, the men's decisions to volunteer for 'Imperial Service' and the voyage to India. It will have to deal with the troops' initial reactions to the country and its people, the nature of their service, their interaction with India's people and the politics of wartime India. The end of the book is reasonably clear too. Saving that the boundaries of what it includes or does not include are still undefined, it will certainly have to deal with the Territorials' service in the Third Anglo-Afghan war, the protracted and messy transfer of India back to the regulars, their return to Britain and the effects of Indian service on Territorial units and their former members. This much is reasonably clear. What is not at present particularly clear is 'the middle bit': what Territorial units actually did in India: how their members lived in cantonments; how they got on with each other, with the Indians they encountered from day-to-day and the British civil community; how they coped with illness and death, with distance and homesickness; with their role as imperial policemen.

Here exposure to the sources begins to help. Let me discuss some of the insights offered by reading twenty-odd collections in the Imperial War Museums' Research Room in May-June 2015. They helped to point to these and other seemingly fruitful questions. I will discuss them more or less in the order in which I encountered them.

Mrs. J.S. Tait, the wife of an official at Bangalore, kept a diary-cum-scrapbook that offers varied and detailed insights into the Territorials' relationship with India's British civil community. Bangalore's British civilians seemed representative of many cantonment communities in organising recreational and welfare opportunities for soldiers. This may have seemed routine in comparison to philanthropic efforts in Britain or the dominions – Australian newspapers are full of reports of refreshment or recreation rooms staffed by middle-class women. British India was no different, it seemed: except that the British community had never had any close relationship

---

6   The regular battalions that remained in India comprised the 2nd King's (Liverpool), the 2nd Somerset Light Infantry, the 1st Green Howards, the 1st Duke of Wellington's, the 1st Royal Sussex, the 1st South Lancs, the 2nd North Staffords and the 1st Durham Light Infantry. Note that, coincidentally, all were English county regiments, two of which had Territorial battalions also in India.

with the long-service regular troops who had formerly comprised India's garrison. 'Before the Great War', Mrs. Tait noted, 'the idea of entertaining private Soldiers was unknown'.[7] Territorials' letters and diaries make the same point. The diary and letters of Walter Saunders, who arrived in Fort William with the 1/10th Middlesex in late 1914 thought that Calcutta civilians 'considered the regular soldier as someone on the level with the lowest caste native'.[8]

Many Territorials' diaries and letters dwell, especially early in their service, on the novelty and discomfort of India's climate. Even arriving in the cold weather of 1914-15 Cyril Burgess wrote of the 'the heat is intense, ... like treading on red hot bricks'.[9] Gunner F.E. Tipper wrote of regretting volunteering to remain on the plains for his first hot weather in 1915 and then of how in the following monsoon 'it started to rain and did not stop till we got to Dehra Dun wet through ... [in barracks] and it came through the roof but it did not matter because we were already wet'.[10] The rhythms of hot weather, monsoon and cold weather punctuate their letters and diaries. Many moved station with a change of season, and those obliged to remain in the plains through the summer received and deserved the commiserations of their more fortunate comrades off to the Hills.

Green to Indian service, the Territorials were coached by regulars seconded from the eight regular battalions that remained in India throughout the war. The newcomers were beset by administrative snarls ('no pay has turned up', a Somerset Light Infantry private complained in the weeks following his arrival) but learned the ropes from old India hands. The Somerset private was soon confiding to his diary that 'we are getting more like regulars every day'.[11] Early in 1915 all the Territorial battalions faced the exacting 'Kitchener tests' in which they faced inspections of their musketry, marching, interior economy and not least their proficiency in maneuvers in the field. (One of the challenges of research has been to trace the relevant official documents. While the holdings of the National Archives of India are rich and extensive, they do not so far appear to include the records of inspection reports of Territorial battalions, nor the files documenting when and why units were posted around India.)

Several collections of Territorials' papers disclose how battalions functioned as social entities. For example, A.E. Serle kept the records of the 1/4th Devonshires' Athletic and Recreation Club at Ferozepore in 1915.[12] Its committee comprised all 31 officers of the battalion, an executive committee of seven officers and NCOs and sub-committees for rugby, association football hockey and cricket. It held about forty football games and as many hockey matches over the cold weather months, as well as inter-company billiards and whist tournaments. Further committees organised

7   IWM, Doc 9772, P394 Mrs. AS [actually J.S.] Tait.
8   IWM, 79/15/1, Walter Saunders, 10th Middlesex.
9   IWM, Doc. 6711, 97/26/1, Pte Cyril Burgess, 1/5th Buffs.
10   IWM, Doc. 13590 05/53/1 Gnr F.E. Tipper, Royal Field Artillery.
11   IWM, Doc. 15428, 07/8/1, Lt Herbert Ewing 1/5th Somerset Light Infantry.
12   IWM, Doc 7350, 76/154/1, Pte A.E. Searle, 1/4th Devons.

a parallel program of vocal and instrumental concerts, a 'Nigger Minstrel Troupe', and 'miscellaneous and variety entertainment'. The cultural life of many battalions encompassed magazines, debating societies, drama troupes and natural history groups, in which Territorial battalions resembled mechanics' institutes in uniform.

The relationship between the Territorials and the political changes India experienced during the war were sharpened by the fact that Frederick Thesiger, later Lord Chelmsford, served as Viceroy 1916-21. He had arrived in India with a Devon Territorial battalion in India, was appointed to succeed Lord Hardinge and in 1918 presided over the 'Montagu-Chelmsford' reforms that effectively conceded the prospect of self-government, which in thirty years became the reality of independence. But the Territorials' presence may have heralded broader changes. While browsing in a bookshop in Kolkata early in 2014 I came upon Nirad Chaudhuri's *The Autobiography of an Unknown Indian*, one of the classic texts articulating and responding to the changes British and Indians experienced in India. I was immediately struck by a passage, in which Chaudhuri, a Bengali student, recounted his impressions of Calcutta just as the Territorials arrived at Fort William:

> At the end of 1914 I began to notice in the Eden Gardens and on the Maidan the presence of British soldiers of a new and very attractive type, who not only wore a more pleasant shade of khaki, but were also very much younger and more refined looking than the old Regulars. ... Their usually solemn expression suggested a dreamy unworldliness which I had not expected on Indian faces...[13]

Chaudhuri found it 'so natural and so easy to idealize' these men. Did they notice and did they react to India's national aspirations, I wondered? (While 'Kitchener' battalions did not formally go to India, some seventeen 'Garrison' battalions went to India from late 1915, and they included men who had joined as wartime volunteers.) The examples offered here are just a fraction of the dozens of Territorial collections that have lain largely unused in regimental and other collections. The research I am presently undertaking in regimental, county and national museums and archives will, I hope, answer this and the many other questions I have about what may be the last major aspect of the British experience of the Great War that remains almost entirely untreated by research.

---

13   Nirad Chaudhuri, *The Autobiography of an Unknown Indian* (London: Macmillan, 1951), pp. 316-17.

14

Tiger by the Tail: Demobilization of the Indian Army of War, 1918-1923

Anirudh Deshpande

Introduction

It is believed that the 'classical period' in the history of the colonial Indian Army came to an end with the outbreak of the Great War in 1914[1]. Towards the closure of this 'classical period' the Indian Army, in comparison with the international standards prevalent at the time, would have reminded a casual observer of the nineteenth century and the military mission of Victorian England in the vast khaki landscape of India. This relic of the past comprised a regular standing force of some 200,000 infantry and cavalry drawn largely from the so called martial races of India. In fact the Indian Army came into existence after the three separate Presidency Armies were merged and re-organized into a single entity in 1895. The equipment of this Indian Army was outdated and, following the upheaval of 1857, it was deprived of artillery except some light mountain batteries which posed no threat to the British garrison in India. When the Indians, clad in field *khaki*, landed in France in 1914 they had to be issued the latest weapons and appropriate clothing suitable for combat operations in Europe[2]. In 1914, and even in 1918, the commissioned officers of the Indian Army were British with the exception of the Indian officers of the Indian Medical Service and those later commissioned at Daly College, Indore. Indians, both educated and uneducated, were kept out of the commissioned ranks of the Indian Army but the ranks of the junior officers like the Non-commissioned officers (NCOs) and Viceroy commissioned officers (VCOs) were open to the Indians. The Indian Army, till 1914,

---

1   T. A. Heathcote, *The Indian Army: The Garrison of British Imperial India, 1822-1922* (London: David & Charles, 1974), prologue.
2   Frederick William Perry, *The Commonwealth Armies: Manpower and Organization in the two world wars* (Manchester: Manchester University Press, 1988), pp. 84-87.

was geared almost exclusively to the task of frontier warfare on the Indo-Afghan border and its leaders thought that its main enemies, most probably backed by Russia, would invade India through the passes like the Khyber Pass. When the First World War began in 1914 this volunteer colonial Indian army was thrust into the scenario of total war for the first time. Unlike the Second World War the First World War, at least during its initial stages, commanded a great deal of popular enthusiasm in Europe. In India the declaration of war, and the subsequent expansion of recruitment, was viewed by the usually cash starved people as a great employment opportunity. The Indian nationalists wholeheartedly supported the Raj during the war for two reasons. First, they expected substantial political concessions, including a British commitment to Indian self-rule, from London and Delhi after the war. Second, they perceived the war as an opportunity for thousands of Indians to receive military training and thereby regain a manhood denied to them by the conditions of colonial subjection prevalent in India. Since the late nineteenth century the disarmament of Indians by the colonial state had drawn criticism from the nationalists on a variety of grounds. Gandhi's record, beginning with his activities during the wars fought by the British imperialists in South Africa against the Boers and Zulus, in the field of supporting the British during wars was consistent till 1918 and our attention to this facet of this apostle of non-violence has recently been drawn by Arundhati Roy in a brilliant essay[3].

The war was also seen as an opportunity to rise up the social ladder by the representatives of those communities, like the *Mahars* of Maharashtra and *Mazhbi* Sikhs of the Punjab, whose members had once been part of the colonial Indian military[4]. The *Mahars*, in fact, never forgot the conspicuous role they had played in ensuring a British victory over a ponderous *Peshwa* army during the famous battle of Koregaon in 1818[5]. The demand for raising a *Mahar* Regiment was quite old and was finally met during the Second World War. After the Second Afghan War, and more due to the influence of the 'martial races' theory, soldiers from these low caste communities had been weeded out of the Indian Army in the decades preceding the Great War. During the Great War the leaders of these communities, who had opposed the upper caste domination of military recruitment in India for a long time, urged the British to resume recruitment from among them. In these circumstances recruiting hundreds of thousands of volunteers in India created no difficulty for the colonial state. Egged on by their leaders the various Indian communities eagerly stepped forward to claim a share in the recruitment pie. War propaganda reached the remote corners of

3   Introduction to B. R. Ambedkar, *Annihilation of Caste*, (New Delhi: Navayana, 2014).
4   The connection between military service and social mobility during the colonial period in the case of the *Mahars* and *Mazhbi* Sikhs is explored in Ardythe Basham, *Untouchable Soldiers (The Mahars and the Mazhbis)* (Delhi: Gautam Book Centre, 2008), (edited by Bhagwan Das).
5   The Battle of Koregaon, with its multidimensional historical implications, has recently been re-visited in Anirudh Deshpande, 'Pride, Dust and Glory – The Third Anglo-Maratha War', *Outlook*, 18th Anniversary Issue, November, 2013.

the country and even the tribal communities of the North East demonstrated their enthusiasm for wartime recruitment. The Indian Army of war raised between 1914 and 1918 was the largest volunteer army in India to date and would be surpassed in numbers only during the Second World War[6]. Between 1914 and 1918 Indian troops fought, and were killed, in large numbers in Flanders, Gallipoli and Mesopotamia. The fighting abilities of the Indians were almost universally recognized and praised and the military capabilities of several Indian communities, hitherto kept out of the peace time army, were discovered or re-discovered on the battlefields stretching from the frozen plain of Flanders to the scorching deserts of Mesopotamia. When the war finally ended in 1918 expectations were running high among the Indian soldiers and leaders. This made the task of post-war demobilization difficult for the British. Several promises related to constitutional reform in India had been made to the Indians during the war. The war time volunteers desired rewards in proportion to the services they had rendered the Raj. The kin of the dead could not be left unattended and the wounded required special attention. In 1918 the British won the war, with American assistance it may be added, but within a year, as this paper shows, the danger of losing the peace in India became palpable[7].

Problems of demobilization

The Indian Army was an organization created in consonance with the British colonial needs of the nineteenth century. Although the Nicholson Committee, under Field Marshal Nicholson, had been established to suggest measures to reform and modernize the Indian Army in 1912, before its recommendations could be taken up the Imperial Government the war broke out[8]. To its credit, the Indian Army gave a fair account of itself during the Great War because of improvisations in its organization and improvement in its equipment, wherever possible. The Indian Army was not geared to participate in a world war in 1914 and its expansion during 1914-18, as mentioned earlier, was unprecedented. Therefore, the first major task of the military planners in British India in 1918-19 was to reduce this army of war to peace time status as rapidly as possible in order to balance the budget and trim military expenditure. To streamline the functioning of the Indian Army, post hostilities, the 4 Command

---

6   This has been examined in detail by Anirudh Deshpande, *British Military Policy in India, 1900-1945 Colonial Constraints and Declining Power* (Delhi: Manohar, 2005).
7   For more on this see V. Longer, *Red Coats to Olive Green: A History of the Indian Army 1600-1974* (New Delhi: Allied, 1981); Stephen Cohen, *The Indian Army* (New Delhi: OUP, 1990); David Omissi, *The Sepoy and the Raj: The Indian Army 1860-1940* (London: Macmillan, 1994); P. S. Gupta and Anirudh Deshpande (eds.), *The British Raj and its Indian Armed Forces 1857-1947* (New Delhi: OUP, 2002); Kaushik Roy (ed.), *War and Society in Colonial India* (New Delhi: OUP, 2006).
8   On Nicholson see T. A. Heathcote, *The British Field Marshals 1736-1997 A Biographical Dictionary* (Barnsley: Pen and Sword, 2012).

System and a new distribution of troops was evolved. The Indian Army was divided into 4 Commands; North, West, South and East. The troops were classified into three kinds; Covering Troops, Field Army and Internal Security Troops. The Covering Troops were expected to handle minor frontier outbreaks and raise a screen behind which a general mobilization for war would occur. The need for these troops arose when the Border Militias, comprising sections of the pro-British tribesmen of the frontier, defected to the Afghan side during the Third Afghan War of 1919. The Field Army of 4 Infantry Divisions and 5 Cavalry Brigades, compared with 9 Infantry Divisions and 8 Cavalry Brigades before 1914, constituted the main strike force of the Indian Army. This was a smaller but better equipped force and it was stated that the provision of modern equipment and adequate ancillary support for the Field Army would be 'an obvious and paramount necessity.'[9] The first thing to do in the process of demobilization was to scale down the army to peacetime proportions without sacrificing the efficiencies gained during the Great War. This had to be done when from 'the purely military point of view, of course, retrenchment was unwelcome' in a country ruled by force by the British[10]. Tremendous expansion had taken place during the Great War and among the wartime additions to the Indian military establishment were units of the Royal Air Force, Mechanical Transport and Signals, Artillery and an expanded Staff and Commands. There was no point in giving all this up because of financial reasons. Further, political and military developments following the Armistice in India militated against retrenchment. The Bolshevik Revolution had succeeded and stabilized in Russia in 1917-1920, the Third Afghan War began in 1919 soon after the European War ended in 1918 stoking Russophobia once again, thousands of Indian troops were stationed in Mesopotamia and in India civil disturbances were threatening to get out of hand. These historical developments queered the pitch for swift demobilization which was necessary to stabilize the mounting deficits of the Government of India in 1918-20.

The principles of the reorganization of the Army in India following the lessons taught by the Great War to the British were presented in the recommendations of the Esher Committee. This politically conscious, though conservative, committee advocated a policy of cautious reform and no radical break from the established traditions of the Indian Army. In the event, and given the precarious financial condition of the Government of India in 1922-23, even the modest recommendations of the Esher Committee were swept away by the urgent and severe measures of retrenchment imposed on the government by the Inchcape Committee (Retrenchment Committee of 1923).[11] The Great War demonstrated that the armaments of an army often played

---

9   Historical Section, Ministry of Defence, New Delhi, *The Army in India and its Evolution, Including an Account of the Establishment of the RAF in India* (Calcutta: Government of India, 1924), pp. 35-3.
10 *Ibid.*, p. 36.
11 For details of reform and retrenchment following the Great War see Deshpande's contribution in P. S. Gupta and Anirudh Deshpande (eds.), *The British Raj and its Indian*

a decisive role in a modern war. The post 1918 army in India was naturally supposed to be a leaner and fitter army compared with its animal transport dependent obsolete ancestor of the 19th century. Thus it was decided that to maintain the increase in firepower gained by the Indian Army during the war its units would be provided armament similar to the kind possessed by its European counterparts. This was easier said than done because soon the planners realized that it was 'practicable' in Indian conditions to adopt a 'lower and more economical scale of provision' in the Indian Army battalions compared with the British battalions. We might also infer a political motive behind this because of the threat posed to the Indian Army by the nationalist rebellion of 1920-22; the circumstances prevalent in India during 1919-1922 easily revived the memories of 1857. Mechanizing the Indian Army in the 1920s was hence fraught with economic and political dangers. The following example illustrates the point. The Great War made the heavy and light machine gun the dominating weapons of the infantry and yet these were kept in short supply to the Indian Army. An infantry battalion on war footing of the British Army was issued 8 heavy machine guns and 34 Lewis light machine guns. In comparison the Indian battalion had to make do with 4 heavy and 16 light machine guns – this meant that in the event of an Indian mutiny the Indian battalion would not stand up to its British adversary.[12] British battalions stationed in India with their full equipment were paid for by the Indian taxpayer.

Due to retrenchment the Army in India in 1923 was smaller than the army of 1914. Despite the disturbed conditions in the country the government managed to reduce the strength of the standing British and Indian troops in India by 18,286 and 18,856 respectively by 1923. General Rawlinson accepted these reductions as an expedient measure to balance the military budget in the difficult times of the 1920s. Official histories of the Indian Army justify the reductions imposed on the Army in India by retrenchment on economic grounds and by suggesting that a reduction in manpower was necessary to free money for technological improvements. Whether all this happened in the interwar period has been examined elsewhere[13]. The reduction in regular troops appears striking when we compare the combatant levels of the Indian Army in 1914 and 1918. However the reduction in British troops was more than made up by the increase in the firepower of the British battalions which could be used mercilessly against an unarmed civil rebellion. In the event of a general uprising the RAF, a British monopoly, could also be pressed into service, as it was in the north west of India following the Great War.

Armed Forces 1857-1947 (New Delhi: OUP, 2002).
12 *The Army in India and its Evolution*, pp. 43-44.
13 Anirudh Deshpande, 'Change by Committee: subjective reform and incomplete modernization of the colonial Indian armed forces (1857-1939)', paper presented at the International Seminar – Renewing the Military History of Colonial South Asia, Jadavpur University, Calcutta, 20-21 January, 2014.

The political economy of demobilization

The end of the Great War was marked by large scale mutinies in almost all the armies which were bled white by it. There were mass mutinies in the German Army and soldiers' councils sprang up in many places in Germany. Large scale mutinies in the Imperial Russian Army turned the tide in favor of the Bolsheviks who seized power in November, 1917 knocking Russia out of the War. The Bolshevik Revolution affected the German army, navy and workers and created a revolutionary situation in Germany in 1918-19. There were mutinies in the French Army too and there was reason to believe that all these events were capable of inspiring mass insubordination in the Indian Army. Discontent in the army and among the civilian population in India was serious enough for the British to contemplate harsh measures against their colonial subjects in 1918. Hardly had the dust of the Great War settled in India when the Punjab Disturbances, as a reaction to the draconian Rowlatt Act, broke out and turned the Indian nationalists against the colonial state from 1919 onwards. The repression of 1918-19 was justifiably seen as an act of government betrayal by the Indians whose hopes had been aroused on multiple counts by the promises made by the British during the War. The surge of mass nationalism (1919-22) could not have come at a more inopportune moment for the colonial state because these were also the years when thousands of war time recruits were being discharged from the Indian Army. Many of these would return to their villages but a substantial number were expected to stay on and suffer in the cities in search of jobs. The opposition to the British sharpened, and threatened the loyalty of the Muslim soldiers of the Indian Army, when the pan-Islamic Khilafat Movement joined hands with Gandhi's Non-Cooperation. The events in the Punjab had unsettled the Sikhs no end and serious mutinies in the Indian Army were therefore expected any time. In October 1921 Gandhi and some Non-Cooperators signed a manifesto according to which it was sinful for Indians to join the colonial Indian Army. This manifesto coincided with the peak of the nationalist movement and alarmed the British no end. Reports also came in of sporadic nationalist attempts made to tamper with the loyalty of the Indian Army. In the *Young India* of 29th September, 1921, Gandhi appealed to the jawans to leave the army and take to weaving *khadi*. Further, Indian troops were expressly requested not to participate in the wrongdoings of a government which had lost the legitimacy to rule the country. The language referring to military service changed completely with the change in the mood of the political leadership. The government was repeatedly accused by the nationalists of using the Indian troops as 'hired assassins' to subjugate the Asian people in general and Gandhi asked the soldiers to leave military service 'at once' if they could support themselves.[14] Fortunately for the colonial state this nationalist propaganda did not lead to the establishment and

---

14   NAI, Secret Simla Records 1 F.NO.303, Se. Nos. 1-48, 1921, GOI, Home Department Political 1921, No. 303 of 1921, Hom/Pol.

development of nationalist organizations within the Indian Army as it did during and after the Second World War. Yet the officials considered the situation serious.

The fact that the official fear of civil unrest spreading to the armed forces was exaggerated was proved during the massive unrest of 1919-21 when the Indian Army remained loyal in general to the British. Indian troops in large numbers were deployed on the Frontier in 1919-20 and against the Moplah Rebellion in the Malabar in 1921-22. At the same time attempts at establishing a Territorial Force met with notable success and in the Madras Presidency the number of applicants so 'largely' exceeded the proposed establishment of this force that the formation of second battalion was soon considered[15]. Nonetheless the Indian response to nationalist propaganda was mixed. It was reported that a great deal of nationalist and *khilafat* literature had permeated the lines in most areas of the country and was keeping the troops animated. There were various organizations and 'agitators' busy dissuading men from joining the post war army as regulars needed to replace the men who retired annually. In Peshawar, for instance, it was reported that the Mullahs were issuing *fatwas* against enlistment and in the Punjab and NWFP several areas reported an actual decline in recruitment for the post-war army. The agitation against the colonial state and its armed forces had become serious and organized with several areas reporting the setting up of anti-enlistment committees. Such committees, often led by local nationalists, appeared in the villages around Jalandhar in November, 1920. In Ferozpur in April, 1921 a Subedar reportedly told a Superintendent of Police that Indian troops would fire on Indians only in the event of being fired upon. As the nationalist movement spread and deepened rumors of British excesses against disobedient Indian soldiers gripped the imagination of the Punjab peasants. From that militarily important province news poured in of the Sikhs coming under the twin influence of nationalism and the rising Akali movement. During the summer of 1921 in and around Amritsar ex-subedars and Sikh jawans were sometimes found openly expressing their desire to rebel against the government in the event of a political breakdown occasioned by nationalism and its repression by the state. The land hungry Sikhs were particularly angry with the colonial state for a number of reasons the least of which was the denial of settlement rights in East Africa and possibly the fertile parts of the Middle East:

> Upon returning to the Punjab many Sikh soldiers found a place in the growing Akali movement, and swelled its ranks with disciplined, trained fighters. The Akalis took special care to press their propaganda on Sikh soldiers on active duty. According to several British Officers, there was much trouble with infiltrators and sympathizers. After the Nankana Massacre in February 1921, black Akali safas (headbands) appeared in Sikh units. The Massacre was followed later in the same year by the affair of the 'Keys of the Golden Temple', and for the first time

---

15 India in 1921-22, A Statement prepared for presentation to the Parliament..., pp. 19-20.

in the history of this agitation recruiting officers reported difficulty in obtaining Jat Sikhs for the Army[16].

These developments caused great alarm to the British and revived the memories of 1857 even though the colonial state believed that it was doing the maximum for the demobilized soldiers in the Punjab. Yet, as the case of the territorial force demonstrates above, the peasantry's reaction to the nationalist and Akali demands was not uniform. While it may have been generally true that the recruitment of Sikhs and Punjabi Muslims was falling in the province in some districts contrary trends were visible. In several districts recruitment was satisfactory and the peasants seemed more affected by the practical benefits of military employment than the rhetoric of nationalist politics. Interestingly the temporary decline in recruitment for the post-war army was explained by an official source in the following words: 'Not many old soldiers are rejoining, but, although the demobilized *sepoys* allege many grievances, they are largely imaginary and it is more reasonable to suppose that they find village life more comfortable and often more profitable than drilling'.[17] In 1919 rumors unfavorable to the British position in the Afghan War were rife in the Punjab and a general belief that despite the end of the Great War there would be no peace seemed to have gained ground. Although the government tried its best to counter these beliefs by issuing contrary communiqués regularly some of its officers felt that mere propaganda was not doing its work and the time had come to tell the people the truth about the Afghan War and other matters[18].

Towards the beginning of 1920 parts of the Punjab had practically slipped out of government control and reports received from various places of the province indicated that 'racial passions' were 'inflamed' among the people in general. This gave rise to a 'great deal of excitement of an undesirable character in several places' in the province and matters had been made worse among the Muslims because the Ali Brothers, leaders of the *Khilafat* Movement, appealed to them not to assist the British in any way.[19] These leaders were 'determined to approach the Muhamaddan Police and the Army and ask them to refuse to fire on Muhammadans in any case or to fight any Muslim enemies of the Government.'[20] In these circumstances the rumors pertinent

16 Cohen, *The Indian Army*, p. 95. Sikh unrest in the Army is also noted in Ellinwood & Pradhan (eds.), *India and World War I* and T. A. Heathcote, *The Indian Army: The Garrison of British Imperial India*.
17 NAI, Delhi Records 1919 Government of India Home Department Political Deposit, Proceedings, July 1919, No. 51: Report on the Political Situation in the Punjab for the second half of July 1919, in connection with the recent disturbances, Index of Fortnightly Reports.
18 Ibid.
19 NAI, Simla Records 1920: Government of India Home Department Political Deposit Proceedings, February 1920, No. 52 Weekly Reports of the Director, Central Intelligence, for the month of January 1920.
20 Ibid.

to the Frontier Campaign in Waziristan gained currency and produced the short-lived anti-British *fatwas* mentioned earlier:

> Reports from various place in the Punjab – more especially in cities and town north of Rawalpindi and in close proximity to Bannu, Kohat and Dera Ismail Khan show that statements are current to the effect that the troops of the Sirkar are fairing badly in their fighting against the Mahsuds; that the Waziris have not been cowed down at all; that they are putting up a stubborn fight and that our losses are very heavy. These statements are coupled with others to the effect that the Bolsheviks have won victories all over the world; that they have gathered round their banner Muslim hordes of Central Asia; and that before long the Bolsheviks, the Afghans, the Turkomans, Tartars and the Persians will combine and attack India. The extremist maintain that the British forces will find it hard to cope with the invaders and that Indian troops, when they see the immense odds against themselves, will refuse to fight[21].

The nationalists, *Khilafat* agitators and sections of the media united against the British precisely at a moment when the state could have done with a bit of good press coverage. *Khilafat hartal* notices were prominent in several newspapers and forbade Muslims from either lending money or manpower to the British. Muslims were told not to recruit as sailors or soldiers destined to serve in Basra, Mesopotamia and other overseas places. Reports also poured in from the United Provinces, another important centre of Muslim and 'martial races' recruitment, of Indian soldiers 'fraternizing' with Gandhi and Shaukat Ali aboard a troop train while these two leaders travelled to the Punjab. The *Khilafat* leaders chose the targeted areas in the Punjab carefully. Districts and *tehsils*, like the area of Rawalpindi and Ludhiana, which had provided a large number of troops during the Great War were selected especially for the dissemination of an anti-British propaganda 'full of rank sedition and undiluted disloyalty.'[22] Appeals to serving and prospective soldiers were published alongside reports which alleged that the British had interfered with the Sikh religion in the Army. For instance the *Akali* of Amritsar (9 September, 1920) alleged that the officers of the Sikh Regiments and their devotees i.e. the subedars, had raised 'obstacles in the ways of the Sikhs in the unrestricted performance of their religious duties.' In Allahbad the *Independent* (13 September, 1921) reported a 'concentrated plan' of the nationalists against military recruitment in the United Provinces. The nationalists, according to this report, were preparing the grounds for a direct appeal to the soldiers to leave the Indian Army: 'If the Government would not bend to the popular will, the Congress would surely and

---

21 Ibid.
22 NAI, Simla Records 1920: Government of India Home Department Political Deposit Proceedings, February 1920, No. 52 Weekly Reports of the Director, Central Intelligence, for the month of January 1920, No, 110, for the month of August 1920.

unhesitatingly call upon the soldiers to withdraw from the service of the Government.' The media in the Madras Presidency also joined the chorus against military service. The nationalist newspaper *The Hindu* (22 September, 1921) published a piece which reported the anti-British speech made by Gandhi in Trichinopoly after the British had arrested the Ali brothers who seemed to have gone too far in their attempts to subvert the loyalty of the Indian Army by then[23]. In this publicized speech Gandhi made much of the fact that he himself had tampered several times with the loyalty of the jawans in the recent past and intended to do so in future to service the cause of *Swaraj*. Indian soldiers were once again asked not to serve the British. In fact shortly after this speech was reported Gandhi wrote an article 'Tampering with loyalty' in the *Young India* (29 September, 1921). In this article he claimed that the Congress had tried to tamper with the loyalty of the Indian troops since September, 1920 and it was his duty to 'spread disaffection openly and systematically' in India because the government had used the sepoy 'more often as a hired assassin than as a soldier defending the liberty or the honor of the weak and helpless.' Further he had not appealed to individuals to desert the military because of his own reasons: 'And if I have not asked individual sepoys to come out, it has not been due to want of will but of ability to support them. I have not hesitated to tell the sepoy, that if he could leave the service and support himself without the Congress or the Khilafat aid, he should leave at once.'

Faced with this powerful attack on the loyalty of the Indian soldier, upon whom the British Raj rested in the ultimate analysis, the Government of India launched a propaganda campaign to influence the Indian troops against the high tide of nationalism prevalent at the time. During 1921-22 a certain amount of success towards this end was reported: 'The military propaganda campaign during 1921-22 in the recruiting areas though inadequate to the needs of the moment had not been unsuccessful. It is difficult to obtain any definite evidence of results but such evidence as is available is sufficient to justify the extension of our programme for another year.'[24] State propaganda to counter the increasing influence of mass nationalism assumed a new importance in 1921-22 and several schemes were pursued by the government to keep the Indian troops contented despite the serious financial crisis faced by the officials. Twenty four Indian officers' associations were organized and selected British officers were sent on tours to the major recruitment areas with an allowance of 12000 rupees. A collection of pensioners was planned for the Prince of Wales' visit to India and a special fund was allocated to this. Serious attention was paid to the image of the army portrayed in the media, especially cinema whose popularity was growing in India. A touring cinema was organized by the recruiting officer of the Bangalore region with a modest outlay of rupees 300 per month to impress the recruits and their families. Though the various army associations organized by the

---

23 Ibid.
24 NAI, Home Department Political 1922 Part B Deposit Proceedings file no 225/11 Subject: Expenditure on Military Propaganda, Hom/Pol.

state were financed by subscriptions it was suggested that a government donation for them would be favorably considered. Throughout the early 1920s the anti-nationalist propaganda drives were meant to concentrate attention on the long established social props of the Raj and it was asserted with great confidence that the 'vast majority of old soldiers and Zemindar element are loyal and only need organizing, for their loyal sentiments to be made effective.'[25] The suggested private donation was a 100 rupees per annum for 1922-23 per association while the army asked for rupees 31,200 for propaganda work. The government found this propaganda work extremely useful and wanted it to be continued but expenditure on propaganda had to be supplemented with savings planned in the army after the Great War. However, things were easier said than done because of the financial crisis of the beleaguered colonial state in the early 1920s – estimates always faced the danger of erosion in case events took an unprecedented turn. Nonetheless, the demand of the army was met and rupees 31,200 were sanctioned for military propaganda during 1922-23.[26]

The government followed up these steps by announcing a number of important military reformist measures in 1921-22. These announcements were made to coincide with the Prince of Wales' highly publicized visit to India. In line with the Esher Committee Recommendations, the government paid special attention to the well-being of Indian troops during these years. To begin with, and to placate Indian opinion, the Prince of Wales inaugurated a Military College in Dehradun. This college was supposed to prepare selected Indian candidates for admission to Sandhurst 'on the lines of an English public school.' The foundations of a Kitchener College were also laid in Delhi with the intention of providing education of a 'High School type for sons of Indian officers.' Foundation stones were also laid down for two King George's Royal Indian Military Schools, one at Aurangabad Serai and another at Jalandhar, to impart education to the sons of Indian soldiers. Further, during 1921, the formation of an Indian Army Educational Corps was also sanctioned to supervise and develop educational standards in the Indian Army[27]. As far as military propaganda was concerned the money demanded was not too much and, given the political imperative underlining it, could be obtained even in the teeth of retrenchment. But when it came to more substantial concessions demanded by the peasantry the Finance Department put its foot down. It was one thing to find 200,000 rupees for the war widows of the Punjab and place it at the disposal of the Punjab Government but quite another to announce substantial remissions of revenue.[28]

After the Great War the demand for a 'general boon' had grown strong especially in those districts of India which had supplied the maximum number of wartime recruits.

---

25 Ibid.
26 NAI, File 225 V-Poll Hom-Poll, 1922: Grant for Military Propaganda, Hom/Pol.
27 India in 1921-22, A Statement prepared for presentation to the Parliament, p. 21.
28 NAI. Delhi Records 1919 GOI Home Dept Pol – Deposit, Proceedings May 1919, No.47, Hom/Pol.

Punjab, as usual, fuelled this demand although expectations of a general reward were reported running high in other provinces as well. The matter was grave because the Punjab, for reasons not necessary to mention here, turned out to be perhaps the most disturbed and rebellious region of British India in 1918-19. In such circumstances it was imperative to take steps to satisfy the well trained men who were returning from the war in droves. The visible effect of nationalist, *Akali* and *Khilafat* propaganda on many such men has been examined above. In general the 'one idea among the masses' was 'that we have been grossly ungrateful' was reported by J. Mackeig Jones to the Home Member Sir William Vincent from the Punjab. In the Punjab among the 'heaps' of *lambardars* [village headmen who wielded considerable influence over the recruits] and soldiers great discontent was visible and urgent measures were required to address this problem which threatened to get out of hand. The British knew that they were responsible for the growing disillusionment among the Punjab peasants to a large extent:

> Our praise of their help in war time had occasionally, perhaps, been immoderate, but it has got home, and the general feeling everywhere was that [the] Government was about to give some just reward. The present feeling among the people is of resentment and disappointment.[29]

Indeed nothing less than an act of an 'Oriental Monarch' appealing to the 'Oriental imagination' was necessary for win the trust of the masses in the atmosphere of distrust created immediately after the Great War. Nothing less than a proclamation remitting one month's land revenue across British India was called for and in fact the government was considering, on the basis of reports of discontent received from several parts of the country, a remission of land revenue for three months in those places from where recruits had flocked to the Indian Army in large numbers.[30]

The Finance Department was not unlikely to be swayed by references to an 'oriental imagination' prone to exaggeration in the colonial discourse. In the Punjab soon after the war several districts, villages and individuals had already been rewarded by remissions of revenue, extension of settlements and land grants to soldiers. Further, there was no precedent of announcing a general boon for the supporters of the British Raj because at the Delhi Durbar held before the war the boons given to the loyal elements among the Indians had excluded a general remission of land revenue. A general boon, which would go against precedent, would create a dangerous weapon which would be used to blackmail the government in future. The usual practice had

---

29 NAI. Simla Records 1919 GOI Home Dept. Political Deposit Proceesings, July 1919, No. 37: Suggestions for allaying the feelings of disappointment prevalent among the rural population of the Punjab and elsewhere at the absence of any announcement of some general boon as a reward for their services during the War, Hom/Pol.
30 Ibid.

been to make special grants of land or assignments of revenue or remissions of revenue in selected cases of long serving distinguished native officers. Despite the weight of tradition behind these arguments many sections within the government remained unconvinced. Numerous officers, obviously shaken by the unprecedented mass movement which was threatening the foundations of the Raj in 1919-20, believed that the times had changed and the Great War had been an exceptional event in the history of the Indian Army. The fact that the anti-British feeling was spreading rapidly in those regions which had done the maximum for the British during the War seemed to justify those who held that exceptional events demanded exceptional responses.[31]

The tension between the urgent need to satisfy the demobilized wartime recruits and regular soldiers and the economic limitations of the Raj surfaced clearly in the objections raised to a general boon by the Finance Department. It compared the proposed remission of land revenue with measures taken by the rulers during the days of Roman decadence to win over their disgruntled plebian subjects. With regard to a substantial increase in expenditure related to satisfactory demobilization the Finance Department raised two important points. First, it asked the military authorities whether such large expenditures were worth the advantages they promised to yield. Second, even before the contradiction between the moderate Esher Recommendations and retrenchment became apparent, it asked whether the finances of the country were in a position to meet such additional obligations. In the view of the Home Department, which was grappling with the rising discontent in the country, a general boon would help the 'rural classes' i.e. landlords, tenants and even the agricultural laborers. This was suggested in a context of rising nationalist influence in the countryside. The Finance Department was not convinced and retorted that the laborers as buyers of grains would in no way benefit from a remission of land revenue. On the other hand experience indicated that the tenants had fared much better due to the war time rise in grain prices. In fact, a remission would assist only those landlords who cultivated their own holdings and this was possible in some parts of the Punjab. Elsewhere the landlords were mostly absentees thriving on rents and a remission would only help them and not their tenants who paid rent. Indeed, the Finance Department asserted, there was no need to encourage further talk of remission in the case of 'notoriously oppressive landlords.' Since the structure of landholding and tenancy was different in Punjab, the United Provinces (UP) and other provinces a uniform policy of general remission, despite its political attractions in 1919, did not make sense. The Finance Department rounded off its argument by asking the government not to overlook these considerations while 'estimating the advantages which may be considered likely to accrue from the expenditure in question.'[32]

The Finance Department calculated the remission cost of 1/12th of land revenue in the Punjab and UP to the tune of 850000 rupees. This was unacceptable at a time

31   Ibid.
32   Ibid: Notes in the Finance Department, June 1919.

when the government of India was facing a great problem of balancing the budget. The receipts from the railways and customs were not as high as expected and the Afghan War, likely to cost 12.5 million rupees a month, had already pushed military spending beyond the budgetary allowances. Even on the assumption that the Afghan War would not last very long at least 60 million rupees over and above the budget had to be urgently found. Further, the agricultural situation was far from satisfactory and already additional *takawi* grants [grant in aid of desperate peasants] of 7.5 million rupees had been sanctioned in the Bombay Presidency where the condition of cultivators had turned grave. To make matters worse the government had to repay its 'floating and unproductive debt' incurred during the Great War. In such conditions it was highly probable that the burden of a 'general boon' would fall upon the Imperial revenues because neither of the local governments in question had expressed themselves in favor of such a measure.[33] The fact that the Imperial revenues, given the massive debt incurred by the British government during the Great War, were in no condition to lift this extra burden was not emphasized by the Finance Department.

There was a general belief in government circles that the Punjab had gained a lot from its participation in the Great War. The Finance Department was actually asking whether there was any point in giving it more. Large areas of the Punjab and the United Provinces had done well during the War because of the rising agricultural prices – a direct consequence of the increased wartime demand for food grains etc. This was evident in the voluminous absorption of currency and precious metals by these provinces in recent years – 340 million rupees ending 31 March, 1919. In the towns the traders had prospered though the working classes had suffered the consequences of inflation. At a time when the government servants, and quasi government servants, had been refused financial relief it was improper to dole out gifts to the Punjab and UP. Moreover, the government had to suppress the appetite for largesse which was insatiable in most cases. The government also had to see that the economic position of India was 'extremely unstable and precarious' and the order of the day was an adherence to 'rigid economy' as regards non-essential expenditure. After this warning the Finance Department summed up its arguments by quoting a passage from the conservative magazine *The Economist* of 10 May, 1919:

> The system of handing doles and grants to anyone who threatens to make himself sufficiently troublesome without them is radically bad and the Government ought to be prepared to face unpopularity rather than squander more of the public funds[34].

The point was not lost upon the Home Department which nonetheless underlined the importance of a concession to the sections of rural classes which had sent a large

33 Ibid.
34 Ibid.

number of recruits to the army. The matter could not only be governed by economic considerations. Above all these concessions were of paramount importance in view of the fact that exaggerated promises had been made to the recruits during the recruitment drives of the Great War. Further, the point that many of these men were lured into the army by 'extravagant promises' could not be overlooked. W.H. Vincent, the Home Member, underlined this:

> My point is that a very large number of men have been recruited for the army and military service generally from the Punjab and the United Provinces. There is reason to believe that many of these men were induced to enlist by extravagant promises, although such promises were not authorized, and it is certain that they all expected that they would be rewarded after the war; and not having received any such reward they are very sore and disappointed for they feel that their services have not been adequately compensated[35].

Despite the objections of the Finance Department Vincent desired the cooperation of the local governments in the case of remissions of land revenue. He also held that with the help of the Revenue and Agricultural Departments of the provinces concerned the government could see to it that the concessions reached the truly deserving people in the rural areas. The Home Department's plea was supported by the fact that in 1919 the Punjab government already enjoyed the discretion to reward good recruiting services by the remission of land revenue in numerous cases.[36]

The Finance Department's position on the matter of foregoing revenue was in line with the economic predicament of the government of India in 1919-20. According to the Finance Department a lot had already been done to satisfy the troops and it was an entirely different matter that many men in the Punjab felt otherwise. The demobilization process, objectively speaking, had greatly favored Punjab over other provinces for obvious reasons. The Punjab had the highest military participation ratio in India thanks to the *Punjabization* of the Indian Army which had gained ground from the 1880s and the theory of the 'martial races.' The demobilization scheme in the Punjab would cost the exchequer two million rupees alone. In the case of villages and sub-divisions of a village, remissions of land revenue amounted to a sum of 150000 per annum for a term of ten years. In the case of particular families or individuals, remissions or revenue assignments ranging between 10 and 250 rupees per year up to a total of 25,000 rupees per annum had been granted. Further, these remissions or assignments were to continue for the entire life of the grantees. In recognition of the exceptional services rendered by the rural population of the Rawalpindi and Jhelum districts, which boasted a recruiting record far above of the other districts of the province, the current settlement was extended from 20 to 30 years and this meant

---

35   Ibid – response of the Home Department.
36   Ibid.

a surrender of revenue in future. This measure was justified on economic grounds and was alone estimated to cost 3 million rupees. In addition to these concessions, there was also a scheme for colonizing an area of 178,000 acres in the Lower Bari Doab Canal region with former soldiers whose land hunger was proverbial. Till 1919 there had been a great delay in selecting these colonists from the several Punjab regiments but the government was confident that eventually the scheme would succeed and confer material benefits to 'many thousand soldiers.' In the North West Frontier Province the term of settlement of the Peshawar district was extended by 5 years. This concession was estimated to cost about 700,000 rupees and was granted as a reward for the good behavior of the Frontier people during the War years. In and around Delhi remissions of land revenue amounting to 26,891 rupees had been sanctioned to villages which had distinguished themselves in the supply of recruits. In the United Provinces land holders of districts under settlement in the Meerut division who were on active service during the War, or who had granted rental remissions to their tenants so that they would enlist, were to a proportionate extent exempted from enhancement of revenue during the period of the next settlement. In Bihar and Orissa, provinces not renowned for military recruitment in the early twentieth century, a remission of rent in the case of tenants on government estates to a maximum of 10 rupees for a period of ten years with effect from 1 April 1917 had been sanctioned but the concession was withdrawn from 1 April, 1919. In the Bombay Presidency a scheme for granting war remissions not exceeding 25 rupees per annum in respect of one individual and special rewards for certain villages which had rendered conspicuous service during the War in furnishing recruits was in operation[37].

Besides the measures listed above, the Provincial Governments had also sanctioned certain specific concessions. For example, the UP government had postponed the inception of settlement operations in the Garwhal district till the end of the War because of its good recruiting record. In the Gujarat district of the Punjab, the new revenue demand after the War was pitched low because it had provided a large number of soldiers. For similar reasons the term of revenue revision was fixed at 30 years for most of the district and, we believe, this was done to provide extra income to the peasants on the assumption that agricultural prices would remain buoyant in the foreseeable future. In addition to the relaxations offered in the field of revenue collection and tenures land grants, *jagirs* and *jangi* pensions (special war pension) were given to the VCOs and soldiers because the loyalty of the troops depended, foremost, upon the contentment of these men. On the basis of such information received the Finance Department concluded that the recruits and their villages had been liberally rewarded and nothing more was needed[38]. In sum, at the end of the Great War 420,000 acres of land were distributed among 5,902 VCOs and Indian other ranks (IOR). In the Punjab the scale of allotment of 2 squares (an unspecified measure of land) to a

37 Ibid.
38 Ibid.

VCO, 1 square to an IOR and 0.5 square to a follower. In the provinces where land was less fertile than in Punjab proportionately a larger unit of land, with the same annual income, was granted to the demobilized soldiers. Another cash reward called the *jangi inaam* was also given[39]. It was granted to 14,100 men for two lives with the following details. The VCOs received 10 rupees/month, IORs rupees 5/month and the followers got 2 rupees 8 annas /month. Two hundred *jagirs* were awarded to specially selected VCOs for distinguished services. These *jagirs* and endowments comprised grants of land with full proprietary rights yielding a net annual income of 400 rupees or an assignment of land revenue for 3 lives in the following order. For the first life 600 rupees/month, second life 300 rupees/month and 150 rupees/month for the third life were granted. Two hundred honorary King's commissions were granted to select VCOs the majority of whom were Risaldar/Subedar Majors about to be discharged from service. These men carried the pay of the rank of a King's Commissioned Officer while still on the active list and double the normal pension of the VCOs on retirement.[40] By all means, and compared with the number of men enlisted during the Great War and the promises made to them, these rewards were modest at best and most likely to cause widespread resentment.

Conclusion

The volunteer army raised by the British in India during the Great War was the largest ever in modern history until it was surpassed during the Second World War. Indians enthusiastically answered the call of recruitment between 1914 and 1918 because of a variety of reasons. The economic reason for a normally cash starved Indian peasant to join the Indian Army as a volunteer fighter was paramount among these. Several Indian communities, most of whom were not officially classified 'martial', from across the sub-continent perceived the Great War as a historical opportunity to receive military training, earn some money and receive other rewards. To these communities the war came as an opportunity to exercise an upward social mobility. Recruitment was also spurred by the pro-British stand taken during the war by the Indian nationalists. The leading Indian nationalists, led by the usually pacifist Gandhi who had earlier helped the British military against the Boers and Zulus in South Africa and the militant B.G. Tilak, became the recruiting sergeants of the Raj in the hope of extracting important political concessions from the British after the War. Gandhi tells us in his *Autobiography* that he supported recruitment during the Great War because he saw the War as a 'golden opportunity' for Indians 'to learn

---

39 Ibid.
40 Historical Section, New Delhi, Bisheshwar Prasad (ed.), *Adjutant General's Branch, Monographs, Vol.III, War System of Accounting & Honours and Awards*, Combined Inter-Services Historical Section (India & Pakistan).

the use of arms' and get the Arms Act repealed.[41] After 1919 Gandhi turned totally pacifist and his position remained unchanged till 1946 when he wanted the army to be turned into a labor corps.[42] Several militant nationalists also wanted Indians to reclaim their manhood by the military means offered by the battlefields of the Great War – the war was perceived as a lesson in discipline sorely needed by the *swaraj* in the making. In sum the mass recruitment drives of the Great War were accompanied by the promises made to the Indians by the Government of India and it was only natural for the Indians to expect substantial political and economic rewards from the Raj after the war.

When the war ended a wave of discontent swept throughout India and, ironically, the most serious civil disturbances amounting to a mass rebellion against the colonial state broke out in the Punjab which provided the largest number of troops to the Indian Army during 1914-1918. Almost everywhere, but once again most poignantly in the Punjab, the returning troops felt that the Raj was not doing enough for them[43]. In 1919-20 discontent in the army was serious enough to be noticed by the authorities in the documents produced at the time. The successful Bolshevik Revolution and the continuation of the war in Waziristan were making things difficult for the British. The *Panama Maru* and *Komagata Maru* incidents had highlighted the blatant racism of British colonialism and inflamed the anti-British passions among the Sikhs in general. The nationalists were disappointed because instead of substantial concessions on the question of self-government the British responded to the post-war situation with the hated and draconian Rowlatt Act. Further, there was enough reason to believe that a large number of Hindu and Muslim soldiers in the Indian Army and the demobilized soldiers returning to their villages were heavily influenced by the anti-British propaganda unleashed by the Non-Cooperation and Khilafat movements in these circumstances. Attempts to tamper with the loyalty of the standing Indian Army were made by the nationalists openly albeit these attempts remained short-lived and the Indian Army remained loyal in general during 1920-22. This loyalty was obtained despite the fact that a 'general boon' demanded by the Home Department was turned down by the Finance Department after the Great War. In the early 1920s, because the finances of the British Empire were in dire straits, the Indian armed forces were subjected to a severe retrenchment and this put paid to a substantial reform and modernization of the Indian Army during the interwar years.

---

41 M. K. Gandhi, *An Autobiography*, (Ahmedabad, 1927), p. 372.
42 Rajesh Kadian, *India and its Army*, (New Delhi, 1990), p.44.
43 S.D. Pradhan, 'The Sikh Soldier in the First World War', in Ellinwood and Pradhan (eds.), *India and World War I* (New Delhi, 1978); Heathcote, *The Indian Army*..., p. 103 writes of Sikh unrest in the Indian Army which surfaced as early as 1914 when restrictions were imposed on Indian immigration to Canada; Cohen, *The Indian Army*...pp. 76-77, mentions post 1918 retrenchment briefly while speaking of the demobilization of the Mahars and Mazbis from the army. He also notes that the Punjab 'was also no longer politically quiet' after the Great War.

Select Bibliography

Alexander, H., *On Two Fronts, Being the Adventures of an Indian Mule Corps in France and Gallipoli* (New York: Dutton, 1917).

Ali, Imran, *The Punjab Under Imperialism, 1885-1947* (New Jersey: Princetown University Press, 1988).

Anand, Mulk Raj, *Across the Black Waters* (London: Shalimar Books, 2014).

Anderson, Lieutenant Colonel R. H., *Regimental History of the 45th Rattray's Sikhs during the Great War and After, 1914-1921* (London: Sifton Praed, 1925).

Anglesey, Marquess of, *A History of British Cavalry 1816-1919, Vol. V*, (London: Leo Cooper, 1994).

Anon., *The Army in India and its Evolution* (Calcutta: Superintendent Government Printing, 1924).

Anon., *The History of the Guides, 1846-1922*, (Aldershot: Gale & Polden, 1938).

Anon., *History of the 15th (IS) Cavalry Brigade during the Great War 1914-18* (London: HMSO, 1919).

Anon., *Statistics of the Military Effort of the British Empire during the Great War 1914-1920* (London: HMSO, 1922).

Atwal, Jyoti, 'Cultural Trauma and Welfare for War Widows in India', *Croatian Political Science Review*, Vol. 54, No. 1-2, 2017.

Atwood, Rodney, *The Life of Field Marshal Lord Roberts* (London: Bloomsbury, 2015).

Barker, A.J., *The First Iraq War, 1914-1918: Britain's Mesopotamian Campaign* (London: Enigma Books, 2009).

Barua, Pradeep, *The Army Officer Corps and Military Modernisation in Later Colonial India* (Hull: University of Hull Press, 1999).

Basu, Shrabani, *For King and Another Country: Indian Soldiers on the Western Front 1914-18* (New Delhi: Bloomsbury, 2015).

Beckett, Ian, Timothy Bowman and Mark Connelly, *The British Army and the First World War* (Cambridge: Cambridge University Press, 2017).

Bhalla, J. S., *History of the Remount and Veterinary Corps 1794-1987* (New Delhi: Directorate General Remount and Veterinary, 1988).

Busch, Brinton Cooper, *Britain, India and the Arabs, 1914-1921* (Berkley: University of California Press, 1971).

Brown, Judith, *Modern India: The Making of an Asian Democracy* (Oxford: Oxford University Press, 1994).
Brown, Judith and Wm. Roger Louis (eds.), *The Oxford History of the British Empire: Vol. IV: the Twentieth Century* (Oxford: Oxford University Press, 2001).
Brown, Judith, 'War and the Colonial Relationship: Britain, Indian and the War of 1914-1918' in M.R.D. Foot (ed.), *War and Society: Historical Essays in Honour and Memory of J. R. Western, 1928-1971* (London: Elek, 1975).

Callahan, Raymond, *Churchill and his Generals* (Lawrence, Kansas: University Press of Kansas, 2007).
Callahan, Raymond, *Triumph at Imphal-Kohima* (Lawrence, Kansas: University Press of Kansas, 2017).
Candler, Edmund, *The Sepoy* (London: John Murray, 1919).
Cardew, Major F. G., *Hodson's Horse 1857-1922*, (Edinburgh and London: Blackwood and Sons, 1928).
Chevenix-Trench, Charles, *The Indian Army and the King's Enemies, 1900-1947* (London: Thames and Hudson, 1988).
Chhina, Rana, *India and the First World War 1914-1918* (New Delhi: United Service Institution of India, 2014).
Chhina, Rana, 'Their mercenary calling: the Indian Army on Gallipoli, 1915' in Ashley Ekins (ed.), *Gallipoli: A Ridge too Far* (Wollombi, NSW: Exisle Publishing, 2013).
Coates Ulrichsen, Kristian, *The First World War in the Middle East* (London: Hurst, 2014).
Coates Ulrichsen, Kristian, *The Logistics and Politics of the British Campaigns in the Middle East, 1914-22* (Basingstoke: Palgrave Macmillan, 2011).
Cohen, Stephen, *The Indian Army* (New Delhi: Oxford University Press, 2002).
Condon, Brig. W.E.H., *The Frontier Force Regiment* (Aldershot: Gale and Polden, 1962).
Condon, Brig. W.E.H., *The Frontier Force Rifles* (Aldershot: Gale and Polden, 1953).
Corrigan, Gordon, *Sepoys in the Trenches: the Indian Corps on the Western Front, 1914-15* (Stroud: Spellmount, 2004).
Creese, Michael, *'Swords Trembling in their Scabbards': The Changing Status of Indian Officers within the Indian Army, 1757-1947* (Solihull: Helion, 2014).
Crowley, Patrick, *Kut 1916* (Stroud: Spellmount, 2009).
Crowley, Patrick, *Loyal to Empire: The Life of General Sir Charles Monro, 1860-1929* (Stroud: History Press, 2016).

Davis, Paul, 'British-Indian Strategy and Policy in Mesopotamia, November 1914 to April 1916' (University of London: PhD dissertation, 1981).
Das, Santanu, 'Indian Sepoy Experience in Europe, 1914-1918: Archive, Language, and Feeling' *Twentieth Century British History*, Vol. 25, No. 3, 2014.
Das, Santanu, *1914-1918 India Troops in Europe* (Paris: Edition Gallimard, 2014).

Das, Santanu (ed.), *Race, Empire and First World War Writing* (Cambridge: Cambridge University Press, 2011).

Deshpande, Anirudh, *British Military Policy in India, 1900-1945* (Delhi: Manohar, 2005).

Dewey, Clive and K. N. Chaudhri (eds.), *Economy and Society: Essays in Indian Economic and Social History* (New Delhi: Oxford University Press, 1979).

De Witt, Ellinwood C. and S. D. Pradhan (eds.), *India and World War One*, (Delhi: Manohar, 1978).

Di Constanzo, Thierry, 'Memory and history of the Great(er) War and India: from a national-imperial to a more global perspective', E-rea, Vol. 14, No. 2, 2017.

Doherty, Simon and Tom Donovan, *The Indian Corps on the Western Front: A Handbook and Battlefield Guide* (Brighton: Tom Donovan Editions, 2015).

Dutta, Vipul, 'India and the First World War', 29 June 2015, Defence in Depth blog, Defence Studies Department, King's College London, https://defenceindepth.co/?s=vipul+dutta

Falls, Captain Cyril and Major A.F. Becke, *Official History of the Great War: Military Operations: Egypt and Palestine: Vol 2 Part II* (London: HMSO, 1930).

Farwell, Byron, *Armies of the Raj* (London: Viking, 1989).

Faught, C. Brad, *Kitchener: Hero and Anti-Hero* (London: I.B. Taurus, 2016).

Fawaz, Leila Tarazi, *A Land of Aching Hearts: The Middle East in the Great War* (Cambridge, MA: Harvard University Press, 2014).

French, David, 'The Dardanelles, Mecca and Kut: Prestige as a Factor in British Eastern Strategy, 1914-1916' *War and Society*, Vol. 5, No. 1, 1987.

Galbraith, John S., 'No Man's Child: The Campaign in Mesopotamia, 1914-1916' *International History Review*, Vol. 6, No. 2, 1984.

Gardner, Nikolas *The Siege of Kut-al-Amara: At War in Mesopotamia, 1915-1916* (Bloomington: Indiana University Press, 2014).

Gardner, Nikolas 'Sepoys and the Siege of Kut-al-Amara, December 1915-April 1916.' *War in History*, Vol. 11, No. 3, July 2004.

Gerwarth, Robert and Erez Manela (eds.), *Empires at War 1911-1923* (Oxford: Oxford University Press, 2014).

Gilmour, David, *Curzon: Imperial Statesman, 1859-1925* (London: John Murray, 2003).

Goold, D., 'Lord Hardinge and the Mesopotamia Expedition and Enquiry, 1914-17' *Historical Journal*, Vol. 19, No. 4, 1976.

Greenhut, Jeffrey, 'The Imperial Reserve: The Indian Corps on the Western Front, 1914-15' *Journal of Imperial and Commonwealth History*, Vol. 12, No. 1, 1983.

Greenhut, Jeffrey, '"Sahib and Sepoy" An Enquiry into the Relationship between British Officers and Native Soldiers of the British Indian Army', *Military Affairs*, Vol. 48, 1984.

Grimshaw, Roly, *Indian Cavalry Officer 1914-15* (Tunbridge Wells: D.J. Costello Publishers, 1986).
Gupta, Partha Sarathi and Anirudh Deshpande, *The British Raj and Its Indian Armed Forces 1857-1939* (New Delhi: Oxford University Press, 2002).

Hadaway, Stuart, *From Gaza to Jerusalem: The Campaign for Southern Palestine 1917* (Stroud: History Press, 2015).
Hadaway, Stuart, *Pyramids and Fleshpot: The Egyptian, Senussi and Eastern Mediterranean Campaigns, 1914-16* (Stroud: Spellmount, 2014).
Haldane, Lieutenant General Sir Aylmer L., *The Insurrection in Mesopotamia, 1920* (Nashville: Battery Press, 2005).
Hamid, Major General Shahid S., *So They Rode and Fought* (Tunbridge Wells: Midas Books, 1983).
Head, Richard and Anthony McClenaghan, *The Maharaja's Paltans: A history of the Indian State Forces 1888-1948*, (New Delhi: Manohar, 2013).
Heathcote, T.A., *Balochistan, the British and the Great Game* (London: Hurst, 2015).
Heathcote, T. A., *The Indian Army: The Garrison of British Imperial India, 1822-1922* (Newton Abbot: David & Charles, 1974).
Heathcote, T. A., *The Military in British India* (Barnsley: Praetorian Press, 2013).
Hudson, General Sir H., *History of the 19th King George's Own Lancers, 1858-1921*, (Aldershot, Gale and Polden, 1937).
Huxford, Lieutenant Colonel H.J., *History of the 8th Gurkha Rifles* (Aldershot: Gale & Polden, 1952).

Jacobsen, Mark (ed.), *Rawlinson in India* (Stroud: Sutton for the Army Records Society, 2002).
Jarboe, Andrew Tait, 'The Prisoner Dilemma: Britain, Germany and the Repatriation of Indian Prisoners of War', *The Round Table: The Commonwealth Journal of International Affairs*, Vol. 103, No. 2, 2014.
Jarboe, Andrew Tait and Richard S. Fogarty (editors), *Shifting Frontiers and Imperial Dynamics in a global conflict* (London: I. B. Taurus, 2014).
Jarboe, Andrew Tait, 'Soldiers of Empire: "Colonial Troops" in the Imperial Metropole and Imperial Propaganda 1914-1918' in Troy Paddick (ed.) *World War I and Propaganda* (Leiden: Brill, 2014).
Jarboe, Andrew Tait, 'Soldiers of Empire: Indian Sepoys in and beyond the metropole during the First World War, 1914-1919' (Northeastern University: PhD thesis, 2013).
Jarboe, Andrew (editor), *War News in India: The Punjabi Press during World War I* (London: I.B. Tauris, 2015).
Jeffreys, Alan, *Approach to Battle: Training the Indian Army during the Second World War* (Solihull: Helion, 2017).
Jeffreys, Alan and Patrick Rose (eds.), *The Indian Army, 1939-47* (Farnham: Ashgate, 2012).

Jeffrey, Keith, '"An English Barrack in the Oriental Sea?" India in the Aftermath of the First World War' *Modern Asian Studies*, Vol. 15, No. 3, 1981.
Jeffrey, Keith, *1916: A Global History* (London: Bloomsbury, 2015).
Johnson, Rob, *The Great War & the Middle East* (Oxford: Oxford University Press, 2016).
Johnson, Rob (ed.), *The Indian Army: Virtue and Necessity* (Newcastle: Cambridge Scholars Press, 2014).

Kant, Vedica, *'If I die here, who will remember me?' India and the First World War* (New Delhi: Roli Books, 2014).
Kazimi, Ali, *Undesirables: White Canada and the Komagata Maru* (Vancoover: Douglas & McIntyre, 2012).
Kempton, Chris, *Duty & Fidelity: The Indian Army August 1914-1922* (Milton Keynes: The Military Press, 2009) 4 vols.
Kerr, Andrew, *I Can Never Say Enough About the Men: A History of the Jammu and Kashmir Rifles throughout their World War One East African Campaign* (Self-published, 2010).
Kaul, Chandrika, *Reporting the Raj: The British Press and India, c.1880-1922* (Manchester: Manchester University Press, 2003).
Kitchen, James E., *The British Imperial Army in the Middle East: Morale and Military Identity in the Sinai and Palestine Campaigns, 1916-18* (London: Bloomsbury, 2014).
Koller, Christian, 'The Recruitment of Colonial Troops in Africa and Asia and their Deployment in Europe during the First World War' *Immigrants & Minorities*, Vol. 26, Nos. 1/2, March/July 2008.
Kumar, Dharma and Tapan Raychaudhuri (eds.), *The Cambridge Economic History of India, Volume 2: c. 1757-c.1970* (Cambridge: Cambridge University Press, 1983).

Leask, I.D., 'The Expansion of the Indian Army during the Great War' (University of London: MPhil thesis, 1989).
Leigh, M.S., *The Punjab and the War* (Lahore: Superintendent Government Printing, 1922).
Lester, Alan, 'British India on Trial: Brighton Military Hospitals and the Politics of Empire in World War I', *Journal of Historical Geography*, Vol. 38, No. 1, 2012.
Lloyd, Nick, *The Amritsar Massacre* (London: I.B. Taurus, 2011).
Lloyd, Nick, 'Losing the Game: Propaganda and Influence in the British Raj, 1917-47' in Greg Kennedy and Christopher Tuck (eds.), *British Propaganda and Wars of Empire* (Farnham: Ashgate, 2014).
Longer, V., *Red Coats to Olive Green: A History of the Indian Army 1600-1974* (Bombay: Allied Publishers, 1974).
Lucas, Sir Charles, *The Empire at War* (London: Humphrey Milford and Oxford University Press, 1926).

MacMunn, George, *The Armies of India*, (Bristol: Crecy Books, 1911).
MacMunn, George, *Behind the Scenes in Many Wars* (London: John Murray, 1930).
MacMunn, George, *The Martial Races of India* (London: Sampson Low, 1933).
MacMunn, Lieutenant General Sir George and Captain Cyril Falls, *Military Operations Egypt & Palestine, Front the Outbreak of War with Germany to June 1917* (London: HMSO, 1928).
Marston, Daniel, *The Indian Army and the End of the Raj* (Cambridge: Cambridge University Press, 2014).
Marston, Daniel P., *Phoenix from the Ashes: The Indian Army in the Burma Campaign* (Westport, Connecticut: Praeger, 2003).
Marston, Daniel P. and Chandar S. Sundaram (editors), *A Military History of India and South Asia: From the East India Company to the Nuclear Era* (Westport: Praeger, 2007).
Mason, Philip, *A Matter of Honour: An Account of the Indian Army, its officers and men* (London: Jonathan Cape, 1974).
Mason, Philip, *The Men Who Ruled India* (London: Guild, 1985).
Maunsell, Colonel E.B., *The Prince of Wales Own, The Scinde Horse* (London: Butler and Tanner, 1926).
Maxwell, R.M., *Villiers-Stuart goes to War* (Edinburgh: Pentland Press, 1990).
Mazumder, Rajit K., *The Indian Army and the Making of the Punjab* (Delhi: Orient Blackswan, 2003).
McLain, Robert, *Gender and Violence in British India: The Road to Amritsar, 1914-1919* (Basingstoke: Palgrave Macmillan, 2014).
Menezes, S. L., *Fidelity and Honour: The Indian Army from the Seventeenth to the Twenty-first Century* (New Delhi: OUP, 2001).
Merewether, J. and F. E. Smith, *The Indian Corps in France* (London: John Murray 1919).
Moberly, F. J., *History of the Great War: The Campaign in Mesopotamia, 1914-1918* (London: HMSO, 1923-27) 4 vols.
Molesworth, Lieutenant General G.N., *Curfew on Olympus* (London: Asia Publishing House, 1965).
Moreman, T.R., *The Army in India and the Development of Frontier Warfare, 1849-1947* (Basingstoke: Macmillan, 1998).
Moreman, T.R., *The Jungle, the Japanese and the British Commonwealth Armies at War, 1941-45* (London: Frank Cass, 2005).
Moore, Robin J., 'Curzon and Indian Reform', *Modern Asian Studies*, Vol. 27, No. 4, 1993.
Moretz, Joseph, *Thinking Wisely, Planning Boldly: The Higher Education and Training of Royal Navy Officers, 1919-1939* (Solihull: Helion, 2014).
Morris, John, *Hired to Kill* (London: Rupert Hart-Davis in association with the Cresset Press, 1960).
Morrow, John H., *The Great War: An Imperial History* (London: Routledge, 2004).

Morton-Jack, George, *The Indian Army on the Western Front: India's Expeditionary Force to France and Belgium in the First World War* (Cambridge: Cambridge University Press, 2014).
Morton-Jack, George 'The Indian Army on the Western Front, 1914-1915: A Portrait of Collaboration', *War in History*, Vol. 13, No. 3, July 2006.

Nath, Ashok, *Sowars and Sepoys in the Great War 1914-1918: Cavalry and Infantry Regiments* (Dhaka: self-published, 2014).
Nunn, Wilfred, *Tigris Gunboats: The Forgotten War in Iraq 1914-1917* (London: Chatham Publishing, 2007).

O'Dwyer, Michael, *India as I knew it, 1885-1925* (London: Constable, 1925).
O'Dwyer, Michael, 'India's Man-Power in the War', *Army Quarterly*, Vol. II, 1921.
Olusoga, David, *The World's War* (London: Head of Zeus, 2014).
Omissi, David, 'Europe Through Indian Eyes: Indian Soldiers Encounter England and France, 1914-1918', *The English Historical Review*, Vol. 122, No. 496, 2007.
Omissi, David, *Indian Voices of the Great War: Soldiers' Letters 1914-1918* (Basingstoke: Macmillan, 1999).
Omissi, David, *The Sepoy and the Raj: The Indian Army 1860-1940* (Basingstoke: Macmillan, 1994).
Onley, James, 'The Raj Reconsidered'', *Asian Affairs*, Vol. XL, No.1, March 2009.

Pati, Budheswar, *India and the First World War* (New Delhi: Atlantic Publishers and Distributors, 1996).
Peers, Douglas, *Between Mars and Mammon: Colonial Armies and the Garrison State in Early Nineteenth Century India* (London: I. B. Taurus, 1995).
Perkins, Roger, *Regiments: Regiments and Corps of the British Empire and Commonwealth 1758-1993: A Critical Bibliography of their Published Histories* (Newton Abbot: self-published, 1994).
Perry, F.W., *The Commonwealth Armies: Manpower and Organisation in Two World Wars* (Manchester: Manchester University Press, 1988).
Pradhan, S.D., *Indian Army in East Africa 1914-1918* (New Delhi: National Book Organisation, 1991).

Robinson, Francis, *Separatism among Indian Muslims: The Politics of the United Provinces' Muslims, 1860-1923* (Delhi: Oxford University Press, 1993).
Robson, Brian, *Crisis on the Frontier: The Third Afghan War and the Campaign in Waziristan 1919-20* (Stroud: Spellmount, 2004).
Robson, Brian (ed.), *Roberts in India: The Military Papers of Field Marshal Roberts 1876-1893* (Dover: Alan Sutton for the Army Records Society, 1993).
Rogan, Eugene, *The Fall of the Ottomans: The Great War in the Middle East* (London: Basic Books, 2015).

Rose, Sonya O., 'The Politics of Service and Sacrifice in WW1 Ireland and India' *Twentieth Century British History*, Vol. 25, No. 3, 2014.
Roy, Franziska, Heike Liebau and Ravi Ahuja (eds.), *'When the War began we heard of Several Kings': South Asian Prisoners in World War I Germany* (New Delhi: Social Science Press, 2011).
Roy, Kaushik, *The Army in British India: From Colonial Warfare to Total War, 1857-1947* (2013).
Roy, Kaushik, *Brown Warriors of the Raj: Recruitment & the Mechanics of Command in the Sepoy Army, 1859-1913* (Delhi: Manohar, 2008).
Roy, Kaushik (ed.), *The Indian Army in the Two World Wars* (Leiden: Brill, 2012).
Rumbold, Algernon, *Watershed in India, 1914-1922* (London: Athlone Press, 1979).
Rutledge, Ian, *Enemy on the Euphrates: The British Occupation of Iraq and the Great Arab Revolt* (London: Saqi Books, 2014).

Sandhu, Major General Gurchan Singh, *The Indian Cavalry: History of the Indian Armoured Corps till 1940*, (New Delhi, Vision Books, 1981*)*.
Sandhu, Major General Gurchan Singh, *I Serve: The 18th Cavalry*, (New Delhi, Lancer International, 1991).
Singh, Amarinder, *Honour and Fidelity: India's Military Contribution to the Great War 1914-18* (New Delhi: Roli Books, 2014).
Singh, Gajendra, 'India and the Great War': colonial fantasies, anxieties and discontent', *Studies in Ethnicity and Nationalism*, Vol. 14, No. 2, 2014.
Singh, Gajendra, *The Testimonies of Indian Soldiers and the Two World Wars: Between Self and Sepoy* (London: Bloomsbury, 2014).
Singh, Lieutenant General Hanut, *'Fakhr-i-Hind'*, *The Story of the Poona Horse*, (Dehra Dun, Akrim Publishers, 1993).
Singha, Radika, 'Finding Labor from India for the War in Iraq: The Jail Porter and Labor Corps, 1916-1920', *Comparative Studies in Society and History*, Vol. 49, No. 2, April 2007.
Singha, Radika, 'The Short Career of the Indian Labor Corps in France, 1917-1919', *International Labor and Working-Class History*, Vol. 87, March 2015.
Slim, Field Marshal Sir William, *Unofficial History* (Barnsley: Pen & Sword, 2008).
Stanley, Peter, *Die in Battle, Do Not Despair: The Indians on Gallipoli, 1915* (Solihull: Helion, 2015).
Stevens, Brian, 'The Expansion of the Indian Army during World War I' *Journal of the Society for Army Historical Research*, Vol. LXXVI, No. 305, Spring 1998.
Stevenson, David, *1914-1918: The History of the First World War* (London: Penguin, 2005).
Stigger, Philip, 'How far was the Loyalty of Muslim Soldiers in the Indian Army more in doubt than usual throughout the First World War?' *Journal of the Society for Army Historical Research*, Vol. 87, No. 351, 2009.
Storm, Eric, and Ali Al Tuma, *Colonial Soldiers in Europe 1914-1945: "Allies in Uniform" in Wartime Societies* (London: Routledge, 2017).

Strachan, Hew, *The First World War, Vol. 1, To Arms* (Oxford: Oxford University Press, 2001).
Streets, Heather, *Martial Races: The Military, Race and Masculinity in British Imperial Culture, 1857-1914* (Manchester: Manchester University Press, 2004).
Sundaram, Chandar, '"Arriving in the Nick of Time": The Indian Corps in France 1914-15' *Journal of Defence Studies*, Vol. 9, No. 4, October-December 2015.
Sundaram, Chandar, '"Treated with Scant Attention": The Imperial Cadet Corps, Indian Nobles, and Anglo-Indian Policy, 1897-1917' *Journal of Military History*, Vol. 77, January 2013.
Syk, Andrew (ed.), *The Military Papers of Lieutenant General Sir Frederick Stanley Maude, 1914-1917* (Stroud: History Press for Army Records Society, 2012).

Talbot, Ian, *Punjab and the Raj, 1849-1947* (New Delhi: Manohar, 1988).
Tan Tai Young, *The Garrison State: The Military, Government and Society in Colonial Punjab, 1849-1947* (London: Sage, 2005).
Tan Tai Young, 'An Imperial Home-Front: Punjab and the First World War', *Journal of Military History*, Vol. 64, 2000.
Tennant, Lt-Col E., *The Royal Deccan Horse in the Great War* (Aldershot: Gale and Polden, 1939).
Tripodi, Christian, *Edge of Empire: The British Political Officer and Tribal Administration on the North-West Frontier 1877-1947* (Farnham: Ashgate, 2011).
Tomlinson, B.R., *The Political Economy of the Raj, 1914-1947: The Economics of Decolonization in India* (London: Macmillan, 1979).
Townshend, Charles, *When God Made Hell: The British Invasion of Mesopotamia and the Creation of Iraq, 1914-21* (London: Faber and Faber, 2010).

VanKoski, Susan, 'Letters Home, 1915-16: Punjabi soldiers reflect on war and life in Europe and their meanings for home and self' *International Journal of Punjab Studies*, Vol. 2, No. 1, 1995.

Wart, Reginal Bramley Van, *General H.H. Sir Pratap Singh*, (London: Humphrey Milford, 1926).
Watson, Major General W. A., *King George V's Own Central India Horse*, (Edinburgh, Blackwood and Sons, 1930).
Whitworth, Capt. D. E., *A History of the 2nd Lancers, Gardner's Horse) from 1809 to 1927*, (London: Sifton Praed and Co, 1924).
Weekes, Colonel H. E., *History of the 5th Royal Gurkha Rifles (Frontier Force) 1858 to 1928* (Uckfield: Naval & Military Press, 2003).
Willcocks, J., *With the Indians in France* (London: Constable, 1920).
Wilson, Trevor, *The Myriad Faces of War* (Cambridge: Polity Press, 1988).
Winter, Jay, *The Cambridge History of the First World War* (Cambridge: Cambridge University Press, 2014) 3 vols.

Winton, Graham, 'British-Indian Army Cavalry: From Mobilisation to the Western Front 1915', in Spencer Jones (ed.) *Courage Without Glory: The British Army on the Western Front 1915*, (Solihull: Helion & Company, 2015).
Winton, Graham, *Theirs Not to Reason Why: Horsing the British Army 1875-1925* (Solihull: Helion & Company, 2013).
Woodyatt, Major General Nigel, *Under Ten Viceroys* (London: Herbert Jenkins, 1922).

Yeats-Brown, F., *Bengal Lancer* (London: Anthony Mott, 1984).

Index

Index of People

Allanson, Major Cecil J.L. 35, 136–137, 140, 145
Allenby, General Sir Edmund 33–34, 38, 232, 236, 238–240, 242, 244, 247–248, 267
Asquith, Herbert 102–103, 107–109, 138, 145, 150, 158, 172
Auchinleck, Captain Claude 18, 26, 38, 42–43, 122, 124, 127, 129
Aylmer, Lieutenant General Sir Fenton 258, 261–262

Barrow, General Sir Edmund 102, 104, 161, 255
Butterworth, Thornton 131, 135, 138, 140, 142–144

Callwell, Major General Charles 102–103, 110, 113, 118, 129
Chamberlain, Austen 160, 165–170, 173, 192, 196, 198–199, 225, 259, 263, 267
Chaudhuri, Nirad 252, 266, 280
Chelmsford, Lord 30, 204, 241, 265, 267–269, 280
Churchill, Winston v, x, 14–15, 20, 29–30, 99, 131–135, 137–145, 147–148, 150–152, 155–158
Crewe, Lord 100, 121, 158, 160, 163, 165, 167, 198
Curzon, Lord 93–94, 108–109, 145–146, 177, 193, 204

Duff, General Sir Beauchamp 19, 30, 93, 111, 114, 120, 261–263
Dyer, Colonel Reginald 148, 205, 226–227

Fisher, Admiral Sir John 93, 99, 133

Gandhi, M.K. 41, 226, 282, 286, 289–290, 297–298
George V, King 166, 187, 235, 243
Gordon, General Charles 22, 47, 54, 112, 137
Grimshaw, Captain Roly 46, 66–67, 119–120, 176, 191

Haig, General Sir Douglas 33, 97–100, 102, 135, 162, 185
Hamilton, General Sir Ian 35, 42, 92, 94, 96–97, 102–103, 139, 177, 200, 253
Hankey, Maurice 102, 135, 170
Hardinge, Lord 19, 121, 156, 158–159, 167–170, 173, 254, 256, 280

Jackson, Admiral Sir Henry 102–103, 105, 107

Khan, Abdul Aziz 45, 81, 117, 147, 160, 194, 225, 227–230, 243, 289
Kitchen, James 34, 176, 182, 186, 232, 238, 248
Kitchener, General Lord 19, 22, 26, 30, 93–97, 107, 109, 112–115, 118–119, 138–139, 150, 158, 169, 177–178, 262, 271, 279–280, 291

Lloyd George, David 33, 204, 265

MacMunn, Major General George 30, 117, 257
Maude, Sir Frederick Stanley 30–32, 38, 170, 173, 201, 267
Maunsell, Colonel E. B. 231, 233–234, 238
Maxwell, Sir John 114–116, 125, 135
Monro, General Sir Charles 30, 176, 185, 264
Montagu, Sir Edwin 38, 204, 226, 265, 268–269

309

Moore, Major General Sir John 79, 83–84, 90

Nixon, Lieutenant Colonel John 167, 173, 179, 256, 258–261, 263

O'Dwyer, Sir Michael 159, 190, 199, 202, 206
von Oppenheim, Baron Max 161, 198, 211–213, 229

Rana, Major Sher Singh 209, 214–215, 218
Roberts, Field Marshal Lord 19, 21–22, 188–189
Robertson, General Sir William 30, 33, 190, 261

Singh, Gobind 188, 192, 194
Slim, Field Marshal William 18, 26, 30, 35

Townshend, Charles 167, 170, 173, 259–260, 262

Vincent, Major Berkeley 97–98, 292, 295

Wavell, General Archibald Percival 34, 144, 147, 232
Willcocks, General Sir James 65, 162, 192, 254, 259

Index of Places
Abadan 101, 199, 253–254
Acre 240, 243, 245
Aden 20, 53, 61, 64, 66, 91, 149, 277
Afghanistan ix, 42, 49, 118, 121, 153, 155–156, 164–166, 168, 171–172, 211, 215, 224, 230
Africa xi, 20, 35–36, 40, 49, 51, 53, 57, 68–73, 86, 91–94, 99–109, 113, 116, 118, 124, 134, 149–150, 152, 155, 174–175, 178, 193, 197, 199, 210–211, 216–217, 226, 250–251, 258, 266, 277, 282, 287, 297
Afuleh 232, 238, 241–242
Aleppo 34, 232, 242, 244, 247
Alexandretta 105, 107, 109
Alexandria 112–113, 115, 145
Amara 28–29, 122, 154, 160, 167, 169–170, 173, 200, 249–250, 256, 258–260, 262–263, 276
America 62, 139, 196, 199

Amritsar 15–16, 148, 192, 199–200, 202–203, 205–206, 226–227, 287, 289
Arabia 56, 80, 164
Arabian Sea 56, 66, 268–269
Argentine 62, 65, 79
Asia iii, viii, xi, 14, 16–18, 30, 38, 114, 116, 137, 148, 155, 179, 189, 198, 210, 229–230, 277, 285, 289
Australia 14, 20, 62, 77–79, 115, 134, 146–147, 184, 251, 272, 275–276
Austria 64, 157, 159

Baghdad 26, 28, 30–31, 56, 101, 105, 154–155, 158, 161, 166–171, 173, 182, 200, 249, 255–256, 259, 263, 267
Baluchistan 53, 80–81, 165
Bangalore 69, 72, 74, 144–145, 181, 276, 278, 290
Basra 26–28, 30, 101, 104–105, 108, 167, 199, 201, 249, 253–258, 260–261, 289
Beersheba 33, 125, 232
Beisan 232, 238, 241–242
Belgium 14, 21, 42, 89, 93, 104, 106, 108, 112, 119–120, 132, 193
Bengal 18, 43, 64, 69, 177–178, 226, 250, 265, 267
Berlin 101, 106, 114–115, 155, 158, 161, 198, 209, 212–213, 221, 223, 229–230
Bombay 21, 44, 59, 62–66, 69–72, 74, 78, 83, 86, 119, 166, 179, 183, 189, 201, 227–228, 253, 266–267, 271, 274, 294, 296
Burma viii–ix, 26–27, 30, 36, 38, 52, 64, 124–125, 129, 161, 188, 198–199, 268, 272

Cairo 25, 113, 116, 119, 129, 268
Calcutta 20, 41, 52, 64, 69–72, 78–80, 85, 119, 154–155, 176, 178–180, 197, 223, 279–280, 284–285
Cameroon 99, 103–104, 107
Canada 146–147, 153, 184, 188, 196–198, 271, 298
Caucasus 115, 162, 214
China 24, 52, 62, 91, 149
Constantinople 127, 131, 133, 156–157, 162, 207, 210–211, 214–215, 217, 219, 229
Ctesiphon 28, 50, 154, 169–170, 260
Cuba 134, 144, 208

Damascus 34, 114, 156, 231, 233, 242–244,

248
Dar es Salaam 102–104, 106, 108
Dardanelles v, 105, 108, 110, 113, 131–136, 138, 140, 142, 144–145, 147, 149–152, 155–162, 164–170, 172, 185, 200, 256, 260
Dehra Dun 47–48, 243, 274, 279
Delhi ii, viii, xii, 13–14, 16, 18, 21, 24, 30, 37, 52, 54, 59, 74, 79, 137, 146, 148, 153–155, 158, 174–175, 181, 183–185, 187, 203, 227, 232, 234, 250, 253–256, 258, 263, 266, 270, 274, 282–284, 288, 291–292, 296–298
Deraa 232, 234, 242–243

Egypt 14, 20–21, 32, 34–35, 53, 57, 64, 66–67, 76, 80–81, 91, 101–102, 104–105, 107, 110–117, 119–122, 124–130, 133–134, 144–145, 149–150, 155, 157–158, 160–161, 168–169, 174, 176, 185–186, 193, 196, 199–200, 211, 226, 229, 245–247, 250–253, 256, 258, 266–267
Euphrates 26, 105, 169, 255–257, 259

Ferozepore 48, 136, 189, 198, 200, 203, 270, 277, 279
Festubert 24, 46–47, 149, 209
Flanders v, 13, 40, 49–51, 130, 174, 233, 283
France v, x, 13–14, 19–24, 26–28, 31–35, 40, 42–45, 48–51, 53, 57–58, 60–61, 67–68, 76, 78, 81, 83, 87, 89, 92–93, 99, 105, 107–109, 111–116, 119–120, 124, 130, 132, 146–147, 150, 162–163, 169, 171, 174, 179, 191, 193–195, 208–209, 211–212, 215–216, 225–226, 229, 232–233, 238–239, 247–248, 250, 253, 260, 271, 281

Gallipoli ii, v, x, xii, 14–15, 20, 26, 28, 30, 35, 40, 45, 53, 57, 108, 110, 131–133, 135–140, 143, 145–148, 150, 152, 160–163, 165, 167, 170, 173–174, 183, 200, 256, 259, 270–271, 274, 277, 283
Gaza 33, 115, 232
Great Bitter Lake 111, 124, 127

Haifa 34, 232, 234, 240, 245–247
Hampshire 52, 138, 271, 274, 277
Helles 132, 136, 142, 145, 165, 200

Holland 201, 209, 221, 225
Hong Kong 163, 188, 198–199

India ii–x, xii, 13–21, 23–26, 28, 30, 32–34, 36–38, 40–44, 48–49, 52–63, 65–70, 72–80, 82–83, 85–104, 106–122, 125, 129, 133–135, 137, 139, 144–149, 153–206, 208–211, 213–219, 221–230, 232–233, 235, 237, 243, 247, 249–259, 261–292, 294–295, 297–298
Indian Ocean 64, 66, 70, 102, 251
Iraq 16, 20, 27, 32, 105, 154, 253–255, 259, 262
Ismailia 119, 122, 124–125, 128
Italy 66, 147, 162, 231

Jerusalem 33, 155–156, 232, 235, 239
Jhelum 74, 203, 295
Jordan 232–236, 238–239, 241–244
Jullundur 147, 164, 203

Kabul 165, 195, 224, 230
Karachi 21, 62, 64–65, 69–70, 81, 116, 144, 224, 266–267
Kent 66, 73, 271, 274
Kenya 35, 70, 92
Kolkata 64, 274, 280
Kut 28–31, 122, 149, 154–162, 164–167, 169–170, 172–173, 200, 249–250, 256, 258–260, 262–263, 276

Lahore 21, 24, 33, 44, 48, 58–59, 64–65, 74, 80, 84–87, 115–116, 130, 157, 159, 169, 198–199, 202–203, 209, 233
Lake Timsah 110, 124, 127–128
Loos 24, 47, 149
Ludhiana 189, 199, 203, 289

Madras 61, 64, 84, 116, 160, 189, 268, 287, 290
Malta 66, 100, 149
Marseilles 21, 45, 65–67, 74–75, 85, 114–115, 119, 137, 191, 195, 225
Mecca 155–162, 164–167, 169–170, 172, 256
Mediterranean Sea 64, 66, 106, 111, 125, 174, 232–233, 264, 266, 269
Meerut 21, 24, 33, 44, 65–66, 74, 85, 87, 130, 169, 198, 233, 270, 296
Megiddo 32, 34, 231, 241, 247

Mesopotamia vi, 14–16, 20–21, 24, 26–35, 38–40, 49, 51, 53, 57, 74, 86, 92, 101, 104–106, 108–109, 121–122, 124, 133–134, 136, 148, 150, 154, 156, 158, 160–161, 164, 167–172, 174, 176, 179, 183, 186, 191, 200–201, 216, 226, 233, 249–260, 263–264, 266–268, 271, 276–277, 283–284, 289
Mysore 41, 53, 74, 237–238, 245

Nazareth 238, 240, 242
Nepal 18, 53, 218, 225
Neuve Chapelle 21, 45, 163, 193
New South Wales ii, 62, 77
New Zealand 33, 77–78, 87, 115, 124, 133–134, 136–139, 146–147, 210, 231, 237, 251
North Sea 99, 107, 225

Orleans 59, 66–67, 81, 87, 191

Pakistan viii–ix, 21, 52, 80, 203, 297
Palestine vi, 14–15, 32–35, 39–40, 51, 83, 114–117, 124–129, 133–134, 176, 182, 186, 200, 226, 231–234, 237–238, 245–248, 250, 252, 266–267, 271, 276
Persia 25, 49, 62, 80, 86, 99, 101, 104, 134, 149, 156, 164–165, 168, 170–172, 217–218, 224, 232, 255
Persian Gulf 20, 32, 53, 101, 251, 253–255
Peshawar 147, 219, 227–228, 287, 296
Port Said 66, 113, 124–125

Quetta 19, 27, 96–98, 118, 180–182, 250

Rangoon 27, 64, 161, 201, 277
Rawalpindi 182, 194, 200, 202–203, 289, 295
Red Sea 66, 111, 232–233
Russia 98–100, 105, 113, 118, 133, 139, 162, 188, 204, 230, 282, 284, 286

Salonika 20, 34, 170, 251, 266–268
Sari Bair 133, 136, 139–140, 145, 151
Secunderabad 59–61, 63, 65–66, 68, 76, 85, 274
Singapore 27, 147, 149, 161–162, 188, 201, 262, 277
Somaliland 37, 97, 219
Somme 40, 49, 132, 144, 277
South Africa 93–94, 100, 108, 113, 118, 134, 197, 282, 297
Southampton 78, 103, 277
Suez v, vii, 14, 21, 32, 44–45, 66, 110–116, 119, 122–130, 133, 161, 200, 232, 251, 264, 269
Suez Canal v, vii, 14, 32, 44, 66, 110–116, 119, 122–124, 126–130, 133, 161, 200, 232, 251
Syria 24, 32, 105, 113, 164, 232, 237, 242, 244, 248

Tanganyika 23, 35, 69
Tigris 26, 28–29, 31, 105, 169–170, 201, 254–257, 259, 262
Turkey 26, 32, 101, 105, 113, 116, 121–122, 124, 126, 156–159, 162, 164–165, 167–168, 186, 210, 214, 217–219, 224, 232

Uganda 70, 91–92, 101, 106
United Provinces 74, 146, 158, 164, 289, 293–296
United States 14, 106, 216
Uttar Pradesh 74, 80, 270

Waziristan 16, 177, 186, 289, 298

Ypres 21, 24, 45, 48, 191, 208, 277

Zanzibar 64, 69, 71, 99, 103–105
Zossen 209, 212–223, 225, 229

Index of Military Formations & Units
British Army x, 15, 17, 19, 22, 25, 27, 36, 42, 45, 52, 58, 73, 84, 88, 92, 94, 108–109, 118–119, 124, 172, 175–176, 178–182, 184–185, 189, 210, 244, 262, 271, 273, 277, 285
British Expeditionary Force 21-22, 24, 33, 47, 57, 83, 89, 110, 162, 191
Egyptian Army 93, 112–113, 124, 149
Egyptian Expeditionary Force 32, 34, 119, 175–176, 232, 268
Indian Expeditionary Force 29, 44, 104, 117, 121–122, 125, 136, 193, 253, 258

Fourth Army 114–115, 234–235, 243

Indian Corps 13, 20, 22–25, 40, 43–50, 74, 132, 137, 146, 162–163, 179, 191–193, 209, 218

Index   313

1st Indian Cavalry Division 58, 60–61, 65–67, 81, 86
2nd Indian Cavalry Division 59, 65, 85
3rd Lahore Division 24, 48, 65, 87, 116
4th Division 238, 241–242, 244
4th Cavalry Division 65, 80, 237, 241
6th Division 26-30, 85, 167, 173, 253, 256–257, 259–262
7th Meerut Division 65–66, 87, 296
42nd (East Lancashire) Division 110, 115–116, 124

6th Cavalry Brigade 234
7th Indian Mountain Artillery Brigade 15, 58, 135
8th Cavalry Brigade 116, 234
9th Cavalry Brigade 59-61, 63, 65-68
10th Cavalry Brigade 242
10th Field Artillery Brigade 85
11th Cavalry Brigade 241
13th Cavalry Brigade 240
15th (Imperial Service) Cavalry Brigade 78, 83, 110, 237, 245
22nd Indian Infantry Brigade 116, 124, 128–129
29th Indian Brigade 15, 35, 116, 125, 135-136, 138–139, 152, 163, 200

2nd Gurkhas 48, 117, 208
2nd Lancers 195, 233, 235, 237, 239–241, 244
5th Light Infantry 27, 161, 201, 277
6th Cavalry 193–194, 237, 248
14th Sikhs 116, 125, 136, 183, 200
15th Lancers 27, 59, 65, 80, 170
19th Lancers 231, 233, 237
29th Lancers 86, 195, 237, 241, 243
29th Punjabis 69, 72, 124
47th Sikhs 189, 193–194, 201
58th Rifles 207, 219, 224–225
89th Punjabis 116, 136, 163, 200
129th Baluchis 43, 45, 209, 225
Bikaner Camel Corps 32, 69, 80–81, 117
Calcutta Light Horse 70, 178, 180
Hampshire Regiment 138, 274, 277
Jodhpur Lancers viii, 15, 34, 41, 65, 69, 235–238, 245–247
Royal Horse Artillery 62, 65, 73
Somerset Light Infantry 179, 272–274, 278–279
Wilde's Rifles 24, 43, 45

British Cavalry 45, 52, 61, 73, 76, 86, 231–233
Desert Mounted Corps 231, 237–238, 244, 248
Imperial Cadet Corps 37, 177, 307
Imperial Service Troops 32, 34–35, 37, 41, 54, 149, 193, 235
Indian Army Reserve 86, 178–179, 186
Indian Cavalry vi, x, 15, 32, 42, 46, 50, 57–61, 65–67, 73, 75–76, 80–81, 84–86, 89, 119, 169, 176, 191, 194, 231–234, 237–239, 242–244, 247–248
Indian Mule Corps 15, 45, 70, 74, 87
Royal Indian Marine 26, 53, 101, 106, 126, 128
Royal Navy ix, 17, 95, 101, 106, 112, 126
Territorial Army 14–15, 180, 273
West African Frontier Force 99, 102, 104

Index of General & Miscellaneous Terms
Boer War *see* South African War
Bolshevik Revolution 284, 286, 298

East African Campaign 20, 35, 71–73, 303
East India Company 17–18, 61, 176–177, 188

German Army 47, 210, 214, 286

Holy War 116, 153, 210, 214, 217, 220

Indian Civil Service 18, 36, 164, 179–180, 199
Indian Mutiny 18, 61–62, 192, 198, 285

Mesopotamia Campaign vi, 26, 121, 171, 249, 252

Second World War ii, viii–x, 13, 15, 31, 38, 124, 132, 135, 139, 147, 152, 172, 174, 179, 183, 186, 231, 269, 282–283, 287, 297
South African War 25, 81, 91, 98, 118, 134, 154, 208

Third Afghan War 16, 18, 172, 186, 227, 277–278, 282, 284, 288, 294
Turkish Army 32, 126, 154, 165, 208, 211, 216, 234, 242

Victoria Cross 24, 40, 48, 241